INTELLECTUAL PROPERTY

Intellectual Property

LEARNED SLAVES AND EDUCATED FREEDMEN IN REPUBLICAN ROME

HARRIET I. FLOWER

PRINCETON UNIVERSITY PRESS
PRINCETON & OXFORD

Published by Princeton University Press
41 William Street, Princeton, New Jersey 08540
99 Banbury Road, Oxford OX2 6JX

press.princeton.edu

ISBN 9780691266169
ISBN (e-book) 9780691270210

Library of Congress Control Number: 2025939586

British Library Cataloging-in-Publication Data is available

Editorial: Rob Tempio and Chloe Coy
Production Editorial: Jaden Young
Jacket/Cover Design: Heather Hansen
Production: Erin Suydam
Publicity: William Pagdatoon
Copyeditor: Natalie Jones

Jacket image: *Still life with coins, money pouch, and writing implements.*
Praedia of Julia Felix (II.4.3), tablino 92, south wall, Pompeii, fine Fourth style wall painting, (MANN, inv. 8598d). Courtesy of Museo Archeologico Nazionale di Napoli. Photograph by Giorgio Albano.

This book has been composed in Arno

Printed in the United States of America

10 9 8 7 6 5 4 3 2 1

MIX
Paper | Supporting responsible forestry
FSC® C008955
www.fsc.org

To the fond memory of Miriam T. Griffin
teacher, scholar, and mentor
1935–2018

"The work of the editors is inconspicuous by design, their labor playing out behind the curtain. Editors work in the service of their authors, not themselves, and their touch is meant to be difficult, if not impossible, for readers to see."

—SARA B. FRANKLIN, *THE EDITOR: HOW PUBLISHING LEGEND JUDITH JONES SHAPED CULTURE IN AMERICA* (NEW YORK: ATRIA BOOKS, 2024), XIII–XIV.

CONTENTS

Preface xi

INTRODUCTION Intellectual Pursuits and the (Formerly) Enslaved 1

ONE Licinius the Flute Player and Gaius Gracchus the Orator 12

TWO In the Households of Cato the Censor and Atticus the Businessman 35

THREE The Homegrown and the Immigrant: Quintus Lutatius Daphnis the Freedman and Archias of Antioch the Greek Poet 65

FOUR Multitaskers: Aurelius Opillus and Lucius Cornelius Epicadus 89

FIVE Foundlings: A Genial "Miser" and a Librarian who Collected Old Jokes 114

SIX Intellectual Prisoners Captured in War: Two Tyrants, a Literary Scholar, and a Fierce Critic 131

SEVEN Conclusion: Glimpses of Educated Men who had been Enslaved 156

Notes 163

Bibliography 219

Index 239

PREFACE

THE CAREERS of intellectuals who were enslaved in Rome during the later republican period are not an easy topic either to investigate or to make sense of. Ancient evidence is sparse and allusive, often paradoxical. Glimpses of individual lives can too easily yield not much more than a catalog of entries that look like brief obituaries, probably distorted both by hindsight and by a desire to stress achievements over harsh misfortunes and the cruelties of enslavement. This examination of the lives of some of the best-attested literate freedmen aims to produce more than a list of names, a column from a directory, or an inventory of the members of a very exclusive club. Rather, the lives of these learned men suggest some of the quirks of individual lived experience within a cultural and literary landscape shaped by collaborative writing practices in the specific context of enslavement.

It is a feature of the Roman slave system that enslaved individuals were called upon to undertake so many jobs, including many that were considered far from menial or debasing in themselves. Within the particular sphere of literary and rhetorical production, the contribution of the enslaved was pervasive and normalized at every level. Men who were or had formerly been enslaved were editors, researchers, writers of drafts, and advisers to their patrons; in addition, these men might also be authors of separate works under their own names. Their influence on Latin literature was surely extensive even as it is impossible for us now to measure in detail. Their lives and experiences were intertwined with those of their patrons in a complex web of interdependence and mutual influence, often over many decades. What we can tease out now is only a tiny fraction of these social and intellectual interactions.

This book has benefited from the help, advice, and encouragement of many others. I would particularly like to thank Cliff Ando, Elizabeth Asmis, Yelena Baraz, Joseph Howley, Bob Kaster, Josiah Osgood, Dan-el Padilla Peralta, and Catherine Steel. Jamie Wheeler contributed essential research assistance. Olivia May caught many errors in her excellent proofreading. Michael Flower has provided his customary, invaluable support and guidance. Sections of this research were presented as lectures at the University of Chicago, at Brown University, and at the University of Texas at Austin. I would like to thank the audiences in these venues for their questions and comments. I am very grateful to everyone who helped me at Princeton University Press, especially Rob Tempio, Chloe Coy, and Jaden Young. The copyediting was done by Natalie Jones. The index was compiled by Beth Nauman-Montana. The final version was drafted while on a sabbatical leave from Princeton University; I am very grateful to the university and to the Department of Classics for their support of my research.

Princeton, NJ
Easter 2025

INTELLECTUAL PROPERTY

INTRODUCTION

Intellectual Pursuits and the (Formerly) Enslaved

"The question is one almost of intellectual property."

BRADLEY 1994, 181.

THIS SHORT study has as its specific focus some of the most highly educated and intellectually prominent among those enslaved in Rome. These individuals formed a recognizable and characteristic group within the ancient metropolis. They typically went on to be manumitted, although not always at a particularly young age or even soon after their talents were acknowledged by an audience of the affluent. The time period treated here falls within the second and first centuries BC, during the later phases of republicanism and the transition to the early principate under Augustus.[1] These two centuries saw a vast increase in the number of slaves, through captives, especially in war but also through piracy, and subsequently in children born to enslaved mothers. As a result, this research topic, although in itself quite precisely defined, is inevitably closely connected to the much broader issues of expansion of Roman imperialism, especially in the Hellenistic East, and also to the emergence of an increasingly ambitious Roman literary culture in the Latin language. Each of these factors played out against the backdrop of a complex intellectual landscape created by multilingualism and ongoing cultural appropriation, especially but not exclusively of Hellenistic culture(s).

My interest in those educated to an advanced level despite enslavement grew out of an initial research project on a single such individual, Quintus Lutatius Daphnis, who was reputed to have been the man who was bought and sold (twice) for the highest price recorded for a person born into slavery in a Roman household (*verna*), at least when Pliny the Elder and Suetonius were writing.[2] It is a revealing aspect of the culture produced by enslavement in Rome that such a high value, perhaps indeed the highest monetary price, would be ascribed to literary knowledge and aptitude rather than to any other skill, talent, or craft among the multitude practiced by the enslaved in Italy during this time period. Daphnis' story will be revisited in chapter 3. The individual chapters of this book examine a series of case studies inspired by the figure of Daphnis, some like him and others with rather different life stories.[3]

At the outset of this investigation, it is important to be explicit about what is and what is not being discussed here. No attempt is being made to write a general history of literate slaves in Rome or of their more typical careers, or of the kinds of training they expected to receive at an elementary level. Rather the focus is deliberately rarefied since the case studies are (inevitably) taken from the most successful and prominent. In other words, the men in these case studies were by definition exceptional, which is also why they were admired in life and were consequently recalled by later generations. Many others will have died young before finishing a course of study that they had begun; yet others, after completing their education, will indeed have been kept in relatively menial tasks or simply been forgotten by posterity despite intellectual achievements and influence during their lifetimes. Behind the individuals examined in the following chapters, we can posit schoolrooms and writing studios filled with other literate individuals who were enslaved, most of whose trajectories and achievements are not recorded in our extant sources.

Similarly, this study is not focused primarily on teachers, in the way that Suetonius' *De Grammaticis et Rhetoribus* took the teachers at various levels as its subject.[4] Nevertheless, to be sure, several of the men under discussion did have distinguished teaching careers, both in private houses and in schools they themselves established and led. Nor is this study concerned in any detail with the complex and time-consuming procedure of book production on papyrus rolls.[5] Yet, each of the case studies deals with authors, several of them highly prolific, whose works must have circulated at least in their own generation, and in some instances for much longer. The everyday use of the written word included the taking of dictation, reading aloud, copying and recopying of letters and of other texts from the mundane to the rarefied. The writing that was integral to running a large household constituted an ecosystem that by its very nature both produced and consumed the labor of many who were literate. All these literate people, as well as the material objects and techniques they used, were and are fascinating in their own right and deserving of attention.[6] Here they provide the background to the lives of the most highly educated slaves and freedmen, who formed an elite within the household, and arguably within the broader cultural networks of the city.

The intellectual formation, aspirations, experiences, and endeavors of prominent enslaved and formerly enslaved intellectuals will guide the discussion that follows. Their interests were often broad, as they collected, sifted, produced, and reproduced information in texts written in a wide variety of genres. Their lives can be measured in basic ways through career trajectory, intellectual networks, students, published works, and sometimes through other more fleeting anecdotes. They worked on command, on commission, but also on their own initiative, often all at the same time. Alongside the outline of their lived experiences, one can see that the recognition (sometimes even explicitly expressed in terms of prestige) that they enjoyed was itself a cultural aspect of Roman intellectual life and self-representation. These men were well known, and they mattered, at least among the intelligentsia in the city. Their patrons and associates included the most prominent Romans of the day. Yet the celebration of their exceptional knowledge and talents took place within the explicit framework initially of enslavement and then subsequently of manumission, itself a Roman citizen status exclusively created by a formal transition from previous enslavement.

Within the increasingly systematic exploitation of a larger and more diverse population of enslaved persons, the intellectual labor of some of the most highly educated became a regular part of larger Roman households.[7] At its most advanced levels, this labor consisted both in the production of new works (presented in spoken and written formats) and in the accessing of an increasingly extensive archive of existing knowledge from the Mediterranean world.[8] Through long years of memorization, educated individuals gained their own command of vast databases of knowledge that their patrons could consult through them. The spectacular virtuosity involved is highlighted by the fact that the Roman patrons had themselves mostly undergone an education that stressed memorization reinforced by rote learning and standardized writing exercises.[9] Yet, the most prominent among their household could be prized for being more learned than they were or even claimed to be. It was for this reason that these enslaved individuals were so valued and admired as repositories of special learning and skill, whether local or acquired elsewhere.

These same intellectuals will also have mastered the other skills associated with literacy, including reading aloud, editing, writing, collating, critiquing, and doing original research. Inevitably, their presence in the households and networks of Romans whom we associate with written texts, such as Cicero and Caesar, Asinius Pollio and Cornelius Gallus, raises complex questions about the very nature of authorship, questions that are also implicit in the life stories of these freedmen. As has already been investigated in some detail, Roman writers tended to go through a complex process of writing and rewriting their texts, sometimes over many years.[10] They drew on networks of friends and peers to advise, react to, critique, and even redraft sections or whole works. Many of these conversations about a literary project took place orally and in person, as an integral part of the social life of the leisured classes. Ideas were exchanged and editing took place in real time and out loud. The process was itself prized, even more than the completion of a draft or a polished version produced by an individual author. In this sense, our whole approach to an ancient text is often and inevitably anachronistic, since we seek and often claim to find one "author," a distinctive voice and point of view in a work that we can now usually only approach in a single written version.[11]

Even as scholars have tried to reinsert at least some understanding of the role of these conversations among friends and peers, who were social equals or distinguished visitors to the city, these same (types of) dialogues and editing sessions will have included educated enslaved persons and freedmen. An incomplete picture results from relegating these individuals to the most basic roles of scribes or readers, as if they were themselves merely tools despite their elaborate educations.[12] It is clear that intellectuals who were or had been enslaved played roles that were essential to these conversations, both within the household and across wider networks of households. The fact that our evidence only allows us to catch glimpses of individual interactions or ongoing relationships between interlocutors should make us all the more eager to try to recover at least some of the flavor of these complex practices that produced ancient texts. Closely related to these basic questions about voice and influence is the larger picture of the role of literary and cultural capital within Roman society, especially but not exclusively in the city itself. Leading Romans were not only refined consumers of literature; many of them also aimed themselves to be writers and even innovators across literary genres.[13] Their intellectual pursuits were a vital part of their self-presentation. In this context, the help of gifted intellectuals, especially ones who could not easily refuse a wide range of requests, became especially and increasingly useful.

Such relationships, and the fruit that they bore, grew and flourished in the very particular context of enslavement, of its various conditions and consequences. A central premise of this study, therefore, is that slavery mattered in Roman society in characteristic and specific ways, including at the most advanced level of knowledge acquisition and literary production. It was not simply that the labor of the enslaved freed wealthy Romans from menial household tasks so that they could pursue their intellectual interests at much greater leisure. Nor was the ability of elites to write merely made much easier and faster by scribes who copied and recopied letters, documents, speeches, and literary texts. Rather the system of household enslavement was based on the labor of these workers, and not least of all on the exploitation of intellectuals who were among the most advanced in their various fields at the time, whether polymaths, comic poets, antiquarians, rhetoricians, creative writers, or literary experts.

Beyond and between the many daily routines of premodern life, whether running a household or writing a book, freeborn Roman writers often relied on the learning of others both to collect relevant material and to produce a new text that they could call their own. Meanwhile, the most successful of these manumitted intellectuals were themselves surely also supported by a literate staff whom they might supervise on behalf of a patron or employ for themselves in their own projects. Even if they had performed many of these same menial tasks themselves at an earlier stage, they moved on to a life of the mind that could eventually yield manumission and a more independent position in Rome, if only through the increasing opportunities to cultivate a wider circle of patrons and students in return for payment.

The wealth of evidence for Roman slaves in business and commerce has perhaps inevitably overshadowed pursuits that were more prestigious in intellectual and literary terms.[14] Petronius' very wealthy freedman Trimalchio, the fictional host of an imaginary vulgar dinner party described in a satirical text, is notable for his ignorance of Greek literature and myth, as well as of good taste and culture more generally. His dinner guests also see literacy as something to be used primarily in commerce or for legal transactions. But Trimalchio represents a particular caricature, who has sometimes loomed too large in readings of freedmen in Roman society more generally.

Similarly, modern prejudices about "secretaries" and about the kinds of work they do, especially as related to the role of women employed in offices during the twentieth century, can also create unconscious, anachronistic biases that distort our picture of what the most literate slaves could and did do in Rome. The almost total absence of highly educated enslaved people doing intellectual work in other historical periods and places means that scholars who study comparative slavery tend to find these particular Roman slaves less relevant to their own research, if they have even noticed them at all. All these tendencies and blind spots are made worse by the scarce evidence, which comes in small fragments from a wide variety of ancient sources.

Nevertheless, recovering at least some of the story of men like Daphnis or Opillus or Epicadus or Melissus is both possible and eminently worthwhile. If the individual ancient life has value, then it does so across the social spectrum. Their trajectories may have been unusually successful, but they reflect the practices and aspirations of many others in a highly competitive market, whether in the case of enslaved boys selected for training or enslavers looking to benefit from their talents. Enslavement will consistently have been exploitative but that does not mean it consistently involved only menial labor. Meanwhile, the independent lives of freedmen as authors were a significant feature of city life but remain largely lost to us.

Stark reversals of fortune in the experiences of a highly educated slave are illustrated by the well-known life story of the renowned and remarkably influential Stoic philosopher Epictetus, who had been born in Phrygian Hierapolis and became the slave of a slave, in the household of Epaphroditus, a freedman of the emperor Nero.[15] Keith Bradley used the story of Epictetus' life as a prime illustration for the paradoxes inherent in enslavement in imperial Rome.[16] Epictetus was enslaved as a child and had been so physically abused at a young age that he walked with a limp for the rest of his life. However, it was also in enslavement that he received his advanced education, including the study of philosophy under the tutelage of the foremost teacher in Rome at the time, the Stoic philosopher Gaius Musonius Rufus.[17] Similar dissonances will surely have marked the lives of many if not most of the individuals in this study of earlier times.

This investigation will offer a series of interlinked case studies of enslaved and manumitted intellectuals, in an attempt to explore at least some of their lived experiences within each social and political setting. Their origins, education, careers, and interests will be examined, as far as the surviving evidence allows. These men came from different backgrounds.[18] Some were *vernae* (home-born), the children of mothers who were enslaved in the households of Roman citizens. Others had been exposed as infants, illegally enslaved, and traded away from their place of birth. Yet others were war captives from all around the Mediterranean, some of whom were enslaved as mature adults who already enjoyed an international reputation for learning, teaching, and scholarship. Yet others were taken in unrecorded circumstances, notably by pirates or traders who preyed on the young and on the vulnerable in society. Their stories touch on habits of breeding enslaved children, trading in educated boys, and lending or sometimes even giving the educated as special gifts or favors. In addition, dowry was a factor in habitual transfers from one household to another at the time of a marriage.[19] Intellectual freedmen were integral to wide-reaching networks of friendship and forced labor. Nevertheless, they are sometimes documented as making at least some choices that were clearly very much their own.

Fragments of works by these men are meager to nonexistent, even in cases where they are said to have been prolific authors of books that seem to have been influential for contemporary and later writers. Consequently, tracing their impact, either on the publications of their patrons or on their own writings, is virtually impossible. Unsurprisingly, the sources that mention them are few; they offer only glimpses of certain conditions of or moments in each individual's life. As a result, this study builds out from such rarely attested moments to create a possible model(s) of their careers, expertise, and personal situations. The interactions of these slaves and freedmen with well-documented Roman patrons, both senators and businessmen, does allow the mapping of at least partial timeframes, networks, and settings, whether geographical or political or cultural. Yet it is obvious that vital information has often been lost or suppressed.

It is also important to note that, in nearly every instance, their own personal opinions, emotions, and relationships remain beyond our reach. This study will, therefore, not try to reconstruct how each individual felt about a devastating change of fortune, a given patron, a particular assigned project, or even about Roman intellectual culture more generally. Some men discussed in this book had been brought up since infancy in Roman households, so that they were truly integrated into Roman society from birth. Others consistently identified themselves as foreigners, even after acquiring citizenship through manumission; they presented themselves not so differently from intellectuals who had come to Rome of their own accord in search of patrons and of ways to support a literary life. One such example of the intellectual immigrant is included in chapter 3 by way of comparison, the poet Archias of Antioch, whose long career is described in some detail but with considerable and cunning distortion by Cicero in a lawcourt speech delivered in 62 that was circulated soon after.

This book is articulated thematically in order to try to give shape to the case studies of individual intellectuals, rather than presenting them in the form of a catalog. The first chapter focuses on a single freedman, Licinius the flute player who worked with and for Gaius Gracchus. This man's contribution to Gracchus' (in)famous rhetorical style raises central questions about the dependence of even the wealthiest and best-educated Roman politicians on the skill and judgment of members of their household. Chapter 2 contrasts two households that were heavily engaged in educating young, enslaved boys at different time periods, those of Cato the Elder and of Atticus, men who lived several generations apart. Atticus' decision to educate every member of his household in Rome can be interpreted as the logical result of earlier experiments with schools at home, such as Cato's. The much-admired Daphnis is the focus of chapter 3, where his trajectory and skills are compared and contrasted with the experiences of Archias of Antioch, a Greek-speaking poet who came to Rome as a young Syrian immigrant in 102. Chapter 4 is devoted to Opillus and Epicadus, two freedmen who were prominent in the 80s and 70s. Their careers demonstrate the fact that the most highly educated were often the closest collaborators of a patron, even when that involved the freedmen taking on more than one job and despite ready access to other skilled helpers. These examples reveal that personal trust could be as important as expertise and might sometimes outweigh it, especially in times of great political unrest and civil war. Roman children who were illegally enslaved after being exposed at birth are the subject of chapter 5. And finally, chapter 6 looks at highly educated war captives, with a principal focus on Tyrannio of Amisus and

Timagenes of Alexandria. The Romans made a habit of enslaving even mature men with high profiles as scholars, writers, and teachers after they had been captured in war.

The most well-known republican writer who was enslaved and whose work still survives will not be examined in detail in this study. He is the comic poet known in English as Terence, said to have been a native of North Africa who had a memorable but short career in Rome in the 160s.[20] His six surviving plays, written in simple, conversational Latin and based on Greek originals, were very popular in the Middle Ages and served as an inspiration for Shakespeare. Publius Terentius Afer is described as having died young while on a journey to Greece, perhaps being only in his mid-20s. He had allegedly been born to an enslaved mother in Carthage. According to this version of his biography, it seems that his mother was a local African woman who had been enslaved in a Punic household while Carthage was still a flourishing city but not at a time of armed conflict with Rome.[21] According to Suetonius, Terence was acquired under unknown circumstances as a child by the Roman senator Publius Terentius Lucanus, who educated and manumitted him.[22] His early success as a writer was said to have gained him many connections with prominent Romans, including Scipio Aemilianus and the latter's close friend Gaius Laelius. Some of these acquaintances were even said to have helped in the writing of his plays, in a pattern suggestive of the kinds of collaborative relationships that produced and were fostered by literary activities.

Terence left behind some property along the via Appia and a freeborn daughter, who later married a Roman citizen of equestrian status.[23] Consequently, Terence seems to have made a profit from his writings and social connections, at least enough to assure his daughter a dowry even years after his death. But much of this traditional narrative might be based on later inferences. It has been interpreted as speculation based on his *cognomen* Afer (the African), Terence's brief period of producing plays, and various other snippets of information. As will be discussed, ethnic names like Afer did not always indicate a place of birth or ethnic origin.[24] Could this man really have risen so far so fast up from slavery in just a few years and have made enough money to guarantee the future of his family in the next generation? If indeed Terence was a freedman who had a meteoric career but died young, then his story serves as a clear illustration of the way in which education and literary talent could lead to fame and fortune. Terence's contested life story illustrates difficulties already experienced by our ancient sources, who were writing later and in very different historical circumstances from his time.

A number of recent publications have served to inspire the methodology of this investigation. These works have faced and come to terms with the central issue of how to reconstruct the lives of persons who stood at the margins of history as formally conceived and about whom the surviving evidence is incomplete. How can we recover at least some of the perspectives and experiences of such individuals, who seem to have been influential in the lives of the prominent men who are the main characters on the stage of history as traditionally constructed? Two recent studies of women at different historical periods illustrate some promising strategies, as well as identifying unique challenges. In 2013 Jill Lepore published her study of Jane Franklin, the sister of Benjamin Franklin. She explains in her appendix on methods and sources how for a long time she had thought that her project was not doable, that she could only write a novel about Jane Franklin Mecom. "But I decided, in the end, to write a biography, a book meant not only as a life of Jane Franklin Mecom but, more, as a meditation on silence in the archives."[25] Lepore uses a wide variety of sources that shed light on the lives of those who came into contact with her main subject. At the same time, in dwelling on the lives of the better-documented family members, she is careful not to lose sight of Jane. Her study brings Jane and the age she lived in vividly to life.

Similarly, in 2019 Susan Treggiari went beyond what had ever been attempted before in recovering the biography of a Roman woman of the republican period, including in her own earlier work on the relatively better-documented women in Cicero's family.[26] Treggiari's study of Servilia, mother of Marcus Brutus the tyrannicide, is a sweeping treatment of several Roman political families and of the ways in which women shaped and supported these kinship groups, especially in times of civil war.[27] Examining the lives and contributions of these women involves both a re-focalizing from their particular perspectives as well as a broadening of one's research horizon beyond the principal actors and events in the senate or on a battlefield. Meanwhile, such a project does not require or even invite us to discount or pass over political or economic history; rather it enriches that central narrative of what was happening in the community as a whole. These and other studies of individual women have influenced this examination of educated enslaved men in republican Rome.

The title *Intellectual Property* is meant to be deliberately ambiguous. It can refer to the enslaved themselves when treated as property within a Roman household. At the same time, it can also indicate their knowledge and ideas, which contributed to shaping both the content and the form of texts that circulated under the names of their various patrons. Intellectual property is a broad concept that goes beyond the simple attribution of authorship to a single individual to the complex question of how ideas and concepts are shared within a literary culture. No literary or rhetorical work is produced in a vacuum; rather it inevitably reflects styles, content, and fashions shared within its cultural and historical setting. This ambiguity inevitably stands at the heart of the present (and perhaps of any) study of learned men who had been subject to enslavement.

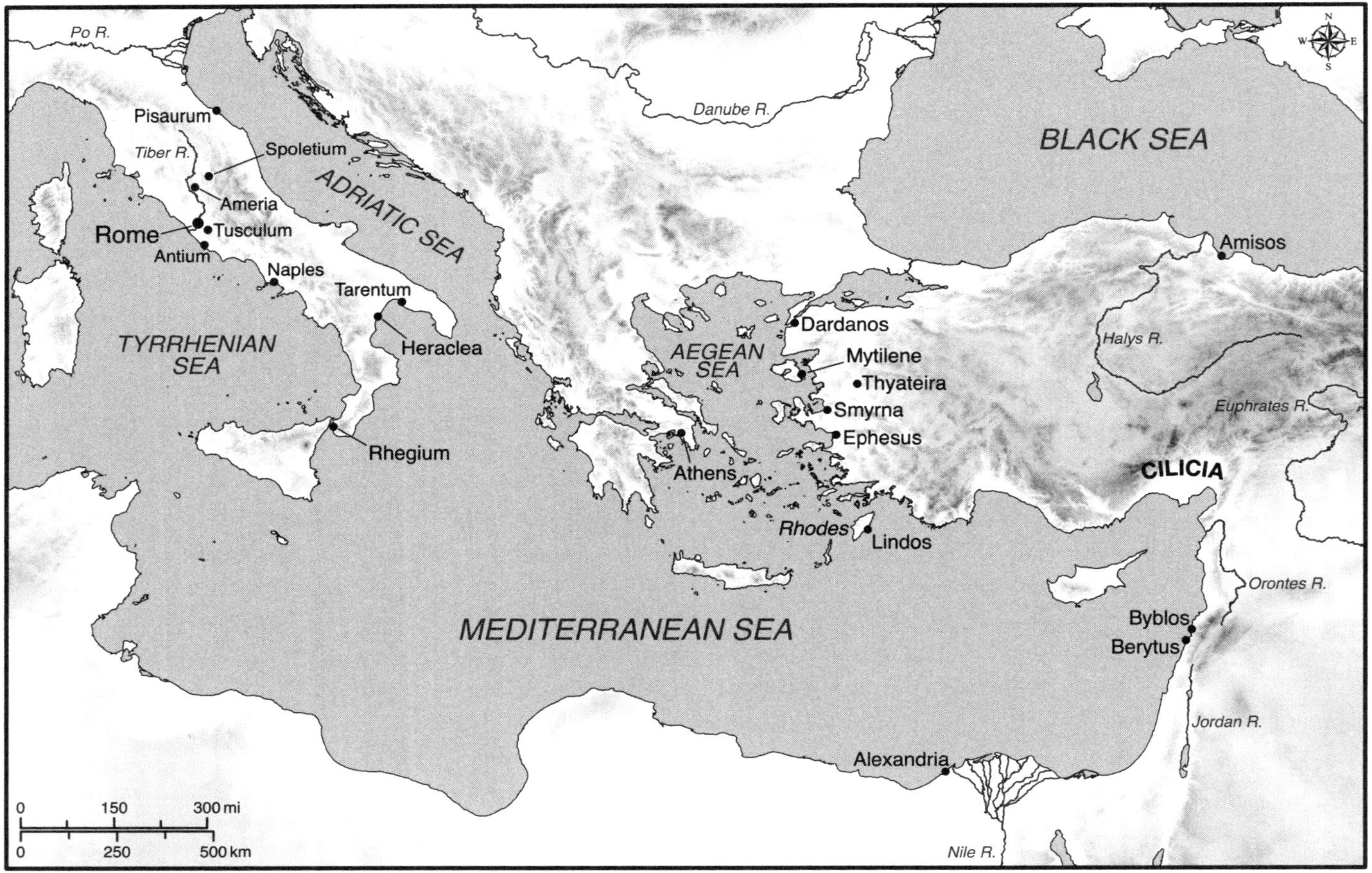

MAP 1: Origins and travel destinations of enslaved and manumitted intellectuals Ancient World Mapping Center, University of North Carolina, Chapel Hill

An example of what can be at stake in a discussion of authorship is raised by John Scheid's 2007 Budé edition of Augustus' *Res Gestae*, the first-person account of his achievements that was published after his death and circulated throughout the empire. In his introduction, Scheid argues that this inscription was produced by Augustus' staff and should not be interpreted as a work written by the *princeps*, although the content and first-person style is in line with the autobiographical writings of earlier politicians.[28] This interpretation, therefore, stresses the contributions of Augustus' literate slaves and freedmen, even as it assigns to them the role of ghostwriters, who are tasked with impersonating someone who is presented in public as the author of a text that he has not himself produced. The research and methodology of the present study eschews the image of the ghostwriter for that of the research assistant who is also an editor, a person (or in this case surely a team of people) who coproduce a final text through an intensely collaborative process.[29] Given the importance of the *Res Gestae*, Augustus would surely have wanted an active hand in shaping and polishing both its design and its final form.

There is plenty of evidence to suggest that these intellectuals, whether still enslaved or already manumitted, were very influential in the lives of prominent Romans such as Cicero and his best friend Atticus. Every aspect of their literary interests and projects was shaped by interactions with these men.[30] Their libraries were arranged and curated by such individuals, who offered invaluable advice about a world of texts, including those beyond what was available in the city of Rome. Their letters, speeches, poetry, prose, and collections of material for all of the above were edited by such helpers. Ultimately, we will never know the extent to which even the most gifted Roman writers relied on the enslaved or manumitted to produce and edit their works and to create an image of themselves as learned and cultivated men. But that does not mean that such an inquiry is fruitless in that it seeks to gain insight into a rarefied world that put so high a value on the acquisition of cultural capital that it created a characteristically Roman system to exploit the persons of intellectuals as repositories of knowledge and skill, whether educated at home or acquired from abroad.

1

Licinius the Flute Player and Gaius Gracchus the Orator

Sed ecce in manibus vir et praestantissimo ingenio et flagranti studio et doctus a puero C. Gracchus: noli enim putare quemquam, Brute, pleniorem aut uberiorem ad dicendum fuisse. Et ille: sic prorsus, inquit, existumo atque istum de superioribus paene solum lego. Immo plane, inquam, Brute, legas censeo. damnum enim illius immaturo interitu res Romanae Latinaeque litterae fecerunt.

CICERO *BRUTUS* 125

But look we have to hand a man of the most outstanding talent and burning eagerness, Gaius Gracchus who was highly educated from a young age. For do not think, Brutus, that anyone was ever richer or fuller in speaking. And he then said: I agree and I think he is virtually the only one of the previous orators whom I read. Certainly Brutus, I said, I very much approve of your reading him. Indeed, his early death was a loss for Roman and Latin literature.

THIS INVESTIGATION begins with the sound of a flute player playing a pitch-pipe in the Roman Forum in the late second century. He is, however, no ordinary musician. He plays individual notes and musical phrases rather than a sustained melody. He stands concealed but close behind an impassioned young orator, who is giving a public speech from the speaker's platform (*rostra*) as he faces a large crowd standing in the Forum area in the political heart of the city. The speaker's back is turned toward the old, republican senate house (*curia Hostilia*) as he looks out over the sizable audience. As he speaks, he strides up and down on the high platform and gesticulates with both hands to emphasize some of his points more forcefully. His toga even slips off his left arm as his movements become more expansive than the traditional costume of a Roman male citizen is designed to accommodate. His voice modulates to express a variety of emotions. The spellbound audience reacts with feeling to each argument. The orator is like an actor on stage but he does not wear the theatrical mask usual in Roman drama. The crowd is captivated by the novelty of his rhetorical performance, which matches the new political ideas he is advocating for so earnestly and with such a range of emotion.

Meanwhile, the flute player must also keep constantly in motion in order to stay close behind the orator. His job is to prompt the speaker, especially if the orator's pace becomes too fast or the pitch of his voice is too high or too shrill. In this way, the flute player helps shape and direct the delivery of a dramatically complex rhetorical performance, even as he monitors the delivery of the young orator to prevent excessive strain on his lungs and to preserve his voice for another speech that he will deliver soon. Sometimes he causes the speaker to speed up a delivery that has become too slow. But the flute player's task is to assist in creating these technical effects without the audience being distracted by his presence. In other words, the flute player and the orator must work together as a team to make the speech as effective as it can be. Even and especially in a heated moment, the orator commits himself to heeding prompts produced by various musical notes on the flute. Much practice and mutual trust are needed to make this dynamic interaction work in a large open-air space, which is filled with the noise and expectation of the crowd. But the flute player is not a prompter simply working from a script. He may know which sections of the oration are more likely to need an intervention, but he must use his own judgment about when and how to prompt the speaker. In this sense, the rhetorical effect of the speech is created by a dynamic interaction between the flute player, the audience, and the orator. Ultimately, the flute player can only be effective if the orator is willing to follow his coaching, as the musician interprets and critiques the speech's effects unfolding in real time, in front of a particular crowd in Rome.

The orator is Gaius Sempronius Gracchus, the foremost political speaker of his generation (and among previous orators second only to Cato the censor) and one of the most celebrated orators of republican Rome.[1] The flute player is a certain Licinius, a freedman of Gaius Gracchus' wife, Licinia, who apparently also helped Gaius Gracchus speak in public before manumission made him a new Roman citizen.[2] In any survey of the roles played by highly skilled slaves, Licinius provides a striking case study that illuminates some of the possibilities, challenges, and limitations inherent in such an investigation. Licinius is named by two ancient sources (Cicero and Plutarch), although the personal name that he used during enslavement and probably as a *cognomen* after manumission is not recorded.[3] He is alluded to simply as a slave or a musician, without being individually identified, by a further five ancient authors (Valerius Maximus, Quintilian, Aulus Gellius, Cassius Dio, and Ammianus Marcellinus). He did not, therefore, succeed in remaining hidden behind the figure of Gracchus, despite the latter's fame and notoriety. On the contrary, his role was noted, appreciated, debated, and sometimes misunderstood and even criticized over a period of five hundred years after the untimely death of Gracchus in 121.

Gaius Gracchus' fame as an orator throughout antiquity rests to a considerable extent on Cicero's appreciation and celebration of his eloquence. Licinius' central role in Gaius' success, in the particular setting of the public meeting (*contio*), was also handed down to posterity, although the freedman's personal identity was not of much interest to later Roman writers. Their vantage point is that of the crowd, which focused on Gracchus speaking, and more specifically of someone standing very close to the front of that crowd, someone who was in a position to catch glimpses of or even to hear, at least occasionally, Licinius playing his flute at certain heated moments. Romans who comment on Licinius' performance are claiming to have some insight into how Gracchus pulled off his most famous, public speeches, ones that also circulated in written form during his lifetime.[4] Subsequently, despite the impressive list of ancient authors who allude to Licinius, he himself has not been a focus for modern scholars and most often appears unnamed in their discussions.[5] This chapter aims to try to reconstruct at least part of his story, within the political and rhetorical context of Gaius Gracchus' career, and to suggest some of what we might learn from a consideration of Licinius' contributions.

Licinius the Flute Player

Licinius' guiding role shaped Gaius Gracchus' public speeches, which were some of the most famous in the tradition of republican oratory as it was recalled by the Romans.[6] This tradition probably originated with the generation of Cicero's teachers, some of whom had themselves heard Gracchus speak or had talked to others who were present at those (in)famous public meetings. Licinius himself seems perhaps also to have survived to recall his patron and their close working relationship. Cicero played a key role in handing on this tradition. He mentions Gaius as an orator on a number of occasions, but refers to Licinius only once, in the treatise *De Oratore*, which was written in 55.

> *Itaque idem Gracchus (quod potes audire, Catule, ex Licinio cliente tuo, litterato homine, quem servum sibi ille habuit ad manum) cum eburneola solitus est habere fistula qui staret occulte post ipsum cum contionaretur peritum hominum qui inflaret celeriter eum sonum quo illum aut remissum excitaret aut a contentione revocaret.*
>
> *DE ORATORE* 3.225

In this way the same [Gaius] Gracchus was accustomed (as you can find out, Catulus, from your client Licinius, a learned man, whom Gracchus kept near him while he was a slave) to have someone/him with an ivory

> flute who used to stand behind him [Gaius] while he was speaking in a public meeting, a skilled person who quickly sounded the right note either to stir him up when he was slowing or to restrain him when he was raising his voice.

In this passage from a dialogue set in the fateful year 91, the renowned orator Marcus Licinius Crassus (cos. 95) vividly recalls the novelty of Gaius Gracchus' speaking style from a generation earlier.[7] The Latin is somewhat compressed, but it is possible to identify the dependent Licinius mentioned here as the same man who stood behind Gracchus, some 30 years before the dramatic date of the dialogue. The chronology is plausible if Licinius was young during Gracchus' short political career in Rome. The physically demanding task of keeping up with Gaius Gracchus' movements, while playing a flute, suggests a job for a young man rather than an older adviser. Alternatively, the Licinius who is called upon as an eyewitness in the *De Oratore* could also be a different freedman of that very wealthy family, the family both of Gaius' wife Licinia and of the orator Crassus, who is the speaker at this point in Cicero's dialogue.

In other words, Licinius the flute player would be significant in any case to someone interested in the history of Roman oratorical style or in the specialized roles of the enslaved or manumitted, but Gracchus' fame as a public speaker puts this Licinius in the same exclusive class of superstars as Gaius Gracchus himself. Ancient discussions of Gaius Gracchus, including some brief verbatim quotations from his speeches, stress both his political ideas and his striking delivery, which was said regularly to have brought even his political rivals to tears.[8] Some confirmation of this is provided by Cicero, who definitely saw Gracchus as the best of the earlier orators, although he was fundamentally and completely opposed to the political initiatives of both Gracchi brothers. Such an opinion was indeed rare for Cicero, who mainly praises orators and politicians who shared his own political views. Nevertheless, Gaius Gracchus was truly exceptional as a speaker in the eyes of Rome's most famous republican orator, Marcus Tullius Cicero.[9]

Unsurprisingly, ancient authors closer to Gracchus' lifetime seem to have had a relatively clearer and more nuanced understanding of Licinius' role in actively helping Gaius during his speeches. They also provide a more coherent picture of what a republican *contio* might actually have been like. A chronological survey of our evidence for Licinius' job reveals the best information we still have access to. Valerius Maximus, writing in the time of the emperor Tiberius, tends to follow Cicero's description of Licinius' role.

> *quotiens apud populum contionatus est, servum post se musicae artis peritum habuit, qui occulte eburnea fistula pronuntiationis eius modos formabat, aut nimis remissos excitando aut plus iusto concitatos revocando, quia ipsum calor*

> *atque impetus actionis attentum huisce temperamenti aestimatorem esse non patiebatur.*
>
> 8.10.1
>
> Whenever he gave a public speech to the people, he had a slave skilled in musical arts behind him, who secretly guided the rhythm of his speech with an ivory flute, either speeding up a pace that was too relaxed or restraining him when he was unreasonably shrill, because he was not himself able, while he was intent upon the passion and impetus of his speech, to be a sound judge of the appropriate tempo.

Similarly, Gaius Gracchus is important to Quintilian, in his discussion of the education of the ideal orator, which was composed near the end of the first century AD.

> *Uno interim contenti simus exemplo C. Gracchi, praecipui suorum temporum oratoris, cui contionanti consistens post eum musicus fistula, quam tonarion vocant, modos quibus deberet intendi ministrabat; haec ei cura inter turbidissimas actiones vel terrenti optimates vel iam timenti fuit.*
>
> *INST.* 1.10.27–28
>
> Meanwhile, let us be content with one example, that of Gaius Gracchus, the preeminent orator of his time. When he was giving a public speech a musician with a flute, which is called a *tonarion* (in Greek), used to stand behind him and help him to modulate the tone necessary (for his delivery). The musician fulfilled this role during his most stormy speeches, when he was either terrifying the *optimates* or already fearing them.

Quintilian imagines a special pitchpipe being used, rather than an ordinary flute. Consequently, his reading stresses the technical aspects of Licinius' job. Both Valerius Maximus and Quintilian give Licinius an active and essential role in shaping Gaius Gracchus' performance by using his own judgment.

Writing in the early second century AD, Plutarch mentions Licinius twice and is still able to recall his name and his membership in Gracchus' household.

> ὁ δὲ τραχὺς καὶ θυμοειδής, ὥστε καὶ παρὰ γνώμην ἐν τῷ λέγειν ἐκφερόμενον πολλάκις ὑπ' ὀργῆς τήν τε φωνὴν ἀποξύνειν καὶ βλασφημεῖν καὶ συνταράττειν τὸν λόγον. ὅθεν καὶ βοήθημα τῆς ἐκτροπῆς ταύτης ἐποιήσατο [τὸν] Λικίννιον οἰκέτην οὐκ ἀνόητον, ὃς ἔχων φωνασκικὸν ὄργανον, ᾧ τοὺς φθόγγους ἀναβιβάζουσιν, ὄπισθεν ἑστὼς τοῦ Γαΐου λέγοντος, ὁπηνίκα τραχυνόμενον αἴσθοιτο τῇ φωνῇ καὶ παραρρηγνύμενον δι' ὀργήν, ἐνεδίδου τόνον μαλακόν, ᾧ τὸ σφοδρὸν εὐθὺς ἐκεῖνος ἅμα τοῦ πάθους καὶ τῆς φωνῆς ἀνιεὶς ἐπραΰνετο καὶ παρεῖχεν ἑαυτὸν εὐανάκλητον.
>
> *TI. GRACCH.* 2.5

> But Gaius was harsh and emotional, so much so that in speaking he was often carried away by anger against his better judgment with a high-pitched voice and uttering abuses and losing the thread of his argument. Consequently, he used Licinius, a talented servant, to help avoid such blunders. He (Licinius) stood behind Gaius while he was speaking with a pitchpipe, designed to indicate tones of voice. Whenever he perceived that Gaius' voice was getting harsh and irregular with anger, he would give him a soft keynote, and then Gaius in turn would let go and soften his voice and his emotions. He would grow gentle and show that he was easy to coach.

> Γαΐῳ μὲν οὖν Γράκχῳ τῷ ῥήτορι καὶ τὸν τρόπον ὄντι χαλεπῷ καὶ περιπαθέστερον λέγοντι διηρμοσμένον ἦν συρίγγιον, ᾧ τὴν φωνὴν οἱ ἁρμονικοὶ σχέδην ἐπ' ἀμφότερα διὰ τῶν τόνων ἄγουσι, καὶ τοῦτ' ἔχων οἰκέτης αὐτοῦ λέγοντος ὄπισθεν ἑστὼς ἐνεδίδου τόνον ἐπιεικῆ καὶ πρᾶον, ᾧ τὴν κραυγὴν ἀνεκαλεῖτο καὶ τὸ τραχὺ καὶ τὸ θυμικὸν ἀφῄρει τῆς φωνῆς, ὥσπερ ὁ τῶν βουκόλων
>
> 'κηρόπλαστος ὀτοβεῖ δόναξ
> ἀχέτας ὑπνοδόταν νόμον.' (AESCH. *PV* 575)
>
> ἐπιθέλγων καὶ καθιστὰς τὴν ὀργὴν τοῦ ῥήτορος·
>
> *MOR.* 456A

> Gaius Gracchus the orator was both a difficult character and too emotional in his delivery. A pitchpipe was made for him, of the kind used by musicians to indicate the correct high or low note for a voice. A servant of Gaius' with this pipe would stand behind him as he was speaking and give him the appropriate, gentle tone by which Gaius was able to moderate his shouting and remove from his voice a harsh and angry tone. Just as one of the shepherd's (in Aeschylus' *Prometheus*) "wax-sealed reed pipe, clear toned, sounds a note that induces sleep." And so he (the flute player) charmed and calmed the rage of the orator.

Plutarch, therefore, seems still to have access to a detailed description of Licinius' activities, which may be based on more than one original source.

By contrast and significantly, Aulus Gellius challenges at some length the fairly unified picture painted by these earlier authors.[10] He places a nameless flute player in the audience and yet assigns him a similar function in crafting Gaius' style and delivery.

> *Ecce autem per tibicinia Laconica tibiae quoque illius contionariae in mentem uenit, quam C. Graccho cum populo agente praeisse ac praeministrasse modulos ferunt. Sed nequaquam sic est, ut a uulgo dicitur, canere tibia solitum, qui pone eum loquentem staret, <et> uariis modis tum demulcere animum actionemque*

> *eius, tum intendere. Quid enim foret ista re ineptius, si, ut planipedi saltanti, ita Graccho contionanti numeros et modos et frequentamenta quaedam uaria tibicen incineret? Sed qui hoc compertius memoriae tradiderunt, stetisse in circumstantibus dicunt occultius, qui fistula breui sensim grauiusculum sonum inspiraret ad reprimendum sedandumque inpetus uocis eius efferuescentes; namque inpulsu et instinctu extraneo naturalis illa Gracchi uehementia indiguisse non, opinor, existimanda est. M. tamen Cicero fistulatorem istum utrique rei adhibitum esse a Graccho putat, ut sonis tum placidis tum citatis aut demissam iacentemque orationem eius erigeret aut ferocientem saeuientemque cohiberet. Verba ipsius Ciceronis apposui: . . .*
>
> *NA* 1.11.10–16
>
> But look, that Laconian pipe music reminds me also of that pipe used in a public meeting, which they say prompted and helped the tone of Gaius Gracchus when he was addressing the people. But it is not at all correct, as is claimed by the uninformed, that a person was accustomed to play a flute standing behind him [Gaius] as he was speaking, and with various tones he would either sooth his spirit and delivery or speed them up. For what would be a more senseless thing than for a flute player to play musical phrases and rhythms and various tunes for Gracchus as he was delivering a public speech, as if for a dancer without shoes? But those who handed on a more informed version, say that a person stood somewhat concealed among the audience, who occasionally sounded a low note on a short pipe to restrain and calm the excessive force of his voice. I think it inconceivable that the famous natural energy of Gaius needed any external prompting or inspiration. Marcus Cicero, however, thinks that Gracchus used that flute player for both purposes, so that with sounds that were sometimes calm but at other times rapid [the flute player] would either urge on his speech that was weak or failing or would reign in a fierce and savage [delivery]. I quote Cicero's own words . . . [here Gellius accurately quotes the passage from *De Oratore* 3.225 cited above].

Gellius' polemical tone demonstrates both his well-attested and keen engagement with second-century literary and rhetorical culture and his personal antipathy to freedmen or enslaved persons in positions of creativity and personal responsibility.[11] Consequently, his aim is to minimize the role of Licinius, even as he effectively displaces him from behind the speaker. At the same time, he erases Licinius' personal identity. In the context of the renewed interest in preclassical Latin prose shared by Gellius and his friends, the figure of Gaius Gracchus loomed large once again, although Gellius is eager to promote his own particular favorite, Cato the censor, above Gracchus, as both the more accomplished speaker and the more inspiring writer.[12]

Gellius' polemic brings out in a suggestive way what he saw in earlier descriptions. Before Gellius' account, Licinius' role had consistently been described in a variety of ancient texts as an active and skillful one that involved making his own decision about how and when to intervene in prompting Gaius to adjust his speaking style. Interestingly, Gellius cannot remove the well-known figure of Licinius the flute player completely from this picture. Yet, on principle, Gellius does not like this function, as he freely admits, because he feels it detracts from Gaius' own, natural talent as an orator. Consequently, Gellius tries to minimize Licinius' contribution by placing him in the crowd and playing down, as far as possible, the kinds of information Gaius may be drawing from the sound of the flute. Gellius' intellectual and social biases have caused him to distort the picture of Gaius' oratorical practice to such a degree that it no longer makes sense in practical terms.

As every other commentator was able to appreciate, Licinius must have stood very near Gaius in order to be heard above the ambient noise of the boisterous crowd, who reacted with emotion to Gaius' forceful delivery. In other words, Licinius must also have stood somewhere on the speaker's platform or perhaps on a step leading up to it.[13] There would be no point in a flute player being positioned within the large audience in the Forum, where he would be much more visible to the crowd but far less audible to the speaker on the platform.

By contrast, Cassius Dio, writing in the early third century AD, returns to a traditional account of Licinius' role, which he does not describe as controversial.[14]

> πρῶτός τε ἐν τοῖς συλλόγοις μεταξὺ δημηγορῶν ἐβάδιζε, καὶ τὸν βραχίονα πρῶτος ἀπεγύμνωσεν, ὥστε μηδέτερον αὐτῶν κακὸν ἐξ ἐκείνου νομισθῆναι. καὶ ἐπειδή γε πολλῇ μὲν πυκνότητι ἐνθυμημάτων πολλῇ δὲ καὶ σφοδρότητι ὀνομάτων ἐπίπαν ἐδημηγόρει, καὶ ἐκ τούτου οὔτε κατέχειν ῥᾳδίως ἑαυτὸν ἐδύνατο καὶ [ἐπειδὴ] πολλάκις ἐς ἃ οὐκ ἤθελεν εἰπεῖν ἐξεφέρετο, αὐλητὴν ἐπήγετο, καὶ παρ' ἐκείνου ὑπαυλοῦντός οἱ ἐρρυθμίζετο καὶ ἐμετρίαζεν, ἢ καὶ εἴ πῃ καὶ ὣς ἐξέπιπτεν καθίστατο.
>
> 25.85

He was the first to walk up and down while speaking in public meetings and the first to bare his [left] arm [from his toga], with the result that neither of these two habits were considered bad after that time. And since indeed he generally gave speeches in public with much intensity of emotion and vehemence of language, and for this reason he was not easily able to restrain himself and so he often was carried away to say what he did not want to, he engaged a flute player and so was brought into line and restrained by that man's playing. And if he ever lost control even under those conditions, he would find his way back.

Dio, whether consciously or not, associates the various innovations Gaius introduced with each other. It is surely the decision to turn toward the Forum and speak to a larger crowd that encourages and even requires the more expansive gestures that tend to displace the toga from the left arm, the new habit of moving around on the platform while speaking, and the need to project the voice further with emphasis and enthusiasm. Dio is less sure about what kind of instrument Licinius is playing or of how he uses tone or pitch, but he is convinced that the flute is effective in making Gaius' speeches so successful in a public setting.

By the time Ammianus Marcellinus is writing near the end of the fourth century AD, the memory of Gracchus' flute player is still familiar enough that no details need be supplied by way of explanation.

> *ut contionaria Gracchi fistula sola post occipitium desit*
>
> 30.4.19
>
> so that only the flute played in the assembly behind the head of Gracchus is missing . . .

Interestingly, the pipe has here become detached from the musician and appears to play of its own accord, even as its position close behind Gaius' head, while it sounds in his ear, continues to be evoked. This passing reference suggests Ammianus' audience is expected to know about the practice, here mentioned with disapproval. For a modern reader the sound of a disembodied pitchpipe serves as a poignant reminder of the part played by Licinius (and so many educated and talented individuals like him), both during enslavement and as a manumitted Roman citizen serving a patron in roles that were vital but so often remained unrecognized, minimized, or deliberately erased in antiquity.

Gaius Gracchus the Orator

An appreciation of Gaius Sempronius Gracchus' impact as a speaker, both on contemporary audiences and on the subsequent history of political rhetoric, also entails an understanding of the careful training he had had and the many hours of practice with Licinius (and surely with numerous others) that produced his final performances. How did the young Gaius Gracchus, who was only in his early thirties at the time of his death, meet Licinius and work together with him to bring about a revolution in political rhetoric? A detailed account of their shared oratorical path has not survived but Gracchus' background and family connections provide the essential context. Gaius' eminent political pedigree destined him for a public career, for which he was prepared by a thorough literary education, army service, and intense rhetorical training.

His famous brother Tiberius, who was nine years older, was himself a leading orator in a much more traditional style.[15] Tiberius' influence and impact have been overshadowed by Gaius' brilliance and innovations, which came to be recognized as a watershed in Roman public speaking and inspired subsequent tribunes of the plebs, notably Lucius Appuleius Saturninus, but surely also other popular speakers, such as Gaius Marius. Plutarch's paired biographies set the pattern of treating the two Gracchi brothers together, a comparison that inevitably made Tiberius seem a less forceful and effective orator than his career suggests.

Gaius, however, did not himself hear any of Tiberius' famous speeches delivered during his tribunate of 133, because he was serving in the army in Spain during the final stages of the lengthy Roman siege of Numantia.[16] In fact, Gaius' early life was marked by long periods of military service, even as his older brother had also built his image of excellence as a warrior. Gaius served twelve seasons of military service instead of the usual ten that were required before standing for public office in Rome.[17] He will, therefore, have been a very young recruit on his first campaign. He later spent two years in Sardinia as quaestor. Upon his return from Sardinia in 124, he burst on the political scene, soon becoming the most influential public orator in the city, a passionate young reformer whose rapid rise was cut short by political disaster and suicide only three years later. The attention he attracted in Rome is also indicated by the crowds that frequented his large house on the Palatine, especially for his famous morning receptions (*salutationes*).[18]

How did Gaius learn to speak so forcefully, at such an early stage of his career? Various opportunities and mentors will have played a role in fostering his natural talent. Gaius was very young, perhaps still a baby, when his father died. But his mother, Cornelia, the daughter of Scipio Africanus, arranged for an elaborate education in the Greek style for her children.[19] After she was widowed, a significant amount of the family's time was apparently spent in Cornelia's villa on the Bay of Naples away from the political sphere in Rome.[20] Subsequently, Gaius' army service provided a close appreciation of speeches delivered in front of the troops and debates in the general's *consilium*, the council of trusted advisers.[21] Perhaps Gaius was even involved in drafting some of these speeches, once he had shown a particular interest in rhetoric. In Numantia he will have heard Scipio Aemilianus (who was his cousin, brother-in-law, and commanding officer), as well as witnessing Aemilianus' triumphant return to the city after his victory in Spain.[22] There is some evidence that Gaius delivered his first public speech(es), upon his return from Numantia, in the immediate aftermath of his brother's murder, when he would have been only about 21 years old.[23] His brother's death overshadowed his own political career and was a regularly recurring, poignant theme of his public rhetoric.[24]

In anticipation of his return to Rome from Spain, Gaius had been named by Tiberius Gracchus as one of the three commissioners to survey and reassign public land (*ager publicus*) under Tiberius' agrarian law.[25] This commission's activities continued despite Tiberius' violent death and are attested by a set of boundary stones, some even found in situ.[26] Each inscription on these markers features Gaius' name. It seems that the commissioners and their team of helpers were very active before their work was challenged in 129 by the same Scipio Aemilianus, who had remained married to Gaius' older sister Sempronia, despite bitter political differences between family members and personal tensions between the spouses.[27] Aemilianus was acting on behalf of wealthy Italian landowners who had become the first to lose public lands that had been illegally appropriated over many years.[28] In the context of the agrarian commission, Gaius Gracchus had the chance to exercise an unusual kind of executive job that would normally be assigned to much more senior politicians, such as his two colleagues. Meanwhile, the very seniority of these colleagues will probably have resulted in more travel and work on the spot for Gaius, who was very much the junior partner in this triumvirate.

Gaius' experience in the army will surely have been useful to him as he traveled in Italy with a team of expert surveyors and explained the implications of the new law to local populations, most of whom had not been in Rome to hear his brother speak about his scheme to redistribute public land in small, inalienable lots to poorer Roman citizens. In this context, Gaius will probably also have been called upon to deliver speeches in public, in addition to more private, high-stakes negotiations with prominent municipal officials and influential local landowners. His initial years as a land commissioner shaped both his skills and self-presentation in the time before he stood for his first political office, a quaestorship for which he was a candidate in Rome in 127.[29]

But how can we fit Licinius the flute player into this picture of Gracchus' educational and career trajectory? The answer to this question depends on when Gaius married Licinia, daughter of Publius Licinius Crassus Dives Mucianus (consul 131 and briefly *pontifex maximus*). Cicero and others thought that Licinius had already worked with Gaius while he was enslaved.[30] Yet, he cannot have been legally subject to Gaius, since all Gaius' property was confiscated by the state after his suicide in 121.[31] In other words, after Gaius' sudden, violent death and the postmortem sanctions immediately imposed upon him, Licinia was not in a legal position to manumit under her own name any persons enslaved by Gaius at the time he died.[32] The most economical explanation is that Licinius came to Gaius as a member of Licinia's own household at the time of their marriage, possibly as part of her extensive dowry.[33]

Gaius and Licinia married young, as was a custom for Rome's most elite families; Cornelia will have played a key role in arranging her youngest son's marriage alliance. Gaius and Licinia are described as already being married while he was serving in Spain with his brother-in-law Scipio Aemilianus (134–133). Gaius may, therefore, have married in his late teens or at the age of 20, perhaps immediately before his departure for Numantia (or possibly even earlier). Licinia would typically have been slightly younger than or about the same age as her husband. Consequently, Licinius, who had received an excellent education, could indeed have been helping Gaius as soon as his return from Spain in 132.[34]

Licinius, the erudite musician with the training in rhetorical arts, should ultimately be associated with Licinia's father, Dives Mucianus (born into the family of the Mucii Scaevolae and adopted by the Licinii Crassi), himself a well-known orator and legal expert.[35] Unfortunately, no fragments survive from the repertoire of Mucianus who was one of Rome's leading politicians when Gaius was an adolescent and while he was completing his army service.[36] Gaius' father-in-law had supported Tiberius' political reforms and was the man designated to replace Tiberius himself on the agrarian commission. Mucianus will have had many interactions with Gaius Gracchus in the immediate aftermath of Tiberius' death, before he himself was killed in 130, after being captured in battle in Asia.[37] Licinius might, therefore, have been assisting Gaius with his speeches as early as the late 130s and could also have accompanied him in his travels in Italy to redistribute public land. Subsequently, he might also have traveled to Sardinia with Gaius for the two years of his quaestorship; it is notable how quickly Gaius became a prominent orator after this return from that junior assignment.[38]

Licinius' background and training reflect the cultural habits and pretensions of the Licinii Crassi, whose proverbially fabulous wealth and political influence were well established by this point.[39] Indeed, the presence in the mid-130s of such a highly educated enslaved musician in the trousseau of a young bride, presumably herself an educated person, evokes both material wealth and its deployment to create cultural capital that was valued in various ways. There is evidence for two Liciniae in the next generation who were known for their rhetorical expertise.[40] Gaius recognized Licinius' talents, with or without the help of his prominent father-in-law, and made use of them for his own political and oratorical advancement.

The figure of Licinius, therefore, creates a further and different connection between Gaius Gracchus and the rhetorical traditions of the Licinii Crassi, his wife's family. In this context, it is useful to recall that Gaius was actually not the first orator to face away from the senate house and its forecourt (*comitium*) by turning to address a larger crowd assembled in the Forum proper. According to Cicero, that distinction belonged to Gaius Licinius Crassus, tribune of the plebs in 145.[41] Very little information has survived about this earlier

Crassus, who is not attested as having had a political career after his tribunate. It is not surprising that his innovation has been attributed by later authors to Gaius Gracchus, the far more famous orator who popularized this same tactic. Gaius, therefore, learned about the tradition of the Licinii both from his aristocratic in-laws and also from their skilled slave(s). That same Licinian ambition to use public speaking for political, juridical, and personal advancement was subsequently carried on by Marcus Licinius Crassus (consul 95, censor 92, some 15 years younger than Gaius Gracchus), so greatly admired by Cicero, who gave him an important role in the *De Oratore*.[42]

As we have seen, Gaius was already familiar with public speeches in military settings, at triumphs, and in local Italian towns. Licinius the flute player helped Gaius to make (some aspects of) an earlier tribune's rhetorical style his own and to realize its fuller potential. Meanwhile, turning toward the Roman Forum created new challenges but also many opportunities for an orator.[43] This orientation soon became the standard one for political speeches. A larger crowd in an expansive open space in Rome resulted in complex acoustics and the need for more expansive, even theatrical gestures in order for communication to be effective. Robust voice and movement training were logical first steps in developing a new oratorical reach and repertoire, one that was designed to withstand and to shape Rome's complex political landscape after the murder of Tiberius Gracchus. Licinius the flute player was one person who played a key role, certainly by the time Gaius was at his most effective, and probably well before, as suggested here. His coaching was attuned both to the reactions of each crowd and to Gaius' particular tendency to get carried away by his own strong emotions, especially anger.

Let us try to re-focalize this well-known narrative from Licinius' perspective. A plausible reconstruction of his life could look something like this. He most probably started his specialized education at a young age in the large and elaborate household of Licinius Mucianus, perhaps as a *verna* (a person, either male or female, born into slavery in a household). As a young man, or even still an adolescent, he was assigned to Licinia's dowry at the time of her marriage in the mid-130s.[44] He will, therefore, probably have been close in age to Gaius and to Licinia herself. He then lived with Licinia in the home of the newly married couple on the Palatine while Gaius was on military service in Spain (134–133). He will have had the chance to experience at least some of the rhetorical and political climate in Rome during these years. And he will have associated closely with Gaius upon his return to Rome, soon after Tiberius' violent death. Mucianus could have been the one to arrange for the two men to work in collaboration, in the tense atmosphere after the disastrous events of 133.

Licinius will have traveled widely in Italy with Gaius and may even have accompanied him to Africa in 121. His talents and training became integral to

Gaius' meteoric career over the next dozen years, until his untimely death. The date of Licinius' manumission is unknown but could easily fall within Gaius' lifetime, in recognition of his vital service, or immediately after Gaius' death, in reaction to the ultimately unsuccessful attempt to deprive Licinia of her dowry.[45] Licinius could also have been present on the notorious occasion when the couple's home was ransacked by a mob incited by the consul of 121, Lucius Opimius.[46] In the year before his death, Gaius had moved out of the house on the Palatine that he had shared with Licinia into a residence near the Forum.[47] Licinius will probably have moved with him, although Licinia and the children seem to have stayed in their usual home. Nevertheless, Licinius was not the one to accompany Gaius on his final flight over the ancient wooden bridge (Pons Sublicius) across the river and to share in his suicide in the Grove of Furrina.[48] He, therefore, experienced firsthand much of the violence, in rhetoric and in deed, first of Tiberius' tribunate and its bloody aftermath, and subsequently of Gaius' short and unusual political career. Licinius seems to have lived for many more years, perhaps eventually as a client of Quintus Lutatius Catulus, and presumably still associated closely with Licinia and her surviving child(ren).[49]

Gaius Gracchus' Rhetorical Style

The rhetorical performances created by the collaboration between Gaius Gracchus and Licinius were shaped by the wider political and rhetorical landscape of Rome in the late second century. Attention has been focused on Gaius' early teachers, who included several learned Greek speakers from a variety of backgrounds. Together with his brother Tiberius, he was influenced by Diophanes of Mytilene from the island of Lesbos, a famous Greek rhetorician, and Gaius Blossius of Cumae, a Stoic philosopher from Campania near the Bay of Naples.[50] Both intellectuals were thought by contemporaries to have contributed to Tiberius' ideas for political reform.[51] Diophanes and Blossius were engaged to instruct her sons by Cornelia, who is herself mentioned as the single most important inspiration for their eloquence because of her learned and fluent way of speaking.[52] Diophanes was executed in the aftermath of Tiberius' death, while Blossius went into voluntary exile in Asia, where he committed suicide after the defeat of the pretender Aristonicus by the Romans.[53] Since Gaius' public speeches fall after Tiberius' death, he cannot at that time have had continued access to Diophanes and Blossius, however close he may have been to them while he was growing up.[54]

Subsequently, Gaius the popular politician was associated with the Syrian rhetorician Menelaus of Marathos (modern Amrit), who is specifically mentioned in relation to Gaius' public speaking style.[55] Menelaus, a freeborn professional rhetorician, who seems to have come to Rome under his own steam (after the sack of his hometown by the Romans in 148 and by way of Alexandria), is attested as an important part of Gaius' support team. Gaius Fannius (consul 122), a leading political opponent of Gracchus', criticized Gaius Gracchus because he had allegedly been helped by Menelaus and by unnamed "others" to compose his speeches.[56] Menelaus may have been a person who introduced Gaius to a range of more emotional and theatrical Hellenistic rhetorical mannerisms, building on elements of the "Asiatic" style in use in the eastern Mediterranean. The meager surviving fragments of Gaius' speeches, however, suggest a plain way of speaking in relatively short sentences, much simpler in style than Cicero's long periodic clauses. The exceptional impact of Gaius' oratory seems, therefore, to have depended to a considerable degree on his dramatic delivery of everyday speech, which cannot readily be recreated in detail even from verbatim quotations.[57]

It is obviously difficult to generalize about Gaius' speaking style based on the few verbatim fragments we have in Latin. It is clear, however, that he made memorable use of short phrases and sentences with carefully chosen words. An example of a tricolon can be found in the following fragment from a speech attacking Lucius Calpurnius Piso Frugi that was delivered in 123:

> *pueritia tua adulescentiae tuae inhonestamentum fuit, adulescentia senectuti dedecoramentum, senectus reipublicae flagitium.*
>
> ORF[4] NO. 48 F43 = ISIDORE *ETYM.* 2.21.4

> Your boyhood was a disgrace to your youth, your youth was a dishonor to your old age, your old age was an outrage to the republic/commonwealth.

This Latin sentence is more reminiscent of the Elder Cato and Sallust than of Cicero, at least to a modern reader. A similar flavor can be found in the longer fragments quoted by Gellius from two speeches, one in opposition to a Lex Aufeia and the other in defense of his own laws.[58] In the latter, Gaius complained about the high-handed treatment of local magistrates in Italian towns by a Roman consul and his wife.

> *nuper Teanum Sidicinum consul venit. uxor eius dixit se in balneis virilibus lavari velle. quaestori Sidicino M. Mario datum est negotium, uti balneis exigerentur qui lavabantur. uxor renuntiat viro parum cito sibi balneas traditas esse et parum lautas fuisse. idcirco palus destitutus est in foro, eoque adductus suae civitatis nobilissimus homo M. Marius. vestimenta detracta sunt, virgis caesus est. Caleni, ubi id audierunt, edixerunt, ne quis in balneis lavisse vellet, cum magistratus Romanus ibi esset. Ferentini ob eandem causam praetor noster quaestores arripi iussit: alter se de muro deiecit, alter prensus et virgis caesus est.*
>
> ORF[4] NO. 48 F48 = GELLIUS *NA* 10.3.2–11

> Recently, a consul came to Teanum Sidicinum. His wife said that she wanted to bathe in the public baths reserved for men. The job of removing the bathers from the bathhouse was assigned to Marcus Marius, quaestor at Sidicinum. The wife told her husband that the baths had not been provided to her fast enough and that they had not been clean enough. For that reason a stake was set up in the forum and Marcus Marius, a most prominent person in his community, was led there. His clothes were removed and he was beaten with rods. When they heard this at Cales, they passed a decree that nobody should use the public baths when a Roman magistrate was present. At Ferentinum, for this same reason our praetor ordered the quaestors to be arrested. One threw himself from the city wall; the other was captured and beaten with rods.

Gellius himself comments on the devastating rhetorical effect achieved here by Gracchus' plain narrative of the abuse suffered by Marcus Marius, a local quaestor, as well as of stark effects on other Italian communities. The nameless consul seems to stand for a typical Roman magistrate of the highest rank.[59] Gaius creates confidence in his narrative through its plain and objective style.[60] Whether his delivery was emotional or matter-of-fact is impossible to recover; in this context either strategy could have been memorable and arresting.

The most obvious fragment that can be associated with an impassioned tone comes from a speech that seems to have been delivered late in his life, again quoted by Cicero in *De Oratore*.[61] The emotion here is closer to despair and sadness than to anger.

> *[Crassus:] quid fuit in Graccho, quem tu melius, Catule, meministi, quod me puero tanto opere ferretur? "quo me miser conferam? quo vertam? in Capitoliumne? at fratris sanguine redundat, an domum? matremne ut miseram lamentantem videam et abiectam?" quae sic ab illo esse acta constabat oculis, voce, gestu, inimici ut lacrimas tenere non possent.*
>
> F 61 = CICERO *DE OR.* 3.214

Crassus is the speaker in the dialogue:

> What was it that [Gaius] Gracchus said, whom you Catulus remember better, the saying that made such a difference to me as a boy?
>
> "Where shall I go, miserable me? Where shall I turn? To the Capitol? But it overflows with the blood of my brother? Or [should I go] home? That I may see my mother, miserable and brought low?"
>
> It is well known that these words were delivered in such a way by him—using his eyes, his voice, his gestures—that his political rivals were not able to contain their tears.

In this case, it is much easier to imagine a dramatic style of delivery, including tone and movement, even as Cicero, who was born some 15 years after this speech was delivered, refers to Gaius' highly effective use of gaze, voice, and gesture on this occasion. Again, the sentences are short and unadorned. Gaius' words are a free but recognizable adaptation of a famous speech given by Medea in Euripides' well-known play of the same name.[62] The theme had been adapted for the Roman stage in Latin by Ennius earlier in the second century, before Gaius was born.[63] Here Gaius uses a well-known rhetoric of despair to recall the tragic figure of Medea at the same time as he rehearses again familiar themes from his own oratorical repertoire, including his brother's violent death in the sacred precinct on the Capitol and his close relationship with his mother, Cornelia, herself a figure of some renown in the public eye.[64] In this version, he has made this ancient theme very much his own.

It is interesting to see Gaius cast himself in the role of a woman and a foreigner without civic rights, at least to those in the audience who recognized the adaptation, with the express intent of arousing popular indignation and pity for him in his moment of extreme crisis.[65] He and his team of advisers clearly expected the emotional appeal of a person who is isolated and wronged to be more effective than the better attested rhetoric of superiority favored by Roman politicians from the kind of aristocratic background that Gaius enjoyed. It would not be surprising if he had sought help from Licinius with the delivery of such an extreme appeal, which evoked an actor on stage in a number of different ways.

Gaius Gracchus' Rhetoric in its Contemporary Context

But how did Gaius' rhetoric fit in with that of others, whether his supporters or his political rivals? This broader question is relevant to the rhetorical culture within which Licinius operated. Again, the surviving evidence is very limited. In fact, no fragments have come down from speeches of Marcus Fulvius Flaccus, Gaius' principal political ally, or of Lucius Opimius, his deadliest rival.[66] Yet both men reached the consulship and must have been at least competent, if not influential, orators. Gaius and his advisers, however innovative their strategies, also surely created content and delivery within the particular rhetorical environment created by the large number of contemporary public speakers, with an eye and an ear to what was being well received. Many of Gaius' attested speeches were attacks on others or expositions in defense of himself or of his policies against critiques voiced by rival politicians. In this sense also, he was continually in dialogue with the public oratory of his day. Yet, it seems doubtful that Gaius himself would have had the time or inclination to attend the *contiones* of others regularly, which makes it all the more likely that informants, perhaps including Licinius himself or other members of the extended household, provided information from their observations about what was being said in public meetings and how rhetorical effects were being received.

This is not the place to give a general survey of Latin political rhetoric in the 130s and 120s, but a brief overview is suggestive of larger trends and fashions. We have evidence for eight other orators who stood in some documented relationship to Gaius Gracchus.[67] Of these six were opponents, two were supporters, and a further two had by 121 changed sides from favoring Gaius to opposing him. It is interesting to note immediately, therefore, that negative speeches have been much better preserved in the citing authors than positive ones. One supporter we know of is Gaius' father-in-law Mucianus, a famous orator and historian, although no fragments of his speeches survive.[68] The other political ally is Publius Decius (tr. pl. 115), who mounted an unsuccessful prosecution of the consul Lucius Opimius in 120 for his role in Gaius' death.[69] In other words, we have no exact title or surviving fragments of speeches in support of Gaius that were delivered in his own lifetime.

The following politicians are remembered for their rhetorical attacks on Gaius: Lucius Calpurnius Piso Frugi (cos. 133), Marcus Livius Drusus (cos. 112), Quintus Aelius Tubero (tr. pl. 129), and Marcus Iunius Pennus (tr. pl. 126). Piso is recorded as opposing Gaius' grain law and as nevertheless coming to collect his share when the distributions began.[70] He is an example of a conservative opponent of the old school, who was concerned about the impact of Gaius' social welfare programs on the public treasury. He is described as an effective speaker in the plain and traditional style. He also authored a history that may have been critical of the Gracchi.[71]

By contrast, Livius Drusus, tribune of the plebs in 122, did decisive political damage to his fellow tribunes Gaius Gracchus and Fulvius Flaccus with his highly effective oratory.[72] He was a formidable opponent, who went on to a distinguished political career. He also had advocated for a program of political reforms of his own. While Gaius was away in Africa for several months (although tribunes of the plebs were supposed to remain in Rome during their time in office), Livius Drusus managed to discredit him and win the populace over to his own political platform. Public speaking was, therefore, a vital tool used both by and against Gaius.

There were also unspecified others in Drusus' circle who criticized Gaius' personal extravagance. They drew attention to the large sums he spent on decorative silver dolphins.[73] It is unclear who these associates of Drusus were or how they circulated their views. It is possible that they included other tribunes of 122, most of whose names are unknown to us, who also used occasions of public speaking to disparage and undermine Gaius, here with a typical charge of personal luxury against a man of considerable wealth.[74] If Licinius stayed in Rome rather than accompanying Gaius to Africa, it would have been highly relevant for him to hear these critical speeches.

By contrast, Quintus Aelius Tubero and Marcus Iunius Pennus were far less distinguished opponents, who were not remembered as leading orators or politicians. Neither seems to have made it to the highest offices. Tubero is described as a mediocre speaker who nevertheless used valid arguments. He was much more skillful as a debater than an orator.[75] The confrontation between Tubero and Gaius reveals some of the negative impact even an undistinguished opponent could have within the public sphere. Pennus, an ambitious man who died young during his aedileship, was more prominent. He was tribune of the plebs in 126, the year in which Gaius was quaestor. Pennus targeted Gaius with some success after he had spoken in opposition to Pennus' bill proposing the expulsion of foreigners from the city of Rome.[76] This rhetorical exchange will have come early in the year since Gaius soon left for two years of service in Sardinia. Here we see Gaius already seeking a public role at the very beginning of his official political career, presumably at a *contio* presided over by a more senior magistrate.

Especially interesting contrasts with Gaius are provided by two leading politicians who had initially supported him but then became harsh critics, Gaius Fannius, consul of 122, and Gaius Papirius Carbo, consul in 120, whose election probably took place soon after Gaius' death. As tribune Gaius had supported Fannius' candidacy for the consulship during the election season of 123, which strongly suggests that he saw Fannius as a supporter, who would not move to overturn his legislation.[77] Although Fannius had an active career in the courts, he was known as a mediocre orator.[78] His most famous speech, however, was a tour de force attacking Gaius' and Fulvius Flaccus' proposal to extend Roman citizenship to Latins and Italians in the second half of 122.[79] This was the political issue that seems to have caused the downfall of the reformers, because it was highly unpopular with many ordinary Romans.[80] Fannius' speech was so uncharacteristically striking that contemporaries apparently suspected that he had had a speechwriter or perhaps several helping him with the text. The speech seems to have survived in written form. It is probable that Fannius felt the need to seek help in countering Gaius' powerful rhetoric. Yet this same Fannius is the very person who (perhaps simultaneously) criticized Gaius for the help he allegedly received in composing orations from Menelaus of Marathus and unidentified others, possibly including Licinius.[81] The heated atmosphere in the later months of 122 apparently led to even greater reliance by orators on a larger circle of advisers, since public speeches were seen as key events in shaping public opinion and in creating political momentum. Fannius was a formidable opponent because he was well informed about the practices of Gaius' inner circle.

Last but not least, Gaius Papirius Carbo was an active and celebrated orator who had a distinguished career both in the courts and in politics.[82] Carbo had been a member of the Gracchan inner circle already in the time of Tiberius; he was chosen in 130 to serve on the agrarian commission of three to implement his political ally's redistribution of land in Italy.[83] He, therefore, also worked closely with Gaius from the beginning of the latter's political career. It was Carbo who, on a notorious occasion, had challenged Scipio Aemilianus to declare his opinion on the murder of Tiberius Gracchus in a public meeting.[84] Yet the only fragments of Carbo's speeches to survive come from his defense of Opimius in a trial before the people on a charge that Roman citizens had been unlawfully executed without a trial, a case that Carbo prevailed in during his consulship.[85] Cicero condemns Carbo as a political turncoat.[86]

Carbo spoke powerfully in defense of Opimius, who may have presided over the election that returned him as consul, arguing that Opimius was justified in defending the republic when he hunted down Gaius, Fulvius Flaccus, and their supporters. His case hinged on a dichotomy that contrasted a wicked Gaius with a noble Opimius, in a scheme that was starkly black and white.[87] The following year, Carbo committed suicide when he was prosecuted under the extortion law by a young Marcus Licinius Crassus.[88] Carbo's eloquence and rhetorical successes did not enable him to survive in the long run. Each of these eight orators, then, together with their advisers, friends, and coaches, shaped the increasingly high-stakes rhetorical and political landscape in which Gaius Gracchus (and so many others) flourished briefly but soon failed.

Conclusion

Gaius' dramatic style of public speaking raises the question of how far oratory in the second century borrowed from the techniques and expertise of the theater to involve and influence larger audiences.[89] This issue is hard to address in a contemporary context because we know little about the stage and its principal performers during Gaius' lifetime. In the next generation, however, there was certainly mutual influence between leading actors and public speakers, including those active in the lawcourts. The most celebrated actor of the first century, Quintus Roscius, went so far as to write a book that discussed acting and public speaking in the same treatise, apparently on an equal footing.[90] Such a comparison was a bold one in Rome's cultural context because public speaking was the preserve of the politically prominent whereas acting on stage brought social stigma with it.[91] Roscius was rare not only for his talent but also for the fact that he seems to have been freeborn rather than coming from a background of enslavement as was common for most actors.[92] He even achieved the status of equestrian rank, thanks to Sulla, and was wealthy enough not to need a salary in the final phase of his career.[93]

Although we know so very little about Roscius' book, it must have argued that acting should be seen as close to other genres of public speaking. It is also said that he and his fellow celebrity Aesopus frequently attended jury trials in order to hear the speeches delivered by Quintus Hortensius Hortalus with the specific intention of picking up techniques they could imitate on stage from the man who was considered the leading orator of the day.[94] Hortensius paid careful attention to every part of his performance, including to his dress. He made extensive use of gesture and movement while speaking.[95] Consequently, he was accused by critics of speaking too dramatically, like an actor, and on one memorable occasion even like a female dancer.[96] This caricature of Hortensius' speaking style, a style that had brought him great success in the courts, suggests the many connections between public oratory and the stage, connections that surely go back to Gaius Gracchus and probably to various of his predecessors whose techniques have not been handed down to us.

With this general context of theatrical public speaking in mind, Licinius the flute player needs to be (re)inserted into our picture of Gaius' coaches, advisers, family members (including his mother Cornelia), and assistants, who worked together on both content and style, especially but not exclusively during Gaius' two tribunates when he was giving public speeches on a very regular basis. It would be interesting to know whether Fannius (or others) publicly criticized Licinius' active role as assistant during Gaius' rhetorical performances, even as he suggested that Menelaus and others were the ones writing Gaius' speeches for him. Licinius clearly played a vital role in shaping Gaius' delivery on the rostra, and surely also in regular practice sessions. He may also have attended other public speeches and received briefings from informants about those he did not attend with a view to gathering information about other orators, whether allies or rivals. Had Licinius been present at dramatic performances to watch actors onstage and to take note of how the audience reacted to them? Had he, in fact, been present at a performance of Ennius' *Medea*, for example, which had helped him coach Gaius' adaptation of a speech from that play? Had his education included acting alongside music? In the time of Cicero, audience reactions at theatrical performances were influential indications of public opinion that were closely watched by politicians and their friends.[97] Once he was manumitted, Licinius would have been much freer to attend a variety of events that would have allowed him to learn from the speaking style of orators and actors in many settings, perhaps even in the company of Gaius himself.

For us, Licinius can and should stand in for so many other freedmen who attended closely upon Roman politicians as they delivered speeches in the most important venues, speeches that were key moments in their careers. A final, comparative example, from some 220 years later, is provided by another unnamed freedman, this man manumitted by the younger Pliny. This Plinius stood behind Pliny while he delivered a speech as prosecutor in the senate during the high-profile trial of Marius Priscus, former governor of the province of Africa.[98] It was mid-January in AD 100 and Pliny had just become consul (for a few months) with the emperor as his colleague. It was the high point of his political career. The emperor Trajan was himself present at the trial and interacted with Pliny's freedman.

> *Caesar quidem tantum mihi studium, tantam etiam curam (nimium est enim dicere sollicitudinem) praestitit, ut libertum meum post me stantem saepius admoneret voci laterique consulerem, cum me vehementius putaret intendi, quam gracilitas mea perpeti posset.*
>
> *EP.* 2.11.15

> Indeed Caesar (the emperor Trajan) afforded me so much concern, indeed so much care (it would be too much to call it anxiety) that he, on several occasions, urged my freedman who was standing behind me that I should take care of my voice and my lungs, at times when he thought I was speaking more passionately than my thin body could bear.

In an interesting parallel with Licinius and Gaius Gracchus, Pliny also had a freedman standing behind him, whom the emperor himself repeatedly prompted to help moderate Pliny's speaking style, in this instance apparently specifically for health reasons rather than for aesthetic effect. On this occasion, Pliny spoke for five hours.[99] It is an unusual description overall since Pliny does not often mention his health or physical strength and claims sometimes to have spoken for even longer than in this case.[100]

How did Trajan communicate with the *libertus*? It is hard to imagine that the emperor himself was also positioned behind Pliny somewhere near the freedman. Surely, Trajan will have been seated in the audience of senators in front, in a prime position facing the speaker and as a principal addressee of this and other speeches in the trial.[101] It is telling, therefore, that he does not signal to Pliny directly to take it easy. He could have used a hand signal, or a nod addressed to the freedman. Alternatively, and perhaps more plausibly, he passed a written note (or a series of notes), by the hand of an attendant of his own, to Pliny's principal assistant, a man who is clearly imagined by Trajan as being able to prompt Pliny's delivery, in addition to whatever other tasks Plinius will have fulfilled during that long senate session. Trajan may have been implying that Plinius was not doing his job properly. Plinius is not described as holding a flute but could have used other prearranged ways to communicate with Pliny, either while he was still speaking or during a break. No other freedmen are attested as being present in the imperial senate, except for attendants of the emperor.[102] Again, we catch just a brief coincidental glimpse of a vital assistant, of whom there may in fact have been many, but who are not recorded in our sources, presumably because they are simply taken for granted. We should try not to do the same with the specialized skills and hard work of these talented and trusted individuals.

2

In the Households of Cato the Censor and Atticus the Businessman

Education is a key to the nature of Roman servitude.

—TEMIN 2013, 129

AS THE example of Licinius has shown, there is often very little detailed evidence for the contexts in which even the most skilled freedmen had originally been educated. This chapter builds on and expands his case study by investigating two Roman households within which education of the enslaved is attested as an important, indeed essential activity. Whether the enslaved members of the household had been born within it or not, training and education was perceived as integral to the well-being and expansion of the economic unit comprised of the family and their staff.[1] A Roman *paterfamilias* was expected to be knowledgeable, and sometimes even innovative, in the ways in which he used specifically designed instruction, training, and education as tools to shape the operations of his household. He was imagined as the ultimate supervisor of each person who worked for him. Ideally his clear and consistent directives would allow his subordinate managers, many of them freedmen, to stand in for him in a range of situations, even as they ensured that his interests were always prioritized. Effective household management became ever more complicated but no less urgent when overall wealth and the number of enslaved persons increased as a result of Rome's rapid imperial growth after the Second Punic War. Roman households produced and acquired individuals educated in a wide variety of skills; these workers in turn made possible the lives of the family members and of their friends.

This chapter will juxtapose the households of two leading Romans who are relatively well documented for us, the senator Marcus Porcius Cato the censor and Marcus Pomponius Atticus (eventually known as Quintus Caecilius

Atticus), Cicero's wealthy equestrian friend. Cato lived before the time of Licinius the flute player and of the other freedmen discussed in later chapters, while Atticus was a slightly older contemporary of Cicero, whom he outlived by many years. Cato and Atticus had very different careers and lived in distinct historical periods, but each was noted for his active involvement with educating enslaved persons within various household settings, both in Rome and on country estates. In other words, Cato and Atticus were heavily invested in slavery as an evolving institution within the historical, political, and social contexts of their long lifetimes. Both men were very successful in their chosen career paths and lived into old age, by ancient standards. While each man originally came from an affluent equestrian background, Cato navigated the path of a new man (*novus homo*) in politics all the way to a censorship, while Atticus became an exceptionally successful businessman. In this sense, each man showed marked ambition in going beyond the social and economic situation he had inherited from his well-established family. The acquisition and training of a large number of slaves was integral to their paths to success and to the lifestyles they ultimately came to enjoy and to use as part of their carefully curated self-representation. A comparison between their households highlights both changes and continuities in enslavement patterns between the defeat of Hannibal at the end of the third century and the emergence of a system of one-man rule after the Battle of Actium in 31.

Marcus Porcius Cato, often referred to as Cato the Elder, was born at Tusculum in Latium in 234 and grew up in the Sabine countryside.[2] His career was built on his outstanding army service, active engagement as a lawyer and public speaker, and the political patronage of a local patrician, L. Valerius Flaccus, with whom he would go on to share both his consulship and censorship. Cato was married twice and had children from each of these unions.[3] His life is illuminated for us by Plutarch's biography of him, by Livy's narrative up to 167, and by the many fragments of Cato's writings and speeches cited by a wide variety of later authors.[4] Indeed, Cato remains the best-documented figure of the second century, largely due to his notorious habit of self-advertisement, which was already commented on by Livy.[5] Cato rose rapidly in politics after his notable military service during the Second Punic War. He served as plebeian aedile in Rome (199) and praetor in Sardinia (198), before becoming consul in 195 at the age of 39. His leadership of Roman troops over two years in Spain earned him a triumph.[6] After holding the censorship for 18 months, starting in 184, he continued to be a notable public opinion maker and influential speaker in the senate for another 35 years until his death in 149 at the age of 85. A prolific author, who circulated his works in his own lifetime, Cato is the earliest Latin prose writer whose writings survive in whole or in part.[7] His stature and influence ensured that he was much remembered both in antiquity and beyond. His aim was to define and revitalize Roman cultural values, military and political objectives, and national ethos in a rapidly changing Hellenized world.

It may seem inappropriate, perhaps even unhelpful, to compare Cato, the vociferous upholder of his own version of traditional Roman values, with Atticus, the famous philhellene who spoke Greek like an Athenian but who avoided both a political career and spending too much time in Rome.[8] Yet there are, in fact, quite a number of ways in which Atticus can be understood to be an heir of Cato in the field of domestic and rural economy, whether through direct or indirect influence. Atticus was well known for having only *vernae* (home-born children of an enslaved mother) in his household in Rome and for educating all of them to a high standard of literacy.[9] This elaborate household system, which Atticus' friend Cornelius Nepos describes as not being a norm in their day, is a logical development of Cato's earlier efforts to structure his household to include a system of training young enslaved boys, whom he might then keep for his own uses or resell at a profit after their education was complete.

The two men also shared a deliberately simple, even ostentatiously plain, personal lifestyle and a highly developed interest in Roman history, the Latin language, and antiquarianism. Atticus wrote works about family history and historical chronology that would have been of great interest to Cato.[10] Atticus' desire to see Roman literature in Latin rival that of the Greeks would also have been appealing and familiar to Cato. Atticus' life is documented for us by two especially valuable contemporary sources, Cornelius Nepos' biography and the 16 books of letters addressed to him by his close friend Cicero.[11] Meanwhile, both Cato and Atticus succeeded in greatly increasing their personal wealth and growing their assets through creative innovation and diversification, initiatives that were made possible by the use of skilled slave labor.

Marcus Pomponius Atticus, born in 110, came from an old Roman family that had enjoyed equestrian status for many generations. His father provided him with a sophisticated education that gave him the tools and contacts for a potential future political career in Rome.[12] However, the violence of the Social War and subsequent civil strife in Rome caused the young Atticus, an orphan by the age of 20, to liquidate (most of) his investments and to relocate to Athens, probably soon after Sulla captured the city in spring 86.[13] It remains unclear whether Atticus had served in the army during the Social War, perhaps even under Sulla himself.[14] Atticus was deeply and personally affected by the violence of the year 88, not least because his cousin Anicia was married to a brother of the tribune Publius Sulpicius Rufus, the man whose actions caused civil war to break out for the first time in Rome.[15]

As a result of his experiences in these turbulent years, when Rome was repeatedly besieged and captured by rival Roman armies, Atticus decided to move to Athens, where he acquired his *cognomen* (man from Attica) while spending much of his time there over the next twenty years. His choice not to marry until much later in life may perhaps also have been linked to his desire not to tie himself to the political fortunes of another family in the way that had caused him so much trouble in the early 80s.[16] Rather he concentrated on developing his business interests through a wide variety of investments as growth opportunities presented themselves in Greece, the Aegean, and Asia in the aftermath of the Mithridatic Wars.[17] In 68, Atticus acquired a large estate at Buthrotum in Epirus, where he raised sheep and farmed.[18] This location, strategically situated between Italy and the Eastern Mediterranean, would serve as a key base and home for the rest of his life.

Early in 64 Atticus returned to Rome, where he now spent much more time, particularly after 58 when he received a large inheritance from his mother's brother, the banker Quintus Caecilius.[19] Under the terms of his uncle's will, Atticus was posthumously adopted as a son and now legally renamed Quintus Caecilius.[20] Atticus' marriage to a certain Pilia, less than 18 months after his change of status and at the age of 54, may perhaps also be linked to the terms of this same will.[21] In any case, he now started spending a significant amount of time in Rome in the fine old house on the Quirinal that he had inherited from his uncle Caecilius. He chose to stay on here even when Caesar invaded Italy in 49.

Atticus is often described as a man who was politically neutral, a businessman who used his neutrality to survive the political crises and civil strife of the first century.[22] In fact, he carefully cultivated many sides in civil conflicts, with the result that he was a Pompeian who was close friends with Julius Caesar, later a confidant of the young Octavian, all the while maintaining an active relationship with Marc Antony throughout the triumviral period. At the time of his death in 32 at the age of 77, Atticus' daughter Caecilia Attica was married to Marcus Agrippa, Octavian's most valuable military supporter and victor at Actium the following year. In other words, Atticus did much more than survive by staying out of politics. Rather he played a complex financial, social, and political game that made him invaluable to each side. He was each person's special friend and vital resource. Meanwhile, he played individuals and factions off against each other in such a way that he consistently came out ahead of the game. There were few wealthy Romans of any class or background who managed to weather political storms in the way that Atticus did. His life is better documented than that of any other equestrian in the first century.

Cato and the Evolution of Roman Slavery in the Second Century

Marcus Porcius Cato grew up in a family that evidently made extensive use of enslaved labor, especially for agricultural tasks and domestic labor, such as cooking. Consequently, Cato will naturally have taken such labor very much for granted, even from his earliest childhood in the 230s and 220s. The distinguished military service of his father and grandfather may have further enriched the family of landowners through war booty, including access to enslaved captives taken in war.[23] By the late third century, the family had enough spare money to support Cato's political aspirations; his rapid progress in gaining election to each magisterial office at a young age shows that he had ample material support, in addition to his many talents and personal achievements. Yet his time as an adolescent in the years before Hannibal's invasion of Italy is portrayed as having been relatively, perhaps deceptively, simple and in tune with the traditional rhythms of life on the land. Cato, probably together with relatives and neighbors, is described as working on the land himself alongside the enslaved workforce.[24] Performing all kinds of tasks on a farm was thoroughly familiar to him, even as he studied and practiced law in local communities. At the end of the day, he easily and quite naturally sat down to share an ordinary meal and common wine with his family's enslaved laborers.[25] In a similar way, he is portrayed as having a casual and even companionable relationship with the enslaved personal attendant who accompanied him during his initial army service.[26] It was from the enslaved members of his family's household that his wealthy patrician neighbor Lucius Valerius Flaccus was said first to have learned the details of Cato's remarkably frugal habits and personal qualities, presumably through questioning.[27]

Cato himself is surely the ultimate source of most of these circumstantial anecdotes in Plutarch's biography. His carefully crafted self-portrait as a man from a humble background who was imbued with traditional Roman values of simplicity and hard work was integral to his political persona. Cato, therefore, seems to have claimed that he was not brought up in a privileged or pretentious way. Plutarch is only too ready to repeat as fact what he has found in Cato's ample writings about his domestic situations. Even if one may suspect that some of the episodes in Plutarch have been exaggerated and taken out of a larger context, either by Cato or by Plutarch, the following basic point is a useful one to keep in mind. Cato was born into a world already heavily dependent on enslaved labor but one that would be radically reshaped by the massive expansion of available war captives with advanced skills, who would flood the labor market in Rome throughout the first half of the second century.[28] But Cato the traditionalist did not resist this novel expansion of slave labor, rather he actively encouraged, developed, and profited from it.

Consequently, his evocations of simpler times in his youth can be understood as fraught with nostalgia for a world that seemed vivid, probably already distorted by hindsight, because it appeared to be vanishing fast or already gone. These descriptions could serve a variety of purposes for Cato, rhetorical, representative, commemorative, and symbolic. Yet, when in his *De Agricultura* Cato instructed his farm manager (*vilicus*) to understand each task himself by working alongside the farm hands, this reads as practical advice gained from personal experience.[29] In his text Cato's ideal landowner has his eye on every aspect of farm management and is the source for the best instructions, from recipes to home remedies, from religious guidelines to time management expectations.[30] At the center of this text, the earliest surviving Latin prose work, is a stylized representation of the effective management of slave labor, largely entrusted to resident managers, both male and female, who seem themselves formerly to have been enslaved. Indeed, the *De Agricultura* itself implies the constant need for those in charge of a farm to instruct the workers to do their jobs properly, even as they are monitoring the performance of each member of the household. Consequently, it is evident that Cato's life and his public image were each closely connected to the changing conditions of the market for enslaved labor as it expanded and evolved during his lifetime. Plutarch's biography is full of references to slavery and its role in Cato's life, even as the surviving fragments of Cato's speeches also repeatedly come back to this topic.

My discussion will attempt to situate the education and training of enslaved members of Cato's household within the overall frameworks afforded by his public career, his writings, and his personal practices. Inevitably, Cato's long and varied life resulted in actions or pronouncements that appear to be illogical or even self-contradictory, but that raise a series of fascinating questions about evolving norms and changing rhetoric related to enslavement. The background to Cato's household is provided by his political, legal, and army career, which brought him vastly increased wealth beyond what he had inherited from his family. Cato had a distinguished military career that gave him direct insight into Rome's expanding role on the ground, both in established and in new provinces abroad. He regularly saw opponents in battle and local civilian populations captured and enslaved by Rome. In his role as a commanding general, he himself was quite capable of enslaving the population of a whole town, as he did in the case of Tarraco in Spain, after this community had revolted from Rome a second time.[31]

Yet, Cato could also sharply criticize a political opponent for "wrongfully" treating free local dignitaries in Italy as if they were enslaved.[32] In other words, he had a view of the institution of chattel slavery that did not necessarily make enslavement the inevitable fate of any opponent or critic of Rome under every circumstance. There was in his worldview, rather, "rightful" enslavement and "wrongful" enslavement, although the distinction may not always be self-evident to us. Meanwhile, as censor, he imposed punitive taxes on expensive slaves below the age of 20, whose inflated prices he consistently criticized, both on a societal and on an individual level.[33] He assessed and then taxed the price of these transactions at ten times their cash value. He was especially critical of high prices paid for young boys who were acquired specifically as sexual companions.[34]

Similarly, Cato used slavery (*servitudo*) in his political speeches as a powerful descriptive metaphor for a condition of political subjection to a foreign empire, a condition he claimed any man would naturally fear and resist. In his famous speech in support of the Rhodians in 167, Cato first used freedom (*libertas*) and its opposite, enslavement (*servitudo*), as evocative terms to argue in favor of allowing Greek states to choose neutrality or even opposition to Rome's ambitions within their own spheres of influence.[35] Despite his own aggressive tactics in Spain in the mid-190s, Cato was much less enthusiastic about Rome's expanding interests in the Eastern Mediterranean after the defeat of king Perseus of Macedon in 168. For this policy position he surely had many reasons, not least his scathing assessment of the greed of Roman leaders who hoped to profit personally from a possible war with Rhodes.

But his speech on behalf of the Rhodians sets out a generous view of political self-determination as the reasonable goal of any political entity, a goal that other political actors, including Rome, should be willing to recognize.[36] The logic of this argument leads Cato to term Rome's domination (*imperium*) in the East a form of servitude that it was natural for Greek states to fear. He could have argued for a policy of more limited foreign involvement purely on the basis of Rome's own self-interest in her current political situation. But he chose instead to make a much more sophisticated, general point about diplomatic relations with Greek states. Cato had his own ideas about what Rome's role should be, both in practical and in theoretical terms, in the larger Hellenistic world. His argument is based on an invitation to the Roman senators in his audience to put themselves in the position of the Greek states and at least try to see things from their point of view. In the context of Cato's speech, enslavement, albeit an inevitable result of war, is portrayed as a natural evil that will inspire hatred of and resistance to Rome, not cooperation with her.[37]

It is within this general context of frequent enslavements associated with Rome's imperial expansion, especially in the Eastern Mediterranean, that one should analyze Cato's own practices within his household and on his country estates. He made a habit of purchasing young prisoners, allegedly at consistently modest prices, with a view to educating them.[38] Did he himself benefit from the taxation measures he introduced that discouraged inflated prices for individuals under the age of 20? It is hard to say. He loudly claimed not to be in the market for the same beautiful boys who fetched the highest prices.[39] But there can be no doubt that Cato appreciated the possibility of exploiting the newly enslaved for his own purposes. This business opportunity was based on establishing training methods within the household, rather than on spending money to acquire individuals who had already undergone an apprenticeship or education elsewhere. Plutarch's description suggests a picture of Cato as a regular frequenter of auctions or other sale venues, a man who himself spoke Greek fluently and could look for potential in a (newly) enslaved child.[40] The implication may be that most of these children were boys, but some were perhaps girls.

Cato's training methods are not described in detail, but Plutarch does refer to a professional teacher, an enslaved *grammatistes* named Chilon, who was a member of Cato's household.[41] Cato decided not to have his older son Marcus (born around 192) taught by Chilon but opted himself to instruct the boy in a wide array of subjects, ranging from reading and the law to riding and swimming. This decision would presumably have come in the late 180s, when Marcus reached the normal school age of 9 or 10 years old.[42] But Chilon is said to have been a skilled and intellectually gifted teacher, who taught many boys. Chilon is not rejected by Cato as a Greek or other foreigner or as an insufficiently learned teacher, but specifically on the basis of his status as an enslaved person. Cato claimed that he did not want his son to be disciplined by a slave (*doulos* in Plutarch's Greek), a practice common in the Roman classroom, or to owe something as important as his education to a person of such low social status. It is interesting to see that Cato felt the need to justify his choice in relation to Chilon, the reputable (enslaved) teacher, which suggests he needed to explain why he was not following what was by now an emerging or even an established custom in the households of other senators.

But who then were the boys who received their lessons from Chilon? It is possible that Cato made money by taking in fee-paying students to be taught by Chilon in the space set aside as a schoolroom in Cato's house in Rome. But if Chilon was already teaching a room full of the sons of Roman senators and businessmen, would Cato have had the same hesitations about having young Marcus join his social equals? Rather, it may be that Chilon's pupils had regularly, at least up until this time, been many boys enslaved by Cato and perhaps by others in the neighborhood who were willing to pay for an education. Cato was not a young father, since Marcus had been born when he was already in his early 40s. Chilon will not, therefore, have originally been employed specifically to teach little Marcus. His schoolroom could have been active long before, as part of the educational system of Cato's household. Chilon could also, perhaps somewhat ironically, have been acquired in the 180s, around the time of Cato's censorship that had targeted luxury and spending, including on young slaves. There is no indication that Chilon left the household when Cato chose to teach Marcus himself; in fact the reverse is suggested by Cato's explanation for not having Chilon teach Marcus. Chilon is one of very few enslaved persons specifically named in our surviving records, despite the large numbers who evidently passed through Cato's household. He was a man with a distinct profile, whose learning Plutarch recalls almost 300 years later.

The name Chilon is, moreover, particularly apt as it recalls the famous Spartan sage, one of the Seven Sages of Greece, a man whose ideas about thrift and the well-considered life suited the image and social message of Cato himself.[43] Chilon could have been a *verna* in Cato's household, or a particularly gifted foreign captive specially chosen by Cato to play a key role in his household. However that may have been, it is interesting to see that Cato himself may have chosen the Greek name Chilon for a learned member of his household in the early second century. Cato's early familiarity with Greek culture is a factor that needs to be kept in mind when considering the role of education in his household.[44]

Chilon's presence as a teacher who was not employed to instruct Cato's son evokes for us a classroom full of other boys, many or most of them enslaved. This picture is confirmed by an unusual scheme that Cato set up in his home, probably in the town house in Rome. Not only did he purchase young prisoners of war himself in order to train them, but he set up a system to encourage his own slaves to acquire young boys themselves and to cooperate as partners with him in a general training scheme. After a year, the pupil would be evaluated for his progress in the educational program that was available within the household. The exact details of this arrangement are not easy to grasp from Plutarch's compressed description.

> ἐδίδου δὲ καὶ τῶν οἰκετῶν τοῖς βουλομένοις ἀργύριον· οἱ δ' ἐωνοῦντο παῖδας, εἶτα τούτους ἀσκήσαντες καὶ διδάξαντες ἀναλώμασι τοῦ Κάτωνος μετ' ἐνιαυτὸν ἀπεδίδοντο. πολλοὺς δὲ καὶ κατεῖχεν ὁ Κάτων, ὅσην ὁ πλείστην διδοὺς ἐωνεῖτο τιμὴν ὑπολογιζόμενος.
>
> CATO MAIOR 21.7

> He also gave money to those of his servants who volunteered; these then bought children, whom they trained and taught for a year at Cato's expense and then sold. Cato himself also bought many of them, paying the amount of the highest price offered.

This was, then, described as a voluntary cooperative venture. Cato provided funds for those who wanted to participate in the business opportunity and they then used this money to purchase boys. Cato also underwrote a one-year training course, which may or may not have been exactly the same for every boy. At the end of the year, Cato had the option of himself acquiring each boy at a fair market price or the boy would be sold, evidently at a profit over the initial investment. There is no mention of the slaveowner being given the option of keeping the boy as his own assistant (*vicarius*).[45]

It is worth trying to clarify (at least some of) what is going on here.[46] What Plutarch does not make plain is that each slave who "chose" to participate must also have invested some of his own savings, from his *peculium,* in the initial purchase of a boy. The scheme simply does not make sense if all the funds were coming from Cato. If that was the case, Cato would himself already own the boys and would have no possibility of purchasing them from another owner at the end of the year. Rather, the slave is the legal owner of the boy, having invested his own money to cover part of the purchase. Cato has incentivized the purchase by contributing some (perhaps fixed) percentage of the sales price while allowing the slave to be recognized as the principal legal proprietor of the boy. Cato underwrites the one-year training period primarily by providing food and clothing for the boy, as well as access to other usual resources to be found in his household, including perhaps instruction from Chilon or others. Learning the Latin language will surely also have been important. It is possible that the boy may regularly have served as an apprentice to his slave-owner, thus encouraging the smooth operation of a training system within the household. It seems unlikely that the famously thrifty Cato would often have paid for lessons outside his home.

In other words, each party must perceive this scheme as at least potentially to their own financial advantage. Although it is, of course, true that Cato ultimately owns the *peculium* of each person he is legally in control of, it is also the case that each enslaved person could have and use his or her own *peculium.*[47] Cato benefited in several ways from such a partnership. As has already been noted, he himself regularly purchased young captives whom he thought good prospects for training. Here we see him encourage his slaves to do the same. Presumably, he does this partly because it allows him to have more boys being educated in his home without paying the full price for them himself. Through this financial scheme, he is managing to get access to the funds in various *peculia* in order to invest them in the slave trade.[48] He allows himself first refusal and opts frequently to buy the ones who have done well after a year. He may then give them more advanced training. Those who look less impressive or whose skills are already available in the household can simply be disposed of in the slave market. It is possible to imagine that Cato's training program also became known and appreciated by other potential buyers. Either way, the boy is legally sold at the end of the year. What is not revealed here is whether the boy's sale price goes entirely to the slave or whether Cato and the slave share the profit according to the percentage each person invested in the original purchase.

In this scheme, Cato's slaves are incentivized to use their own resources, which must, therefore, have been considerable, to invest in the rapidly evolving slave market. In imitation of Cato's own practices, they were given the opportunity to invest in a young boy of their own choice who would be educated within the household. Their financial interest in this enslaved child or adolescent only extended for a single year at a time under a fixed arrangement. Then the results of the training would be assessed in some agreed upon way. Ownership of the boy would pass either to Cato or to someone else at the current market price. The slave investor will then have received his money back; he surely hoped and expected to make an additional profit. Otherwise, there would have been no point in the exercise, and it could hardly have attracted volunteers, since Plutarch states that no one was required to participate. The fixed time period for the investment may also have been attractive to the slaveowners since it will have limited their liability and provided a return within a predictable time frame.

Inevitably, this arrangement involved the enslaved members of Cato's household directly in the larger slave trade in Rome, presumably mostly through the purchase of readily available young males. These boys were apparently easy to come by but not hard to resell, especially once they had acquired even a basic training of some kind. Cato's household was set up to educate such young boys; they were another annual product generated by the household unit, not unlike wine or olive oil or wool from the sheep. Meanwhile, a number of Cato's regular household members had evidently amassed the personal means to invest in this cycle of purchase and training, at least with his help.[49] Perhaps these profits allowed them to buy their own freedom sooner. Cato will also have benefited from enlisting their enthusiastic and self-interested involvement in selecting and training the boys and their subsequent contentment at making a profit, when the outcome was successful. We are not informed about what happened in cases of failure. Cato and each slaveowner perhaps shared the loss if a boy died before the year was over.

An episode from Cato's time in Spain in the mid-190s seems to provide a further allusion to the practice of buying children to train for profit. Cato, first as consul and then as proconsul, was very careful to ensure that he himself and all those around him behaved according to a set of strict norms he had personally established.[50] He took only five of his own attendants to wait on him during his time on campaign, although he surely had a large household at home.[51] One of these chosen attendants, a man named Paccius, decided to buy three young male prisoners of war after a victory.[52] This purchase would logically have followed Cato's example of looking for newly enslaved children to train. Paccius, who seems to have been a freedman at this time, had the money to acquire the three boys for himself, but by doing so went against the express directives of Cato, who had insisted that no one on his staff should be seen to derive any profit from his command.[53] It is likely that prices in Spain under local circumstances were significantly lower than in Rome; Paccius was tempted to exploit an investment opportunity that seemed too good to pass up, despite the additional logistics involved in transporting and then training the boys. It would not have made sense to take this risk if Paccius had been returning to live in Cato's home in Rome.[54] When Cato discovered what had happened, Paccius committed suicide rather than trying to explain or justify what he had done. Cato then sold the boys and deposited the money in the public treasury. Presumably a different commander would not have objected to this kind of personal purchase, but Cato was at pains to stage his life in the simplest terms while he was serving as a Roman magistrate abroad.[55]

The only other named member of Cato's staff is a certain Quintio, a freedman who acted as a business agent.[56] Here again we see an example of a man who has received an advanced education, with the result that he has gained his freedom, either by purchase or gift, and become a close and trusted associate of Cato. Cato made use of Quintio's services when he decided to start investing in maritime ventures, which were always particularly risky and very different from his usually conservative holdings. Plutarch did not approve.[57] Cato was only willing to invest when the shipping company in question had fifty ships to its name, each with a separate owner. Cato then took one share, which was, therefore, a fiftieth of the whole, thus spreading his risk across many voyages. Quintio evidently checked the accounts, at least in Cato's own share but perhaps also in others. He accompanied Cato's ship on all its voyages to keep an eye on what was going on. Clearly Cato had selected Quintio as both a gifted accountant with a shrewd business sense and a man whom he could trust. His unusual name (Fifth), which plays on the word for "five" in Latin, may refer to his selection for additional training to deal in precisely such a business, one based on various multiples of five.

Beyond those few named as individuals who worked for Cato, we can posit many others who had received specialized training in order to carry out his specific instructions, often in his absence. Each of these men will have been literate so that communication through letters and by means of written directives would have been possible. As Cato's landed possessions grew, both in Rome and through the estates he purchased or inherited, he instituted a system of guidelines in order to keep their inhabitants healthy, productive, and firmly under his control at all times. Plutarch's picture is mostly confirmed by the *De Agricultura*, an eclectic text that Cato seems to have worked on over many years. The detailed description of the many roles that Cato expects his *vilicus* to fulfill implies a thorough education, leadership qualities, and the ability to read instructions in writing and to communicate through letters when necessary.[58] The same is true, to a somewhat lesser extent, of the *vilica*, who may or may not be married to the *vilicus*.[59] The *vilicus* is presumably usually a freedman of Cato's, whom he had trained himself and come to trust. This farm manager is in a similar situation to that of Quintio the shipping expert, although he is represented as apparently the only free male on the medium-sized farm described in Cato's text. He was expected to set the tone and to be concerned with the well-being and contentment of his workforce. Cato interestingly suggests that harmony and a sense of community promotes the efficiency that was so vital in making a farm productive.[60]

Meanwhile, in Rome, Cato's life was consistently busy, even into his old age, with politics and lawsuits, which inevitably involved giving frequent speeches in front of various audiences. We have surviving evidence for 80 of the 150 published speeches Cicero knew of. At the same time, Cato was writing many other texts, including most notably his *Origines*, the first Roman history prose work in Latin, and his *De Agricultura*. He also circulated works on such varied subjects as military tactics, the law, a collection of his own sayings (*sententiae*), and a poem about Roman traditional customs.[61] While he had more time to devote to writing at the end of his life, the texts we know most about tend to consist of collections of material that were added to over time. The *Origines* is evidently a project that Cato worked on over many years and expanded beyond the original scope of a possible "first edition."[62] It was itself probably a much-elaborated version of a more basic Roman history book that Cato had written for his older son in his own hand in big letters, probably in the 180s.[63] He also added some of his better-known speeches to the *Origines*, possibly in edited versions. Some speeches, such as the Rhodian oration, were therefore, "published" more than once, initially close to their original delivery, then in the *Origines*, and perhaps also in one or more collections of speeches, although some of these may also have been put together after Cato's death. Cato was a collector of information with many ongoing interests, a man who obviously enjoyed editing and reediting these assemblages over time.

All of this literary activity in itself implies the availability of a staff of educated assistants and copyists, possibly also researchers to gather information and check references. One such unnamed individual is introduced in the following passage from Cato's speech *de sumptu suo*, whose date and context are not firmly established.[64]

> *M. Porcium in ea oratione, quae* ***de sumptu suo*** *inscribitur, in qua sic ait:*
>
> *Iussi caudicem proferri, ubi mea oratio scripta erat de ea re, quod sponsionem feceram cum M. Cornelio. Tabulae prolatae: maiorum benefacta perlecta: deinde quae ego pro republica fecissem leguntur. Ubi id utrumque perlectum est, deinde scriptum erat in oratione: "Numquam ego pecuniam neque meam neque sociorum per ambitionem dilargitus sum." "Attat, noli noli scribere," inquam "istud"; nolunt audire. Deinde recitavit:"Numquam ego praefectos per sociorum vestrorum oppida imposivi, qui eorum bona <coniuges> liberos diriperent." "Istud quoque dele; nolunt audire: recita porro." "Numquam ego praedam neque quod de hostibus captum esset neque manubias inter pauculos amicos meos divisi,*

ut illis eriperem qui cepissent." "Istuc quoque dele: nihil eo minus volunt dici; non opus est recitato." "Numquam ego evectionem datavi, quo amici mei per symbolos pecunias magnas caperent." "Perge istuc quoque uti cum maxime delere." "Numquam ego argentum pro vino congiario inter apparitores atque amicos meos disdidi neque eos malo publico divites feci." "Enimvero usque istuc ad lignum dele." Vides in quo loco respublica siet, ubi quod reipublicae bene fecissem, unde gratiam capiebam, nunc idem illud memorare non audeo ne invidiae siet. Ita inductnm est male facere impoene, bene facere non impoene licere.

FRONTO *EP. AD ANTONINUM IMPERATOREM* 1.2.11–12

I requested the tablet be fetched on which my speech was recorded, about the case concerning the judicial wager with Marcus Cornelius. The tablets were produced. The public services of my ancestors were read out; next what I had achieved on behalf of the state was read. When both these parts had been read out, the next section in the speech was written as follows: "Never did I squander my money or that of the allies in order to buy favors." "Oh, no," I said, "Don't, don't write that! They do not want to hear it." Then he read, "I never appointed prefects in the towns of your allies, men who plunder their goods, wives, and children." Delete this also, they do not want to hear it. Continue reading. "Never have I divided booty, either that taken from enemy soldiers or the share due to the general among a small number of my friends, so that I would have taken it away from those who had captured it." This too delete; they do not want anything less than this; there is no point in reading it aloud. "I never granted travel passes, so that my friends might gain a lot of money by means of permits." Hurry to erase this also as far as possible. "I never distributed the allowance for the distribution of wine among my attendants and friends. Nor did I make them to the detriment of the public treasury." Indeed, erase that section down to the wood. Regard, therefore, the state of the commonwealth, when under present conditions I do not dare to recall that which I rendered as a service to the state, actions from which I used to gain credit, lest I gain a bad reputation. As a result it is a norm to do bad things with impunity, but it is not allowed to do good without being punished for it.

This scene imagines Cato calling for a speech he had given in a court case to be read aloud from a written version recorded on wooden tablets coated with wax. The person reading the speech and making the corrections seems to be a secretary, most probably one of the educated slaves or freedmen who worked for Cato. This passage refers quite naturally to the use of such an assistant, as well as to the interaction of reading aloud from a written text with the simultaneous editing of that same text. Roman writing tablets were designed precisely for such relatively easy rewriting of a text in comparison to the much more expensive papyrus, which was written on in ink.[65] It is not clear whether the text being edited represents a version of the speech drafted before or after delivery by Cato or even circulation. This quotation may be the earliest direct evidence for a literate assistant working together with an orator or writer to produce a text, one that is related, more or less closely, to a particular oral performance but one that can also then take on a life of its own as a published piece. The large number of erasures Cato imagines making would have created a text with so many lacunae that recopying would in any case have been necessary, regardless of the format, which would have been another task for a secretary. Meanwhile, the topic of expenditure and Cato's personal parsimony is one that he returned to on many occasions throughout his career as a magistrate, perhaps with similar phrasing and emphasis.

Cato's writings show familiarity with Greek literature, including Homer, Herodotus, Xenophon, and Demosthenes.[66] Cato will have owned copies of the writings of these and of many other authors, copies kept in a home library that also needed regular attending to. The *Origines* was based on extensive research in a wide variety of subjects dealing with Italian geography, history, social customs, and local traditions, topics that drew on specialized knowledge and sources. Beyond direct testimony to the use of slave labor in the household, Cato's career and lifestyle strongly suggest the presence of educated slaves and freedmen in his household over the decades, perhaps throughout his life in Rome. Despite the allegedly small size of his home in Rome, he seems to have made use of many skilled assistants.[67] In addition, he was clearly known as someone who was often in the market for young boys but also frequently selling those whom he had trained but decided not to keep. The expansion of his business and landed interests will regularly have required additional staff. Cato himself saw slave labor as closely linked to education and to productivity of every kind. Skilled and educated slaves, a certain number of whom went on to be manumitted, were themselves products integral to the economy of his household. He is explicit about his aim to be a producer who enriched himself through diverse business ventures, rather than a consumer who spent down his inherited resources.[68]

Atticus, the Entrepreneur and Man of Culture

Like Cato, Atticus was a man of equestrian background who lived in a rapidly changing world, one in which he was remarkably successful at making money and consequently at expanding his various households. Again like Cato, perhaps even under his influence, Atticus seems to have been a strategic and innovative entrepreneur, who set his own distinctive guidelines for each member of his staff to follow.[69] Unlike in Cato's case, however, most of Atticus' new acquisitions and investments were outside Italy, which made him possibly even more dependent on reliable managers to ensure that houses, farms, ranches, cargoes in ships, and many other types of business ventures were operating smoothly and according to his own specific requirements.[70] In addition, Atticus' refined literary interests led him to maintain extensive book collections, compose his own works, host readings of new publications, and produce copies of recent books for friends.[71] Education and training of enslaved persons was just as important to Atticus as it had been to Cato. Although a rich array of contemporary evidence survives about Atticus, members of his household are only occasionally named or described in any detail for us. Nevertheless, his staff provides a fascinating case study of investment in and profit from educated slaves, of whom a few freedmen are as usual the most visible to us.[72]

As far as we can see, as an adult Atticus spent most of his time in four principal locations where he owned homes, namely Athens (especially from 86/85 to 65, but also occasionally later), Rome (from 65 onward), his extensive estate at Buthrotum in Epirus (from 68 onward), and (apparently to a much lesser extent) a country house in Italy at Ficulea, on the via Nomentana within easy reach of Rome.[73] In addition, he owned land elsewhere and regularly made business trips in the Aegean and further East.[74]

His life in Rome is visible to us after he inherited his uncle Caecilius' fine old house on the Quirinal in 58.[75] However, he must have spent time in the city on a regular basis before, especially during the annual election season, in order to maintain his network of connections with the powerful and the ambitious. It would have been impossible for him to wield the political and financial influence he exercised without frequent trips back home from Athens.[76] After his move to the Quirinal, Atticus surely kept his place in Athens, even as he maintained many friendships there throughout his life.

Indeed, Atticus started to spend much more time in Rome from the mid-60s onward, perhaps partly with a view to cultivating his elderly and childless uncle, who ended up leaving him HS 10 million in addition to his house.[77] It is striking that we effectively know nothing of where he stayed in Rome during the previous decades; he surely had an establishment of his own, perhaps a family house that he had already inherited as a young man.[78] Nor do we know what happened to this family house after he moved to the Quirinal to a carefully curated life there with his new young wife Pilia. In other words, even as we can see Atticus expand his estates and regularly adapt his own life to new political and economic opportunities, much remains hidden, some of it perhaps deliberately edited out by Atticus himself. It is not unlikely that he acted as one of the earliest editors of Cicero's letters and that some gaps in the collection reflect material he decided not to pass on to posterity, for whatever reason.[79]

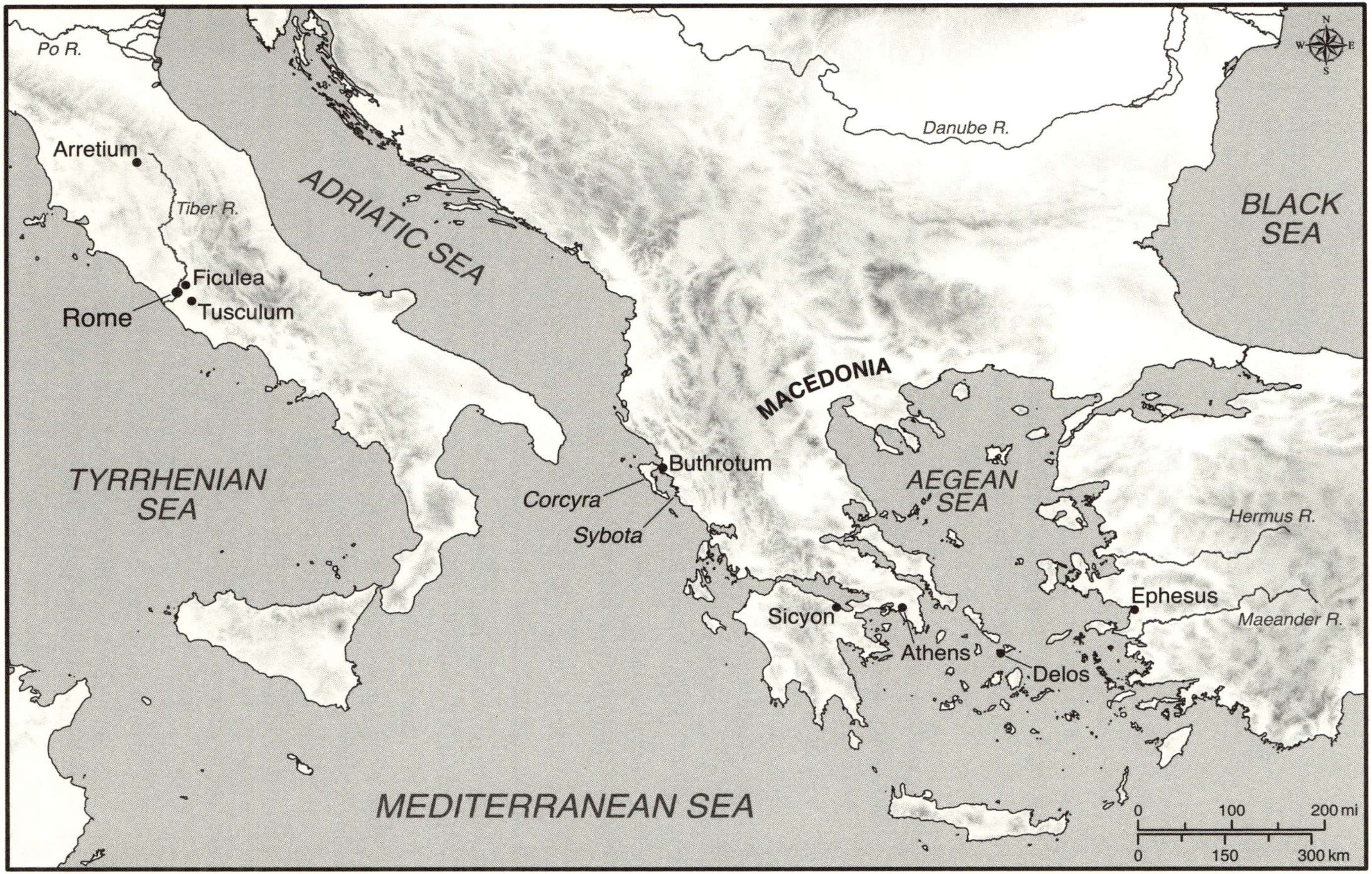

MAP 2: Atticus' real estate holdings and business sphere. Ancient World Mapping Center, University of North Carolina, Chapel Hill

Nepos' well-known description of his close friend Atticus' enslaved staff as entirely composed of *vernae*, all of whom were said to be literate and highly educated surely applies principally to the household on the Quirinal, which was set up when Atticus was in his early 50s. Nepos seems to have written this part of his account while Atticus was still alive but near the end of his life:

> *Usus est familia, si utilitate iudicandum est, optima; si forma, vix mediocri. Namque in ea erant pueri litteratissimi, anagnostae optimi et plurimi librarii, ut ne pedisequus quidem quisquam esset, qui non utrumque horum pulchre facere posset, pari modo artifices ceteri, quos cultus domesticus desiderat, apprime boni. Neque tamen horum quemquam nisi domi natum domique factum habuit; quod est signum non solum continentiae, sed etiam diligentiae.*
>
> ATT. 13.3–4

> He (Atticus) maintained a household staff that was excellent, if judged for its utility, and hardly average, if evaluated on the basis of the attractive appearance of its members. For it included highly educated young men, the very best at reading aloud and a large number trained in literary skills, so that there was not even a single male servant who could not do both of these (reading and writing) very well. In the same way, the other craftsmen, who were employed in maintaining a domestic household, were exceptionally good. He did not employ anyone of these who was not born in his household and brought up at home, which is an indication not only of thrift, but also of economy.

This is the refined household that was so thoroughly familiar to Nepos and to so many others over the last 25 years of Atticus' life. The description is obviously idealized but indicates something of the overall effect that Atticus was aiming at.[80] An entirely self-sufficient household designed to produce within itself only the best-educated staff reflected the experiences and aspirations of Atticus' life up to that point. Atticus' home also reveals the value he placed on literacy and education in general, in a society where most Roman citizens were presumably illiterate.[81] His home shows how he wanted to present himself and his family in the context of life in the city of Rome. He now had a new name and lifestyle as a more regular resident of Rome, a husband, and then a father. By this time, he also owned so many estates elsewhere that he could indeed supply a big house in Rome with nothing but *vernae*, who had all been specially chosen and trained to a high standard with his own curriculum and apprenticeship programs. His educational initiatives clearly took shape before he had a child of his own to educate.[82]

It is not possible to imagine that Atticus had previously managed to set up his other households, notably in Athens in the mid-80s and then again in

Epirus in the early 60s without ever acquiring a slave through purchase.[83] When Atticus arrived in Athens, he was only in his mid-20s and had liquidated most of his assets in Italy.[84] He surely did not travel over with as extensive a staff as he would later employ once his business interests had spread throughout the Eastern Mediterranean. Similarly, whether or not one thinks he had owned land in Epirus before, in 68 he clearly made a major new investment in a villa with an extensive estate.[85] This acquisition allowed him to cultivate a variety of agricultural products, including especially large herds of animals who were pastured on his own lands. In the second book of Varro's *De Re Rustica*, a dialogue set in the year after Atticus bought this land in Buthrotum, he is presented as owning a large estate in Epirus and as being an expert on raising sheep, as well as other animals. The land in Epirus required a much larger and differently trained group of agricultural workers than the ones he employed before and most probably continued to use for his money-lending business in Athens. Each time Atticus expanded into a new area of investment, he did not leave his older ventures behind. Rather as he became richer he diversified, both financially and geographically, in different economic and political circumstances.

Nepos' account of Atticus' educated slaves is embedded in a longer discussion of his lifestyle that stresses its characteristically thoughtful combination of refinement and frugality. Nepos ranges from a description of the old house on the Quirinal set in its splendid park to Atticus' tasteful furniture and modest monthly expenditures, despite frequently entertaining a wide range of acquaintances at home. Nepos claims to have been a regular visitor, who even had access to the details of Atticus' own household accounts.[86] The following sentence sums up the overall point Nepos is trying to make in this part of his biography:

> *Elegans, non magnificus; splendidus, non sumptuosus: omni diligentia munditiam, non affluentiam affectabat.*
>
> ATT. 13.5

> Elegant, not pompous; glittering, not extravagant; he [Atticus] diligently aimed for good taste, not excess.

We are invited to believe that Atticus' home set a standard for refined taste with a sophistication that was redolent of old money, Roman traditionalism, and intellectual engagement. In this context we may recall that the future emperor Augustus was, as a young man, very much taken with the elegant lifestyle (*elegantia vitae*) of Atticus, the worldly man of letters whom he consulted as a sympathetic mentor.[87] In a society in which educated slaves had fetched exorbitant prices for over a generation, Atticus had worked out a way to have the most impressive and cultured household staff while spending significantly less on this enterprise than others were. By using his own educational system to train these men, Atticus also reproduced his values and interests both within his own home and in the wider social circles with which his freedmen came into contact.

At the same time as he invested in slaves with literary and technical skills, Atticus also owned other highly trained staff, notably gladiators.[88] By the middle of the first century, these highly trained fighters had become an investment vehicle for wealthy Romans, who used them to put on combat displays (*munera*) and also as personal bodyguards in the increasingly unstable political situation in and around Rome.[89] Needless to say, the gladiators were very expensive both to acquire and to maintain in special barracks with expert trainers and special equipment. Atticus invested in such a troupe, which he lent to friends for their displays. Cicero informs us that, if he had been charging a fee, Atticus could have recouped his initial outlay after their third public appearance.[90] This information also suggests what is unsurprising, namely that by this date the fights were being elaborately staged precisely to avoid too many severe injuries and casualties. Otherwise, the owners would never have been able to make a profit from a rapidly reduced troupe. Atticus seems to have provided gladiators to both sides in the well-known clash between Milo and Clodius, an ongoing series of street battles that culminated in the murder of Clodius on the Via Appia near Rome in January 52.[91] Atticus was, therefore, a businessman who traded in skilled slaves for profit, both purely financial and in terms of influence, even during the unstable mid-50s.

Atticus' named freedmen who appear in our sources tend to be most visible to us once they step out of Atticus' house and interact with others. This situation highlights the fact that Atticus had so many educated people working with and for him that he could afford to have them help his close friends, sometimes for extended periods of time. These friends, by definition, therefore, did not themselves have access to the same level of expertise within their own households. Atticus' ability to help out in this way did favors that were not easily repaid in kind within the complex economy of Roman friendship. Such favors also reveal how exceptional Atticus' personal investment in his educated staff had become. Cicero, as Atticus' best-documented friend, inevitably provides most of this information.

Cicero's own household is documented in some detail, yet relatively few slaves or freedmen are named or described personally.[92] The detailed information that has survived about Tiro, Cicero's confidant and literary adviser, including a book of letters addressed to him, has tended to obscure the fact that other experts like him were apparently not readily or consistently to hand within the household.[93] Yet, we can be reasonably sure that Cicero did have a considerable staff at home, at his Palatine house in Rome and at least a basic, local team at each of his country villas.[94] In fact, we hear from Cicero's letters about almost as many freedmen from other households who worked for him at some point, presumably for a wage, as about his own freedmen.[95] In other words, when Cicero needed a doctor, an architect, or a learned librarian to reorganize his library at Antium, he did not call on members of his own household to complete these tasks.[96] He even asked Atticus to provide two trained assistants to help the librarian with the gluing of the papyrus rolls and the labeling of the shelves in his library.[97] This work has sometimes been categorized as "menial," but Cicero seems to think that experts are needed or will, at least, do a much better job than his own people.[98] This general situation forms the essential background to the freedmen of Atticus and of others who worked for Cicero.

During Cicero's long marriage to Terentia, her ample resources were managed by her freedman accountant Philotimus, who was also in charge of the house on the Palatine and communications by messenger.[99] Despite regular friction with Cicero over a range of matters, and some suspicion of fraud while Cicero was away as governor of Cilicia in 51 and 50, Philotimus remained the main accountant in the household until Terentia's divorce from Cicero in the mid-40s.[100] At that time Cicero was required to repay Terentia's dowry and simultaneously lost the services of Philotimus. We then see Cicero turning to Atticus who provides his friend both with regular financial advice of his own and with the services of an accountant named Eros, who was probably a freedman by this time.[101] In other words, even by the age of 60, Cicero did not have an accountant of his own; he had clearly been reliant on Terentius Philotimus, probably for many years, despite the fact that the latter inevitably owed his main allegiance to Terentia not to Cicero himself. Philotimus was a man of property, who himself was a slaveholder and eventually held a public religious office when he became a *Lupercus*.[102]

Cicero did not himself acquire a reliably trained personal accountant of his own during the years of Caesar's dictatorship. In fact, he soon made a series of costly errors, including a brief and disastrous marriage to his young ward Publilia, whom he married for her money but then immediately had to repay when a rapid (second) divorce ensued.[103] During this series of unfortunate events, it is easy to focus on Cicero and lose sight of the dependable Eros. There will have been a great deal for Eros to sort out, with many houses to run, debts to service, two divorces within a short period of time, and financial complications caused by the difficulty in recovering Cicero's daughter Tullia's dowry after her own divorce from her third husband, Dolabella.[104] Atticus was consistently supportive and most importantly was able to recommend and provide the services of Eros.[105] In this way, as in the case of the gladiators,

Atticus' ample and exceptional staff gave him leverage in making himself indispensable. Meanwhile, Eros will have expected compensation, perhaps from both Cicero and Atticus.

The best-documented freedman of Atticus in Cicero's employ was a brilliant intellectual named Marcus Pomponius Dionysius, who was so close to Cicero that at the time of his manumission he had taken the latter's *praenomen* (first name) rather than calling himself Titus Pomponius after Atticus himself.[106] If this was indeed Dionysius' own free choice, then it is remarkable testimony of his relationship with Atticus' friend during his enslavement, which came to an end before Atticus changed his own name to Quintus Caecilius. Consequently, Dionysius' citizen name indicates that he was often with Cicero well before being first attested in the correspondence, in November of 56.[107] This first reference describes Cicero's eagerness to spend an extra day of vacation simply with Dionysius, whom he refers to as if he is on very familiar terms with him. In another letter Cicero casually mentions that Dionysius is already awaiting him at his villa at Tusculum before he arrives there.[108] Yet would Dionysius have chosen to be called Marcus in the early 50s when Cicero was in dire political trouble? It seems more likely that this name was selected during or immediately after Cicero's consulship of 63, at a time when his political career was at its height. Dionysius was a man who knew how to make his way in the world and his connection with Cicero was designed to be one more step on that path.

Cicero, in turn, admired Dionysius greatly, employed him to teach his son and nephew, had a special guest room built for him, and generally just enjoyed spending time talking to him.[109] In 51 Dionysius, certainly with Atticus' approval, accompanied Cicero to Cilicia to serve as tutor for young Marcus and his cousin Quintus, who were in their mid-teens by then.[110] At this time, Cicero was still very taken with Dionysius and not impressed by the complaints of his pupils about their teacher's impatience, high standards, and bad temper. However, on returning from the East, Dionysius chose to rejoin Atticus and to spend his time engaging in his own business ventures rather than returning to Cicero late in 50 or in 49, when Caesar invaded Italy. To no avail, Cicero repeatedly begged both Atticus and Dionysius to restore the former situation.[111]

Cicero was mortally offended by what he considered Dionysius' ungrateful and high-handed behavior. An extensive and bitter row ensued, despite efforts on the part of Atticus and Tullia to effect a reconciliation.[112] Subsequently, Dionysius did not return to Cicero's house for any length of time, although he does seem to have apologized in person and at some length.[113] Atticus thought that Cicero had behaved harshly to Dionysius and was apparently unwilling, probably indeed unable, to insist that Dionysius return to Cicero's employ.[114] Inevitably, much attention has been focused on Cicero's remarkably emotional statements, first praising Dionysius effusively but later condemning him in equally exaggerated and hyperbolic terms. Nevertheless, it is possible to draw some at least relatively more objective conclusions about Dionysius himself, his character, and his life.

We know that Dionysius was manumitted, as an adult, before 58. If we date his acquisition of Roman citizenship to around 62 (for example), then he would have been born by the mid-80s, or perhaps somewhat earlier. He could, in fact, have been born around the time when Atticus moved to Athens (c. 85). Cicero calls him a Greek; he will then not have been a *verna* in Atticus' household.[115] He could have been a young child or even already in early adolescence when he was enslaved, in the aftermath of Sulla's capture of Athens. In any case, it is tempting to imagine him in Atticus' household in the late 80s in Athens.[116] He clearly had an independent personality and a formidable intellect, finely honed by the environment around Atticus.[117] He did not feel the need to indulge the well-born boys who were his pupils. Cicero's assessment of his learning and talent is virtually unparalleled in the surviving letters.[118] Dionysius became a man of property with his own household of enslaved persons and a business in loans.[119] He also married and had a son of the same name, who became a well-known rhetorician.[120] His career as a Roman citizen seems to imitate Atticus' in a number of ways, with its combination of banking, investing, and maintaining a wide range of intellectual interests.

The fact that Dionysius refused to rejoin Cicero's household in 49 also speaks to shrewd judgment on his part. Unlike Terentia's Philotimus, Dionysius did not have political allegiances that he had already declared in public.[121] Cicero was once more in a difficult position politically and would make a series of hesitant yet injudicious political choices over the next several years. By contrast, Atticus was so well connected that he could afford to stay in Rome, claim neutrality, and soon be on very good terms with Caesar. Rejoining Atticus was a wise move on the eve of a new civil war. Indeed, Atticus may also have needed Dionysius, perhaps almost as much as Dionysius needed his patron at this key moment of crisis. Meanwhile, Cicero was clearly demanding and temperamental, even as his son was effectively now too old for a tutor like Dionysius. At the end of the day, Dionysius did not see himself as a professional teacher. He was an entrepreneur of personal means who could afford not to teach teenagers. There was ultimately much more money to be made in finance than in the classroom. Atticus' patronage allowed Dionysius to develop a career trajectory of his own and to become an independent man of means, even as he still spent time in Atticus' household, including extended stays at Buthrotum in Epirus.

We only catch fleeting glimpses of other freedmen in Cicero's correspondence with Atticus, although each in his own way adds to a larger picture. Asides mentioning members of Atticus' household by name claim familiar, warm relationships with educated men, incidental details that have not been edited out by those who put together the collection of Cicero's letters that has come down to us.[122] From such references we learn that Atticus' own closest secretarial assistant, his Tiro, was named Alexis, an individual whom Cicero says he knows well. Alexis is attested in letters dated between 50 and Cicero's last surviving letter written to Atticus on November 12, 44.[123] Alexis frequently drafted Atticus' correspondence, although the letters Atticus wrote to Cicero were usually in his own hand.

Alexis had, it turns out, been specially trained to imitate Atticus' handwriting so that his texts should be indistinguishable from the ones Atticus wrote himself.[124] With Alexis' help, Atticus was able to appear to respond in person to many more correspondents and to continue to be writing himself even when he was ill, especially at times when his malarial fever would return.[125] Cicero, however, prided himself on being able to spot a letter written by Alexis, which was a way for him to demonstrate his close personal familiarity with Atticus, but also with Alexis himself. Alexis will have been extraordinarily talented to be chosen for this key position on Atticus' personal staff. One wonders whether there was a competition within the household for this job of acting the part of Atticus in writing.

Another talented person who is attested as living with Atticus is a certain Phemius, a musician who was named after the lyre player who entertains Penelope's suitors in the *Odyssey*. Presumably he will also have played the lyre, a very common instrument in a Roman context. We hear of him briefly in Epirus because Atticus asks Cicero, while he is governor of Cilicia, to procure a special horn for Phemius.[126] This Phrygian-style horn was apparently not available in Rome, despite the many musicians active in the city. As it turns out, it was not easy for an increasingly irritable Cicero to find this rare item but he does eventually manage to put in a special order. Other sources do not mention Atticus as having a keen interest in music, but he clearly did. For present purposes the special horn is interesting because it is repeatedly described specifically as being *for Phemius*. Atticus could easily have written to his friend simply asking for this type of musical instrument, a not untypical exchange of favors between wealthy Romans. But Atticus' letter, which does not survive, evidently explained that the horn was specifically for Phemius to play. Again, we see that Cicero is expected to be familiar with Atticus' staff on a personal level and to appreciate their varied, individual talents. The implication is that Cicero will have heard Phemius play other instruments before and understand that Atticus is very excited about the prospect of hearing Phemius perform, presumably for an audience, on a rare horn. Each of these references conjures up a series of interactions, often involving shared cultural and intellectual interests but also attesting to human relationships.

Beyond the world depicted in Cicero's letters, Suetonius informs us about Atticus' most notorious freedman, Quintus Caecilius Epirota, who outlived his patron, apparently by many years, to become a well-known intellectual in early Augustan Rome.[127] As Epirota's citizen name reveals, he was manumitted after 58 under Atticus' new adoptive name. He is of interest to Suetonius because he opened a fashionable school for older boys in the 20s and was a leading literary critic, who gave public lectures on contemporary poetry, including on the works of Vergil. Suetonius' account of Epirota's life is succinct and compressed but filled with unusual details that link the world of Augustan culture with the household and interests of Atticus, who died in the year before the battle of Actium.

In his account of famous teachers (*grammatici*) in Rome, Suetonius gives the following account of Epirota's career.

> *Q. Caecilius Epirota, Tusculi natus, libertus Attici equitis Romani, ad quem sunt Ciceronis epistolae, cum filiam patroni nuptam M. Agrippae doceret, suspectus in ea et ob hoc remotus, ad Cornelium Gallum se contulit vixitque una familiarissime, quod ipsi Gallo inter gravissima crimina ab Augusto obicitur. Post deinde damnationem mortemque Galli scholam aperuit, sed ita ut paucis et tantum adulescentibus praeciperet, praetextato nemini, nisi si cuius parenti hoc officium negare non posset. Primus dicitur Latine ex tempore disputasse, primusque Virgilium et alios poetas novos praelegere coepisse, quod etiam Domitii Marsi versiculus indicat: Epirota, tenellorum nutricula vatum.*
>
> GRAM. ET RHET. 16

> Quintus Caecilius Epirota, born at Tusculum, was a freedman of Atticus, a Roman of the equestrian order to whom letters were addressed by Cicero. When he (Epirota) was teaching the daughter of his patron (Caecilia Attica), the wife of Marcus Agrippa, he was suspected in his relations with her and was dismissed for that reason. He joined himself to Cornelius Gallus and lived together with him on very friendly terms, a relationship that was held against Gallus himself as one of the most serious reproaches leveled against him by Augustus. Then after the disgrace and death of Gallus, he opened a school, but on the condition that he teach only a few pupils, who were adolescents. He taught no boy who had not assumed the toga of manhood, except in cases where he was unable to deny this favor to a parent. He is said to have been the first to give a public seminar in Latin, and the first to begin to give commentaries on Vergil and other new poets. This is referred to in a verse by Domitius Marsus: "Epirota, nurse of tender bards."

Epirota, despite being named "the Epirote," was born at Tusculum in Latium, and was eventually manumitted by Atticus, Cicero's friend. Epirota had, therefore, been enslaved by Atticus himself; Suetonius implies that he was a *verna*. Yet Atticus did not own an estate at Tusculum, but the Cicero brothers each had houses there. Consequently, Epirota's mother, herself enslaved by Atticus, was in Tusculum when her son was born. It seems unlikely that Atticus traveled to visit his friends with a heavily pregnant woman as one of his attendants. Nor is there any other evidence that he ever sent an enslaved woman to work in Cicero's household. The more logical solution to this apparent puzzle is to posit that Atticus had sent Epirota's mother to work for his own sister Pomponia, who was married to Cicero's brother Quintus.[128] Quintus Cicero owned a villa in Tusculum that we know he was trying to sell by 61.[129] He had probably acquired it a few years earlier, in the early 60s around the time when Marcus Cicero bought his own beloved Tusculan villa.[130] Consequently, Quintus and Pomponia will have spent time in Tusculum during the 60s and will also have had a household staff there, including apparently at least one female servant supplied by Pomponia's brother Atticus. But this woman's legal status had remained unchanged; she had not been given as a gift to Pomponia. As a result, her son, despite being born in Tusculum and not in one of Atticus' homes, was classified as a *verna* of Atticus.

In fact, the name Epirota serves as a confirmation of such a reconstruction. Atticus acquired his large estate at Buthrotum in Epirus in 68. In Varro's *De Re Rustica* set in the following year, several Roman landowners in Epirus, including Atticus, are referred to as *Epirotae*, which is to say "the Epirotes."[131] This is a special kind of joke in the case of Atticus, who had already received a name from his long time spent living in Athens. So he was called "the man from Attica." Similarly, the newborn boy was named "the man from Epirus" after Atticus himself, who was now being called by this new name in a playful way, even apparently by family members. In his case Epirota never replaced his more usual nickname of Atticus. In Epirota's case, however, it also served to remind everyone in Tusculum whom the boy actually belonged to.[132]

The name was apt, perhaps even prophetic, in the sense that Atticus must have become very close to the talented and charismatic Epirota to choose him as the personal tutor for his only child, his beloved daughter Caecilia Attica. Epirota, then, will have received an advanced literary training in Atticus' household, one that allowed him to go on to a remarkable career as a literary critic and public intellectual.[133] He seems to have been already manumitted when he was teaching Attica. She is described by Suetonius as being married to Marcus Vipsanius Agrippa during these lessons. That marriage is usually dated to 37, when Attica was around 14 years old.[134] If Epirota was indeed born in the early 60s, he would have been about 30 around the time of this brilliant marriage. Given her age, Attica will most probably also have been taught by him before her marriage. However, as Attica matured and lived away from her father's house, her relationship with Epirota was perceived to be inappropriate and he was dismissed in disgrace from Agrippa's household. This episode is best dated to the mid-30s since it is unlikely that Attica would have continued to take lessons once she was in her late teens or early twenties.[135]

It goes without saying that we are not in a position to evaluate whether Epirota did indeed have a scandalous relationship with Attica or whether he was falsely accused, whether by Attica herself or by another member of the household who resented his somewhat unusual presence.[136] Private tutors for women, especially after marriage, were much less common than for young men.[137] On the one hand, Epirota certainly had access to personal time with Attica; on the other hand, she was a newly married woman, and soon a mother. He was putting his whole life in jeopardy if he was not above suspicion in a new household. Interestingly, he now also lost the support of his patron Atticus and went to live with the politician and poet Gaius Cornelius Gallus, another rising star and close associate of the future *princeps*.[138] What is clear is that Augustus remained absolutely furious with Epirota. He was still angry about Epirota's behavior toward Attica in 27 or 26, when Gallus fell from favor and was accused by Augustus of a variety of misdemeanors.[139] According to Suetonius, Gallus' close association with Epirota was very much held against him by Augustus at that time. Gallus committed suicide rather than face the *princeps'* displeasure. By this date, however, Agrippa was married to Marcella, Augustus' niece. We do not know what happened to Attica, who may have died young.[140]

Epirota, then, emerges as a highly controversial figure, an exceptionally favored freedman who allegedly squandered his position as a result of an adulterous affair with a newly married teenager half his age. He then brought disgrace on his new patron Gallus, a man whose ambition and self-importance ruined his own meteoric political career. Epirota surely knew Gallus well before turning to him for help in a crisis; they seem to have been about the same age and shared a deep interest in contemporary poetry. Gallus was ready to take Epirota into his home regardless of what Atticus, Agrippa, or Octavian thought at the time of the scandal. Epirota appears to be independent and well connected. Epirota will have lived with Gallus in Rome before his new patron left for the East, in the late 30s. Gallus would go on to be the first Roman governor of Egypt after the death of Cleopatra VII, where his personal self-aggrandizement is well attested. Did Epirota accompany Gallus to Egypt as part of his retinue of friends and associates? This seems a distinct possibility given how closely Augustus associated Gallus with Epirota in 27.[141] If they had not seen each other for several years, then the accusation of living together as intimates would seem out of place. It was only after Gallus' disgrace and suicide that Epirota opened his school in Rome, in the 20s.

Epirota was, then, truly a notorious man by the time he set up a new kind of school for boys in their late teens in Rome, a school that catered to pupils who were older than the ones usually taught by the regular *grammatici*.[142] But prospective parents were apparently not put off by Epirota's earlier career mishaps or by the publicly declared displeasure of the man who now called himself Augustus. Perhaps the negative publicity even helped Epirota? He only took a few students at a time and organized at least some sessions in a novel seminar format, with discussion between teacher and pupils in Latin rather than the usual lectures, a number of which were apparently in Greek.[143] Teaching older students will presumably also have meant a higher turnover of pupils, as young men moved on from school into the first stages of their careers. According to Suetonius, he only accepted younger students to whose parents he owed particular favors. The very fact that such parents formed an identifiable group also hints at Epirota's broad circle of connections among the elite of the city. One is tempted to imagine that his fees were high, based on personal attention to his protégées and an advanced curriculum not available elsewhere.[144] The line of poetry by Domitius Marsus quoted by Suetonius suggests that Epirota was known for training new poets, not simply for teaching poetry to future politicians and financiers.[145]

The concept of a small, exclusive school with a progressive curriculum evidently made something of an impact in Rome. Epirota appears entrepreneurial, as well as being learned. His closeness to Cornelius Gallus indicates an interest in neoteric love elegy, an enthusiasm they both may have shared with Atticus himself.[146] Epirota was an innovator also in his presentation of lectures on the contemporary poets, including Vergil. At first only the *Eclogues* and *Georgics* will have been available since the *Aeneid* was not in circulation until after Vergil's death in 19. But Epirota, by now perhaps in his late 40s, could have survived Vergil to continue his teaching and lecturing. We cannot know how influential he was in creating a curriculum or a style of instruction that was more widely used outside his own school or whether Augustus was ever reconciled to his presence on the literary scene.[147] Epirota was surely familiar with many other literary figures of the day, including Parthenius, who was close to Gallus, and probably the cultural circle of Maecenas, friend of Horace, Vergil, and Augustus.[148] Despite his personal rift with Atticus, Epirota's interests and innovations carried Atticus' own taste and emphasis on education into the new imperial age.

Conclusion

In contrast with the previous chapter about Licinius, this chapter has proposed a series of smaller case studies drawing on the households of Cato the censor and of Atticus. In this context, a juxtaposition of the classroom of Chilon in

Cato's house in the 180s with Epirota's literary school for adolescents in the 20s is suggestive in a number of ways. There is clearly so much that we will never know. However, the importance of education by and for the enslaved within and beyond the households of the wealthy is evident. The growth of Roman slaveholding that came with expanded imperial aspirations was accompanied by a renewed focus on training these workers, whether in crafts, trades, agriculture, entertainment, or the various literary pursuits that were integral to elite households. In the early second century, even and perhaps particularly a traditional Roman like Cato could see the opportunities for the slaveholder in educating the young, many of whom had been enslaved in war. There was money to be made in slave trading by buying at low prices and selling at higher ones; education was one of the most obvious ways to achieve the goal of making a profit. Meanwhile, the expansion of Cato's investments in manufacturing, ranching, and agriculture on newly acquired estates all depended on an efficient and loyal workforce. Education was so central to Cato's household that he even encouraged his own slaves to join him as partners in an ongoing enterprise based on an annual cycle of buying and selling young boys.

Despite the significant increase in the number of slaves in central Italy, Romans continued to manumit regularly, whether in exchange for a fee or as a gift. Freedmen were in some ways even more useful to their former patrons, since as Roman citizens they could engage in many more activities, especially in business and in management roles. Although we do not know the names of many of Cato's freedmen, he clearly relied on such educated, formerly enslaved men to run his farms and oversee his business interests. Although he himself had grown up in a very different environment before the Second Punic War, Cato embraced and developed the much-expanded use of slave labor in his writings and through his own practices. He surely served as an inspiration to many other Romans.

Atticus' extraordinary household in Rome, in which every member of staff was fully literate, represents the ultimate development of what Cato was just starting to envisage and experiment with. Atticus' system of education could produce intellectuals like Dionysius, whom Cicero considered second to none, and Epirota, intimate friend of Cornelius Gallus and a leading literary critic in the interpretation of Augustan poetry. Both of these men had independent careers, which allowed them some degree of choice even in times of civil war and societal dissolution. Dionysius was not compelled to work for Cicero. Epirota flourished in Rome despite Augustus' personal enmity. Dionysius was able to combine his literary interests with a career in business. Epirota could set up a completely new type of literary school for a new age; he was not limited to teaching an elementary curriculum to young children. Atticus was an exceptional entrepreneur, who could see the potential of educating as many enslaved persons as possible. His staff of experts added to his reputation for refinement, as well as to his ability to help himself stay ahead in a rapidly changing world and to rescue his friends when they were in trouble. The assistance he afforded people of all sorts saved his own life and fortune in many desperate situations. Meanwhile, his vision of educating his household in Rome will have set them apart from the general population of Roman citizens, many of whom were illiterate or only barely able to read and write on a basic level.[149]

3

The Homegrown and the Immigrant

QUINTUS LUTATIUS DAPHNIS THE FREEDMAN AND ARCHIAS OF ANTIOCH THE GREEK POET

servitia rectiora politioraque inmenso pretio, et cuius ipsum etiam puderet, sic ut rationibus vetaret inferri.

He (Julius Caesar) acquired rather special and educated slaves at great expense, which even he himself was ashamed of, with the result that he ordered the prices not be recorded in his account books.

—SUETONIUS *DIVUS IULIUS* 47

THE FIRST CHAPTER focused on the figure of a freedman whose job it was to stay hidden behind his patron, both physically and metaphorically, as he coached him to give a rhetorical performance that was attributed entirely to that patron, one of Rome's greatest orators. Only those in the know referred in passing to his contribution, which was not easy to explain and consequently often misrepresented. By contrast, this investigation now pivots to examine the case of a younger contemporary of Licinius, a man who was much talked about, both before and after his manumission, whose learning was celebrated during his lifetime and remembered for generations. This man's renown contributed to his patrons' self-representation as men of culture and learning. He was openly in competition with other intellectuals, including freeborn foreigners who came to Rome to earn their living, men who served in some of the same intellectual roles and cultivated the same patrons.[1]

This chapter examines the life of the individual who was bought and sold for the highest recorded price in the history of Rome, at least for someone born into a state of servitude in Italy (a *verna*). His name was Daphnis and he had been born and educated in the household of a Roman citizen, a certain Attius, originally from Pisaurum (Pesaro), a Roman colony on the Adriatic coast.[2] Daphnis became a highly educated man. The attention he garnered and the upward mobility he experienced, which eventually resulted in freedom and Roman citizenship, are directly attributed to his literary skills. As noted in the preface, in a world of enslavement that included many highly trained individuals in a variety of fields, it is interesting to see the highest recorded price being paid for literary learning rather than for any other accomplishment or talent.[3]

According to Pliny the Elder and to Suetonius, our two principal informants, Daphnis was twice sold for the fabulous price of HS 700,000, most probably within the city of Rome itself.[4] That sum of money is hard to give a precise value to in real terms and is well beyond other prices recorded in the meager surviving evidence.[5] After an attempt to recover the life story and experience of this rather particular individual in Rome in the late second and early first centuries, my discussion will explore the social, economic, and cultural background that could produce a phenomenon like Daphnis. Beyond his own remarkable talents and special skills, which there is no reason to doubt, lies the story of a sophisticated and complex market for highly trained slaves, a world that we only catch glimpses of in the ancient evidence and that has consequently remained relatively unexplored in modern scholarship.[6]

Daphnis features in passing as an early figure in Suetonius' account of professional teachers in Rome, the *De Grammaticis et Rhetoribus* (written in the early second century AD). As a result, he is not given a detailed biographical profile. Nor, in fact, is there any evidence that he ever was a teacher, either of grammar and writing or of rhetoric. In other words, he is a famous example whom Suetonius simply wants to allude to in his survey of prominent teachers, mostly freedmen, if only because of Daphnis' notorious price; but he does not obviously fit into the group of educators in Suetonius' compilation, whose subject is rather precisely conceived.[7]

Daphnis' life story raises three interrelated questions:

1. Why was Daphnis so expensive? Is there a sense of relative value within the range of luxury spending that we can recover?
2. How can we understand Daphnis in his own historical and social context, at a period earlier than that of the better-documented intellectuals of the later first century and beyond?
3. What does such a high price for an educated person, whether understood in absolute or in relative terms, tell us about literary culture in republican Rome and about the relationship of that culture to the labor of the enslaved?

In order to address these three questions, I will examine Daphnis' life, which was articulated by four distinct "career" stages. This narrative unfolds in the context both of the Roman slave market more generally and then specifically in light of the evident value assigned by members of the city's political elite to learning in many forms in the context of their own daily lives at home. In the second part of the chapter, the life of the poet Archias of Antioch will provide a suggestive foil for Daphnis by exploring the career of a freeborn, Greek-speaking poet who became a prominent intellectual at Rome and moved in many of the same social circles as Daphnis.

Who Was Daphnis?

Daphnis was born into a Roman household in an unknown year in the later second century; he was categorized as a *verna* in Latin, which is to say the home-born child of an enslaved mother.[8] From this particular start in life, he clearly received an excellent and elaborate education, surely beginning from his early years. In other words, he was selected and trained based on intellectual promise, and perhaps also on personal characteristics of other kinds, such as sociability and wit. He was then sold for HS 700,000 to Marcus Aemilius Scaurus, a patrician who was consul in 115, censor in 109, and was *princeps senatus* for 25 years.[9]

> *Pretium hominis in seruitio geniti maximum ad hunc diem, quod equidem compererim, fuit grammaticae artis Daphnin Attio Pisaurense uendente et M. Scauro principe ciuitatis, HS septingenta milia licente.*
>
> As far as I have been able to find out, the highest price paid for someone born in slavery was for the Daphnis, learned in the arts of the grammarian; the seller was Atius of Pisaurum and Marcus Scaurus the leading citizen bid 700,000 sesterces.
>
> PLINY *NATURAL HISTORY* 7.128

Scaurus was a leading orator who was very active in the law courts. To Cicero, Scaurus was a giant among the previous generation of statesmen.[10] It would have been hard to find a more prominent purchaser, especially in that last decade of the second century.

Subsequently, after an unspecified time period, Daphnis was sold again, presumably by Scaurus, to Quintus Lutatius Catulus, a well-known politician, author, and patron of the arts, who held the consulship in 102.[11]

> *Pretia vero grammaticorum tanta mercedesque tam magnae, ut constet Lutatium Daphnidem, quem Gaius Melissus per cavillationem nominis Πανὸς ἀγάπημα dicit, septengentis milibus nummum a Q. Catulo emptum ac brevi*

> *manumissum, L. Appuleium ab Aeficio Calvino equite Romano praedivite quadringenis annuis conductum ut Oscae doceret.*
>
> Actually, the prices paid for grammarians were so great and the fees paid were so large, that it is an established fact that Lutatius Daphnis—whom Gaius Melissus calls "Pan's delight" in a joke about his name—was bought by Quintus Catulus for 700,000 sesterces and was soon freed, and Lucius Appuleius was hired by Aeficius Calvinus, a very wealthy Roman knight, at the rate of 400,000 sesterces a year to teach at Osca.
>
> SUETONIUS *DE GRAMMATICIS ET RHETORIBUS* 3.5–6

The cash price (HS 700,000) is recorded as having been the same, although it is inevitably unclear whether inflation or other factors may have caused a fluctuation in the real value of this sum over the intervening years. Catulus soon manumitted Daphnis, who then went on to have a new life as a freedman, a Roman citizen named Quintus Lutatius Daphnis, for a further unknown time period. The fact that he (apparently) did not open a school indicates that he had enough resources of his own, as well as having access to the continued patronage of Catulus and of other leading men, that he did not need to teach.

In this fourth phase of his life, Daphnis seems to have written a work of historiography in Latin entitled *Communis Historia* (*Shared History* or perhaps in the plural *Communes Historiae, Shared Histories*), which had at least four books, and perhaps more.[12] Only 12 brief fragments survive, which are cited by much later authors, notably the *Origo Gentis Romanae,* a short and controversial anonymous text usually assigned to the late fourth century AD.[13] Consequently, the general shape and purpose of Daphnis' history remain elusive. An equivalent that has been proposed is a general or universal history in the style of a Polybius or a Timaeus, a work that somehow compared or contrasted Romans with Greeks.[14] On the other hand, the surviving fragments relate to Aeneas, early Roman history, and Italian origin stories, in other words to material that would have overlapped with Cato the Elder's famous *Origines,* the earliest historiographical work written in Latin.[15] Daphnis' history may have contained one of the first synchronized chronological systems, one later used and adapted by such leading scholars as Atticus, Varro, and Nepos for their own chronological publications.[16]

The identity of the Lutatius who is named as the author of this *Shared History* has been long debated, but he is surely Daphnis (as first suggested by Otto Jahn in 1843) rather than his prominent patron Catulus.[17] Q. Lutatius Catulus, the well-known man of consular rank who produced works in several genres, including elegiac couplets and prose autobiography, is consistently referred to by ancient sources simply as Catulus, never as just Lutatius.[18] Moreover, fragment 8 of the *Communis Historia* portrays Aeneas as a traitor who betrayed

Troy to the Greeks in return for money and a free passage, a version that was obviously at odds with the family traditions of the Julii Caesares, who were Catulus' close relatives.[19] Daphnis appears, therefore, to have written in an independent voice, at least once he was a free Roman citizen. Such confusion over the authorship of a lost text is symptomatic of the challenges involved in recovering the stories of educated freedmen as authors in their own right.[20] Suetonius chose not to include independent authorship as a topic in his discussion of learned freedmen who were also teachers, despite the fact that some in his catalog wrote very well-known texts.[21] Meanwhile, the traditional pattern of naming freedmen after their manumitters can easily result in the elite Roman himself getting credit in later accounts for a work produced by someone he had formerly enslaved, a work that may have been conceived and written after the actual author's manumission.

The Roman citizen Quintus Lutatius Daphnis, then, was a man of means who could afford to spend his time writing historiography, a genre that had been associated with authors of senatorial rank in the second century.[22] His accomplishments had allowed him upward mobility in the highly competitive intellectual environment of the city of Rome. In his previous life of enslavement, he had himself been a true luxury item, enjoyed at home by leading men, and not required to take in pupils to earn money for his various owners. Buying, owning, selling, and freeing him were each gestures that displayed a refined literary taste together with exceptional opulence.[23]

Daphnis' career is all the more striking in the context of the slave trade in Rome in the second century, a time that saw a huge influx of unfree labor to the Italian peninsula and to the capital city itself. The vast slave supply can be directly linked to Rome's expansion of influence in the Eastern Mediterranean, a source of captives in great numbers, including a significant cohort who were already highly educated in a wide variety of skills and crafts practiced in the Hellenistic world.[24] Prisoners from Rome's military campaigns were brought back directly to Italy or were sold to slave traders soon after they were captured. Consequently, such newly enslaved individuals initially came into Roman hands outside a monetary system but soon acquired a price as they were sold and resold in a rapidly growing and evolving market.[25]

At this historical period, slave labor in Rome was, by definition, a plentiful and presumably often inexpensive commodity. As a result, we can see the development of very specialized tasks for skilled individuals and also of the huge domestic staffs kept in the private houses of the elites by the first century.[26] Educated captives, especially from the Hellenistic East, brought new knowledge and skills, but even these, relatively more expensive prisoners, are well attested early in the second century.[27] Men like Scaurus and Catulus, both of whom profited significantly from their legal, political, and military careers, will have had households of very many specialized slaves in Rome.[28] This was the world of rapidly growing personal wealth and extravagant spending, at least for and by the most successful few, that Daphnis was born into. He was a *verna* but not one who was initially enslaved by an ancient or fabulously wealthy Roman political family. Perhaps his parents had been captured in war. In that case, he may have been part of a second wave of those born in enslavement, a demographic echo of an influx of imported captives from the East after one of Rome's many wars.

Unsurprisingly, much recent scholarship on Roman slavery has focused on the large numbers of those involved, the big picture, and the overall effects on the Roman economy of so many able-bodied people arriving in the community, not gradually, but in successive waves after military victories.[29] Most of these individuals were not educated and did not end up in a Roman domestic setting. Rather, they worked in menial tasks, in the production of goods for use or sale, or in agriculture, which remained the largest economic sector throughout antiquity. Their labor produced more wealth for owners and, at second hand, for merchants and traders, even as the unfree might displace a free worker, who hired himself out for a daily wage. The Roman economy and the demography of Italy cannot be studied without taking account of the rapid expansion of enslavement during this pivotal period of imperial growth in the second century.

By contrast, Daphnis' life story opens up a rarefied world of astonishing prices and irrational expenditure on luxury goods, an elite world associated with high culture, with literary consumption and production, and consequently with the relative value accorded to an advanced education. Understandably, this environment of very highly educated but enslaved people has received less attention; it is certainly less relevant to the big picture of enslaved labor in the Roman economy. Nevertheless, Daphnis cannot have been an isolated phenomenon. Behind "the most expensive *verna*" stand two necessary preexisting conditions for such a high price. These conditions are a consumer-driven high-end luxury market and (consequently) a sophisticated training system for educating the enslaved, who would make such high prices in this market possible. In other words, Daphnis must have faced fierce competition, especially since he was marketed as a homegrown product, not an exotic novelty that could fetch a high price based on local scarcity or uniqueness. Surely many involved in the slave trade would be buying or breeding boys to train in the hope that they would make a significant profit in the long run. Yet obviously, years of education were needed. How many, one wonders? The initial investment of money and time would be considerable, but the potential profit margin was evidently thought to be attractive enough to justify the attendant risks.[30]

A suggestive but allusive comparison can be found in the brief and tragic life of an enslaved comedian named Panurgus, whose fragmented story forms the background to Cicero's *Pro Roscio Comoedo*.[31] In this speech, Cicero describes how a certain Gaius Fannius Chaerea had entered into a type of partnership with the famous comedy actor Quintus Roscius to train the promising enslaved boy Panurgus as a stage performer. Under this plan both men had a legal share in Panurgus and would split the profits from his performances, once Roscius had educated him. After significant initial success, the scheme was abruptly cut short when Panurgus was killed under unspecified circumstances by a man named Quintus Flavius who was from Tarquinii. Subsequently, Flavius gave Roscius a farm in compensation, an estate that was eventually valued at HS 100,000. Cicero's speech deals with a complex financial dispute between Roscius and Fannius about how the proceeds from the compensation should be shared between them. Cicero, acting on behalf of Roscius, claims that the amount of the compensation paid was determined by the skill and training Panurgus had received.[32] Unfortunately, virtually no detailed information survives about Panurgus' origins, his program of training, what roles he played on stage, and about the circumstances of his violent, perhaps accidental death at a young age.

Luxury, Price, and the Labor of the Enslaved

Let us consider briefly how much HS 700,000 might have been worth in the late second or very early first centuries. It is important to start by noting that prices rose and the markets for luxury goods evolved in major ways after the Social and civil wars of the 80s, as a result of Sulla's massive redistributions of Roman and Italian wealth in his dictatorship, and then again with the vast imported wealth acquired and distributed first by Pompey and then by Julius Caesar after their extensive conquests.[33] But Catulus died in the early 80s and will surely have bought and freed Daphnis well before the crisis with the Italian allies came to a head late in 91. The HS 700,000 that was paid for Daphnis belongs to an earlier time, not to the republic after Sulla. It is thus even more difficult to put the figure into a relationship with other expensive prices. Before the later first century, the equestrian census rating was set at HS 400,000; some scholars have posited a date around 140 for the introduction of this standard to express the social status of an *eques*.[34] It is possible, therefore, that Daphnis cost almost twice the equestrian census, even when he was first sold, probably near the end of the second century.

In this context one may cite the example of a political ally of Scaurus, the tribune Marcus Livius Drusus, who was assassinated in 91. Drusus was considered to be the wealthiest man in the Rome of his day; he owned 10,000 pounds of silver.[35] By contrast, Titus Pomponius Atticus' father, who died around this same time, left his son an inheritance of HS two million, which was considered to be a significant sum at the time.[36] It should be noted, however, that the elder

Pomponius also had a daughter, Pomponia the future wife of Quintus Cicero, who will have inherited her share. In addition, he will have left the customary legacies to friends and dependents. So Atticus' father's total fortune will have been closer to around HS five million (or more?) at the time of his death.

Slave prices had been high, or at least been considered to be high, before the later second century.[37] The existence of a tax on expensive purchases suggests that buyers were obliged to maintain and make available to the censors records of the amounts they had spent at the slave market. It is impossible to know how systematically such taxes were actually implemented or for how long. Most republican sumptuary legislation targeted public games, expensive houses, and the cost of banquets in private houses.[38] The result of comparisons indicates that, unsurprisingly, Daphnis' price is hard to make sense of in any nuanced way within the parameters of the scarce economic data points available to us.[39] Meanwhile, it is important to note that Daphnis was mortal. In this sense, he could obviously not be thought of as any kind of long-term investment, like a house or a piece of fine furniture. He would eventually die; he might die at any time, as the Romans were only too well aware. Thus the relatively high degree of risk involved in buying him was self-evident. He represented a quite exceptional purchase that should or would logically only be made with "spare" cash. It is hard to believe anyone would lend money against him as a security. In this sense, Daphnis was treated as a true luxury in the context of the Roman economy.

Daphnis' Education and Career

I will move on now to examine the circumstances in which Daphnis was twice sold before being manumitted. M. Aemilius Scaurus is the first purchaser we know of; he is presumably the one who acquired the young Daphnis from his original owner.[40] This purchase was made at an auction, which suggests that the enthusiasm of other bidders may have helped to drive the price up beyond what was customary. The setting of a public auction might also explain how this particular sale became so notorious. On the other hand, private sales would also make good business sense for more skilled slaves. A shrewd and experienced dealer could have been able to get several wealthy customers to bid against each other privately. Indeed, it may also have been the case that other prominent Romans felt the way Julius Caesar did; they did not want anyone to know what they had paid for their most expensive acquisitions, so they would need to buy them behind the scenes so that they could keep the prices out of their account books.[41]

Can we date this first sale more precisely than putting it before the death of Scaurus in 89? Another way to put this question is to ask: when do we think that Scaurus would have had the money to buy Daphnis? Scaurus, who was probably born in the late 160s, had a slow start in politics because of early financial constraints. Later he acquired a notably bad reputation for enriching himself, particularly in the period after his consulship of 115.[42] It seems safe, therefore, to say that he acquired Daphnis after 115. Additional moments of profit are attested over the next few years. During and immediately after official trips to North Africa in 112 and 111, Scaurus was accused of taking "bribes" from the Numidian king Jugurtha on the eve of the Roman war in Africa.[43] Similarly, he is said by Pliny to have profited significantly from his close connection to Gaius Marius, who held his first consulship and took over the war against Jugurtha in 107.[44] These opportunities for personal enrichment suggest a time window in the decade between 115 and 105, with the most likely date range falling between 110 and 106. During these years, Scaurus was elected to the censorship (109–108) and was at his most influential in Roman politics. It is interesting to see new money that surely came from imperial sources abroad, possibly directly or indirectly from Numidia, being spent on an expensive homegrown intellectual.

How old was Daphnis when he commanded such a high price? He cannot have been a child. He was being bought and sold for his talents but also for the education he had already received. In this context, one may posit that he was somewhere between 18 and 25 years old, a time when young males typically fetched their highest prices.[45] If we imagine, just for the sake of argument, a first sale in 110, that could put his birth in the later 130s or very early in the 120s. His literary skills will already have been on display in some way to a select audience in preparation for the initial sale, since his trainer will have been aiming to increase his own profit margin in relation to the cost of upkeep and education that he had born, perhaps for over two decades. Clearly, Daphnis was perceived to offer much more than an ordinary scribe or an actor who read aloud. Such educated members of an elite household were not uncommon.[46] Nor does it seem credible that he was simply a handsome boy sold for sexual purposes, who also happened to have done well at school. Again, sexual services provided by slaves were not rare or necessarily always as expensive as the exceptional cases criticized by Cato earlier in the century. While the name Daphnis may suggest he was attractive in his youth, it also has other, more literary connotations that fit in with what Daphnis himself had to offer.[47]

These considerations bring us to the question of who had trained Daphnis. According to Pliny, he was sold by a certain Attius of Pisaurum.[48] This man seems likely to be his trainer, whose household he was born in, or someone who bought him at a young age in order to train and resell him. The Attii or Accii were a well-known and wealthy family in Pisaurum in the later first century.[49] They seem to have been among the original settlers of the Roman colony in 184. The descendants of their freedmen included the poet and tragedian Lucius Accius, who was prominent as a playwright and literary figure in Rome for the last several decades of the second century and who seems to have lived into the 80s.[50]

It is obviously tempting to identify this famous Lucius Accius the tragedian, himself the son of two freed people, as the probable owner and trainer of Daphnis. In other words, Daphnis' price makes at least somewhat better sense if he had a well-established pedigree that linked him to individuals who could vouch for the education he had received and to an intellectual and artistic milieu that was already recognized as prestigious in Rome. If Daphnis had indeed been born in Pisaurum, he surely did not grow up there. It is unlikely that he received his specialized training in a provincial place.

Lucius Accius the tragic poet was active in Rome from about 140 onward, so probably before Daphnis was born. The connection of Daphnis to this particular Lucius Accius is further supported by the range of learned works, now lost, that are attributed to Accius, who is best known to us for his tragedies. The compositions attributed to him other than dramas included a hexameter poem in many books (possibly 27) entitled *Annales*, whose five extant fragments deal with etiologies and the local origin stories of festivals. This material is similar to what Daphnis was later writing about in his *Communis Historia*. In addition, there were works by Accius on literary and theatrical history, astrology and farming, philosophical questions apparently set in a bucolic landscape, and an influential intervention about spelling conventions in Latin.[51] The choice of the name Daphnis as a literary allusion makes sense in this intellectual milieu. Lucius Accius was a very successful man, who benefited from the patronage of Decimus Iunius Brutus Callaicus, consul in 138.[52] Accius' high profile in Rome in the later second century and the rich variety of his literary output suggests that he himself relied upon educated slaves and freedmen in his own household. As Lucius Accius' apprentice, Daphnis would have been exposed to a sophisticated environment of learning, in which information of many sorts was being collected, sorted, and reproduced in both prose and verse formats, with the help of (a larger or smaller group of) assistants and advisers. In this context, innovation was taking place on the level both of genre and of performance.

Alternatively, Daphnis might have been born in the household of a different Accius in the same family, who sent him to be trained by the famous poet in Rome. The family itself had been educating slaves for more than a generation. The poet Accius' parents, who both gained their freedom and citizenship before their son was born (c. 170s?), might originally have been captives or might have been born in Italy and educated while enslaved. Although the details of this literary and genealogical pedigree are not preserved, the fame of the poet Lucius Accius speaks to the upward mobility through education that he had received from his freed parents in the mid-second century. He, in turn, apparently trained and profited from specially selected enslaved boys, who helped in his own literary workshop. Accius' career spanned the turbulent years of the Gracchi and beyond, when Latin literature was being refined and reinvented by men like the satirist Gaius Lucilius and the politician Catulus, the next purchaser of Daphnis.[53]

Quintus Lutatius Catulus was very well connected in politics and in Rome's literary circles. He was one of the first elite Romans to write elegiac love poetry based on Hellenistic models in his own name and the first man to deliver a public eulogy from the speaker's platform (*rostra*) in the Forum for a Roman woman, his mother, Popilia.[54] Cicero claims that Catulus' consulship in 102 marked a high point of Hellenism in Roman culture.[55] Catulus surely knew both Accius and Scaurus personally. He will, therefore, most probably also have been familiar with Daphnis, perhaps from an early age. According to this reconstruction, Scaurus will have owned Daphnis for a number of years before Catulus was elected consul.

But when did Catulus buy Daphnis from Scaurus? He would not have had the money to do so before his victory over the Cimbri in 101. Catulus only reached the consulship in his fourth candidacy, in the elections held in 103, when he was already in his late 40s. Few men had the financial resources or the sheer perseverance to stand for the highest office as often as Catulus did (each year consecutively in 107, 106 and 105, and finally successfully in 103). Money must have been tight for him during these years. Subsequently, after he had shared the military success of 101 and the attendant recognition with his consular colleague Marius, Catulus seems to have gained a great deal of wealth from Celtic booty. His ambitious building program in Rome in the 90s is well attested.[56] In addition, he lived in an exceptionally expensive house on the Palatine in Rome, as well as owning a magnificent villa at Tusculum in Latium.[57] Catulus, who started with modest means, had expensive tastes, perhaps even as a young man, but his later affluent lifestyle can be securely connected with his recent and dramatic enrichment after 101.[58]

Catulus acquired Daphnis for HS 700,000, thus paying Scaurus the face value of his initial investment, and then soon set Daphnis free, in what was a truly lavish gesture of generosity.[59] In several senses, therefore, this second sale, which was probably a private transaction between acquaintances (friends?), was just as notorious, if not even more so, than the first. Catulus' actions were commemorated by Daphnis' new name, Quintus Lutatius Daphnis (rather than Marcus Aemilius Daphnis, if he had been manumitted by Scaurus). Everything we know about Catulus' life, therefore, suggests that he will have bought Daphnis no earlier than 100, and perhaps more plausibly in the early 90s. This timeline also fits in with the order in which Daphnis is introduced in Suetonius' *De Grammaticis et Rhetoribus*, a text that proceeds through its examples chronologically. Catulus' freeing of Daphnis was a public demonstration of the cash still at his disposal, even *after* he bought several new private houses and funded both an exquisitely fine, round marble temple in the Campus Martius and a portico on the Palatine to house Gallic weapons captured on the battlefield.

So why did Scaurus agree to sell Daphnis? Daphnis was a "collector's item" by now, an individual who may have been in Scaurus' household for as long as a decade or perhaps even longer. A partial answer can perhaps be found in Scaurus' changed personal circumstances at the very end of the second century. Scaurus' only son had died by suicide after retreating from his post guarding the passes into Italy in 102, when the Cimbri invaded over the Alps and initially met with very little resistance.[60] Although at least 60 years old by now, Scaurus soon remarried to a young, aristocratic wife and started a new family, with a daughter and two sons born in the early 90s.[61] Expenses associated with making this fresh start, as well as the personal interactions of Scaurus with Catulus, who had been his late son's commander in chief, were soon followed by the high-profile transfer of a famous intellectual. Scaurus' position as leading man in the senate (*princeps senatus*) and Daphnis' service to him, which will have been well known in political and literary circles, allowed Daphnis to avoid any loss of "market price," despite being older when he was acquired by Catulus.

As already noted, there was a famous joke that was associated with Catulus' purchase of Daphnis for a high price and perhaps also his granting of freedom almost immediately. This joke, which was presumably originally made at the time of that sale, was included by Gaius Maecenas Melissus, the freedman of Maecenas discussed in chapter 5, in his authoritative collection of jokes entitled *Ineptiae* or *Ioci* (*Trifles* or *Jokes*), a work in 150 *libelli* (small books or pamphlets) compiled during the time of Augustus.[62] According to this witticism, Daphnis was referred to as *Panos agapema* or "Pan's delight." Daphnis is cast as the mythical Sicilian goatherd with whom the god Pan falls in love. Thus Catulus is identified as Pan and Daphnis as his beloved. At around this same time, Catulus had written an elegiac love poem about his romantic feelings for the famous comic actor Quintus Roscius.[63]

constiteram exorientem Auroram forte salutans
cum subito a laeua Roscius exoritur,
pace mihi liceat, caelestes, dicere uestra,
mortalis uisus pulchrior esse deo.

By chance, I had taken up my position to face the Dawn in prayer, when suddenly Roscius came up from the left; may I be permitted by your allowance, o heavenly deities, to declare that he, though a mortal, appeared more beautiful than a god.

QUOTED BY CICERO (*DE NATURA DEORUM* 1.79)

With this poem in mind, the joke about Daphnis has been interpreted as hanging on the high price Catulus paid for him. Surely, only a man madly in love would pay such a sum for a slave.[64]

But we can detect an extra dimension to the humor that helps explain why this was a "really funny joke" that was remembered for a century. The traditional love object is a boy or young man, as the goatherd Daphnis is described in myth and depicted in Hellenizing art of the period.[65] Yet by the early 90s the historical Daphnis was no longer a very young man. He will probably have been at least 30 and perhaps as old as 40, while Catulus himself was about 50. A consideration of the chronology and historical circumstances reveals the more complex humor in this jest. Catulus is cast as Pan but his beloved is no youngster and may not, in fact, by then or even ever, have been very handsome. Hence the idea that Catulus is madly in love with Daphnis, *as if* he was a beautiful boy, can be seen as funny on several levels in Roman terms. This joke also deliberately seeks to undercut Catulus' prestigious gesture of buying and freeing a man who is a mature intellectual appreciated for his literary skill.

Daphnis was, I argue, manumitted around the turn of the first century and went on to publish his historical work under his own name. He surely continued to be part of Catulus' literary circle and may even have lived in his house or in another property owned by him. He may have helped Catulus write what are described as two distinct works of autobiography, one a letter in an elaborate style (in the first person?) and the other a third-person memoir in one book in the plain style of Xenophon, dedicated to the poet Aulus Furius.[66] Scaurus also wrote a memoir entitled *De Vita Sua* in three books, which seems to date to the late 90s.[67] It would be unsurprising if Scaurus continued to be on familiar terms with Daphnis and sought his assistance with a variety of projects. It is unfortunate that the 90s are such an obscure decade in Roman history, which makes the context of Daphnis' life in Rome during these years difficult to sketch. Both Scaurus and Catulus died in the early 80s and no more is known of Daphnis' subsequent life.

Archias of Antioch, a Greek Poet in Rome

A partial analogy can be found between the life of Daphnis and the much more fully attested experiences of Aulus Licinius Archias, a poet originally from Antioch in Syria who arrived in Rome in 102 when Catulus was consul and made an independent career there.[68] In 62, forty years after this poet first came to the city, Cicero was successful in defending Archias' legal claim to Roman citizenship.[69] Cicero's speech in defense of Archias vividly portrays a world of educated Romans eager to serve as patrons to a poet who traveled with them on campaign and celebrated their achievements in Greek verse. Archias moved in the same milieu as Daphnis and spent a significant amount of time with Q. Catulus, and with his son of the same name. In fact, Daphnis and Archias will surely have known each other, and may even both have lived in Catulus' house together, in the 90s, although Archias was perhaps somewhat younger than Daphnis.[70] Aemilius Scaurus was also a person who took time to hear Archias perform in person.[71] The network of prominent Romans who are mentioned by Cicero in connection with Archias will have been thoroughly familiar to Daphnis.

Archias' experiences as an immigrant provide both a comparison with and a contrast to those of the freedman *verna* Daphnis. In his defense speech, Cicero claims that he is telling us a great deal about Archias' career in Rome; he was freeborn and had come to the city of his own free will. Yet his status as a dependent poet made him subject to the demands and preferences of the same leading Romans, as well as eventually to becoming a target in their fierce internal political struggles.[72] It may seem ironic to note that even as an older man Archias, a freeborn immigrant, had to defend his claim to Roman citizenship in court, while Daphnis had received his as a gift under the Roman laws of manumission.[73] At the same time, Archias' career represents for us some of the risks and rewards of the professional intellectual in late republican Rome. Daphnis socialized and competed with men like Archias on a daily basis. Subsequently, he may even have been present in court to hear Cicero defend his comrade of many years.[74]

Cicero himself was only four years old and was living in Arpinum when Archias arrived in Rome. Consequently, Archias was part of the intellectual landscape that shaped Cicero's experience of Rome as a young man. By the time Cicero was in his mid-40s, his familiar relationship with Archias could form a natural part of his own intellectual and social self-representation.[75] As many have noted, the speech in defense of Archias' claim to Roman citizenship contains exaggerations, distortions, and a number of significant and strategic omissions.[76] It is a lawcourt speech designed to win a particular case by any and every means at hand; in no way should it be considered a simple or objective account. It was delivered in 62, many years after the central events it describes, with the result that anachronisms prompted by contemporary concerns are almost inevitably present.[77] Nevertheless, the speech does provide insightful evidence about Archias himself and about the world in which he had enjoyed a successful career. Cicero's speech on behalf of Archias has been much read and reinterpreted by generations of different readers since its rediscovery by Petrarch in 1333.[78] The defendant poet himself, however, has often not been a principal focus of attention.[79]

Cicero will surely have won this case since his speech was published soon after its delivery.[80] Consequently, it seems fair to assume that the written version we have largely reflects what was said in court on the day; Cicero's performance will have been fresh in people's memories. The fact that he published the speech shows that he was pleased both with its form and with the way in which it had been received by the jurors and the general audience (*corona*) in the court. It provides a snapshot of a courtroom enthralled by the dramatic rhetoric of a recent consul, a famous orator at the height of his political career who was only just beginning to be aware of the dire political consequences of some of his recent actions. The present analysis of this speech will consider its rhetorical approaches by taking into account both what Cicero says and (at least some of) what he omits, on the assumption that the basic facts he states are not completely false. Ultimately, however, it is not possible for us to evaluate the legal strength of Cicero's case or to surmise what the prosecution had said.

Archias Becomes a Roman Citizen

According to Cicero, Archias of Antioch became a Roman citizen through a legal process in 89 in the immediate aftermath of the Social War and under the terms of the *lex Plautia Papiria*, some 13 years after he had first arrived in Rome.[81] He changed his status by appearing before the urban praetor Q. Caecilius Metellus Pius within the 60-day timeframe specified by that law and by providing the presiding magistrate with proof that he was living in Rome at the time and was a citizen of Heraclea, a Greek city in southern Italy.[82] Consequently, his new Roman name (Aulus Licinius) appeared on Metellus Pius' list of newly enfranchised Italians, an archived document that Cicero was able to produce in court in 62.[83] Archias' transition to his new status as Aulus Licinius happened a full decade (or more) after Daphnis was manumitted and became Quintus Lutatius.[84] The date of Archias' arrival, in the consulship of Marius and Catulus, and of his enfranchisement in 89 are the two most clearly fixed points in the poet's earlier career.

Yet Cicero's account is misleading because he is determined to stress Archias' natural talent and unique abilities, which were integral to the value he wanted the jury to assign to his client as a member of the Roman community. Consequently, Cicero describes Archias as having been very young, perhaps even still an adolescent, when he arrived in Rome.[85] Yet other parts of Cicero's own narrative make this chronology seem implausible. In fact, Archias appears to have been a grown man, with an established reputation by the time he came to the city in 102.[86]

Archias had been born in Antioch, the capital of Hellenistic Syria, and completed his education there.[87] He then set out to travel as a professional poet. Before reaching Italy, he made a tour of Greece and of several, unnamed Greek cities in Asia Minor. These career stages will all have taken some time to complete and there is no reason to think that Archias was a child when he set off from home. Similarly, he spent time in Italy traveling around before coming to Rome. Before 102, he had already received honorary citizenships in Naples, Rhegium, and Tarentum, which suggests he must have made an impact locally in each place.[88] He may also have been living in Heraclea, a colony of Tarentum, at some point before he came to Rome.[89]

Archias had a reputation as a poet that preceded him and was easily able to make contacts with leading Romans, as soon as he arrived, including notably with both consuls of 102. All this suggests a series of networks and a man who was shrewd and skillful at making an impression. It will surely have been some years since Archias left Antioch, after completing his formal education in his home city. Cicero never mentions his father's name, despite the fact that many Greek speakers regularly used a patronymic to identify themselves in Rome, nor indeed any precise details of his social background.[90] In other words, Cicero has omitted Archias' family background and obscured his age, in such a way that hides the path of someone who was surely a largely self-made man. Perhaps his birth family was Syrian and did not identify as closely with the Greek language and culture as Archias himself later would.[91] His peripatetic life does not suggest an established man of independent means but a young person trying to make a career and a living. Ultimately, Cicero's picture of the boy genius is at odds with his own description of Archias' extensive travels as a young man.

Above all, Cicero stresses Archias' intimate and immediate connection with the family of the Licinii Luculli, whom the poet lived with in Rome and who remained patrons even during the trial itself, 40 years later.[92] This fact has suggested the tempting hypothesis that Archias was invited or even brought to Rome in 102 by a Licinius. The obvious candidate to introduce Archias into Rome's high society was Lucius Licinius Lucullus, the father of the two Luculli whom Cicero knew.[93] This older Lucullus had been in Sicily as pro-praetor in command of a military action against a slave revolt during the year 103.[94] He could have met Archias on his travels in southern Italy and brought him back to Rome upon his return, in 102. This explanation neatly accounts for Archias' rapid rise in Roman society and his presence in the house of the Licinii, where the two brothers in the next generation, Lucius and Marcus, were still teenagers.[95] Cicero does not specifically mention their father who appears a likely candidate to be Archias' first patron in Rome, presumably because this Licinius was soon convicted of financial crimes and exiled, apparently never returning to Rome. Some have imagined that he went into exile at Heraclea, but no direct evidence is available for where he went or for how long he survived living in exile.[96]

Plutarch's laudatory biography of the younger Lucius Licinius Lucullus tells us a great deal about his life, including especially about his love of Greek culture, and also provides information about his brother Marcus, who appeared in person as a witness during the trial.[97] Archias is not mentioned by Plutarch.[98] Yet some logical inferences suggest themselves. Almost as soon as he arrived in Rome, Archias was exposed to a complex and highly divisive political landscape in the city, including tension between the two consuls, pressure from an invasion of Italy by the Cimbri, and the fragility of his first patron Licinius' own political position.[99] Within a year (or two at most) Archias' initial sponsor was exiled and the poet will have found himself in urgent need of other patrons. Yet he apparently chose to stay in Rome rather than returning to one of the Greek cities where he had lived before, and he went on to flourish in the metropolis.[100] His close and sustained relationship with the two younger Luculli speaks to a special bond formed during their difficult teenage years after their father's exile, a connection that was intellectual, but surely also emotional and personal.[101]

Cicero aims to impress the jury with a catalog of Archias' prominent sponsors and patrons, whose social and political prestige is meant to suggest how brilliant and useful Archias is.[102] This list includes a significant number of prominent men who died, mostly in violent circumstances, in the late 90s and early 80s, as a result of the civil strife that broke out during and after the Social War.[103] From this catalog a picture of Archias' life in Rome in the 90s emerges. He was part of a familiar inner circle who were very much idealized by Cicero as the great men of the previous generation. Archias also lived for an unspecified length of time at the house of Catulus (cos. 102) and his son (cos. 78), which must have been during this same decade, perhaps when the Luculli were less able or willing to support him themselves. Catulus was, therefore, happy to entertain Archias, and be entertained by him, around the same time that he manumitted Daphnis. The two writers will have shared in the same cultural activities and network of acquaintances. Yet Archias, who may not initially even have been planning to move to Rome at all, did not have an easy time in a city already torn by fierce political differences and ongoing concerns about the number of free noncitizens in its large population.[104]

At some point before the end of the 90s, Archias traveled to Sicily with Marcus Licinius Lucullus, then in his early 20s, on a private journey that included a stop in Heraclea on the way back to Rome.[105] It was on this trip that Archias was made an honorary citizen of Heraclea, both on his own merits and through the local influence of the Luculli, according to Cicero. It is this event that is attested to by the witnesses present in court, Marcus himself (by now a man of consular rank in his mid-50s) and a delegation of leading citizens from Heraclea.[106] The official records of the town had been lost in a fire during the Social

War.[107] During his trip to Sicily with Marcus, we again see Archias' closeness to the younger Luculli, well before they became leading politicians.

Heraclea is not, however, located on the road from Sicily to Rome; a significant detour was needed to reach it and then to return back to that main highway heading north.[108] In other words, Marcus and Archias made a deliberate trip to Heraclea, a place where Archias had apparently spent some time before and where young Marcus was said to have local influence, presumably through established family connections. It is possible that they went there to visit Marcus' father in exile. However that may have been, Archias received a grant of local citizenship at his own request, according to Cicero. Again, there are surely several factors that are not mentioned in the speech that will have motivated both the journey to Heraclea and the request for local citizenship at that time. Similarly, Cicero is remarkably economical in what he says about the Social War, which forms the essential historical background to the law of 89 and, consequently, to Archias being in a position to apply for Roman citizenship at a time when many inhabitants of Italy were being enfranchised.[109]

After Archias became Aulus Licinius, he is most closely associated with Lucius Licinius Lucullus, Marcus' older brother. The poet accompanied Lucius on two extended campaigns in the East to fight Mithridates VI, king of Pontus, thus causing him to be absent from Rome for many years. Lucius had been serving as quaestor to Sulla in 88. He traveled East with Sulla's army in 87 and stayed on after the Peace of Apamea, not returning to Rome until 80, after Sulla had already staged a coup and imposed a new constitution as dictator.[110] The Luculli were consistently close to Sulla in the Social and civil wars, both politically and personally. Lucius was entrusted with publishing Sulla's memoirs after his death in 78.[111] Yet Cicero does not mention Sulla at all in his defense of Archias. It is evident that Archias must have known Sulla well and have interacted with him frequently during the 80s.[112]

When Sulla first marched on Rome in 88, Lucius seems to have been the only officer to join him in this unprecedented action.[113] Was Archias with that army as a witness to the first time the city of Rome was attacked by a Roman army? This seems a distinct possibility, since he was a member of Lucius' entourage that was due to travel East with that same army. Did Archias also write poems about Sulla? Or verses that discussed Lucius' role in Sulla's military campaigns? Cicero is very cautious in what he says about Archias before the recent expedition against Mithridates. It is, of course, possible that Archias was abroad with Lucius simply as a friend and entertainer, a composer of light verse and congenial dinner companion. Yet given his later role as an author of propaganda poetry in Rome's ongoing struggle against the Pontic king, we may suspect that he also composed similar poems that praised Rome's military and imperialistic initiatives during that first war.

Archias' position as a dependent poet took him away from the salons of Rome to long years of army life and extensive travels through Greece and Asia Minor, areas in which his previous experiences could have made him useful to his patrons. He will have seen firsthand the effects of Roman military campaigns, the siege and capture of Athens, and the bitter fighting in Asia. His poetry in Greek would have been useful in presenting a positive picture of Roman military and political initiatives, in contrast to the elaborate self-image of Mithridates, who himself claimed to be a Hellenistic king, a worthy successor of Alexander the Great who had come to rescue the Greeks from Roman aggression, greed, and cruelty.[114]

Archias traveled extensively with Lucius and his personal companions, who would have included freedmen from his household. Archias will also have interacted with those close to other leading Romans—for example, Sulla's trusted freedman Epicadus and Aurelius Opillus, another learned freedman who served as companion and literary adviser to Publius Rutilius Rufus, a Roman politician in exile at Smyrna who spent time with Sulla in Asia.[115] These two intellectuals will be discussed in chapter 4. On campaign and in territory (re)conquered by the Romans, Archias had a range of experiences that differed significantly from the much more academic existence of Daphnis and others in Rome. During the 70s, Archias presumably returned to the city and lived there, even as he witnessed the brilliant careers of the two Luculli brothers.[116] It is unclear whether he also traveled to Africa with Lucius in the mid-70s.[117] Subsequently, he went as an officially recognized and remunerated staff member of Lucius in his second campaign against Mithridates (73–66).[118] Lucius was now the commanding general and Archias was a member of his support team. We know that Archias wrote an epic poem in Greek about the war in more than one book, traces of which may perhaps be found in some more colorful sections of Plutarch's life of Lucius Lucullus.[119] During this time, Archias will surely also have met Tyrannio of Amisus, a war captive who is discussed in chapter 6.

Archias returned to Rome with Lucius in 66, after his patron had been replaced by Pompey as Rome's commander against Mithridates. His close association with Lucius, whose hostility to Pompey became a key element in Roman politics throughout the 60s, eventually led to him being targeted by the well-attested accusation of fraudulently pretending to be a Roman citizen.[120] Lucius Lucullus waited for three years before the senate granted him a triumph over Mithridates in 63.[121] Opposition to this honor was organized by supporters of Pompey and others who resented the wealth and influence of the Luculli brothers. The intensely partisan politics of the 60s are chronicled for us in great detail by Cicero and Plutarch.[122] Yet the citizenship trial of Archias in 62 should not be seen as merely a minor episode in the protracted fight between the Luculli and Pompey. Rather, Archias was targeted in his own right, a fact that shows he had a public profile by now, precisely within the type of elite circles that Cicero refers to in his speech.[123] His poetry, despite the fact that it was surely all in Greek and not aimed at a wider audience in Rome, mattered enough that it was worth trying to get rid of him. At the same time, a considerable effort was expended by people who cared to save him from being banned. Cicero and Marcus Lucullus spoke on his behalf and someone paid for a delegation from Heraclea to travel to Rome for the trial.[124]

Cicero, of course, represents the prosecution's case as completely baseless. Yet, Archias had, in fact, been away from Rome for many years since becoming a citizen in 89, probably for at least half the intervening time period.[125] The question of where he was legally domiciled was, therefore, probably the most plausible part of the attack on him. In addition, he may well not have presented as an Italian or as a Greek from southern Italy. The flavor and style of his personal Hellenism is not recoverable for us. There is no mention of him ever having voted in Rome, but he was clearly behaving "like a Roman citizen" in other ways, at least in the mid-60s.[126] Cicero tries to use instances of such actions in his defense, but these activities surely will have drawn attention to him and made him vulnerable, precisely because he was still obviously a foreigner but not a freedman.[127] His recent poem about the Mithridatic war has been taken as the decisive factor in drawing the ire of Pompey's supporters, even before Pompey's return to Rome.[128] The impact of this epic is further revealed by the fact that Cicero was so eager for his own consulship to be the subject of Archias' next composition.[129] Here again, Archias emerges as a fascinating and talented individual. Although Cicero clearly won the lawsuit on his behalf, which constituted a significant favor by any measure, Archias soon chose not to write an epic for the very disappointed Cicero.[130]

A number of conclusions seem to follow from this somewhat surprising turn of events. Archias was indeed comfortably established in Rome and was now much in demand, including by the Caecilii Metelli, who are said to be the subject of his next composition. Cicero, even as a man of consular rank, simply did not have the clout or the resources of other patrons in Archias' circle. In late 62 or early 61, Archias could perhaps already see the political dangers in writing about Cicero's consulship, even before the fallout from the Bona Dea scandal or the subsequent formation of a novel political alliance between Pompey, Caesar, and Crassus.[131] Archias had just written a controversial epic and was perhaps not in the mood for another one.[132] He was, therefore, politically astute and well informed, which made him fully able to make his own decisions. He did not comply with Cicero's request, despite his own previous promises and the fact that the Luculli continued to support Cicero; they went on to do so even during his exile and they worked for his return.[133] But Archias had his own plans and a position of some independence, even if he was (still or again) living at the house of a Lucullus.

To conclude this section, it is worth reflecting briefly on the range of poems Archias was composing. Cicero praises him for his ability to produce improvised verses in Greek on demand for an audience on any subject currently under discussion.[134] After an initial performance, he was also in the habit of improvising another version on the same topic but in a completely different style. We may imagine such a scene at a dinner party, where subjects in contemporary politics and literary culture were raised by diners. Some of these verses were probably laudatory of contemporary figures who were patrons or potential employers, in a tone similar to the one he would use for the Luculli. Other verses may have been satirical and humorous or even vituperative commentaries on current events. Here again we see Archias needed to be very well informed about the political issues of the day.

When he first arrived in Rome, he composed some verses about the Cimbric War, which pleased Marius but apparently did not displease Catulus.[135] Archias achieved a fine balance between two rival generals, a rare feat indeed. Cicero's stress on his mastery of different styles, apparently one of his trademarks, suggests that he worked in a range of meters and genres, as many other Roman authors from different backgrounds tended to do, including Archias' friend Lucius Lucullus.[136] Some of Archias' poetry probably consisted of epigrams in the Hellenistic style, although no surviving verses can definitely be attributed to him.[137] Such poems tend to be on more personal and less political topics, perhaps for the birthday of a patron, for example.[138] He may also have given lectures on literary topics.[139] He clearly did circulate poems in written form, in addition to his well-known oral performances.[140] The poem he wrote about the Mithridatic war was in more than one book and was, therefore, most probably an epic in hexameters. Archias had accompanied a general on campaign in the way Ennius had, but Archias' Greek poetry will not have found the same audience in Rome, despite Cicero's comparison of the two poets. Archias' role in republican political and literary culture demonstrates the importance of Roman self-representation within the larger Greek world, as Cicero argued at some length.[141]

Neither Archias nor Daphnis is described as having worked as a *grammaticus*, a teacher of young boys.[142] Each man excelled in his area of expertise and on the basis of his personal charisma. Above all, these two intellectuals moved in the same social circles and enjoyed the patronage of the same leading men. Daphnis will naturally have interacted with a large number of freeborn immigrants to the city. It is striking to see a man like Catulus spending the money to acquire and manumit Daphnis at the same time as he was willing to support other intellectuals who were living in his house. But a high price for Daphnis had obviously been paid upfront, whereas Archias could be employed or let go on a temporary basis and entirely at will. Each of these men contributed to Catulus' self-representation within the larger network of his peers.[143] A cultivation of a wide range of literary pursuits in both Greek and Latin was integral to the lifestyle of republican elites.

Conclusion

The remarkable life of Daphnis sheds some light on a range of Roman habits with regard to the roles of the enslaved who were learned. In the second and first centuries, such highly trained individuals were specially educated, sometimes alongside the family's own sons; they were bought, sold and resold, given as gifts, and regularly freed. The focus of our meager surviving sources is inevitably principally on the wealthy Romans and to a much lesser extent on their freedmen. But many more would have been involved in making this market function. Its logic was driven by the fact that it was high profile and highly lucrative in republican Rome. Men of consular rank, both from old families and the more recently upwardly mobile, displayed their wealth and fine literary taste by collecting these learned intellectuals, even as they might collect books or art objects or villas. These wider assemblages included *vernae* such as Daphnis alongside decorative foreigners such as Archias.

The competition to identify a likely candidate among the enslaved and to educate him successfully from a young age will have been intense.[144] The stakes were high and it made sense to train several boys at once in the same school, rather than to invest in just one, who might not survive. As discussed in chapter 2, learned men like Atticus educated their whole household staff at home in town with their own chosen curriculum and teachers. By the 50s, Atticus had no intention of paying a high price for a Daphnis. After a boy was educated, he would need to be marketed in the right way and to the kind of customers who were able and willing to pay, if he was to realize a high price. Each stage in this system speaks to the interplay of entrepreneurship with the development of the most impressive curriculum and the most effective training methods. Men like Atticus competed with those from lower social strata who trained boys. Atticus did not (any longer) buy, or so he claimed, but he may well have sold on a regular basis. Cato the Elder bought and sold every year in an annual rotation.

A consideration of this market brings us back to the question of what services literate freedmen provided before and after their manumission. The focus here has been on the most expensive and learned, but a large household would contain many literate individuals from a variety of backgrounds.[145]

There were secretaries who took dictation, maintained correspondence, and kept account books. Copyists produced fair versions or duplicates of books, speeches, documents, and legal texts. Readers read aloud in a variety of settings, to larger or smaller audiences. Tutors taught children, whether free or enslaved. Daphnis will have mastered more than these basic skills, and he will also have been able to do most of the tasks mentioned so far, as well as perhaps being an expert supervisor of others in these various occupations.

We may imagine that Daphnis was an intellectual who had command of a wide range of knowledge, much of which he will have accessed from memory.[146] He was probably a polymath, who also wrote well and was a skilled conversationalist. He could act as a researcher, editor, or literary collaborator for his various patrons and their friends.[147] He might inspire and advise; he had the potential to be a type of intellectual "friend." In addition to his knowledge base and literary skills, he could also provide the kind of emotional support that comes from shared interests.[148] Moreover, all these services were obviously available on command, which would not be the case with a social equal. Daphnis' learning might be used in a purely private setting or might be displayed, especially in the house to invited groups of friends or people who needed to be impressed.

Four distinct but interrelated features emerge as concluding themes to this discussion. First, Daphnis' life, in its four stages between childhood and citizenship, holds a particular fascination, purely in its own right. Second, his trajectory reflects the overall value placed on literary skill, knowledge, and production during a key time period, the historical moment when the Latin language was said to be reaching its fully "classical" form in the early first century. Third, the high price paid for Daphnis and his consequent renown, even for Romans in later generations, raises many types of questions about luxury as a concept and about elite taste within a rapidly expanding urban economy. And last, Daphnis' movements reveal at least some of the complex interactions between wealthy Romans and their educated staff and dependents, not only within their own homes but also in a web of literary connections between various elite households and their many occupants.

Archias of Antioch has been introduced here both as a complementary foil to Daphnis, because he moved in the same social circles at the same time period, and also very much in his own right. Cicero's description of Archias' experiences and social networks maps onto those of Daphnis in numerous ways, only some of which are explored here. Yet, the two men will not have been interchangeable in the range of services or the precise expertise they offered. Archias remained very much a foreigner in the city, even decades after he managed to acquire Roman citizenship in the wake of the Social War, a fact that made him employable but also a target for attack. His language was Greek and his poetry, while appreciated by select audiences in Rome at sessions of improvisation or in published form, was surely also designed to present Roman imperialism to a wider Mediterranean audience in the Greek East. At the same time, he was no less dependent on powerful patrons among the Roman intelligentsia than any other intellectual discussed in this study. The significance of his contribution is reliably indicated by the fact that he became a target of Lucullus' political enemies after the end of the war with Mithridates, a conflict he had described in an epic poem in Greek that celebrated a victory of the Romans near the end of a decades-long conflict with a formidable Hellenistic king.

4

Multitaskers

AURELIUS OPILLUS AND LUCIUS CORNELIUS EPICADUS

Librum autem, quem Sulla novissimum "de rebus suis" imperfectum reliquerat, ipse supplevit.

He himself (Epicadus) edited the very last book that Sulla had left behind unfinished, a work entitled *About His Achievements.*

—SUETONIUS *DE GRAMMATICIS ET RHETORIBUS* 12

THE PREVIOUS three chapters, through their focus on elaborate households such as those of Cato, the Licinii, and Atticus, at quite distinct historical periods over more than a century, have raised several issues that invite further exploration. Two central areas have already emerged as being of special interest, namely the wide range of tasks a highly educated individual could be called upon to fulfill and, consequently, the complex personal bonds implied by the extent to which even very wealthy patrons chose to rely on their most trusted freedmen, the few mentioned by name among so many others who remain nameless. While both of these topics deserve consideration in their own right, the interconnections between them provide a particular focus for further research into the lived experience both of patron and of freedman. The most educated in the household might spend the most time with the patron and, therefore, be most closely involved both with his political career and with his personal interests.[1]

Once such an exceptional amanuensis had been entrusted with more than one key role, his interdependence with his patron was inevitably enhanced. Some of the various jobs of individual high-profile freedmen are tangible items that can be documented from our sources. Personal relationships are inevitably a different matter, since most of them are lost to the historian. Yet examining one aspect without at least evoking the other leaves obvious gaps in a discussion. Ultimately, talent and a personal relationship that resulted in a sense of trust will both have contributed to a choice to employ the same individual for several tasks that required clearly different skill sets and specialized training in each case.

One common approach that has been fundamental to the study of enslavement in the context of large Roman households is based on analysis of the job titles to be found listed in epitaphs from family tombs.[2] Such extensive burial areas contained the remains of dozens of household members, assembled in death in a configuration that mimicked their communal living and working relationships. The tombs of the enslaved, and of many freedmen, were frequently characterized by the use of job titles to designate the deceased. These inscriptions might serve as oppressive labels and yet at the same time as affirmations of personal skills and contributions to a lived community. They have tended to suggest a consistent picture of persons who could be assigned very specific tasks within a complex environment in which human labor was in essence cheap and plentiful.

Most of these individuals only have a single job mentioned in their inscription, an end-of-life label that may obscure what had actually been a career in various different trades or crafts, at least in the case of those who lived to a more advanced age. These named tasks, we imagine, took up the bulk of each person's time. The household of Livia, wife of Augustus, is a frequently cited example, the home of a long-lived woman whose upbringing and habits were firmly rooted in traditional, republican aristocratic precedents.[3] Her domestic staff of over 1,000 attested people, over many years, included individuals with 46 distinct job descriptions. Such a reconstruction that features large numbers of specialized household staff has appeared to be confirmed by the extensive slave quarters archaeologically attested in some late republican houses in the center of Rome.[4]

The two case studies of highly educated freedmen under discussion in this chapter are designed both to build on and to contrast with this normative model of a large household that formed a natural ecosystem for highly specialized training and employment at virtually every level, as may have been the case in the households of Cato and Atticus discussed in chapter 2. Aurelius Opillus, whose first name (*praenomen*) is lost together with the identity of his manumitter, and Lucius Cornelius Epicadus, freedman of the dictator Sulla, will surely have met on a number of occasions, probably first in Rome and then again in Asia Minor during the Mithridatic War in the 80s. Opillus spent many years living with Publius Rutilius Rufus (cos. 105), who went into exile in the Roman province of Asia after he had been unjustly convicted of extortion in that same part of the world. Sulla reorganized the province after concluding the Treaty of Dardanus with Mithridates; Rutilius assisted him and spent what seems to have been a considerable amount of time with him in the mid-80s. These years also gave Opillus and Epicadus a chance to encounter each other again, even as they stayed close to their patrons in times of exceptional political uncertainty and complex violence.

Like Daphnis, whom they will also have known personally, Opillus and Epicadus were highly educated intellectuals who were on intimate terms with the leading political figures they worked for after they had acquired Roman citizenship. Catulus (who freed Daphnis), Rutilius, and Sulla also happened to be among the tiny number of Roman politicians who made the unusual decision to write autobiographies in Latin in the early first century.[5] In his consulship and for some years after, Sulla was married to Caecilia Metella, the widow of Aemilius Scaurus (the original purchaser of Daphnis), the author of a recent Latin memoir in three books.[6] Opillus and Epicadus' lives were certainly shaped by the unprecedented and dramatic changes of fortune experienced by their patrons during the first decades of the first century. It was these highly unusual times that also served as inspiration for their autobiographies, innovative works designed to give their own versions of events and to shape their self-representation at a time when traditional means of image making and commemoration were failing along with the decay of republican political culture.

The role of the most trusted associate will only have become more important to Rutilius and to Sulla as they even lost their status as Roman citizens, at the same time as they were both on the front lines in the bitter conflict with Mithridates VI, a Hellenistic king who aimed to eliminate the Roman presence in Asia Minor. It was a time of vast change in Roman politics and culture, a transformation further effected by Sulla on his return to Italy from Asia with his invading army. Meanwhile, Rutilius made the decision to stay on in the province after he refused Sulla's offer to return to Rome. Each man gave up his previous role in Roman politics, Rutilius to become a citizen of Smyrna and a writer of political history in both Greek and Latin, Sulla to become dictator and author of a new republican system. Opillus and Epicadus not only had front-row seats as witnesses to this whole series of dramatic events, but they were also participants, in their own particular roles, as well as having an editorial hand in published accounts of their patrons' lives, texts that would be influential in shaping how future generations understood these controversial events and their protagonists.

Aurelius Opillus

As the older of our pair of freedmen, Opillus will take precedence in this discussion.[7] We meet Opillus, notable for his rare Oscan personal name, early in the pages of Suetonius' account of teachers in Rome, the *De Grammaticis et Rhetoribus*.[8] He is only the third in the roughly chronological list of 36 teachers and rhetoricians discussed by Suetonius. His Oscan name implies that he was born in Italy and may have had a family background in one of the Oscan-speaking peoples of the central peninsula (such as the Samnites) or alternatively in Campania, where Oscan was commonly in use before the Social War.[9] Small fragments of Opillus' works preserved in much later grammarians reveal him to have been a prominent author, whose writings survived well into late antiquity.[10] He is consistently and closely associated with Publius Rutilius Rufus (cos. 105); the two even appear as a pair in a letter written by Quintus Aurelius Symmachus in AD 378.[11] Interestingly, however, Symmachus cites them in a rhetorically elaborated list of famous pupils who were ungrateful to their teachers, although Opillus was surely never Rutilius' teacher in any formal sense. In other words, their personal closeness was recalled even in contexts where the actual details of their perhaps somewhat unconventional relationship had become obscure. Rutilius and Opillus simply belonged together and were remembered as a pair even some 470 years after they set off into exile from Rome.

Born before the middle of the second century, Opillus is the earliest individual to be discussed in this study; his life is both suggestive of the opportunities for at least some educated freedmen in Rome before the time of the Gracchi and is also characterized by a series of unusual personal choices that make him seem a distinctly individualistic figure. He is said to have grown old at the same time (*simul consenuit*) as Rutilius Rufus in Smyrna (probably spelled Zmyrna at the time), which implies that they were close in age to each other. Rutilius was, therefore, probably born around 158, which would make him a contemporary of Gaius Marius.[12] The following reconstruction assumes that Opillus was also born around that same time, although he could equally well have been either a few years older or younger than Rutilius. In any case, they belonged to the same generation and probably to the same age cohort within their generation.

Opillus' ethnic identity and early life are hard to discern from the surviving evidence. His Roman *praenomen* is lost.[13] His Oscan personal name could suggest either that he had not been born into enslavement or that he had been enslaved as a child in an Oscan-speaking context. Later Romans had trouble spelling this name, and Suetonius takes the trouble to try to put this ongoing debate to rest. He claimed that the correct spelling (OPILLUS) was revealed by the acrostic at the start of the work entitled *Pinax* (*Tablet* or *Catalog*?).[14] As a freedman Opillus bore the family name of the prominent Aurelii, a plebeian *gens* of political distinction and considerable wealth in Rome at the time. Yet Suetonius does not mention any one of these prominent Aurelii as Opillus' manumitter or patron. Rather he says that Opillus was the freedman of a certain Epicurean (*Epicurei cuiusdam libertus*), a phrase that appears somewhat dismissive in tone. Suetonius seems to be saying that he knows the identity of this Epicurean Aurelius but does not feel it is worth recording his name for his readers, presumably because the name would not mean anything to them or they would not benefit from identifying this individual. The clear implication is that this patron was not himself socially prominent, and certainly not a senator of consular rank like Rutilius. In this context, the label Epicurean indicates someone who teaches philosophy, not a wealthy Roman with an interest in philosophy. It may be more likely, therefore, that Opillus was the freedman of an Epicurean who was himself a freedman of the Aurelii, an educated person who had been attached to the household of this family in the past and who consequently also bore and handed on their family name.

A connection of some kind with the political Aurelii can help to explain Opillus' relationship with Rutilius Rufus. Rutilius' sister was married to an Aurelius Cotta, by whom she had three sons, each of whom went on to be elected consul.[15] The eldest one, C. Aurelius Cotta (cos. 75), had, as an emerging orator, spoken in defense of his famous uncle Rutilius at his corruption trial in 92.[16] But this Aurelius was surely not Opillus' patron. If that had been the case, Suetonius would have referred to him differently because of his political and social rank. In addition, Cotta was not obviously an Epicurean. Rather, Opillus emerges through his talent and hard work from among a wider circle of intellectuals, who had lived in Rome in association with the Aurelii for a generation before the birth of Gaius Cotta, the consul of 75. His patron may well have been the man who also taught him philosophy at a young age.

If this reconstruction is accurate, then Opillus' life mirrors, at least in its earliest stages, some of the experience of the famous later Stoic philosopher Epictetus, who was educated and manumitted by the emperor Nero's wealthy freedman Epaphroditus.[17] During his enslavement, Epictetus had also been trained as a philosopher, under the tutelage of the prominent equestrian Gaius Musonius Rufus, and subsequently went on to teach philosophy in Rome. After the emperor Domitian expelled the professional philosophers from the city in AD 93, Epictetus founded his own successful philosophical school at Nicopolis in Epirus. Similarly, Opillus also first launched his career in Rome as a teacher of philosophy, presumably no earlier than the 130s.

We may doubt, however, that Opillus was himself a dedicated Epicurean on the model of his patron. Opillus' close personal association with Rutilius, one of the leading Stoics in Rome, would surely have complicated matters if that had been the case.[18] In addition, Opillus was living with Rutilius throughout the years of his exile, when the image of Rutilius as the "Roman Socrates" was created and disseminated.[19] With the help of Opillus, Rutilius worked consistently and largely successfully to shape his own self-image for posterity as a philosopher-statesman who had been unjustly convicted by greedy and selfish jurors of the equestrian class. The distinctly Platonic and Stoic themes cultivated by Rutilius were in many ways the antithesis of Epicureanism.

Opillus may, therefore, have offered more general lectures on philosophical topics, probably delivered in Latin, rather than specifically promoting the doctrines of a single philosophical school. None of the works attributed to him are labeled as being philosophical, but Suetonius describes him as the author of many books.[20] One small surviving fragment does have a slightly philosophical tone. It offers a four-part definition of a "necessity" (*necessarium*) as something that one cannot stop doing or without which one cannot live or cannot live well or something that cannot be forbidden.[21] This definition could have come from a philosophical work. Opillus will also have come across Rutilius at public lectures given by Panaetius, the famous Stoic who was teaching in Rome from about 138 to 129.[22] After Panaetius returned to Athens to lead the Stoic school, there will have been more scope for other teachers of philosophy in the city, as well as an audience accustomed to engaging in philosophical debates. Opillus, about 30 years old by now, was in the city to take advantage of that opportunity.

It was not an easy matter, however, for a freedman (or perhaps for anyone else) to make a living in Rome simply from teaching philosophy during this time period. Consequently, Opillus branched out, first into teaching rhetoric, which was the essential tool for young Romans who were aiming at a political career. Then he also moved on to giving instruction in "grammar," which was the basic curricular foundation for the educated classes and was much closer to rhetoric than its title initially suggests. Suetonius says that Opillus first taught philosophy (*philosophia*), then rhetoric (*rhetorica*), and finally grammar (*grammatica*), all at a school he was in charge of in Rome.[23] It would be surprising, however, to see Opillus move completely from one subject to another in a teaching career. The order of subjects Opillus taught is listed in the reverse of their prestige value, since the youngest students studied grammar, after which they moved on to rhetoric, and sometimes then also to philosophy, with the latter not being required in any way but still gaining in popularity during Opillus' lifetime. Did Opillus really have a career that moved in reverse, possibly as a sign of repeated early failures to attract fee-paying students?[24]

As Suetonius himself points out earlier in his discussion, it was common for teachers of Opillus' generation to give lessons in both rhetoric and grammar at the same time, whereas schools later tended to become more specialized.[25] This will surely also have been the pattern for Opillus himself. It was bold to start out with philosophy but probably not practical in the longer term to give instruction only in that one advanced subject. Other changes in his personal circumstances may also lie behind his choices. For example, the death of his patron the Epicurean could have left Opillus in need of new, more reliable sources of income to support himself. We are first introduced to Opillus in 92 when he was already at a relatively advanced age (perhaps in his mid-60s), when he made the momentous decision to close his school in Rome and follow Rutilius into exile in Asia.[26] Consequently, it is not easy to reconstruct the details of his life before then as a teacher and intellectual living in Rome. Yet, it was in that earlier life that he had evidently become a close friend of Rutilius, a relationship that would lead Opillus to give up everything he had in Rome in order to set out on a new and uncertain path.

Suetonius' wording does not, in fact, indicate that Opillus gave up each subject in order to move on neatly and decisively to the next one in the list. Such a reading creates more problems than it solves. It is more natural to interpret Suetonius as saying that as it grew Opillus' school branched out to offer instruction to students of different ages. Expanding his school would have provided more opportunity for profit and for developing a curriculum that took younger boys through the basics first and then kept them on at older ages. He may have made use of his own enslaved staff, or of his freedmen, to make this expansion possible on a larger scale. Opillus' close friendship with Rutilius also suggests that he was still moving in the circles of those in Rome who were interested in philosophy, a milieu in which he would have had the chance to interact with others whom Rutilius was familiar with over the years, for example Scipio Aemilianus, Posidonius of Apamea, and the satirist Gaius Lucilius.[27] We should, therefore, imagine Opillus in 92 as the well-respected and established head of a flourishing school, one probably not housed in the domestic quarters of a patron but in premises that Opillus had himself secured as a rental, or even in property that he owned.

It is essential to note that even if Opillus had indeed been a freedman of Rutilius' in-laws, the Aurelii Cottae, he would not have been under any obligation to go into exile with Rutilius Rufus or with any other third party, that is to say with a person who was not his own patron. As the case of Cicero and M. Pomponius Dionysius has clearly demonstrated in chapter 2, such a demand would have fallen outside what a freedman owed his manumitter. In fact, Rutilius Rufus himself, while in office as urban praetor (c. 119), had introduced a new norm that put further limits on the services that freedmen were required to offer their patrons.[28] No one forced Opillus to close his school and follow Rutilius. Rather, he chose himself to make this radical life change, a decision that must have been based on his close personal and intellectual friendship with Rutilius. Similarly, Opillus' consistency in staying with Rutilius even during very unpredictable and dangerous times in the 80s is testimony to his ongoing commitment to their shared life together.

Opillus might easily, therefore, have had a teaching career that spanned some 35 years or more in the city of Rome. Yet, when he left the city, he is said to have closed his school rather than handing it to a successor or partner.[29] There is no evidence that he ever opened another school in Asia. If he was the same age as Rutilius, then he would have been about 70 years old by the time they settled together in Smyrna. The trajectory of Opillus' teaching career in Rome strongly suggests that he had not traveled abroad with Rutilius Rufus before 92. In particular, he could not have been on Rutilius' staff during the latter's recent time in Asia from 94 onward since he had been teaching in Rome during these years. In fact, there is no reason to believe that Opillus had ever been to Asia before, or perhaps even anywhere outside Italy.

The general background of Opillus' career in Rome serves as the essential setting for his stark departure in 92, a personal choice that will perhaps also have had political and philosophical dimensions. There is no other evidence for any reason why he might have felt under pressure to leave Rome, but we are obviously not informed about his private life. Nor is it clear to what extent he could have foreseen or feared the imminent violence of the Social War that broke out at the end of 91, a conflict that pitted many Oscan speakers against Latin speakers with terrible suffering on both sides.[30] As a Roman citizen, he should have been able to weather that storm without much difficulty, regardless of his original ethnicity and family background.

Rutilius Rufus' trial and conviction on a charge of extortion became one of the most notorious and frequently cited examples of a miscarriage of justice in Roman legal history.[31] It took place in the highly charged atmosphere, one fraught with political divisions, that immediately preceded the Social War and the closely contemporary outbreak of the first war with Mithridates. Rutilius had recently returned from the Roman province of Asia where he had been serving as legate to its outgoing governor, the eminent jurist Q. Mucius Scaevola (cos. 95).[32] The two men had attempted to implement reforms to curb the exactions regularly imposed on provincials by Roman tax farmers (*publicani*) of the equestrian class. Scaevola and Rutilius envisioned a new way of governing a Roman province, a policy that would have significantly reduced the profits accruing to rapacious tax farmers. By way of taking revenge for this unwelcome innovation, a jury composed of members of the equestrian class condemned Rutilius for extortion in Asia as soon as he was back in Rome. The irony of this unjust verdict was not lost on Rutilius or on many others in Rome. He, rather than Scaevola, was the man to take the fall for this attempt at political reform, partly because he had been the one to implement many of the changes made on the ground in the province. Meanwhile, Rutilius did not go into voluntary exile, as was the custom for many Roman elites, but stayed in Rome to face a harsh sentence after he was convicted. As a result, he was deprived of his status as a Roman citizen, was formally condemned to exile, and all his property was confiscated by the state, including a country villa at Formiae.[33] Rutilius was now in a situation of personal crisis and would not reach his eventual new home in Smyrna for several years.

Scaevola seems to have provided Rutilius with some funds.[34] Rutilius' wife, Livia, also came from a very wealthy family and could have helped him with her personal resources.[35] She stayed in Rome when her husband left. Rutilius himself, however, was not at this point in his life in a position to play the role of the wealthy patron to an educated freedman. When considering Opillus' choice to close his school, which was presumably his main source of income, and go into exile with Rutilius, it is important to take the full extent of Rutilius' new financial and civic condition into account. Opillus had surely been a Roman citizen himself for many years by now and was a well-established figure in intellectual circles. As already noted, Opillus had not been in Asia with Rutilius and had had no direct involvement with what had happened there. We will never know whether his political sympathies lay with Rutilius and Scaevola or whether he preferred to stay detached from the politics of Rome's empire. Clearly, regardless of politics, his personal and intellectual relationship with Rutilius made him want to share his friend's fate, which would have been by no means predictable immediately after his conviction.

Given these circumstances, we should at least entertain the theory that Opillus was himself in a position to underwrite at least some of the initial costs of their new life together. Opillus was perhaps not a man of modest means; he may have had plenty of financial resources and apparently had no family he left behind in the city. Closing the school will have been one part of liquidating his assets in Rome, which could have included the building that housed the classroom(s). Neither Rutilius or Opillus ever returned to Rome, and we do not know if one outlived the other. At the time of their departure for the East, however, Opillus was a Roman citizen with his fortune intact, while Rutilius was stateless and had just lost all of his own property.

Most details of Rutilius' and Opillus' shared experiences after 92 are not revealed in our sources. What is clear, however, is that they lived through remarkably adventurous times during Mithridates' invasion of Asia. Circumstances made them move more than once before they eventually settled together in Smyrna, several years after leaving Rome. Rutilius made a point of returning to live in the province that he had been convicted of mistreating, where he famously was said to have received a warm welcome from the Greek cities, many of which would soon revolt from Rome.[36] He had worked hard to enact the kinds of reforms that could perhaps have prevented the imminent revolt from Rome and the massacre of Italians that soon followed. Now he chose to return to the province that was shortly to become the target of Mithridates.

It may have taken Opillus and Rutilius some time to travel from Rome to Asia, especially if they chose the overland route and made stops along the way. Their first attested place of residence was Mytilene on Lesbos, a city that was among the most hostile to the Roman imperial presence in Asia.[37] They both seem to have lived there as resident foreigners, perhaps for several years, without the benefits of local citizenship. This choice is surprising in a number of ways, not least because Mytilene was far from being a secure place of refuge for an exile, as events were soon to reveal. This was a community that was one of the first to welcome Mithridates when he invaded, and to hand over leading Romans to him as captives before being required to do so.[38] Subsequently, the massacre of Romans and Italians carried out at the instigation of the Pontic king was particularly fierce here. After the Peace of Dardanus, Mytilene was one of the few cities that continued to resist when Sulla arrived in the area with his army. Was Rutilius really unaware of the political climate on Lesbos despite having just spent an extended time in Asia over the last two years? He must have had a reason to settle here, especially if many other attractive options were indeed available to him at the time.

Despite the harsh anti-Roman atmosphere in Mytilene, both Rutilius and Opillus escaped from the island of Lesbos to the mainland. Rutilius, probably in his memoirs, claims that he changed into Greek clothes and escaped unnoticed by passing as a Greek-speaking person who was not from Italy.[39] The same must, therefore, have been true of Opillus, who was much more entitled to wear a toga at that time than Rutilius was. Under Mithridates' sweeping orders, issued from his new headquarters in Ephesus, they were both subject to summary execution (and to being left unburied).[40] Other prominent Romans, however, had been taken prisoner earlier and handed over to the king.[41] It remains unclear, therefore, whether Rutilius and Opillus escaped in disguise from Mytilene before or after the general massacre of the Roman population in Asia. If before, then they must have weathered that terrible storm in another location. In either case, the two clearly took the initiative and had a sufficient command of the Greek language to make their escape in dire circumstances in which so many of their countrymen perished on the island. Friends, who were willing to take considerable personal risks, probably also helped. Their ages (c. 70 years old) may have made it easier for them to pass as locals, since most businessmen from Italy will have been younger and many are attested as having families with young children and more extended households that made an undetected escape much more difficult. One assumes that Rutilius and Opillus were traveling light.

Other Italian survivors of what was effectively a genocide also used disguises and a majority traveled to Rhodes, whose navy provided powerful protection and whose politicians were firmly pro-Roman.[42] Ships must, therefore, have been available in various places along the coast that were able and willing, presumably for a fee, to provide transport to Rhodes for those fleeing persecution. Rutilius and Opillus, however, chose another path and may have traveled from Mytilene more or less directly to Smyrna.[43] Again, this choice is not easy to explain. Smyrna is much nearer Ephesus (c. 50 miles away), which the king was using as his capital. Unsurprisingly, Smyrna was firmly in Mithridates' camp by 88.[44] It would have been an exceptionally bold move to hide in plain sight by moving to Smyrna, in the vicinity of Mithridates himself.[45] On the other hand, it is also possible that Rutilius and Opillus did not arrive in Smyrna until somewhat later and spent time in hiding at an undisclosed location after escaping from Mytilene.[46] Meanwhile, it is important to keep in mind that Opillus as a Roman citizen of Italian ancestry was just as much of a target as Rutilius.

Not everyone from Mytilene had fond remembrances of Rutilius after his departure. In 62, after the death of Mithridates, Theophanes of Mytilene, a close associate of Pompey, claimed to have found a document (*logos*) written by Rutilius among the papers of the Pontic king.[47] Theophanes alleged that this *logos* proved that Rutilius had been the one to plant the idea of killing all the Romans and Italians in Asia in Mithridates' mind. Even Plutarch considered this accusation to be totally implausible and attributed it to resentment over Rutilius' treatment of Pompey's father in his (influential) historical writings.[48] Whether or not Theophanes had actually gone to the trouble of forging a letter or speech to incriminate Rutilius, or only claimed to have seen something that never actually existed, this allegation shows that Rutilius was still remembered for his time in Asia over 25 years after the massacre of 88. While it seems unlikely that Rutilius was ever working on behalf of Mithridates (even as a double agent planted by Rome?), it is not difficult to see that his unusual travels and ability to survive in extreme situations led to pointed questions and malicious rumors about his political affiliation.

By 85, after a treaty had been agreed upon with Mithridates, Rutilius (surely together with Opillus) is attested as being in the camp of the Roman commander Sulla, near Thyateira (Akhisar) in Lydia, at a distance of about 100 kilometers from Smyrna.[49] Sulla evidently had no qualms about working with Rutilius. Dio suggests that Rutilius set out from Smyrna to meet up with Sulla, after his Roman army had crossed into Asia.[50] Rutilius must, therefore, have been well informed about Sulla's movements and confident about his reception in the Roman camp. At that time, Sulla had been declared an enemy (*hostis*) by his political enemies in Rome, so he was in an even more tenuous situation in the eyes of Roman law than the ordinary exile Rutilius.[51] Rutilius, by now in his early 70s, was working for Sulla at this point and was his envoy in negotiations with the rival Roman general Gaius Flavius Fimbria.[52] Rutilius may have traveled around in Asia with Sulla during his time there; he could have provided useful insights into local conditions. The two shared intellectual interests, as well as some of the same political concerns, although probably not the same ideas about which solutions might work in Rome.

Subsequently, Rutilius refused Sulla's offer to return to Italy with his army, although the two were clearly friends, and spent the rest of his life in Smyrna, where he was awarded local citizenship and also had financial support provided for him.[53] As had been his established custom, he maintained a simple personal lifestyle. In all of this, Opillus stayed with him and chose to share this new life in Smyrna, rather than returning with Sulla or simply striking out on his own at some point during these turbulent years. Quintus Servilius Caepio (cos. 106) had retired into exile at Smyrna more than 15 years earlier, near the end of the second century, so there was an established precedent for a Roman settling here.[54] Rutilius was visited by a young Cicero and his brother Quintus in Smyrna in 78 and is represented as being still alive a little later, as a participant in Cicero's imaginary dialogue *De Natura Deorum*.[55] Rutilius' presence helped the community in Smyrna to reconcile with the Roman authorities after their support of Mithridates.[56]

It is impressive to see Rutilius and Opillus use Smyrna as a base to produce a series of texts in differing genres that circulated widely in Rome and beyond, allowing these two to have a significant impact. From many perspectives, this Ionian city must have seemed a considerable distance from Rome in the late 80s and 70s. Yet Rutilius, despite his status as an exile, remained connected to his original native place, even as he had clearly been integrated into Sulla's network of influence in Asia during the mid-80s. His literary projects were twofold. He worked on parallel publications that retold the story of his own life and more broadly of the historical times he had lived through from his own point of view. A general history of the time period was written in Greek in the third person in the tradition of Hellenistic historiography.[57] This work was clearly aimed at a broader Mediterranean audience, including many in Asia and Greece who had been the supporters or victims of Mithridates and the audience for his self-presentation as a Hellenistic king who would combat Roman aggression. This Greek account overlapped in significant ways with Rutilius' first-person autobiography in Latin, a work in at least five books and perhaps on a much larger scale.[58] Opillus will most likely have served as an assistant and adviser in these ambitious, ongoing compositions.

Rutilius followed in the footsteps of three other consuls, Catulus, Scaurus, and Sulla, in choosing to write about his experiences and achievements in his own voice for a contemporary audience. The rather fine memory of him that has been handed down in most extant sources suggests that his writings were influential in shaping how people remembered the events of his long career and especially his high-profile trial and subsequent adventures in Asia.[59] His account will have been a reaction to the episodes of civil war in Rome since his departure and to the political revolution introduced by Sulla during his dictatorship. At the same time, it is relevant to keep in mind that Pontus was still ruled by Mithridates VI, an ambitious king who was biding his time for further conflicts with Rome. It is not impossible that Rutilius lived to see the final war with Mithridates that broke out just over a decade after the Treaty of Dardanus.[60]

During these same years in Smyrna with Rutilius, Opillus was working on his own, completely separate program of literary research and publication. Suetonius says that Opillus wrote many books, some of which may, of course, date to before his departure from Rome. Only two titles have survived. A nine-volume work called *Musae* (*Muses*) had each book named after a different Muse. A single surviving fragment from this work consists of a definition of *indutiae* (truce) cited by Aulus Gellius. The work may have been a miscellany or anthology along the lines of Gellius' own *Noctes Atticae*. Opillus also published something called *Pinax* (*Tablet* or *Catalog*?), which might have been a type of bibliography in a Hellenistic style or could have been a completely different thing entirely, such as an art historical work whose title could also be translated as *Picture Gallery*. It was this book that started with an acrostic of Opillus' name. Opillus was considered an expert on the plays of Plautus and published a definitive list of which plays were genuine and which others were later attributions to the famous playwright. He may also have produced an edition of the poems of the contemporary poet Gaius Titius. His other books may have included works on philosophy or other topics. The range of his learning was evidently considerable.

Opillus' life was unusual and varied. It was shaped by his many academic interests and deep learning, as well as by his special personal relationship with Publius Rutilius Rufus. He had a long career as a teacher in Rome and was probably one of the earliest Italians to give instruction in philosophy (in Latin?) in the city. As a result, he may well have enjoyed a degree of financial success and independence. The few fragments of his works to survive are all rare Latin words cited by much later grammarians, words that do not necessarily tell us much about the content of the original texts they had been lifted from. What one can discern is his deep love of the Latin language and of unusual expressions covering a wide range of topics. Perhaps he was the author of a dictionary or encyclopedia of some kind. This philological inclination fits in with an Italian origin and early, intensive exposure to Latin, even if Oscan had probably been his first language. Yet this was also a man who had managed to save his life by "passing" as a Greek speaker in Asia when he was well into his 60s, if not already 70. Opillus' multilingual ability reminds of the earlier poet Ennius, who had famously claimed that he had three hearts (*tria corda*) because he was fluent in Greek and Latin, as well as being a native speaker of Oscan from Apulia.[61] As is typical but also intensely frustrating, our sources reveal only brief but vivid glimpses of a fascinating life, which can be supplemented in his case by what we know of Rutilius' travels after he was condemned and sent into exile.

Lucius Cornelius Epicadus

While in Asia in the mid-80s, Opillus will have spent time with Sulla and consequently also with members of Sulla's immediate entourage. This will have brought him into contact, probably not for the first time, with Epicadus, one of Sulla's most trusted freedmen.[62] Conversations between Sulla and Rutilius, dialogues that included Opillus and Epicadus as active participants, could easily have shaped the literary works of each of these men, both those produced in collaboration and some that were more individual intellectual projects. Caecilia Metella, Sulla's wife who had previously been married to Aemilius Scaurus, may also have been an interlocutor who had a contribution to make, but we do not know if she and her children traveled on to Asia with Sulla or stayed in Greece to await his return. While in Rome, Sulla was well known for socializing on a regular basis with an exceptionally wide range of intellectuals and artists.[63] He will have sought out literary conversations in other settings as well. He cultivated Rutilius for political reasons, but their shared cultural interests will also have influenced their personal interactions, as was so often the case for educated Romans of the political class.[64]

Epicadus' exceptional closeness to Sulla makes him a fascinating case study and a suggestive parallel to the relatively more elusive Opillus.[65] The ways in which Sulla called upon Epicadus to fulfill several essential roles reveal both Epicadus' many talents and his personal qualities. Sulla, probably more than any other Roman of his generation, had access to the services of vast numbers of enslaved individuals, many of them captured in war or confiscated during the proscriptions. As dictator, he manumitted 10,000 picked young men to serve as his network within the city of Rome.[66] He will also have had an extensive household before the civil wars. Within this rarefied atmosphere, Epicadus evidently stood out and was trusted by Sulla, especially at the end of his life. Unsurprisingly, very few names and profiles of individual freedmen of Sulla's have been handed down to us. This pattern is in line with what we see in the households of Cicero and of Atticus in the next generation; there are only a few more named individuals in the case of each of those households, despite the much greater wealth of information about the 60s, 50s, and 40s.[67] Getting at the identities and experiences of individuals like Epicadus is inevitably challenging and involves a re-focalization of well-known events from a different perspective.

In fact, the other named freedmen Cornelii who are associated with Sulla are specifically mentioned in connection with their profiteering in the proscriptions of the late 80s. These are individuals who had been part of Sulla's household and had been manumitted before his return to Rome in 82. They are Tartula, Scirtus, and most notoriously Chrysogonus, who was a target of the young Cicero in his speech in defense of Sextus Roscius from Ameria.[68] Chrysogonus was held up as a stereotype of a wealthy freedman who breaks both law and convention while his patron is too engaged on important matters of state to be able to do anything to stop behavior that he would evidently have disapproved of, at least according to Cicero. By definition, therefore, Chrysogonus did not live in Sulla's household or accompany him on a daily basis. Rather he had a house of his own in the exclusive Palatine district, where Cicero would eventually move himself some 20 years after he defended Sextus Roscius.[69] Although Chrysogonus was still in a favored position, he was in fact far from being Sulla's closest assistant.

By contrast, Epicadus, the man who would be chosen to complete Sulla's unfinished memoirs after his death, is not mentioned by Cicero or others commenting on the politics of the 80s or 70s. Rather we meet him in the pages of Suetonius' *De Grammaticis et Rhetoribus*, although nothing is said explicitly there, or anywhere else, about him as a teacher, either in a school or in a private household.[70] His presence in Suetonius' book appears to be a bit mysterious. The chapter that discusses him is short, which might perhaps indicate that some text has been lost here. An account of a possible teaching career and of his other publications could have been the subject of an additional sentence or two, but this is simply a hypothesis.[71]

Epicadus bears a common Illyrian name, but not one that was often found among enslaved persons in the city of Rome.[72] Like Opillus, he stands out for his unusual *cognomen*. Does this indicate that he was a prisoner of war captured by Sulla sometime in the mid-80s, at a time when the Romans were fighting in northern Greece? This theory seems untenable in light of a number of considerations, including the kinds of tasks assigned to Epicadus by Sulla, the specialized books he is known to have written in Latin under his own name, his role in completing Sulla's memoirs, and, above all, the overall chronology of his interactions with Sulla. It is simply hard to imagine that a newly captured foreigner from outside Italy, who did not arrive in Rome before 82, would immediately have been chosen by Sulla to be his special assistant in his priesthood or his closest associate in compiling his memoirs. The origin of Epicadus' name must, therefore, be sought elsewhere.[73]

Epicadus will have been somewhat younger than Sulla (who was born in 138), since he went on to have a close relationship with Sulla's son Faustus, who was very young when his father died.[74] Faustus was judged too young to speak at Sulla's funeral in the spring of 78, when a leading orator was commissioned to deliver the traditional public eulogy that was usually entrusted to a family member.[75] Epicadus claimed to be as much Faustus' freedman as the *libertus* of his father.[76] This remark cannot be a legal statement but is rather a description of his personal closeness to the family of the Cornelii over two generations.[77] His relationship to Faustus necessarily implies that Epicadus outlived Sulla to see his son grow up to adulthood. If not serving as a private tutor to Sulla's three surviving children, then Epicadus could have stayed on in the household as a more informal mentor, while he was working on editing Sulla's posthumous publications. He may also have been busy with Sulla's extensive private library, although there were probably other librarian(s) who were more formally in charge of that collection.[78]

In fact, Epicadus had already been legally manumitted by Sulla earlier, most probably before Faustus was born, since he served Sulla as his *calator*, a priestly assistant who was usually a freedman chosen from the household of the priest he worked with. As Suetonius makes clear, therefore, Epicadus had two distinct roles in relation to Sulla, first as his *calator* during his time as *augur*, and subsequently as the main editor of his memoirs, a posthumous role that surely built on an extended earlier engagement with Sulla's large-scale autobiographical project.[79] Both these tasks were vital to Sulla; they demanded separate skill sets and special loyalty, in addition to a recognized ability in making independent decisions that furthered Sulla's interests. In addition, Epicadus was also the author of several literary works published under his own name, which will be discussed after the treatment of his jobs for his patron.

Epicadus' role as *calator* was defined by the tasks that job entailed and by the length of time Sulla served as *augur*. Each of these two topics, however, is controversial and not directly attested. Hardly any *calatores* are ever named in literary sources; most names are recorded in inscriptions of the imperial period, whether epitaphs, dedications, or donations made by one or more *calatores*, or in the detailed records of rituals kept by the Arval brothers.[80] It is remarkable, therefore, to see Suetonius mention the office of *calator* as a job for a named freedman. In this instance again, the unusual character of his book about teachers and rhetoricians needs to be acknowledged. Ironically, this sentence is also the only explicit testimony we have for Sulla holding the prestigious priesthood of *augur*.

The most important Roman priests were assisted by personal *calatores* (also spelled in a more archaic way as *kalatores*), one for each priest.[81] These *calatores* were chosen from among the freedmen of the priest himself and enjoyed an official designation as what might be described as the principal assistant in the various roles undertaken by that particular priest. *Kalatores* spelled in the archaic way are epigraphically attested as early as the sixth century, during the regal period.[82] The title is sometimes translated as "herald" because one very visible function of *calatores* was to call for silence and to remove any inauspicious speech or menial action from the vicinity of a priest who was about to begin a religious ritual.[83] In this sense, the *calator* was essential to the successful performance of each ritual by the priest on behalf of the community. At the same time, a priest regularly made use of other attendants, specifically called heralds (*praecones*), whose job it was to clear their path as they traveled around the city.[84] The task of the *calator* was, therefore, by definition more technical and separate from that of an ordinary herald, who might also be present. The *calator* accompanied the priest in every official duty. By his presence, in his person, and through his actions, his *calator* marked out the status of the priest and served as a guarantor of ritual correctness. It is vital not to underestimate the skill and poise needed for this role, which required a strong public presence and a clear understanding of ritual requirements across a range of situations.[85] Epicadus was, therefore, Sulla's right-hand man during his time as *augur*.

For other ritual functions of *calatores* beyond that of heralds, by far the most detailed ancient source is the records kept by the Arval brothers in the sacred grove of Dea Dia at a short distance from Rome.[86] This priesthood enjoyed what seems to have been a revival and a higher social profile under Augustus and his successors. The inscriptions were carved on an annual basis and placed inside the sacred grove of the goddess. They provide details of rituals performed, meals shared, and other events related to the cult, either inside the grove or in Rome. There were 12 brothers in the priesthood, and the emperor served as the 13th priest in each reign. Although these texts are much later and record rituals of a college of priests who were principally attached to a single deity most often worshipped in a specific location, they do give us some general idea of the kinds of tasks that were undertaken by *calatores*, either individually or as a group, most of whom are not named in the inscriptions. Given the generally conservative nature of Roman ritual habits and some clearly archaic features that are preserved in the cult of Dea Dia, these practices can be interpreted as reflecting traditional roles for the various participants.

From these inscriptions the following practices seem to emerge as habitual. When a priest became an Arval brother, a freedman *calator* from his household also joined the priesthood at the same time as his assistant.[87] This *calator* paid an entrance fee (*introitus*) from his own resources and was also initiated and recognized as a member of the collective group of *calatores*. If the original *calator* was later replaced by a successor, no second entrance fee was required.[88] The association of *calatores* also had a common fund that could be used to make donations, for example of a generous gift of incense for the funeral of Matidia, the mother-in-law of Hadrian, in AD 120.[89] When only a single *calator* is mentioned in a ritual, he is understood to be the *calator* of the priest presiding over that particular ritual. In this sense, a *calator* shared in the seniority and rank of the priest he worked with and for; they operated as a ritual pair.[90]

Calatores were involved in a wide range of ritual situations, both inside and outside the sacred grove of Dea Dia, a hallowed area that only certain people could enter. They assisted during ceremonies but also had a special role in taking responsibility for transporting ritual objects and implements (*tuscanicae*) back to the houses of the Arval brothers in Rome at the end of these being used inside the grove.[91] They are often mentioned as operating alongside others involved in rituals, notably the children and the public slaves. They may have supervised these other two groups.[92]

It is notable that *calatores* regularly performed recurring rituals independently and without the presence of the brothers. These included habitual expiatory sacrifice connected to the sacred space of Dea Dia's grove. An example is when a blade was introduced into the grove, either to remove a dead tree or branch or to inscribe the annual priestly records on stone.[93] Maintaining the integrity of the grove's sacred space was essential to the worship of Dea Dia. In other words, *calatores* were expected to be in charge of religious rituals on behalf of the brotherhood as a whole and, by extension, of the broader Roman community that was protected by this ancient goddess.

The Arval records, therefore, suggest that *calatores* were indeed religious experts in their own right. Their roles went well beyond the designation of the English term "herald." Meanwhile, it is important to keep in mind that the surviving Arval inscriptions, even in their original and most complete form, would not have been designed to give a complete picture of every task performed by *calatores* and other ritual assistants. Most of their attested roles required *calatores* to master religious knowledge and ritual practice themselves, whether through books of ritual instruction or by means of an apprenticeship of some kind.[94] Each priesthood will have had its own specialized knowledge and practices, in addition to more general norms in Roman religion. Since a *calator* entered on his job at the same time as his patron, the pair will have been learning the new rules of the office together.

It is interesting to see that Roman priests preferred their own freedmen rather than for example assistants who already had the appropriate religious training. The *calator*'s patron, especially if he was a busy man, may well have relied on his freedman to acquire the new knowledge quickly in the beginning and to serve consistently as an adviser and reference point. The *calator*'s role as one who prevented ritual flaws shows that he needed to have a clear understanding of what these might consist of. Overall, the *calator*, himself a Roman citizen, was expected to be deeply imbued with traditional Roman religious practice and ritual norms. Being literate and educated would obviously have been useful. Personal resources were also required for the entrance fee, which was not refundable.

Despite the fact that *augurs* were among the most prominent priests in Rome, we know very little about their *calatores*. Only a single inscription survives with the name of the *calator* of an *augur*, an epitaph that is usually dated to the Augustan period but that could also be a little earlier.[95] This simple text inscribed on travertine memorializes a man who died relatively young but had, like Epicadus, served his patron in two quite distinct functions.

> *L(ucius) Iunius Silani / l(ibertus) Paris, dispe(n)s(ator) / calator augur(is) / vixit annos XXXII / in fr(onte) p(edes) XII, in ag(ro pedes) XII*
>
> Lucius Junius Paris, freedman of (L.? Junius) Silanus, steward, *calator* of an *augur*, lived 32 years, 12 feet in front, 12 on the side (*the size of the square burial plot*).

Paris was a *calator* to an *augur* and that same man's steward (*dispensator*) or chief financial officer.[96] In other words, he served as both a religious and a financial expert, which indicates that he was literate, numerate, and considered highly trustworthy. His connection to the prominent political family of the Junii Silani suggests that his patron was probably a wealthy man with an elaborate set of accounts to manage.[97] A *dispensator* in such a large household would usually train for that managerial position by first working with the accounts in various less exalted capacities. It would obviously be interesting to know which of these two jobs was first entrusted to Paris, the religious office or the financial one. Holding both at the same time will have kept him very busy and constantly close to his patron.

A handful of other inscriptions reveal the following about some other *calatores* of the imperial period. *Calatores* are attested for several priesthoods in Rome; there will surely have been many more than we have evidence for.[98] One young man, who died at only 15 years old, is described as *studiosus eloquentiae* (a diligent student of rhetoric).[99] His epitaph gives us another brief glimpse of the learning associated with *calatores* and of the training they received during their school years. Apparently, some were indeed already manumitted and serving as official *calatores* in their teenage years. The *calatores* of all the *pontifices* and *flamines* eventually formed an association that made dedications from their own funds in a variety of religious contexts.[100] Some of these contain substantial lists of *calatores*, all of whom seem to be freedmen. Many of the monuments and inscriptions associated with *calatores* are on a grand scale.[101] In the imperial period, these were men who had access to financial resources and had a public presence in the city.

The only other *calator* for whom we can trace a career path is T. Tettienus Felix, who was *scriba librarius aedilium curulium* (scribal assistant to the curule aediles), *viator aedilium plebis* (messenger for the plebeian aediles), and *accensus consulis* (attendant to a consul) in addition to being *calator*, probably to the *pontifex* T. Tettienus Serenus, a man of consular rank.[102] Felix's offices suggest a close link between *calatores* and the world of the *scribae* and other literate *apparitores*, who were so close to Roman magistrates. Most of the *scribae* were freeborn and some were of equestrian rank, although the *scribae librarii* were more often freedmen.[103]

In light of this epigraphical evidence, therefore, it seems likely that Epicadus was educated in the Latin language and in Roman religious customs from a young age, quite possibly within Sulla's own household. He was clearly a diligent student. He will have been manumitted and will perhaps have acquired some money of his own before being chosen and initiated as Sulla's *calator*.[104] He was certainly remembered for this role that he must have held for some time, most prominently at the end of Sulla's life, during his dictatorship and subsequent second consulate. It is natural, therefore, to imagine that Epicadus' time as *calator* did overlap with all or most of Sulla's augurate, however long that lasted.

The length of Sulla's augurate continues to be a much-debated topic.[105] Nevertheless, the most economical reconstruction of his priestly career is not hard to discern. As we have seen, Suetonius clearly states that Sulla was *augur* and that Epicadus was his *calator*. We know that Epicadus outlived Sulla for many years, so he must have served in this role in the last years of his patron's life. Priesthoods were conferred for life within the Roman system and there is no indication that anyone before Julius Caesar held more than one priesthood at the same time.[106] Appian records Sulla's urgent demand, delivered in 84 before he returned to Italy from the East, to have an unspecified priestly office restored to him.[107] Sulla had been declared a *hostis* (enemy) and had been deprived of his citizenship status and property in 87.[108] It is not surprising to see that Sulla, a patrician who had reached the consulship, had also held a priesthood before reaching his 50s. Since he was deprived of every other social, legal, and political position, it is also logical that he was no longer recognized by the government in Rome as a priest who could act on behalf of the community. Once Sulla had taken the city by storm and established himself as dictator, he will have been in a strong position to regain the priestly status he had been requesting. That priesthood should surely, therefore, be the augurate, which he is clearly attested as holding in the late 80s.

Other reconstructions that posit him holding a different priesthood earlier or holding two simultaneously as dictator are not based on any explicit ancient evidence, even as they complicate the picture of what was legal or even desirable for him to do.[109] Rather, we should recognize that Sulla was evidently *augur* before his election to the consulate of 88 and that he claimed to remain in office for the rest of his life, as was the norm.[110] He did not hesitate to act as a *proconsul* in the East between 87 and his return to Rome. He would surely also have behaved as an *augur* since many leading generals had held this priesthood while on campaign with a Roman army. A coin he minted in Greece in 84 features the *lituus*, a staff with a crook that was a symbol of the augurate, which is suggestive but does not provide proof of his status or his thinking.[111]

His son Faustus' coins also make references to this same priesthood.[112] If Sulla was already augur in 89, then he may well have held the office for some time before, given his prestigious family background and successful political career.

Sulla's career in the 90s is not attested in precise detail.[113] He seems to have spent a significant time away from Rome, mostly in the East. Consequently, his initiation as *augur* in Rome, if it occurred in person in this decade, should logically fall either in the early 90s or at the very end of the decade, immediately before the Social War.[114] However, it is also possible that Sulla became a priest in the late second century, perhaps even as early as his election to the quaestorship in 107 or soon after his return from Numidia with the conquering army of Gaius Marius in 105.[115] Marius himself became an augur in 98 or 97.[116] The rift between the two men did not develop until somewhat later; it is possible that one or the other had a hand in promoting his colleague to this prestigious priesthood.

Can Epicadus' age suggest a possible model for Sulla's priestly career? If Epicadus was indeed Sulla's original *calator*, who entered into office at the same time with him, then a date in the second century becomes harder to argue for because Epicadus clearly outlived Sulla by many years, perhaps as many as 20 or even 30. If we imagine that Epicadus lived into the decade of the 50s, when Faustus Sulla was himself chosen to be *augur* and then elected as *quaestor*, that would indicate one possible way to reconstruct his life.[117] Taking Epicadus' probable lifespan into consideration, a date in the 90s seems more likely for Sulla's initiation as *augur*.[118] Such a date could fit in with Epicadus being in his late 50s or into his 60s by the time Faustus was old enough to enter politics in the 50s. Epicadus' life can shed light on Sulla's, even as Sulla's obviously does on Epicadus'.

Regardless of how one evaluates these various dating puzzles, it seems most likely that Epicadus was indeed a member of Sulla's household in the 90s, accompanied him to the East after his first consulship, and then returned with his army to invade Italy and capture the city of Rome by force for a second time. Epicadus' life will have been shaped by Sulla's highly unusual choices, by his profound personal religious engagement, his bold military strategies, and his brutal dictatorship in Rome. It was his very closeness to Sulla, combined with his recognized literary talents, that made Epicadus the obvious choice to edit and complete Sulla's memoirs after his sudden death early in 78. As a witness to Sulla's most important experiences over many years, Epicadus was a natural ally and collaborator in helping to present Sulla's version of events to posterity. Meanwhile, it seems worth noting that *augurs* are the best-attested authors among those who held priesthoods in Rome.[119] That condition helps to provide a framework that naturally connects Epicadus the *calator* with Epicadus the literary editor and writer.

Sulla did not hesitate to act confidently as a Roman general, in effect *the* Roman general, in the war against Mithridates. In his capacity as commander with *imperium*, he was the man in charge of the auspices for his military campaigns. At the same time, he will also, I argue, have behaved "like an augur," as far as possible according to the circumstances in which he found himself during these years.[120] Most of our information about *augurs* comes from their roles in the city of Rome rather than in the military sphere.[121] Having his *calator* at hand, especially on public occasions, would have helped to remind Romans who saw Sulla that he was making confident claims to his full previous civic status, despite recent political events in Rome. In this sense, Epicadus was all the more important to Sulla, for whom religion was, in any case, a constant defining aspect of his daily life and of his self-representation to others.[122] In a highly unusual political climate, each man helped to define the status and function of the other.

Similarly, Sulla's memoirs presented a story about his personal destiny as shaped by exceptional divine favor.[123] Although it extended to 22 books, it was unfinished at the time of his death. The ultimate scope he envisioned is not recoverable from the meager fragments that have survived. However, something of its flavor is to be found in Plutarch's biography of Sulla. The sprawling narrative contained a very detailed account of his life that may have been cut short before it treated much in his dictatorship in detail.[124] Many circumstantial details were enhanced by descriptions of landscapes and probably by speeches. Religious experiences were central to this account, including dreams and visions, oracles, and the predictions of local prophets from numerous religious backgrounds.[125] The tone could be baroque and sometimes apocalyptic. Sulla also included details of his own psychological states at various key moments. The messages he regularly received from the gods through many different channels of communication served to confirm that he was the leader chosen for Rome and that all his actions, however violent and unprecedented, were in accord with divine will and even at divine command.

Sulla's huge and highly original first-person text was surely many years in the making; it is implausible that all of this was conceived and written in the last 15 months of his life.[126] Moreover, the narrative, with its minute details and circumstantial descriptions, was based on an elaborate system of notes and records that were kept by and for him over the years.[127] Sulla made a point of boasting of his administrative skills, which relied on keeping track of supplies with the same attention to detail that he gave to his catalog of grudges. Sulla had been planning this work for a long time. Catulus and Scaurus had set precedents with their autobiographies on a much smaller scale. Meanwhile, Rutilius Rufus had most likely been working on his for some time before he met up with Sulla in Asia in 85. Sulla had a great deal to explain and his status as an outlaw will have given him the same kind of motivation as Rutilius, a need to give a shape to his story during his own lifetime and not to let his political enemies distort or erase the memory of his achievements.

There can be little doubt that Sulla made use of a professional staff to keep his records and to do research and fact-checking for his memoirs. Epicadus emerges as the most likely man in charge of this project, both before and after Sulla retired to Campania.[128] As a result, he was also chosen, whether by Sulla himself or by his close friend Lucullus, to finish the memoirs and see them through to publication.[129] Two interrelated questions emerge, both essentially unanswerable on the basis of our extant evidence. First, how much influence did Epicadus have on the memoirs as a whole? This question can be broken down as follows. Had he worked on the project from the beginning and consistently over many years? How far did he shape the overall design and purpose or the characteristic narrative techniques? What might any given episode owe to him?

Second, what did Epicadus do to finish the text after Sulla's death? How much did he add? It is clear that Epicadus should probably be recognized as the author (with help from others?) of three items: Sulla's final illness and sudden death, his dream in which he sees his *genius* calling to him, and the description of his public funeral.[130] Beyond these specific items, it is impossible to be sure what else Epicadus may have added, adjusted, edited, or changed. It seems clear, however, that the parts written after Sulla's death were composed in a style very similar to the main body of the work.[131] While this editorial choice may not come as a surprise, it does tend to confirm the overall impression that Epicadus had indeed been working on this project before. He was thoroughly implicated with it. This role also carried over into his relationship with Faustus, who could rely on people like Epicadus to tell him about his father and to create continuity within the family.

Traditions about Sulla's death are twofold; he either died slowly and painfully of a horrible, wasting disease or suddenly within less than 24 hours after an acute health crisis.[132] These accounts are effectively mutually exclusive. It is not difficult to surmise that the second version was written by Epicadus, since it fits in with all the predictions that Sulla would die at the height of his good fortune and in a manner that revealed divine favor. It is also easy to imagine that the first version is a reaction to the idealized end of the memoirs. It is interesting to see how Plutarch, who made extensive use of Sulla's memoirs, was resistant to some of the parts at the end that he knows were written by Epicadus. Plutarch also prefers to have Sulla die a painful death that teaches a moral lesson about the consequences of the wicked things he had done. Appian is more willing to accept the benign version, even as he also includes other material from the memoirs that Plutarch has chosen not to cite.[133]

Epicadus was commissioned to find a way to end the memoirs on a suitably high note, although the text itself and its ending were probably far from being what had originally been planned.

Epicadus, then, was a man with many gifts and talents, who was able to maintain a close relationship over many years with an exceptionally demanding and ruthless patron, a man who made himself dictator and who wrote a new republican constitution for Rome. During this time, Epicadus was called upon to fulfill a wide variety of roles, surely more than we can perceive. He was a writer and organizer, of a staff of writers and copyists, but also of the material they were reworking and shaping. He was a religious expert with special expertise in the complex rules that governed augural law. He had a front-row seat that allowed him to observe the political and religious crises of his age. He became a mentor and friend to young orphans, at the same time as the steward of Sulla's legacy.

Meanwhile, Epicadus was also an author in his own right. His works were very different from those he helped Sulla compose and publish, but perhaps equally original. He wrote a study of Roman nicknames (*De Cognominibus*), a distinctive feature of the life of the political classes but also a typical marker of freedman status.[134] This study will have involved collecting the history of many leading families. By contrast, Epicadus also seems to have produced the first work on poetic meter in Latin (*De Metris*).[135] In addition, he had antiquarian interests that may have resulted in an encyclopedia of some kind.[136] In other words, he was both a collector of information and also a literary critic and social historian. In complete contrast to the stereotype of the wealthy freedman Chrysogonus created by Cicero, Epicadus was a cultivated individual who was integral to Sulla's household, especially after his return from the East. Epicadus stayed on after Sulla's death and had a hand in shaping the final form of his memoirs, a key text that influenced how many understood Sulla and his age. This work survived to be read by Augustine.[137] Epicadus was close to Faustus, as the young man aimed to emerge as Sulla's heir. Epicadus will perhaps have been too old to serve as Faustus' *calator* when he became *augur* in his father's footsteps, but he may have lived to see what was surely a splendid family celebration on this occasion.[138]

Conclusion

Suetonius' close focus on teaching, especially in Rome, the topic that is the organizing principle of his innovative collection of biographies, has tended to divert attention both from the books these same learned men were writing and from some of the other important roles they fulfilled. In addition, the fragmentary state of so much literature from the republican period has obscured what were genuine contributions to learning and to the later development of a wide variety of genres in Latin literature. Many of the most intellectually inclined of Rome's politicians were themselves active across a wide range of literary genres, even as they innovated in going beyond established expectations. These men worked closely with learned interlocutors and assistants, especially freedmen, some of whom had been their teachers, others their collaborators and personal companions. The interactions between these freedmen and their patrons mirrored and influenced the intellectual conversations shared by these same patrons with friends and acquaintances of their same social class.

As this chapter has argued, remarkable patterns of interaction and interdependence can be discerned in the households of Rutilius Rufus (especially in exile) and of Sulla, both leading politicians who made a significant impact on Roman political life, whether at home or in the imperial sphere abroad. Each of these men worked closely with just a few freedmen, highly educated individuals, who were familiar with the outlook, taste, and ambitions of their patrons. Such a collaborator was often the freedman of his patron, as Epicadus was of Sulla. It is indicative of the profound significance of religion to Sulla that his *calator* was also his closest collaborator in the composition of his uniquely ambitious memoir. Sulla depended on Epicadus for the successful performance of the duties of his priesthood and, subsequently, for the completion and dissemination of his memoirs. If asked, he would surely have acknowledged these debts and have had much more to add about their complex emotional and intellectual bonds over many years. A similarly close relationship then developed between Epicadus and Sulla's surviving son Faustus.

By contrast, Rutilius had a different associate, a freedman philosopher and teacher with a more independent position in Rome. Opillus' shared life with Rutilius demonstrates that a close and lasting collaboration could extend well beyond an individual household and even outside the specific social and legal bonds created by enslavement and manumission. In Rutilius' hour of need, when he had been deprived of his property, including his enslaved household, and his position in society, it was Opillus who was willing to share his new circumstances, even at immense personal cost. Rutilius' own freedmen may have chosen to keep their distance from a patron who had lost his Roman citizen status. Rutilius' and Opillus' adventures together included surviving uncertainty, privation, refugee conditions, and even large-scale genocide. They emerged as residents of Smyrna, who went on to produce an impressive dossier of publications during their shared years of retirement, with Rutilius no longer an active politician and Opillus no longer a busy teacher. Their choice to live and work together in this way speaks to the vital role this type of relationship could play, both for the *nobilis* and for the freedman. After Rutilius had lost everything else, he still had the companionship and support of Opillus.

5

Foundlings

A GENIAL "MISER" AND A LIBRARIAN WHO COLLECTED OLD JOKES

> Marcus Antonius Gnipho was "the most famous Latin *grammaticus* of the first third of the [first] century [BC]"
>
> RAWSON 1985, 74

THIS CHAPTER and the next explore some of the most celebrated intellectuals who had *not* been born into slavery but were nevertheless enslaved, sometimes illegally according to Roman law, as a result of adverse life circumstances that ranged from exposure as newborns to capture in war later in life. Partly as a response to the complex social realities that shaped the many conditions of enslavement in Roman society, Latin has more than one noun that can be translated into English by the word "slave." *Servus* is the most commonly used term, which also has a general meaning in designating legally imposed servitude.[1] By contrast, as we have already seen, the less frequent but typically Latin noun *verna* specifically designates a person born to an enslaved mother within a Roman family's own household (*familia*).[2] A *verna* is, therefore, a distinct sub-type of *servus,* one who was born into slavery in a Roman home and often continued to live in servitude in that same household, such as Daphnis who is discussed in chapter 3. Meanwhile, there is a contrast, on occasion implied but sometimes more explicit, between the *verna* as an insider and the *servus* as an outsider to a Roman home. A *servus* might be a foreign captive or a victim of piracy or a person of less well-attested provenance, someone acquired through the commercial slave trade. How many prospective buyers asked questions about a person's birth and background? How many were told less than the whole truth about the origins of enslaved individuals?

One apparently not-insignificant source of enslaved persons in Roman society, as attested by extant ancient sources, was newborn children exposed at birth by their parents (*expositi*). Exposure of infants was a practice that was both legal and socially acceptable at all levels in Roman society.[3] It is impossible to know how many Roman children were exposed at birth, for a wide variety of social and economic reasons, but it is usually assumed by scholars to have been a considerable number. Presumably many of these exposed infants soon died; others were quickly collected and raised by someone else.[4] A freeborn child who was exposed and (illegally) enslaved was, therefore, technically not a *verna* born into slavery; neither could this child be legally (re)classified as a *servus*. Nevertheless, many (perhaps most?) exposed babies who survived infancy were raised as if they were slaves either within the households of the person who had rescued them or they were traded to others as legally enslaved, with or without their true origins ever being revealed.

This chapter looks at the lives and careers of the two men who are the best known of the very few named *expositi* we have information about in a Roman context: Marcus Antonius Gnipho, teacher of the young Julius Caesar, and Gaius Maecenas Melissus, close associate both of Maecenas and of Augustus.[5] These two prominent and influential intellectuals with differing literary interests both lived in the city but more than a generation apart. They will be introduced here in a reverse-chronological order.[6] The fascinating and highly unusual experiences of Gnipho and of Melissus illustrate some of the effects of infant exposure in Roman life, as well as adumbrating a complex relationship between them and home-educated *vernae* such as Daphnis (discussed in chapter 3) or war captives, such as Tyrannio of Amisus and Timagenes of Alexandria, leading intellectuals who will be discussed in chapter 6.

Infant Exposure: A Succinct Introduction to Roman Social Practice and Legal Paradox

Infant exposure was a common and accepted practice in many, if not most, ancient Mediterranean cultures. Rome was no exception. As Soranus describes in his gynecological handbook, it was routine for a midwife to assess a newborn for viability soon after birth.[7] Based on her practical experience, she could then make a professional recommendation as to the chances that the infant would survive and thrive. She is envisaged as the first person to give an opinion about whether the child should be raised or not. But the actual decision to raise a child belonged legally to the father (or male head of household), who could choose to expose a child for a wide variety of reasons, without providing a detailed explanation, either privately or publicly.[8]

Economic factors will have been decisive for many less affluent parents, but doubts about paternity, marital discord, or other personal challenges and considerations, will all have contributed to the choice to expose a newborn of either sex.[9] Gnipho and Melissus were both born as viable male babies but were nevertheless exposed at historical moments that may have been as much as 75 years or more apart. The decision to raise or not to raise a baby was expected to be taken during the first week of life, before a traditional naming ceremony recognized the newborn as a family member and consequently also as a member of the wider community.[10]

It is important to note that exposure was not the same as infanticide, which was presumably also practiced but was not much discussed, for obvious reasons.[11] Rather, exposed infants seem usually to have been swaddled and deposited during the daytime in a public location, often a customary one, where they could easily and openly be picked up by another person, whether by prearrangement or without any contact.[12] Exposed babies do not seem to have been handed directly to selected foster parents under a formal agreement of any kind, another possibility that existed as an alternative option within the Roman community.[13] In cases where the exposed child was successfully raised by another, we can, therefore, glimpse a complex interrelationship over many years between the hardships experienced by the biological parents at the moment of exposure and the future profit anticipated, at that very same time, by the person who had initially taken possession of that same baby. Through the mechanism of exposure, a child that was a burden to one family could become an economic opportunity for another family or for a person engaged in enslaving the vulnerable in society.

Clearly, therefore, some were willing to pay for the rearing of a child, starting from the very beginning of life with the prompt hiring of a wet nurse, in the expectation that they would eventually profit from the sale of that person to a slave dealer or directly to a slaveholder.[14] In order for the practice to have continued in the customary way, such a profit must sometimes have been realized, or at least have been perceived to have been achieved in the long run. Unsurprisingly, there is virtually no extant information about exposed children who were simply passed off as family members, perhaps in cases of infertility or after the recent death of an infant.

In the cases of Gnipho and Melissus, by contrast, the *expositi* themselves claimed to know something about the circumstances of their free birth and subsequent enslavement. These cases show that such knowledge could, at least in a few instances, be preserved (or at least plausibly be claimed to have been preserved) and passed on, first to the exposed child himself, and subsequently, by that same individual once he was an adult. In this situation, the act of exposure had become an integral part of his life story. Beyond examples cited in legal codes, Suetonius is the only source to mention historical examples of exposure that have come down to us.[15] In the cases of Gnipho and Melissus, this information seems to go back to autobiographical statements made by these same men, although the exact contexts of these claims are now lost. How and why was such information passed on to a child? Who told him and under what circumstances? Or was he brought up initially in a group of children who had all been exposed, a situation that would have made his origin more obvious? After hearing this story, why would a person want to repeat it? Many questions can be raised, especially in relation to the well-known individuals discussed in this chapter; few answers are available.

Meanwhile, it is important to keep in mind that exposure itself was completely legal, as well as not being unusual, in Roman society. Yet, at the same time, the enslaving of a freeborn Roman child, including one that had been exposed, was never legal. From these two circumstances a series of paradoxes arose within the Roman legal system, self-contradictions presumably created precisely by the regular enslavement of exposed infants.[16] Under Roman law, a father had absolute legal power to expose a newborn under his *patria potestas*. Despite being subject to *patria potestas*, that child was not acknowledged as a family member and did not bear the family name (in almost every case).[17] Yet, the child did not, as a result of the exposure, lose the status of a freeborn citizen. Rather, a legal process was in place for such a person to reclaim their original status at birth (*vindicatio*), but only with the help of a citizen who was legally able to bring a suit (often a relative).[18] In republican Rome, the urban praetor adjudicated these cases. Such a lawsuit, if upheld on the basis of the available evidence, freed the individual from illegal enslavement by proving that they had, in fact, been a free person all along.

Somewhat ironically, the same father who had exposed an infant could, therefore, bring such a suit to reclaim his paternal rights in relation to his child. Neither his *patria potestas* nor the freedom and citizenship status of his child had been voided by the act of exposure that had taken place within the very particular social vacuum that was the first week of life for every Roman baby. Other persons, including women, could also bring such lawsuits, especially if a father was not available.[19] The development of Roman law in this area of family life shows that such cases must have been not entirely uncommon, although perhaps not easy to win. Under imperial Roman law, such a case could eventually be settled even without the cooperation or agreement of the *expositus*, the person who was the actual subject of the suit.[20] In other words, free status was recognized as an absolute condition in law, an inalienable right, regardless of the personal preferences of the (possibly illegally) enslaved individual. The inherent and inalienable freedom of the Roman citizen was, therefore, of concern to the whole community, to its magistrates, and eventually also to its emperors.[21]

Consequently, it seems safe to conclude that many of the *expositi* who survived were indeed illegally enslaved, but that an unknown number of these were later legally recognized as freeborn. A variety of evidence could presumably be adduced in court, including witnesses and tokens or documents placed with the exposed child, items that had preserved a family's hope of reuniting with that child in the future under more favorable circumstances.[22] Inevitably, the *expositus* could not give any direct evidence about what had happened immediately after birth, however much a version of that story might have become part of his or her self-understanding. The possibility of an *expositus* being reclaimed by a family member at a future date will presumably have encouraged some slave traders to move *expositi* well away from their birthplaces, where their true identity might often have been an open secret.[23] Such a move had happened, to varying degrees, for both Melissus and Gnipho.

Melissus, Friend of Maecenas and Protégé of Augustus

General discussions of infant exposure in Roman law and society frequently cite the well-known case of this Melissus, who was manumitted by Augustus' close friend and adviser Maecenas.[24] Melissus has attracted attention because a few more details of his personal situation are recorded. His rise to prominence in Roman society illustrates an exceptional trajectory, since he started life as an *expositus* in Spoletium, about 80 miles from the capital, and eventually became the founding librarian for the new Greek and Latin libraries in the Portico of Octavia. In recognition of his profound literary knowledge, Melissus was personally recruited by Augustus to organize the new libraries in the portico that the *princeps'* sister Octavia was recreating, adjacent to the new theater that would be named in memory of her son Marcellus after his untimely death. In other words, by the 20s BC, Melissus, now a manumitted Roman citizen, was recognized as a leading intellectual in Rome, a man courted by the most influential in the city. He seems to have held his job as chief librarian for many years, a job that will have given him a comfortable and prominent position at the center of the Augustan cultural renewal that transformed the city over the next decades.[25] Melissus will have made his own distinctive contributions to the development of this new literary landscape.

Suetonius gives Melissus a generous entry in his *De Grammaticis et Rhetoribus*; he evidently had more information about him than about many of the earlier figures he mentions.[26]

> *C. Melissus, Spoleti natus ingenuus, sed ob discordiam parentum expositus, cura et industria educatoris sui altiora studia percepit, ac Maecenati pro grammatico muneri datus est. Cui cum se gratum et acceptum in modum amici videret,*

quamquam asserente matre, permansit tamen in statu servitutis praesentemque condicionem verae origini anteposuit; quare cito manumissus, Augusto etiam insinuatus est. Quo delegante, curam ordinandarum bibliothecarum in Octaviae porticu suscepit. Atque, ut ipse tradit, sexagesimum aetatis annum agens, libellos Ineptiarum, qui nunc Iocorum inscribuntur, componere instituit, absolvitque C et L, quibus et alios diversi operis postea addidit. Fecit et novum genus togatarum inscripsitque trabeatas.

GRAM. ET RHET. 21.

Gaius Melissus was born a free person in Spoletium but he was exposed at birth because of discord between his parents. He received an advanced education as a result of the care and close attention of the man who raised him. He was given as a gift to Maecenas as a teacher of young boys. Since he [Melissus] realized that he was pleasing and treated like a friend by him [Maecenas], he [Melissus] remained in a state of enslavement and preferred his present condition to the legal status conferred by his true origin, although his mother was bringing a suit to free him. For this reason, he was soon manumitted and even personally introduced to the intimate circle of Augustus. At his [Augustus'] request, he undertook the task of setting up the libraries in the Portico of Octavia. In addition, as he himself records, during his sixtieth year he started to put together his little books of *Trifles*, which are now called by the title *Jokes*, and he published 150 of them. To these he later added other publications on diverse topics. He also created a new genre of comedy in Latin and called the plays *Trabeatae* [plays in short cloaks].

The unusual level of detail surrounding Melissus' exposure and his mother's unsuccessful attempt, many years later when he was already an adult, to reassert his status as a Roman citizen will ultimately have come from an account that he circulated himself, although the context and format of that autobiographical narrative is now lost.[27] The inhabitants of Spoletium had acquired Roman citizenship after the Social War, a generation before Melissus was born.[28] His parents were, therefore, presumably both Roman citizens, but trouble in their marriage, resulting probably in a divorce, led to his exposure as a newborn.[29] His family name is lost; Melissus will be a name given to him after he was enslaved.[30]

It is notable that the person who educated Melissus to an exceptionally advanced level with considerable personal care, simply called the *educator*, is recognized with some gratitude but not named. This *educator* subsequently gave the fully trained Melissus as an (expensive!) gift to Maecenas, who emerged as a very prominent and influential man during the early triumviral period.[31] At the moment of being gifted, Melissus was described as being a *grammaticus*, a teacher of young children, although he himself characterizes his education as being beyond what was required for that job. *Grammaticus* may perhaps also be used as a general term for an educated man. The *educator* may therefore have been a cultivated and wealthy man who moved in Rome's highest intellectual and political circles, a man who invested in educating the enslaved in his household and used them as currency to further his own social and political networking.[32] He will have lived in Rome and that is where Melissus acquired his advanced education, in both Greek and Latin. If such a reconstruction is accurate, Melissus' education recalls the experiences in the household of Atticus discussed in chapter 2 or Daphnis' education treated in chapter 3.

Consequently, the *educator* will not necessarily have been the same person who picked Melissus up as a newborn in a public square or on a street corner in Spoletium. It seems more probable, therefore, that Melissus was first illegally enslaved by a local person, possibly a neighbor, or by a traveling slave trader who resold him in Rome, either as a baby or, at a more handsome profit, as a young boy who was already showing intellectual promise. If such a reconstruction is correct, then Melissus chose in his own account of his life to pass over the initial stage(s) of his childhood, a time he might have remembered less fondly than his subsequent experiences within the household of the *educator*. As we have seen, it was tempting for those who enslaved *expositi* to move children away from their birthplace; Spoletium was several days' journey from Rome for a person traveling on foot or in an ordinary oxcart.[33]

However, in this case, the mother of the exposed child later reappeared in Rome and was able to initiate a lawsuit to try to liberate her son from illegal slavery. Her case, although it was ultimately unsuccessful, is in itself highly suggestive. She appears to have been a woman with some education, since she was able to understand how such a lawsuit could be brought. She may have traveled from Spoletium to Rome for this very purpose. Melissus' father seems, therefore, to be deceased by this time or he would have been called upon to sue in this context in order to assert his legal right to *patria potestas*. Melissus, as paraphrased by Suetonius, refused to cooperate with the woman's case but did not deny that she was his mother. He did not label her as a fraud, which would presumably have been the easiest way for him to stay in the household of Maecenas.[34]

The case of the mother must have been brought while Melissus was still enslaved, but while he was living in the household of Maecenas. The implication of the case and of its aftermath is that the fully educated Melissus lived for some time with Maecenas before being manumitted.[35] Maecenas, however, did not have children of his own. Consequently, in his role as *grammaticus* Melissus would most likely have taught the enslaved children in the household.[36] He may, in fact, have been specifically given to Maecenas by the *educator* for this task, as an enslaved teacher of enslaved children. Melissus' career reveals again the systematic way in which wealthy Romans, like Maecenas, Atticus, the *educator*, and others, invested in an educational system for the enslaved within their own homes. Meanwhile, manumission did not come automatically for the highly educated or for those serving as teachers.

Melissus' mother sued to free her son, but he refused to cooperate and declared a desire to stay on within the household of Maecenas. Her case then failed. By the imperial period, as we have seen, Melissus' personal opposition to the lawsuit would have been irrelevant.[37] It is possible that the legal situation was different at the time of this lawsuit (perhaps in the later 30s or early 20s?) and that Melissus' opposition was taken into account in court. Alternatively, the mother may have dropped the case in order to fit in with his preference to remain enslaved.[38] Such a scenario seems less likely.[39] It seems more probable that the case failed either because at this point Melissus' agreement was indeed legally required or for lack of sufficient evidence at the time of trial.[40] Melissus may himself have been in possession of some crucial piece of evidence that was needed to prove who he really was, a token or other item that his mother expected him to produce in court. In other words, it is possible that the mother appeared suddenly and simply assumed that Melissus, a person whom she had not been much in touch with since his birth, would naturally prefer to be a freeborn citizen. Her lawsuit will, in that case, have reflected her own desire, for a range of personal and economic reasons, to have the well-educated Melissus back as a legal son who owed her support and gratitude for rescuing him from slavery.[41]

But if the mother had succeeded and Melissus had been recognized as a freeborn Roman citizen, his connection to Maecenas would have been rendered void. If he had not been legally enslaved, then he could never be manumitted by Maecenas, a legal act that would join the two men and create a range of expectations and obligations for their future relationship.[42] Melissus claimed that he was at the time of the lawsuit already on close and friendly terms with the great Maecenas, but that his flattering decision to stay on in the household led to rapid manumission and even to a special introduction to Octavian/Augustus.[43] There could, of course, be a degree of strategic editing and exaggeration in this narrative. The motives of the individual players in the drama are inevitably obscure. Yet the basic trajectory of Melissus' career remains attested and apparently in a form that he later himself circulated in public. Suetonius' wording suggests that Melissus, at least later in life, essentially wanted to have it both ways. He asserted that he had been born free to a mother who had tried to restore his legal status, but he also claimed personal agency in choosing to remain enslaved to Maecenas, whose exceptional favor toward him he openly advertised.

Maecenas was a very rich man whose political influence grew steadily throughout the 30s.[44] It is apparent that even in a famously opulent household the size of his, the young Melissus had managed to attract his attention.[45] Melissus was, therefore, probably doing more than teaching young, enslaved children how to read and write in an elementary classroom. Rather, he had become personally close to Maecenas and gained special credit for his refusal to support his mother's lawsuit. For his part, Maecenas apparently cared if Melissus stayed on in his household or not.[46] Whether manumission would soon have been forthcoming in any case for Melissus even under other circumstances is impossible to know. However that might have been, Melissus' career benefited greatly from his early association with Maecenas and his extensive literary and social circles.

Yet Melissus was also, in several ways, a self-made man. Even as Maecenas seems to have receded from public life, starting early in the 20s, Melissus soon acquired the ultimate patron in Augustus himself and a plum job organizing the new dual library that was closely associated with several members of the *domus Augusta*.[47] Melissus' deep learning and attractive personality recommended him to Augustus, who had learned freedmen of his own whom he could and did place in similar jobs.[48] This promotion makes best sense, therefore, if Melissus had already been a leading intellectual within the distinguished circle of poets and writers around Maecenas during the 30s.[49]

The Greek and Latin library spaces being built during the 20s in what was formerly known as the Portico of Metellus were planned in conjunction with the construction of the adjacent Theater of Marcellus.[50] The redesigned portico had a school attached to it and perhaps also a dedicated hall for senate meetings (*curia*). Consequently, Melissus' earlier teaching career could have recommended him for the job, if as librarian he was also expected to maintain an active involvement with this new school and its pupils. In effect, Melissus was a teacher, a scholar, a writer, a librarian, and an intellectual influencer who shaped the way in which one of Rome's most prestigious new cultural locations was designed and used.

Over what seems to have been a long life, Melissus apparently tried his hand at several genres of writing, perhaps including scientific treatises and philological works. As usual, surviving fragments are meager.[51] But he was remembered for an (unsuccessful?) attempt to invent a new genre of comedy in Latin, named *trabeata* after the short cloaks (*trabeae*) traditionally worn by Roman *equites*, and for a collection of jokes in 150 separate small books (*libelli*), which he says he started putting together at the age of 60. The small books of jokes were probably pamphlets, which he will initially have circulated separately in installments, rather than as an encyclopedia of Roman humor. In other words, Melissus was himself a comedian, a producer of comedies, and a collector of jokes, both new and old. He may have been a playwright who had staged his comedies under his own name, perhaps even in the theater next to the library where he worked. In Augustan Rome, a schoolroom was to be found next to a library and a theater, spaces that could easily interconnect. Melissus certainly had enough backing from prominent men with an interest in Latin literature to put on performances of his plays.[52] There would have been little point in trying to launch a new style of comedy without performances for a live audience. If one was to go a step further, one might even wonder whether it was seeing one of his comedies performed on stage, either in Rome or on tour, that brought Melissus to the renewed attention of his long-lost mother, who had at least some idea of what had happened to him later in life.

Marcus Antonius Gnipho, Tutor to Julius Caesar

The other foundling whose origin is recorded by Suetonius was known by the unusual Greek (nick)name of Gnipho (Γνίφων: "miser" or "tight-wad"), a name that is rarely attested.[53] Since Gnipho died at around the age of 50 in the mid to late 60s, he did not have the chance to meet Melissus, who was probably born around that same time or a little later.[54] Yet Gnipho's spectacular success in Rome as a leading rhetorician and expert on the Latin language can be seen as paving the way for Melissus and others from a similar background. Some prominent pupils of Gnipho's boasted of their relationship to him, as was the case with Lucius Ateius Philologus, a learned war captive from Athens who is discussed in chapter 6. Others put Gnipho's name on their own publications in the hopes of attracting a wider audience among the reading public.[55] Gnipho's profound influence on his former pupil Julius Caesar will be the focus of the next section.

Again, Suetonius is our main source for Gnipho's life, which he describes in the following way.

> *M. Antonius Gnipho, ingenuus in Gallia natus sed expositus, a nutritore suo manumissus institutusque (Alexandriae quidem, ut aliqui tradunt, in contubernio Dionysi Scytobrachionis: quod equidem non temere crediderim, cum temporum ratio vix congruat) fuisse dicitur ingenii magni, memoriae singularis, nec minus Graece quam Latine doctus; praeterea comi facilique natura, nec unquam de mercedibus pactus, eoque plura ex liberalitate discentium consecutus. Docuit primum in Divi Iulii domo pueri, deinde in sua privata. Docuit autem et rhetoricam, ita ut quotidie praecepta eloquentiae traderet, declamaret vero nonnisi nundinis. Scholam eius claros quoque viros frequentasse aiunt, in iis M. Ciceronem, etiam cum praetura fungeretur. Scripsit multa, quamvis annum aetatis quinquagesimum non excesserit. Etsi Ateius Philologus duo tantum volumina*

> *de Latino sermone reliquisse eum tradit; nam cetera scripta discipulorum eius esse, non ipsius; in quibus et suum alicubi reperiri nomen, ut hoc *.*
>
> GRAM. *ET RHET.* 7.
>
> Marcus Antonius Gnipho was born a free person in Gaul but was exposed. The man who brought him up manumitted him and arranged for his education—at Alexandria, as some people report, as a fellow student of Dionysius Scytobrachion (although I am not inclined to believe this easily, since the chronology hardly fits). He was said to have been prodigiously clever, with an exceptional memory and equally learned in both Greek and Latin. Besides he was described as being friendly and having an easygoing nature. He never set a formal fee structure and for this reason he made more money [than other teachers] from the generosity of his students. He first served as a teacher in the house of the deified Julius when Caesar was still a young boy, and then in his own private establishment. But he also taught rhetoric [in addition to grammar], with the result that he presented lessons on oratorical excellence every day, but he only declaimed his own speeches on market days. They say that prominent men also made a habit of attending his school, among them Marcus Cicero, and even in the year when he [Cicero] was [urban] praetor. Gnipho wrote many books, although he did not live past his fiftieth year. Ateius Philologus, however, reports that he only left behind a work entitled *On the Latin Language*, in two volumes. For, Philologus says that the other books, on which Gnipho's name also could be found in some places, are by his pupils, not by him.

Not much seems to be missing at the end of this biographical sketch, which gives us a vivid picture of a man who was greatly admired as a teacher, scholar, and a generally kind and charming individual.[56]

Suetonius stresses Gnipho's friendly and accessible manner, which provided a welcome contrast to the severity that was customary for and even expected of a Roman schoolmaster. By not charging his pupils a set fee as was the norm, Gnipho cleverly made more money than other instructors, at the same time as he won a reputation for being accessible and user friendly. Indeed, the fact that he could set up a school independently on his own premises in itself indicates that he was financially secure. The name Gnipho seems, therefore, to have originated as a joke based on the man's behavior, which was consistently the polar opposite of mean or miserly or ungenerous in any way.[57] The name would not have made much sense for a baby or a very young child; he will originally have had a different name that is now lost. It is a further indication of his easygoing nature that he did not substitute anything more dignified or honorific for his pejorative nickname, as some other learned freedmen did, including his own distinguished pupil who chose the name Philologus for himself.[58]

Gnipho had been exposed at birth in a place simply described as "Gaul," but he is attested as tutor to the young Julius Caesar in Rome around the year 90 and presumably for a few years subsequently. Consequently, he was probably born in the decade of the teens in the second century and far from Rome. But who was this amiable Gnipho and where was he really from? Answers are hard to come by. Around the year 114, the term "Gaul" would usually signify either the Roman province of Narbonensis in the South of France, or Gallia Cisalpina, the area of northern Italy north of the Po River.[59] Each of these localities has been proposed as Gnipho's native place, but explicit evidence is lacking.[60] Since his Greek nickname was surely not given to him as a baby, it provides no indication of whether or not he was born in one of the Greek-speaking cities along the Mediterranean coast.

Clearly, Gnipho had been moved far away from where he was exposed, probably by slave traders or pirates. The identity of his parents is lost and it seems possible that they were not Roman citizens. His status will, therefore, have been more ambiguous than that of Melissus, a man who came to know who his birth parents were, exactly where he had been born, and under what circumstances he had been exposed. By contrast, Gnipho, although perhaps not born to Roman citizen parents, had neither been born into enslavement nor enslaved as a result of war. Yet a claim to free birth in a Gallic context was recalled as part of his life story, surely also by the man himself, and may contain an assertion of a Celtic ethnic background. What the term *expositus* signified outside the legal framework of Roman citizenship is not self-evident.

Gnipho was subsequently acquired, at a young age, by a person who raised, educated, and manumitted him—a man described as his *nutritor*, a term that evokes the raising of a child from infancy. That man's name will have been Marcus Antonius, the same name that Gnipho acquired upon manumission, perhaps some time before he became tutor to Julius Caesar around the period of the Social War. It seems likely, therefore, that Gnipho entered the household of this Antonius in Rome in the late second century and was educated there. This Antonius had the resources and cultural interests to send Gnipho to Alexandria in Egypt for the completion of his higher education, a long expedition that may be dated to sometime in the early to mid-90s, when Ptolemy X Alexander was pharaoh. In Alexandria, which was the Ptolemaic capital of Egypt and one of the greatest centers of Hellenistic learning in the Mediterranean world, Gnipho will have studied philosophy and rhetoric and perhaps other subjects taught in the advanced schools, including natural science or even medicine.[61]

For chronological reasons, Suetonius is (rightly) doubtful that Gnipho could have been a student in Alexandria at the same time as the enigmatic Dionysius Scytobrachion; Suetonius does not, however, doubt that Gnipho studied in Alexandria, even at a time when relatively few wealthy Romans would have traveled that far.[62] Athens or Rhodes or some of the other Greek cities were more obvious destinations for study in the early first century. In addition, the adolescent Gnipho cannot simply have traveled to Egypt on his own, he must have had some traveling companions with him. Did he need to be manumitted in order to make travel and study abroad practical? Or did another, more senior freedman travel with him to supervise his (and others') studies? Alternatively, did he travel to Egypt as the companion to a young family member who was studying there?[63] Or did several of these conditions need to be met in order to make such an exotic trip happen?[64]

The spectacular investment in Gnipho's education, which at the time must have seemed extravagant by almost any measure, is a remarkable testimony both to the cultural horizons of this Marcus Antonius and to the special attention Gnipho had garnered within his household. Suetonius highlights Gnipho's facility with languages (Latin and Greek) and his exceptional memory, both qualities that were particularly prized within Roman intellectual culture. While Marcus was a traditional *praenomen* for the Antonii, the most likely individual to be identified as Gnipho's *nutritor* seems to be the famous orator and politician Marcus Antonius (consul in 99), the grandfather of Cleopatra VII's husband of that same name.[65] This earlier Antonius was one of the most celebrated rhetoricians of his generation and a man who had enjoyed a fine political career. He is not known to have traveled to Egypt himself but was active in the Roman province of Asia and in Cilicia.

Antonius' family was close to the patrician Julii, a connection that helps explain how Gnipho came to teach Julius Caesar (perhaps together with a few other boys his own age?) privately in Caesar's own home in Rome.[66] Again, the timing and circumstances are remarkable. Gnipho had by now completed his advanced studies in Alexandria and was one of the most highly educated individuals in Rome. Yet he was soon employed to teach a young boy at an elementary stage of his education (the *puer* Caesar), in a curriculum that would have started with the basics and could not have made full use of the advanced knowledge that Gnipho had acquired abroad. If he was a freedman at this time, which seems likely, he would have undertaken this assignment as a special favor, and probably in return for a generous fee. Gnipho was kind and easygoing, or so we are told, and whatever he may initially have thought of being asked to teach Caesar, he will have found in him a bright and engaged pupil, who seems to have been strongly influenced by Gnipho's teaching before he eventually went on to more advanced studies on Rhodes with Apollonius Molon in the mid-70s.[67]

Gnipho, we are told, either wrote many works or only a single composition entitled *De Latino Sermone* in two volumes. According to his pupil, who chose for himself the name Philologus, many other students ascribed their published works to him, perhaps after his death. These works may have been based on notes they had taken during their time studying with him. Gnipho made a tremendous reputation for himself in Rome as a teacher of rhetoric, a subject that was taught to older boys once they had finished their basic education. In other words, despite an advanced education in Greek, the part of his career that was especially remembered seems focused on the Latin language and its use in oratory, although he may have given speeches in both Greek and Latin. Gnipho also gave public declamations, whether in the form of lectures or of performance pieces, on market days (*nundinae*), so perhaps as often as every eight days. These were days on which the city was crowded with people coming to buy or sell goods at the many specialized markets. Gnipho was such a famous orator that even Cicero, in 66 when he was urban praetor, regularly attended Gnipho's lessons on oratory in the afternoons and perhaps also his declamations on market days.[68] Cicero was apparently not the only politician to try to learn as much as he could from Gnipho.

Yet Gnipho's death, at the height of his fame in Rome, means he probably did not live to see Cicero speak in public as consul or Catiline conspire against the state or his own pupil Caesar mount a large campaign of conquest in Gaul in the 50s.[69] After traveling from an unspecified Gallic location to Rome, from there to Egypt and then back to Rome again, Gnipho was active as a teacher and scholar in that city from the late 90s until the mid-60s, a span of more than 25 years. Within that historical period, roughly between the outbreak of the Social War and the defeat of Mithridates VI, Gnipho represents a truly republican phenomenon, a man who bridged the intellectual landscape between the *verna* Daphnis and Melissus, a Roman citizen who had been exposed at birth. After initially being supported by an Antonius (and perhaps by his extended family), Gnipho seems to have been able to make enough money from teaching, consulting, and speaking in public to run a famous school independently on his own premises. Yet his prominence and prestige apparently did not make him forget his start in life as a baby exposed in a Gallic environment.

Julius Caesar, Scholar of the Latin Language

Gnipho's most prominent pupil was obviously Julius Caesar, an ambitious and very busy man, yet one who consistently continued to write prose and sometimes also poetry throughout his life.[70] In chapter 56 of his biography of Caesar, Suetonius provides us with the following booklist for Caesar: assorted juvenilia (later suppressed by Augustus) were followed by the books about the Gallic and Civil wars, a work *On Analogy* (*De Analogia*) in two books, a posthumous attack on the younger Cato (*Anticatones*), and a poem entitled *Journey* (*Iter*). Several collections of letters, both official and personal (some written in code), also survived for Suetonius to read. He does not mention any of Caesar's speeches, but some will surely have circulated; Caesar was a persuasive and popular orator. Caesar's well-known extant works, the *Commentarii*, have naturally been the focus of most attention. But his whole oeuvre also needs to be taken into consideration in creating a picture of his intellectual engagement and of how he expressed himself, despite or perhaps because of the increasingly exceptional trajectory his political and military career took over the years.

Caesar's intellectual interests included philological and linguistic questions that were close to the kinds of material cited by later grammarians for Gnipho (*De Sermone Latino*) and for other freedmen authors discussed in this study. Caesar understood issues of how Latin should be spoken and written not simply as part of an academic or antiquarian project or even an aesthetic choice but as political, cultural, and central to Rome's political life at home and abroad. He was writing his two-volume work on grammar, style, and word usage during his winters in camp and seems to have finished his final draft in 54. These were the very same years in which he was composing the annual installments of his prose work on the Gallic war, a brilliant piece of self-justification written in a strikingly plain and accessible style.[71] The report from the war in Gaul may have been composed to be read aloud to audiences in the city, in the manner of a speech. These two projects clearly informed each other in complex ways that are no longer recoverable for us.

But would anyone have called Caesar a *grammaticus*?[72] Perhaps not at that time in the 50s—or at least not to his face. But his view of the Latin language had been shaped by his learned teacher Gnipho, among many other intellectual influences. His powerful arguments for plain speech and correct diction were part of a much larger, ongoing debate in Rome about the Latin language and about rhetorical style that many of his contemporaries were engaged in during these same decades.[73] In this instance, we again see that in the Roman imagination "grammar" was thought of as integral to "rhetoric," which in turn shaped a political culture in which public speaking was so central.

Caesar would not have used any of the rare words that have survived from Opillus' writings and his self-presentation was deliberately and starkly different from what Sulla and Epicadus had crafted in the former's memoirs.[74] Caesar was surely familiar with these publications and others like them, but carefully chose a different path from their authors, both linguistically and politically. Gnipho was a crucial early influence on how Caesar experienced and used the Latin language, as well as how he became familiar with Greek linguistic theories developed in Hellenistic Alexandria. Caesar's books on the Latin language can be seen as a tribute to Gnipho and to others who shared his interests and outlook.

Conclusion

The nature of our surviving sources about these *expositi*, principally the compressed and abbreviated biographies put together by Suetonius, afford us only brief glimpses of a few memorable moments in the lives of Melissus and Gnipho. But these glimpses are suggestive of the roles learned freedmen could and did play in the intellectual life of the city. One such vignette evokes a scene of Gnipho declaiming a speech on a market day in 66, in an age when republican oratory was still very much flourishing. Was Caesar (an emerging politician in his mid-30s who had so far had only a few opportunities to speak in public) in the audience to hear his former tutor, one of his intellectual inspirations and personal mentors?[75] At that time, Caesar was a candidate for an aedileship in the following year. Did he continue to visit Gnipho's classroom in the way that more senior politicians and orators like Cicero did? Gnipho's afternoon classes were unlike many others in the city because a relaxed atmosphere was created by the genial instructor and leading orators of the day could often be found in attendance, sitting with the teenagers who were Gnipho's officially enrolled pupils and perhaps contributing to a general discussion about language, style, and rhetoric.

Some 65 years later, with a system of one-man rule now firmly established under a leader who had recently taken the title *pater patriae*, Melissus could be found fulfilling his role as head librarian at the Greek and Latin libraries in the Portico of Octavia. At 60 years old, Melissus started to put together his little books of jokes and witticisms, which he had probably been appreciating and even collecting for many years already, in the libraries and in the theater. Melissus included some jokes that were by now about 100 years old, such as the mockery of Catulus and Daphnis discussed in chapter 3. Melissus will have sifted through primary material of many kinds to find such popular sayings, which were not obviously part of comedies or other more formal literary publications. The libraries could provide him with ample source material, at the same time as the whole complex was full of students and scholars, a ready audience for him to try out his favorite political or social satires and witticisms. Melissus, the comic playwright and grand old man of Roman humor, had survived his patron Maecenas, by now dead for some years, to become an established influencer in his own right in the cultural setting of Augustus' new Rome.[76]

Both Melissus and Gnipho had been charismatic and charming figures in very different styles, each vividly memorable in his own way. Yet their names do not reveal either who they really were or where they had come from. Rather these nicknames came to serve as brand labels for their intellectual projects, at the same time as obscuring and even misidentifying their origins.

Meanwhile, they shared humorous and casual nicknames with the most well-born Roman male citizens, including the boys and young men they taught as their pupils.[77] Both Gnipho and Melissus recalled their start in life as babies cast out from their families, stories they did not choose to discard along the way as they became celebrated and more financially independent. Presumably, many if not most *expositi* had no idea that they had been exposed at birth because no one ever told them. Some others among their number were eventually reunited with family members and restored to the status of freeborn citizens. Meanwhile, each of these accounts tends to erase the crucial role played by slave traders (and others) who actually took possession of the exposed infants in the public locations where they had been placed, specifically in order to make a profit from enslaving them illegally, even at historical periods when many other sources of enslaved bodies, including prisoners captured in wars, were readily available in Rome.[78]

6

Intellectual Prisoners Captured in War

TWO TYRANTS, A LITERARY SCHOLAR, AND A FIERCE CRITIC

Perbelle feceris si ad nos veneris. offendes dissignationem Tyrannionis mirificam librorum meorum . . .

You would do an excellent thing if you came to visit us. You will come face to face with Tyrannio's amazing organization of my books . . .

Cicero in a letter, sent from Antium to his friend Atticus, June 56

ATT. 4.4A.1 = *SB* 78

οὐ γὰρ ἠξίου Λούκουλλος ἄνδρα διὰ παιδείαν ἐσπουδασμένον δοῦλον γενέσθαι πρότερον, εἶτ' ἀπελεύθερον. ἀφαίρεσις γὰρ ἦν τῆς ὑπαρχούσης ἡ τῆς δοκούσης ἐλευθερίας δόσις.

For Lucullus did not think it right for a man valued for his learning to be enslaved first, nor then to be manumitted. For the gift of what appeared to be freedom entailed the taking away of his existing liberty.

—PLUTARCH *LUCULLUS* 19.9

WHILE THE PREVIOUS CHAPTERS have discussed writers, intellectuals, and teachers, most of whom were either born into a condition of enslavement or were enslaved very early in life, this chapter will investigate four leading intellectuals who were captured in foreign conflicts outside Italy and brought to Rome as enslaved prisoners of war.[1] Such highly educated men came from a wide variety of ethnic and social backgrounds but shared in a common Hellenic culture, which had become widespread albeit with distinct local variations, especially in the eastern Mediterranean. These men, whom we may call prisoners of war, came to occupy a very particular category all their own among educated freedmen in Rome; some, including the four investigated here, were considered among the most prominent intellectuals of their day.[2] They made significant contributions by introducing various aspects of Greek culture to a Roman audience. Meanwhile, they presented competition for those educated in Italy who were seeking manumission and an independent life as teachers and scholars after enslavement.

This chapter will examine the lives and careers of four individuals, as a tiny cross-section of those who were most able to make a new life after undergoing capture in war and loss of the free status that they had been born with. Two men came to Rome as established intellectuals with what was effectively already an international reputation and two were probably in their early twenties, fully educated in Greek at home but not yet mature scholars or teachers in their own right. One of the older individuals was selected after capture to be the chosen booty assignment of a high-ranking officer in the Roman army. His fate highlights the value placed on learned, foreign prisoners of war for a wide variety of economic and cultural reasons. Such special prizes of war were not then resold but were manumitted by their captors (or by members of their immediate family), after an intervening time of enslavement that has become obscured by their subsequent prominence in Rome. Another seems to have been acquired by a centurion, perhaps as his share of the booty or in exchange for payment. The remaining two men were sold off outside the immediate circle of the Roman army, one to a member of the Roman general's own household staff (perhaps another special favor at a discounted price) and the other at a more open, albeit surely specialized, luxury market in Rome. Interestingly, therefore, three of the four seem to have been spoken for before the prisoners of war from each war reached anything like a slave market in Italy.

The four captives, in order of appearance here, are Tyrannio the Elder (born Theophrastus, son of Epicratides and of Lindia, from Amisos on the Black Sea); his pupil and successor known as Tyrannio the Younger (originally Diokles, son of Artemidorus, from the coast of Syria); Lucius Ateius Philologus (an unidentified Athenian captured during Sulla's siege of Athens in 86); and the remarkably eminent Timagenes of Alexandria in Egypt, brought to Rome by Gabinius in the mid-50s. Several of these men styled themselves as if they were resident foreigners in Rome. Timagenes, for example, does not seem to have made use of a Roman freedman name (presumably Faustus Cornelius Timagenes). The earliest of these to arrive was the Athenian who would later choose for himself the suggestive name of Philologus (scholar, lover of language); he will have reached Rome in the late 80s when Sulla marched on Rome a second time.

Then, some 15 years later, the first Tyrannio arrived in the early 60s, a native of the city of Amisos on the Black Sea that was part of the kingdom of Mithridates VI of Pontus. Both these men had seen their home cities ravaged by the Romans and their whole community uprooted. By contrast, Timagenes was enslaved in 55 in the aftermath of Gabinius' unauthorized invasion of Egypt to restore King Ptolemy XII Auletes to his position as pharaoh. The city of Alexandria had been taken by the Roman army and some of its inhabitants were evidently enslaved, although the circumstances of these events raise many questions. Egypt was returned to the rule of a pharaoh named Ptolemy, albeit an unpopular one, and her traditional government and culture remained essentially intact under a type of Roman hegemony. Finally, Diokles was brought to Rome from what is now Lebanon, apparently in the aftermath of the battle of Actium, although there is some debate about these circumstances.

The lives of these men, therefore, span much of the first century, from the clash with Mithridates VI and Sulla's sack of Athens through the turbulent triumviral period in the 30s, to the emergence of Augustus as *princeps* after the Battle of Actium. These four individuals were not only witnesses to but also active participants in the political and cultural transformation of Roman society and culture during these years. The main focus of this discussion will be on Tyrannio of Amisos and Timagenes of Alexandria, two individuals who were taken prisoner as mature scholars and who went on to have the greatest impact in Rome over many years. The careers of the other two men, who had been captured at a younger age, will serve as a complement and supplement to the two principal personalities.

Before proceeding to reconstruct their stories, as far as is possible from the surviving evidence, one famous episode from the late third century provides a salutary reminder of the ways in which Romans had debated the treatment of prominent captives earlier in their history. In the aftermath of the siege and capture of Syracuse in 212, the much-lamented fate of Archimedes, the most famous scientist and inventor of his time, who had been killed by Roman soldiers, stood as a cautionary tale of what might happen in the wake of a Roman victory.[3] In capturing a city at the end of a siege, especially when that siege had been long and brutal for all involved, it was quite possible for the conquerors to end up being responsible for the death of an irreplaceable genius, a great mathematician who had added to the sum of human knowledge. But if such an intellectual does not die in the siege of his hometown, what happens to him next?

The differing versions of Archimedes' death, which questioned whether this killing was accidental, and of Roman reactions to the tragic loss it entailed, reflect echoes of a complex and ongoing conversation in Roman political culture. This discussion centered on the very nature of Roman imperialism and on its relationship to the sophisticated Hellenic scientific and literary culture that Romans were increasingly coming into contact with. As the great city of Syracuse was laid waste, Archimedes' death did not go unnoticed; rather it could be represented as a senseless destruction on many levels despite the key role Archimedes' engineering expertise had played in prolonging the bitter siege. By the time Sulla was besieging Athens or Lucullus was capturing Amisos, Roman military leaders had very different, well-articulated plans for the most educated men they might capture, with a finely balanced regard for the age, expertise, and standing of each person within their local communities.[4] Such calculations of relative value were based, therefore, both on the past achievements and on the future potential for exploiting high-value prisoners, who were far from all being treated in the same way as most other captives.

Two Tyrants, One from the Black Sea and the Other from Syria

The man who went by the nickname Tyrannio (Τυραννίων, the tyrant) was the leader of a famous school in Amisos.[5] During the third war the Romans fought with king Mithridates of Pontus, Amisos was subjected to a lengthy siege by Lucius Licinius Lucullus, whom we have already encountered as a patron of the Greek poet Archias.[6] This region would soon become the Roman province of Bithynia, with Amisos eventually chosen as its capital by Caesar.[7] After settling in Rome, Tyrannio would go on to be a much-admired teacher and scholar, cultivated by many leading Romans, including Cicero, Caesar, Atticus, Varro, and others. His most famous pupil was the geographer and historian Strabo of Amaseia, who also came from the region of Pontus.[8] Tyrannio was a prolific author in his own right and one of the few true experts on Aristotle in Rome at the time. Yet it would be an oversimplification to represent him as a famous intellectual who had a successful school in Amisos, which he then transferred to Rome to even greater acclaim, after his home city had been sacked.[9] Before earning accolades in Rome, he passed through enslavement as a fate that was apparently not one he was able to avoid, although his captors seem to have been well aware of who he was and had every intention of using that knowledge for their own purposes.

Tyrannio was enslaved in 71 when Amisos fell to the Romans, with significant damage resulting to the city's infrastructure and devastating loss of life.[10] In many ways, therefore, Tyrannio was lucky, because he escaped a violent death and was recognized as a person of value who had the potential to contribute to Roman society. Plutarch's account of Tyrannio's enslavement and distribution as a prestige booty item is exceptional in explicitly raising central issues, both about Tyrannio's own situation as a prisoner in war captured by the Romans and more generally about why and how Romans enslaved leading intellectuals in the Greek East in the first place. Not many ancient texts address such fundamental questions since enslavement of prisoners of war was generally taken for granted by the Romans and by most other societies they came into contact with.[11] Consequently, it is worth taking a closer look at what Plutarch says and which sources he seems to have been using.

Plutarch's account of the siege of Amisos and its aftermath can be found in his biography of L. Licinius Lucullus, who was the commanding general in charge of the war in this region and who brought the siege to a successful conclusion.[12] The narrative is, therefore, naturally centered around the figure of Lucullus, a well-known Hellenophile whom Plutarch admired (with some reservations).[13]

> τότε καὶ Τυραννίων ὁ γραμματικὸς ἑάλω· Μουρήνας δ᾽ αὐτὸν ἐξῃτήσατο καὶ λαβὼν ἀπηλευθέρωσεν, ἀνελευθέρως τῇ δωρεᾷ χρησάμενος. οὐ γὰρ ἠξίου Λούκουλλος ἄνδρα διὰ παιδείαν ἐσπουδασμένον δοῦλον γενέσθαι πρότερον, εἶτ᾽ ἀπελεύθερον. ἀφαίρεσις γὰρ ἦν τῆς ὑπαρχούσης ἡ τῆς δοκούσης ἐλευθερίας δόσις. ἀλλὰ Μουρήνας μὲν οὐκ ἐνταῦθα μόνον ὤφθη πολὺ τῆς τοῦ στρατηγοῦ καλοκαγαθίας ἀποδέων.
>
> PLUTARCH *LUC.* 19.8

> At that time Tyrannio the grammarian was also captured. Murena requested him for himself (as his share) and once he had possession of him, he manumitted him, in this way making a degrading use of his war prize. For Lucullus did not think it right for a man valued for his learning to be enslaved first, nor then to be manumitted. For the gift of what appeared to be freedom entailed the taking away of his existing liberty. But Murena was not for the first time found very wanting in relation to the gentlemanly behavior of his commanding officer (Lucullus).

The section that describes the commander Lucullus giving Tyrannio as (part of?) a requested booty assignment to his cousin Lucius Licinius Murena, who was serving as his legate and who had himself been in charge of the siege at various times when Lucullus was away fighting elsewhere, comes at the end of the description of the capture of Amisos. This account of Tyrannio's fate is an integral part of the extremely laudatory narrative of Lucullus' role as commander in chief.

Amisos was a community that had been reliably loyal to Mithridates and had offered the Romans stiff resistance. Many circumstantial details suggest that this section of Plutarch's biography is heavily based on a source that reproduces Lucullus' own version of what was a highlight in his military career.[14] It is possible that Lucullus himself was the source, perhaps in a memoir that was influenced by the style of his close friend Sulla's memoirs; several similarities to Sulla's self-presentation can readily be identified in this description of what happened at Amisos.[15] One may especially note the strongly apologetic tendency in this narrative of a brutal series of events, the focus on a single main character whose emotions, words, and personal feelings are described in detail, and a marked tendency to denigrate opponents such as the Athenian general Callimachus, the man in charge of Amisos, and even trusted fellow officers such as Murena. The use of some direct speech for Lucullus' laments is also a telling feature.[16] In light of the fact that Pompey would later be chosen to replace Lucullus as commanding officer and would bring the long war with Mithridates to an end, it is not surprising to see Lucullus (and his admirers including Plutarch) magnify his own achievements in capturing Amisos, even as he is trying to deflect any criticisms about the destruction of a major city, a recognized center of Hellenic culture and learning. What Plutarch presents us with seems to be a much-compressed synopsis of a longer account that was vividly descriptive, highly emotional, and distinctly apologetic.

In imitation of the great Scipio Aemilianus who lamented as Carthage burned, Lucullus weeps over the bloody destruction of the city, a reckless carnage blamed on his greedy and ruthless soldiers, whose desire for booty he is unable to control.[17] He claims to be generous to many, especially to the surviving pro-Roman Athenians who have been trapped in the city by the siege.[18] It is essential, therefore, to read the brief concluding section about Tyrannio "the grammarian" (*grammatikos*) within the general context of this overall narrative, into which it fits quite neatly. At the same time, we should not allow ourselves to be misled by this laudatory version, but we should take note of Lucullus' evident desire to deflect concerns that have been voiced about his treatment of the famous Tyrannio, who was a prominent teacher in Rome by the time when Lucullus would have been writing a memoir.

But what actually happened to Tyrannio after the Romans captured Amisos and destroyed much of the city? Despite the alleged chaos created by the undisciplined and bloodthirsty Roman soldiers, Tyrannio was not killed but taken prisoner and soon identified as a valuable asset. This development reveals a detailed knowledge on the part of the Roman officers of the intellectual and cultural landscape in Amisos and clear communication lines with soldiers under their command. They had surely instructed their soldiers whom to bring to them as the most sought-after prisoners in a variety of categories.[19] Lucullus and Murena (or others in their employ) were clearly aware of Tyrannio. Murena then asked specifically for Tyrannio in the initial distribution of the most valuable booty to the highest-ranking officers in the Roman army.[20] Lucullus, as the commanding officer, was ultimately in charge of this important allotment of prizes, a mechanism that was designed to reward those who had supervised a siege that had lasted more than a year.[21]

Did Lucullus the learned philhellene not realize who Tyrannio was or why Murena, surely one of the first in the rank order to make his request for the top prizes, asked for him as a personal share? Similarly, neither Lucullus (nor Murena) initially intervened to remove Tyrannio from the group of desirable prisoners on offer to Roman officers as prizes. Rather, Tyrannio's experience as a prisoner of war should be understood as the result of business as usual for the Romans after the capture of a major city. In this context, it is obviously interesting to see Tyrannio, the fierce intellectual, treated as an especially desirable prize, alongside what will surely have been a considerable accumulation of prestigious objects of value and other recently enslaved leading citizens of Amisos, a major city in the region.

Murena subsequently manumitted Tyrannio, perhaps not until they both returned to Rome in 68, thus making him a new Roman citizen named L. Licinius Tyrannio.[22] It is not easy to see how Tyrannio, even if he had been freed soon after being distributed as booty, could or would have traveled to Rome independently of his new patron and without any resources of his own. Rather, he will have spent the next several years accompanying Murena on his military expeditions, including his campaign in Armenia, quite possibly as an enslaved member of Murena's household and entirely dependent on him in practical terms regardless of his legal status.[23] Murena evidently enjoyed spending time with a man like Tyrannio and publicized his act of manumission or perhaps his intention to manumit once he returned to Rome. In other words, Murena not only manumitted Tyrannio but boasted of his generous act, which garnered him attention both in the army and in Rome. Murena relished his new role as Tyrannio's patron. A largely positive reaction to Murena's actions is, in fact, suggested by Lucullus' attempt to denigrate his cousin's literary interests and generosity, which he should really have shared and approved of.

With a noticeable lack of logic, Lucullus immediately criticized Murena for treating Tyrannio as a slave in the first place and for subsequently claiming the legal right to manumit him. According to Plutarch's version of these events, Lucullus asserted that a great intellectual like Tyrannio should never have been enslaved at all. This piece of sophistry is as clever as it is unconvincing. Who had enslaved Tyrannio after the capture of Amisos? It was the Roman army under Lucullus' command. Lucullus had not intervened to release Tyrannio from enslavement either before or after the distribution of the most desirable booty to the Roman officers. Perhaps, therefore, an inattentive Lucullus had been upstaged by Murena, who was then crowing over his prize and showing Tyrannio off to others? The precise details and motivations inevitably elude us. Nevertheless, it is clear that Lucullus subsequently criticized Murena harshly for his patronage of Tyrannio. This critique might seem slightly less gratuitous if Murena had indeed kept Tyrannio enslaved throughout the remaining military operations before he returned to Rome.

However that may have been, Lucullus was only able to (try to) make a point at the expense of his cousin by calling into question the whole Roman approach to enslaving educated prisoners, in particular individuals who already had an international reputation. Two Licinii, Lucullus and Murena, were responsible for enslaving Tyrannio. Yet, in a highly unusual move, Lucullus then shows that he is indeed capable of criticizing the systematic Roman enslavement of prisoners, regardless of age, social class, education, talent, or other personal qualities. A modern reader might see this argument as hypocritical, especially coming from the commander who evidently had the power to dispose of booty and captives in the initial time period immediately after the end of the siege. Lucullus' preferential treatment of the Athenians in Amisos serves as obvious contemporary confirmation of such an interpretation. Yet Lucullus was bold enough to assert that he personally did not agree and thought that Tyrannio should in effect never have been treated as a prisoner of war. He was able to articulate such an argument and to claim to be superior to his cousin Murena while doing so, although he had not acted on this progressive policy at the time.

Who, then, was this tyrannical teacher, who was immediately recognized as a scholar by leading Romans and who went on to such a prestigious career in Rome? The man known by the nickname Tyrannio(n) (the tyrant) was a certain Theophrastus, son of Epicratides, who had been born in Amisos.[24] Surprisingly, his mother's name is also recorded; she was Lindia from Alexandria in Egypt. His parents clearly had some resources for they provided him with an excellent education. In Amisos, his teacher Hestiaios had already named him "the tyrant" at a young age for his offensive behavior toward his fellow students. In a pun on his father's name, he had jokingly called himself "son of Korymbos."[25] This naming game evokes a whiff of a playful but competitive classroom of boisterous young students. But the nickname Tyrannio stayed with Theophrastus throughout his life. It may reflect his self-fashioning as a bold intellectual who did not suffer fools. He traveled to Rhodes for more advanced studies, probably in the 80s. There he attended the lectures of Dionysius Thrax, himself a famous former pupil of the most renowned scholar of the Alexandrian philological tradition, Aristarchus of Samothrace.[26] Upon his return to Amisos, Tyrannio opened a school that was so popular that his local rival Demetrios of Erythrai felt compelled to move his own educational establishment elsewhere.[27] A number of extant writers refer to Tyrannio, but consistently by his nickname, including Cicero, Strabo, Plutarch, Diogenes Laertius, Sergius, and the *Suda*.[28]

Tyrannio's prominence in Amisos at the time of the Roman siege suggests that by the late 70s he was not a very young man. He was probably already in his 30s and may have been over 40.[29] He was a mature intellectual whose activities will have contributed to the cultural profile of his hometown. Despite what were probably several years spent in various army camps and on the march in the entourage of Murena, Tyrannio went on to a career in Rome that was, if anything, even more distinguished than his initial trajectory in Amisos. After reaching the city around 68, he will have been launched by the Licinii, perhaps beyond the patronage of Murena, who is not attested in our sources after his consulship in 62. According to the *Suda*, Tyrannio was eventually rich (*plousios*), which suggests that he had income streams beyond the fees he could collect from his pupils. He is the only freedman grammarian in Rome attested as having an extensive personal library, which he presumably had not brought with him from Amisos.[30]

Tyrannio's school became very well known. In the mid-40s, Strabo may have traveled from Pontus to Rome partly to study with him. Tyrannio is described as a prolific author and a man whose wide learning attracted the attention of Cicero, Caesar, and Atticus. His specialized knowledge of geography inspired Strabo and is referred to by Cicero, who himself consulted Tyrannio, as an expert on this subject.[31] Caesar is said to have encouraged or requested that Tyrannio write a work on Greek meter, a study that was presented to a discerning audience in a reading hosted by Atticus in his home on the Quirinal.[32] Works attributed to Tyrannio include discussions of Homer and of Homeric exegesis and of systems of grammar (*theoria mimeseos*) and spelling conventions.[33] He also wrote commentaries on Nicander and Alcman.

It was Tyrannio who was able to identify and organize the manuscripts of little-known works by Aristotle and Theophrastus that Sulla had brought to Rome in the late 80s as booty from Athens.[34] These books had been part of the library of the Athenian politician and bibliophile Apellicon.[35] They came to be housed in the private library at Cumae that Sulla's son Faustus had inherited from his father. Tyrannio was able to do far more to catalog this collection than Sulla's own professional librarians had been able to over the many intervening years. Tyrannio was credited, therefore, with renewing the study of Aristotle and with introducing the teachings of Aristarchus in Rome.

Similarly, in the mid-50s, it was Tyrannio who, presumably for a handsome fee, reorganized Cicero's books in his library at Antium after they had been damaged by Clodius' gangs when Cicero's houses were looted during his exile in 58.[36] Every aspect of the restored book collection was overseen by Tyrannio himself, with the assistance of two special library workers sent by Atticus. Tyrannio could evidently identify damaged papyrus scrolls and then arrange for their texts to be repaired or completed as necessary. At the same time, he oversaw the making of special labeled bookcases and probably the general system used to store and retrieve papyrus rolls.[37] However, he subsequently refused to render similar services to Quintus Cicero for his own library.[38] In sum, it would be difficult to overstate Tyrannio's intellectual influence within his new environment. According to the *Suda*, he lived to an advanced age, perhaps, therefore, into the mid-20s.

The name Tyrannio, originally given to an overbearing schoolboy by his teacher in Amisos in the early years of the first century, became, as it were, the brand of a school and of its whole intellectual enterprise. Consequently, Tyrannio's successor as head of school also called himself Tyrannio (known as the younger), in an effort to suggest continuity and fidelity to a standard and style of learning that had evidently drawn an audience in Rome. Such a succession is not often attested and serves as a final testimony to Tyrannio's influence, which lived on in the city after his death, even in the evolving political and cultural environment of the later first century. The second Tyrannio had also been brought to Rome as a prisoner of war. His name was Diokles, son of Artemidorus, and he had grown up in coastal Syria, apparently in the area of modern Lebanon.[39] The *Suda* calls him a Phoenician (*Phoinix*) by birth. He was an educated person but still a young man, so perhaps around the age of 20, when he was enslaved. He was acquired by a freedman named Dymas, who saw to his further education, notably at the school of the famous elder Tyrannio, where he evidently flourished and became close with his teacher. Dymas then presented the fully educated Diokles as a present to a Roman woman named Terentia, whom the *Suda* identifies as the wife of Cicero.

Diokles' life story comes from the *Suda* and has been much debated with regard to its chronology and, consequently, its historical and political context. A brief reassessment will be offered here, if only to clarify the remarkable succession to Tyrannio of Amisos' famous school. The *Suda* describes the occasion of Diokles' capture as the war between Antony and Caesar (in this context Octavian), which is to say the campaign that culminated in the Battle of Actium in the late 30s.[40] Dymas, who gave Diokles to Terentia, is described as a freedman of this same "Caesar," which would make him a member of Augustus' household, the *familia Caesaris*.[41] Terentia is identified as the wife of Cicero, although the orator had by now been dead for over a decade.

For a variety of reasons related to chronology, some scholars have tried to reposition the capture of Diokles almost 20 years earlier, to the war between Caesar and Pompey.[42] However, such a reimagination brings with it as many problems as it seeks to solve. While it is indeed true that the name "Caesar" is in the *Suda* elsewhere only used for Julius Caesar, and not for Augustus, the name Antony is clearly in the text and is not easily confused with that of Pompey, Julius Caesar's rival.[43] Chronologically, the later civil war is indeed possible, and Tyrannio himself is said to have lived to be very old. Conversely, if we move Diokles' arrival in Rome to the early 40s, then he would surely have waited many years to succeed Tyrannio or Tyrannio would have "retired" relatively early. It seems preferable, therefore, to keep the dating in the *Suda* as it stands. Dymas will have given Diokles to Terentia when his education was complete, which would have been a few years after his arrival in Rome in the aftermath of the Battle of Actium.

The identity of Diokles' manumitter Terentia is a separate and even more complex question.[44] Obviously, it is fascinating to see evidence of a woman from a prominent family being given a highly educated slave as a present by a freedman from a different household. In this case, the gift is remarkable because the individual in question was soon to become the head of Tyrannio's well-established school, which would presumably have brought him a steady income, a share of which would have come to his patron. He may also have inherited his wealthy teacher's library, his library staff, and other valuable assets. In other words, this was a truly magnificent gift, one that would keep on giving. Such a gift, even if it was given in return for a favor already received, will have been designed to create a powerful sense of obligation and goodwill. Needless to say, a close relationship between the freedman Dymas and this particular Terentia is not otherwise documented.

But who was this fortunate Terentia, the beneficiary of Augustus' freedman Dymas' generosity? Cicero's wife lived to be very old so she is certainly a possible candidate, although she can seem relatively unlikely for a number of reasons.[45] She was not central to Roman political or intellectual life either in the mid-40s around the time of her divorce from Cicero or two decades later in the mid-20s, the two windows of opportunity presented by the context of a civil war between a Caesar and his adversary. Consequently, another younger Terentia seems more likely, especially around the time when Octavian took his new name of Augustus, in which years Cicero's former wife would have been in her early 70s. It would have been easy for the wrong label to be attached to a Terentia, since Roman women were hard to identify because of their lack of a personal name. Cicero's wife is the most well-known Terentia in the surviving sources for the first century, so the most likely to be invoked in cases of uncertainty.

The best-attested alternative candidate is a younger Terentia, the wife of Maecenas.[46] This woman was a generation younger than Cicero's wife and was a long-standing member of the literary and cultural circles of her powerful husband Maecenas and of Augustus himself. Although she and Maecenas may eventually have divorced, that did not happen until 12.[47] Around the mid-20s, Maecenas was still close to Augustus, even if he no longer played the kinds of political roles that he had enjoyed during the 30s, when Octavian was the triumvir in charge of Italy and Rome.[48] The long-standing closeness of their two households can help explain how Dymas came to know and cultivate this

Terentia. Nevertheless, according to this scenario, it is still telling that Dymas gave Diokles, the fledgling Tyrannio II, to Terentia instead of to her famous husband Maecenas, who had been presented with the remarkable Melissus as a gift, probably sometime earlier.[49] We may go a step further in imagining that Augustus, who was later said to have had an affair with this same Terentia, will have approved of this spectacular present.[50]

The two Tyrannios are, then, inextricably linked in our sources, through questions of chronology and of the authorship of texts. In order to understand Tyrannio of Amisos' career in Rome, the chronology of Diokles' arrival and education needs to be addressed. Similarly, the list of publications has been much discussed as regards to which Tyrannio wrote which work, a question that is of less concern for the purposes of this discussion.[51] In each of these senses, the original Tyrannio of Amisos can be said to have succeeded. He created a school and a brand of scholarship across various disciplines that outlasted his own long lifetime and distinguished career. He shrewdly chose a successor, another former captive, who was able and willing to carry on his legacy in Rome into a new age, a man who gave up his own name to follow in the footsteps of his teacher. Through his own influence and through the background of his chosen successor, Tyrannio was connected to the highest political and intellectual circles in the city even in times of civil war and great political change.

Moreover, this man (Theophrastus, son of Epicratides) managed all of this apparently without making much use of his new Roman citizen name; rather he styled himself Tyrannio of Amisos, as if he was one of the many Greek-speaking scholars who had chosen to move to Rome as the city had grown and as other cities around the Mediterranean fell on hard times, often as a result of various wars the Romans were involved in.[52] In his case, the use of an old nickname helped negotiate a somewhat singular status that he was able to create and define for himself. He shared the experience of former enslavement after capture in war with his pupil and successor the Syrian Diokles, son of Artemidorus. Diokles had also been a specially chosen prisoner, one acquired, probably at a bargain price, by a member of the conquering general's own staff, Dymas, freedman of Octavian.[53] Neither of the two Tyrannios, therefore, ever came up for sale on an open market.

Dymas may have acquired the young man Diokles in the East, while traveling with his patron Octavian, or in Rome at an event organized for a select audience of household members to gain access to items of booty from recent campaigns. A scenario abroad would parallel the one attested for Cato the Elder as consul in Spain over 160 years earlier.[54] As discussed in chapter 2, Cato had instructed his personal staff that they could not profit in any way from the war while he was in command and he enforced his orders strictly. Octavian, and probably most of his contemporaries, had a very different policy. Meanwhile, the freedman Dymas, like Murena before him, was on the lookout for an educated man whose future career could enhance the standing and social networks of his first Roman patron. Dymas could only afford a younger scholar but through care and good fortune managed to achieve a similar outcome to that of Murena, a man from an aristocratic background.[55]

A Literary Scholar from Athens: Lucius Ateius Philologus

A uniquely attested earlier parallel to the experience of the two Tyrannios is apparently provided by the man who, after manumission, came to be known as Lucius Ateius Philologus.[56] We have already met this individual in chapter 5 as a prominent pupil of the great rhetorician Marcus Antonius Gnipho, the tutor to Julius Caesar. Philologus is thought to have been captured at Athens in the aftermath of Sulla's siege, which concluded in a Roman victory on March 1, 86. Philologus' original name and family background are lost but he appears to have been an Athenian citizen, since he was an educated young man. He may have been still a teenager when he was enslaved. In theory at least, no Athenian citizens were enslaved when Sulla took Athens, but there may obviously have been exceptions to this stated policy.[57] The aftermath of the long siege was the ransacking of the city and a bloodbath enacted by Sulla's soldiers, veterans of the brutal Social War during which illegal enslavements had also occurred in Italy.

Philologus' Roman family name of Ateius, and his other attested connections to the family of the Ateii, have been taken to indicate that he was brought to Rome by a Lucius Ateius, a centurion who was known to have served in Sulla's army.[58] This man was the grandfather of the famous jurist Lucius Ateius Capito, who claimed to have known Philologus well.[59] Ateius the centurion could have received Philologus either as a chosen prize or a random booty assignment or he may have purchased him on-site.[60] Alternatively, a less official or even clandestine transaction may have resulted in the young man eventually reaching Rome and the household of the Ateii. Philologus seems, therefore, to have come to Rome in the vanguard of Sulla's attacking army, probably in the autumn of 82, some 15 years before Tyrannio arrived from the East with Murena. Philologus was probably about the same age as Tyrannio but arrived in Rome at a much earlier stage in his life.[61]

The rising fortunes of the Ateii as a family group did nothing to impede Philologus' own notable career. He will probably have been a pupil of Gnipho soon after his arrival, an educational opportunity for him and a solid investment for the Ateii.[62] He may have been a well-known teacher in the city when Asinius Pollio was a boy, which would have been in the mid to late 60s.[63] In the later 50s he traveled to Asia and Cilicia as teacher to two young patrician Claudii.[64] In other words, Philologus moved in the most exclusive social circles and was evidently much in demand.

Some manuscripts of Suetonius list a previous nickname as Praetextatus ("wearing a *toga praetexta*," a toga with a purple border), for which Ateius was said to have substituted the more dignified Philologus ("the scholar," "the lover of learning") at an unknown date.[65] If he had indeed ever been known as Praetextatus, that name could have had a number of meanings. Certain freedmen did wear the *toga praetexta* on very special occasions, notably for the festival of Compitalia, if they were presiding over the festivities and sacrifices.[66] In such a case, *praetextatus* would be an honorific title, reminding others of the leadership role the individual had played in his local community. By contrast and more commonly, *praetextatus* was applied as a description to a young freeborn Roman male, who had not yet put on the plain toga of the adult man but still wore the dress of the younger boys.[67] In this context, the adjective usually designated a "school-boy," but Philologus had obviously never been such a Roman schoolboy.

In his case, the name would, therefore, be a kind of joke that took its meaning from a complete reversal of status and background. A "schoolmaster" was nicknamed "school-boy." If this had been the case, it might be easy to see why he wanted to change his name to something more dignified once he had the opportunity to do so. Choosing a name that said "scholar" instead of "schoolboy" could also make sense in the context of his career. At the same time, a reversal of the name could also function as a joke for those who had known him as "school-boy." In the end, this man was no Gnipho, nor even a Tyrannio, men who stuck with the comical nicknames they had acquired early in life.

Philologus seems to have lived to see Octavian's triple triumph and perhaps even into the new age of Augustus. He was an amazingly prolific author in his own right on many subjects. One suspects, therefore, that he, like so many others, had a professional staff of researchers and editors on hand. He also wrote specialist works on commission for leading Romans. For the spectacularly wealthy historian Sallust he produced a concise summary of Roman history as a handy reference work.[68] For Asinius Pollio, who wrote a history that continued on from Sallust's work, Philologus compiled a Latin style guide, which he delivered with specific advice about how to write a narrative history.[69] His own encyclopedic tendencies are revealed by his collection of knowledge about many subjects (*Hyle*, supposedly in 800 books) and a literary catalog (*Pinakes*, in 3 books).[70] By contrast, a specific discussion of whether Aeneas had really been in love with Dido (or rather with her sister Anna?) will presumably have predated Vergil's memorable treatment of this episode in *Aeneid* 4.[71]

Ateius Capito's possibly posthumous remark that Philologus had been "a grammarian among orators, an orator among grammarians" could be taken as a compliment or as a more dismissive, even denigrating characterization.[72] At the same time, Philologus' prominence is especially revealed by the fact that Suetonius had access to letters of his that were evidently kept and circulated long after his death, perhaps even as a collection.[73] These letters to a friend (Laelius Herma) seem the obvious source for small details about Philologus' life. The Mithridatic wars brought vast upheavals to the Eastern Mediterranean, seismic changes that included the displacement of many Greek-speaking intellectuals, some through enslavement, others through economic or political pressures in a rapidly changing world.[74] Rome absorbed many of these men, whether they were themselves willing or unwilling. Both Philologus and Tyrannio of Amisos came to Rome as captives in this ongoing series of conflicts between two empires in collision.

A Fierce Critic from Alexandria: Timagenes

While each individual discussed so far in this chapter was a leading intellectual in Rome, the most prominent of all by quite a stretch was to be Timagenes of Alexandria, who went on to enjoy a long if highly controversial career in Rome after arriving in the city in the mid-50s.[75] Interestingly, this intellectual powerhouse, although brought to Rome from Egypt by Gabinius, the Roman governor of Syria who restored King Ptolemy XII Auletes to the throne, was not initially distributed (or perhaps even made available?) to anyone on campaign. Rather, Timagenes was apparently sold off in Rome, perhaps at a public auction, albeit probably as an exotic, luxury item.[76] No one in Gabinius' army had, therefore, laid claim to him. His case demonstrates the harsh fate that could await a captive, even a mature person with an exceptional reputation, and even without being captured after an infamous siege, such as Sulla's of Athens or Licinius Lucullus' of Amisos. Gabinius' incursion into Egypt had been brief but strategic and was not aimed at conquest or at establishing a new Roman province there.[77] Meanwhile, Timagenes was clearly already an exceptional scholar even in the context of Alexandria's rich literary scene. His experience of enslavement raises many issues, especially in Rome where scholars such as Gnipho, Philologus, and Tyrannio of Amisos were already well-known figures in intellectual circles at the time of his arrival.

Timagenes was quite possibly the most important historiographer writing in Greek in the second half of the first century.[78] He has been much discussed in modern scholarship as an important source for a wide range of later writers in both Latin and Greek.[79] In addition, he was a master rhetorician active as a teacher and probably also as a public speaker. Younger contemporaries who were heavily influenced by him include Strabo of Amaseia and Nicolaus of Damascus, writers who came to spend time in Rome of their own free will. Although fragments of Timagenes' works are now scarce, many ancient authors refer to him and especially to his brazen outspokenness, which was eventually to cost him the friendship of Augustus, apparently sometime in the 20s. Soon after Timagenes' death, a separate account of his life was written by Evagoras of Lindos, a scholar of Egyptian history, who may have been his pupil.[80] Evagoras, Dionysius of Halicarnassus, and Timagenes all combined the study of history with a keen interest in rhetoric and linguistics.

But who was Timagenes and how did he come to be captured by the Romans? His father was a moneychanger (*argyramoibos*) or banker, whom the *Suda* describes as having been in the employ of the pharaoh.[81] It should be noted, however, that there is no independent evidence from Egyptian sources for the existence of such an official at the royal court.[82] It may be, therefore, that the father had a fairly lowly administrative role, or worked as an assistant to a more senior person in finance. Again according to the *Suda*, Timagenes was an "Alexandrian" (*Alexandreus*) and possibly an "Egyptian" (*Aigyptios*), in other words someone of local indigenous descent rather than from one of the many other communities of immigrants in the city. He grew up in the thoroughly Hellenized environment of Alexandria. If this information is accurate, Timagenes seems to have been a local boy whose upwardly mobile parents had given him a good education in the Hellenic style of their metropolis. He had become a well-known intellectual before Gabinius' invasion. He may, therefore, have already been in his 30s or even 40s when he was enslaved, some 25 years before Octavian finally conquered Egypt and went on to make himself pharaoh as successor to the Ptolemies.[83]

Although enslaved Egyptians are already mentioned in the republican period, by far the biggest influx of such individuals came into the city after the Roman conquest of Egypt in 30.[84] In republican times, free Egyptians living in Rome were mostly from a royal background or from the priestly classes. By contrast with any of these, Timagenes was a leading Alexandrian who had been enslaved as a result of what can be termed a "special military operation." This eventuality should surprise us more than the experiences of any of the other enslaved intellectuals discussed in this chapter. There is no reason to think that Timagenes was actively serving in the army that opposed Gabinius' invasion, which could have resulted in his becoming a prisoner of war during or immediately after a military engagement. If he was not a soldier or an army officer, but a teacher of rhetoric in Alexandria, why would he have been enslaved as a result of Auletes' restoration?

Indeed, we may go a step further and ask how many Egyptians were brought to Rome as slaves in the wake of Ptolemy XII's restoration in 55. Epigraphic evidence does attest to two other individuals with Egyptian names, who had been enslaved by Gaius Rabirius Postumus, the man left in charge as *dioiketes* of Egyptian finances by Gabinius.[85] Rabirius was soon driven out of Egypt for his rapacious practices and will presumably have brought these individuals, a (married?) couple named Hermodorus and Demaris, back to Rome with him as part of his household.[86] As we have already seen, the case of Timagenes was quite different because he was not enslaved in the household of a Roman who was in Egypt with or soon after Gabinius. A plausible reconstruction of events could posit that Timagenes had been a vocal opponent of the unpopular pharaoh and had spoken publicly against him and his return, as many others in Alexandria had in the years since the king had left that city in 59.

Alexandria was known for its volatile and highly divisive political climate, partly fostered by its many private political clubs (*hetairiai*), which enhanced the aggressive and partisan discourse typical of the city's population.[87] A number of these political focus groups had targeted Auletes as a weak and corrupt ruler, a man who was in the pocket of the Romans and who had recently ceded the island of Cyprus to them.[88] In this urban landscape, public rioting and political violence were endemic. Conversely, Ptolemy Auletes himself was a ruthless man who exacted fierce vengeance from his political opponents after he returned to the throne. Many critics, including his own daughter, were killed in sweeping purges, which were accompanied by confiscation of property.[89]

Timagenes, not as prominent or troublesome as a treacherous courtier or a rebel military leader, was, therefore, caught up in these events and soon ended up a captive on a ship bound for Rome. Under the political circumstances of the day, in the late spring and early summer of 55, it is hard to believe that this was a mere coincidence or a simple matter of being in the wrong place at the wrong time. Rather, Timagenes the tiresome rhetorician was handed over to the Romans as someone out of favor with the new, restored regime of Ptolemy Auletes. He may, therefore, have been a member of one of the political clubs in Alexandria. Alternatively, or at the same time, he could have spoken publicly in opposition to Auletes' restoration, in the rhetorical schools or in other public places, such as the great library, which was the city's intellectual hub.

Timagenes might even have been involved in some way with the embassy of around 100 prominent Egyptians who had gone to Rome in 57, under the leadership of the philosopher Dio, to petition the senate not to restore Auletes.[90] Attention has naturally been focused on the high-profile murder of this same Dio, who was poisoned while staying in Rome in what was the second such attempt on his life.[91] Cicero's protégé Marcus Caelius Rufus was tried and acquitted of this murder. In fact, members of the Egyptian delegation had already been attacked as soon as they arrived at Puteoli on the Bay of Naples.[92] Many were killed before the murder of Dio, with the result that some others opted to return to Egypt rather than continuing with their dangerous mission. Ptolemy Auletes was responsible for these crimes. The intrusion of this type of extreme political violence created something of a scandal in Rome even in the unstable decade of the 50s.[93] It is indeed possible that Timagenes had also been one of their number and had escaped back home, perhaps before ever reaching the city of Rome.[94]

Alternatively, and perhaps more plausibly, Timagenes had not been a leader of the first rank but a vocal and influential supporter in one or more of the political initiatives to oppose Auletes. For if he had been truly prominent, he would presumably have been targeted with so many of the others whom Auletes soon eliminated. In Rome Timagenes' subsequent reputation for outspokenness and vituperation serves to confirm the theory that he was already a political critic, as well as a teacher and scholar, in his earlier career in Alexandria. In this context, Timagenes' enslavement makes sense as part of a secondary purge beyond the summary execution of the opposition leaders, a decisive intervention that removed a group of less powerful political voices from Alexandria, while at the same time making some money or buying some other favors from the Romans who stood to gain from these enslavements. This could have been an especially attractive proposition at the end of a military campaign that had not produced many captives to sell or even much other booty. Auletes was deeply indebted to the leading Romans whom he had bribed at vast expense to restore him and to continue to keep him on the throne with a garrison of Roman soldiers.[95] Killing wealthy opponents in what amounted to a proscription allowed him to confiscate their personal property to alleviate his own financial obligations. Timagenes was evidently less wealthy, a situation that confirms the picture of him as a largely self-made man, but that condition may have saved his life in these circumstances. Selling his person was more profitable for the pharaoh than killing him.

Timagenes, then, suffered a stark reversal of fortune and was transported to Rome with the rest of Gabinius' Egyptian booty. In Rome he was then soon acquired, whether at a private sale or at a public auction, by Faustus Cornelius Sulla, son of the dictator, presumably at a high price.[96] Faustus was, at various times in his life, very wealthy but also a notorious spendthrift. Apparently, he was happy to collect intellectuals like Timagenes, who might complement the vast library of rare books that he had inherited from his father.[97] It is unclear how soon Faustus, who died in 46 almost a decade after Timagenes arrived in Rome, manumitted him. Timagenes may, therefore, have spent some time in enslavement and seems to have been dependent on Faustus, with whom he probably lived, during those early years of the later 50s and then the early 40s. Again, we may note that arriving in Rome as an enslaved captive without any personal possessions at all inevitably made a person completely dependent on a first patron, regardless of how soon a formal change of legal status occurred with manumission. Timagenes seems soon to have returned to teaching and lecturing, perhaps in order to earn money to pay back at least some of what Faustus had spent on his purchase.

After Faustus' death, in fact probably sometime before, Timagenes spent time in the circle of Marc Antony, who effectively became a second patron.[98] They may already have met in Egypt at the time of Timagenes' enslavement since Antony had served as a legate to Gabinius during the Roman invasion.[99] Timagenes was close to Antony in the 40s and well into the 30s, which would have brought him into contact with the young Octavian, whose sister Antony married in 40, and probably also with Asinius Pollio, at whose country estates he would live in old age. In addition to cultural and literary interests, Timagenes could have served as a very useful adviser on Egyptian and even on Parthian matters, especially to Antony as he set off to follow in Caesar's footsteps to fight the Parthians.[100] Timagenes was remembered as having introduced Antony to Alexas of Laodicea, who was an influential figure at the court of Cleopatra VII.[101] Timagenes will presumably have stayed in Rome as a teacher rather than have returned to Egypt with Antony, at least for most of the time. In any case, Timagenes will surely have been familiar with Cleopatra VII from her visits to Rome in the 40s. She was in Rome with her son Caesarion at the time of Caesar's assassination.[102]

Despite his closeness to Antony and perhaps also to Cleopatra, Timagenes managed to switch to the camp of Octavian at some point before Actium. This maneuver would have been much easier to make if he had indeed been based in Rome rather than if he had moved back to his home city of Alexandria in the entourage of Antony.[103] It is fascinating to see Timagenes emerge as a relatively independent scholar and teacher in Rome and as a person in tune with the shifting politics of the late 30s.

After Actium, Timagenes was very much in favor with Octavian and may even have been living at his house in Rome, around the time when the *princeps* took the new name of Augustus in 27.[104] Yet, what had been a warm, probably long-standing intellectual relationship ended in bitter recriminations when Augustus formally renounced his friendship with Timagenes and forbade him from ever entering his house again, at some point later in the 20s.[105] This very public row echoed down the ages but was clearly intensely personal rather than political in any formal sense of that term. Augustus became enraged by Timagenes' satirical public comments, many of them probably meant to be humorous, about himself and about his wife Livia and their whole *domus* (family and household?).[106] There is no reason to imagine that a Helleno-Egyptian historian like Timagenes mourned a lost Roman republic.[107] He may not even have mourned the end of the Ptolemaic dynasty, which he had studied in great detail, even if he had a higher opinion of Cleopatra VII than he had had of her father Auletes. He could indeed have had regrets about the Roman conquest of Egypt, yet he had evidently managed to be on close terms with Octavian the conqueror and new pharaoh in the initial years after his return from the East. Timagenes, by now probably (at least) in his 60s, was neither a political martyr nor a person with a covert plan either to overthrow the new government in Rome or to restore the Ptolemies in Egypt.[108]

Rather, Timagenes was an outspoken public intellectual from a completely different cultural milieu, one in which personal political satire about rulers and their family members was an integral and accepted part of everyday life. Biting satire, perhaps most notably including denigrating names like Auletes (flute player) that parodied the formal regnal names of pharaohs, had a long history in Hellenistic Egypt.[109] Augustus was now officially pharaoh, at least in Egypt. Timagenes' very intimacy with Augustus' family, and particularly with Livia, afforded him the special opportunity of hitting close to home with revelations and risqué jokes about matters private to the new *princeps*. Apparently, he was unable to resist this temptation, despite his previous experiences as the political target of an absolute monarch. Timagenes was overconfident about what his most important patron would find funny or even acceptable. It is clear, however, that Augustus' reprisal against his former associate also took a specifically private form.[110] Asinius Pollio, another close friend of both men, did not hesitate to take Timagenes into his own household where he would live for the rest of his life.[111] Others in Rome also continued to cultivate him and there is no good evidence to suggest that he lost his overall position in society.[112] Timagenes was no Cornelius Gallus or Terentius Varro who might pose any kind of tangible political threat to Augustus.[113]

Meanwhile, Timagenes was unbowed, even defiant, in the face of Augustus' anger. He retaliated by burning a work in several volumes that he had written in praise of Augustus, a surely encomiastic account of Augustus' rise to power that was probably a separate composition already available, at least in some circles in the city.[114] Augustus excluded Timagenes from his house; Timagenes in turn destroyed his own publication, thus excluding Augustus from his work.[115] This gesture would have taken on additional force if the book in question had been commissioned by Augustus himself. It might, therefore, be possible to describe Timagenes as having been a court historian to Augustus for a few years (possibly before and) after Actium, someone who was able write an account of the Roman conquest of Egypt that might have made the enterprise seem like good news to a Greek-reading public in the eastern Mediterranean. After the breakup, Augustus called Timagenes a wild animal.[116]

We should note again, however, that Augustus' very bitter feelings did not affect Timagenes general situation in Rome, nor even Augustus' ongoing association with Asinius Pollio. As their mutual friend, Asinius Pollio allegedly tried to smooth things over between the two, but Augustus would have none of it. Pollio is then said to have offered to expel Timagenes from his own home also, should Augustus demand this action.[117]

> *Si iubes, Caesar, statim illi domo mea interdicam.*
>
> SENECA *DE IRA* 3.23.8
>
> If you give the order, Caesar, I will immediately ban him from my home.

It is not easy to catch the tone of Pollio's question to the *princeps,* which may have been rhetorical. Did Pollio really invite Augustus to insert himself into Pollio's own household in this manner? Was this a defiant challenge or a flippant joke or simply a way to end an awkward conversation that had already gone on too long? Augustus' response, which recalled how he had himself reconciled Pollio and Timagenes on a previous occasion, sounds rather wistful. Augustus (or perhaps Livia?) really could not stand any more of Timagenes' brashness and his unremitting need to be provocative. But Augustus did not want to be the cause of a rift between Timagenes and Pollio, whom he had reconciled to each other after an earlier, perhaps similar incident involving hurt feelings.[118]

Timagenes was said to have authored many books, but we only know of his magisterial history of kingship in the Mediterranean world and beyond, entitled *On Kings* and of the destroyed work about Augustus (if it was indeed a separate work rather than a section of *On Kings*).[119] *On Kings* was a sweeping work that offered a universal history arranged geographically by region and chronologically by the reigns and dynasties of monarchs. It included the Hellenistic kings, successors to Alexander the Great, as well as the Hasmonean kings of Judea. There is much that we do not know about this work, which was surely influential and was highly praised by later writers, notably Quintilian and Ammianus Marcellinus.[120] We do not know its length in number of books or its chronological scope or its main themes. Presumably it started with Alexander the Great and reached at least to the end of the Ptolemies with the death of Cleopatra VII, but this overall framework is hypothetical. Fragments are scarce and some possible excerpts on papyri are not certainly by Timagenes.[121]

The popular hypothesis that Timagenes was somehow an "anti-Roman" historian is based on scant evidence and seems distinctly unlikely given his continuing popularity in intellectual circles in Rome throughout his own lifetime and beyond.[122] Rather, he had probably conceived the broad format of his history long before being enslaved by the Romans; it was an immense project that would have taken many years to research and then to formulate. It represented a revival and apparently an expansion of Hellenistic universal history, notably the works of Polybius and Posidonius, with a focus on Greek culture but showcasing a well-articulated interest in other peoples, such as Judaeans and Celts.[123]

Seneca the Younger records another critical saying of Timagenes, but only in paraphrase; it seems that Timagenes was in the habit of expressing this opinion.[124]

> *Timagenes felicitati urbis inimicus aiebat Romae sibi incendia ob hoc unum dolori esse, quod sciret meliora surrectura quam arsissent.*
>
> *EP.* 91.13 (AD 64)
>
> Timagenes, resentful toward the good fortune of the city (Rome), used to say that the fires in Rome only caused him grief for this single reason, namely that he knew that something "better" would replace what had burned.

Here again the statement, probably meant to be satirical and humorous, is specific, not general or formal. Seneca glosses Timagenes in saying that he was an opponent of the "well-being" or "good fortune" of the city, meaning Rome. In the particular context of urban fires, which were an acknowledged problem in the time of Augustus and before, Timagenes seems to criticize the *princeps'* ambitious programs of urban renewal. Regardless of how one interprets what Timagenes said and how Seneca (mis)represents it in a secondary context, this was a specific joke about rebuilding in Rome after a fire. After a fire, an old neighborhood might be swept away to make way for a different urban configuration. The Augustan city that Timagenes experienced was indeed in the midst of making a huge transition to being more like the kind of urban environment that he had been used to in Alexandria. It is possible that Timagenes was thinking of the destruction Alexandria had undergone more than once at the hands of the Romans. He may be saying that he himself, as a foreigner, is not sorry in general to see Rome burn but that even then he regrets her ability to rebuild rapidly. Yet even the force of the word "better" (*meliora*) might be ironic or sarcastic, which would change the meaning of the saying significantly.

At the same time, Timagenes is described as having been a "sophist" (i.e., a teacher of rhetoric) in Rome, even soon after his arrival in the 50s ("in the time of Pompey") and continuing on into the time of "Augustus," over 25 years later.[125] There is no reason to think he had to retire from teaching because of his personal dispute with Augustus. The school he had founded in Rome was apparently later taken over by a freedman of Asinius Pollio, a man originally from Tralles, a city in southern Asia minor.[126] Like Tyrannio, therefore, Timagenes established an educational approach that outlasted his own long activity in the city. In old age he spent most of his time at Pollio's villas in the countryside, at Tusculum and in the Alban hills.[127]

Unlike Tyrannio, Timagenes did not apparently become financially independent at any time during the several decades he spent in Rome. He seems always to have lived with a Roman patron, first Faustus Sulla, then probably Marc Antony, whose house he could have continued to live in after Antony left for the Eastern war. It is unknown whether Timagenes ever traveled with Antony, for example to Athens in the early 30s. He would probably have lived in Antony's household in Rome at times with his wife Octavia.[128] During the 30s, Timagenes seems to have been cautious enough in what he said, and to whom he said it, to survive in the evolving political climate of this unstable decade. A close connection with Octavia would also have helped him with her increasingly powerful brother; she was not dismissed from Antony's house until 33 when she moved in with Octavian.[129] Perhaps Timagenes moved with her. As noted previously, the phrasing of Augustus' ban on Timagenes can be taken to mean that he too had been living in the *princeps'* house before he was banished sometime before the year 20. Then Pollio, who surely outlived him, took Timagenes in and gave him a number of pleasant homes to spend time in.

Timagenes was far more than a renowned teacher or well-known public speaker or an expert adviser on Egyptian politics. He was a historian writing in Greek who was one of the leading intellectuals of the early Augustan time period, which is in itself an impressive claim in an age of remarkable literary and cultural renewal in Rome.[130] He revived and reinvented universal history as a genre, but without a focus on Rome, or perhaps on any other capital or kingdom, as its central focus point.[131] While he will presumably have promoted the idea that Hellenistic civilization was ultimately superior to others, his detailed and thoughtful treatment of other cultures displays a genuine interest in their customs and history, and in a new and ambitious project of world history that seems to have gone beyond what anyone had ever attempted before.[132] His combative personal style had made him an attractive interlocutor for the most powerful Romans of the day. His dramatic row with Augustus, which was evidently far from being a secret in Rome, seems only have added to his allure for others among the educated classes.

Conclusion

The experiences, outlook, and contributions of educated prisoners captured in war are inevitably different from those of individuals born into enslavement in Italy or enslaved illegally as infants. Such men who came to Rome as adults brought with them not only their experiences of life as free citizens in another community but also their learning based on the educational systems that they had previously experienced, whether as students or as teachers. Mature scholars such as Tyrannio and Timagenes were highly influential in Rome over many years. They naturally replicated the academic styles of eastern centers of learning including Alexandria, Amisos, and Rhodes. Tyrannio's knowledge of Aristotle's works was so detailed that he could identify damaged or defective papyrus rolls that others in Rome had been unable to assign. These men were treated by their captors as valuable assets to be deployed as prizes, gifts, or investments that could bestow cultural capital, as well as bringing in income. They both founded schools that were successful enough to be passed on to a successor. Their publications made Rome a center of Hellenistic literary production in a wide variety of fields, including linguistics, philology, geography, and historiography. They gained for themselves positions of independence, as scholars and critics, sometimes even in financial terms. We are told that Tyrannio was a wealthy man with a vast library of his own, not simply someone who was employed to consult in arranging the libraries of others.

The distinguished nature of the careers these men were able to shape for themselves in Rome, combined with the fact that our surviving sources do not often refer to them by their Roman freedman names, has tended to obscure their passage through slavery. Their names lay claim to an identity that is more Greek and less Roman. As a result, we do not know how long each man remained legally enslaved after capture in war. Modern discussions often pass quickly over their enslavement; some scholars choose not to mention it at all, although being a captive was the reason why they had come to Rome in the first place.[133] This chapter has tried to reconstruct a more detailed chronology for each individual, which suggests that enslavement may often have lasted for several years, for example in the case of Tyrannio and his patron Murena. As was the situation for other intellectual freedmen, manumission was by no means uniformly swift or something that could simply be taken for granted.

Unsurprisingly, Lucullus' assertion, passed on by Plutarch, that a man like Tyrannio should never have been enslaved in any case has resonated with later readers.[134] In other words, it is not difficult to give an account of the careers and intellectual projects of a Tyrannio or a Timagenes while interpreting their enslavement by the Romans as a brief interlude, an unfortunate detour in an otherwise remarkable and consistent career. The long lives of these men also allow this reading to seem more plausible. As the present reconstructions have tried to show, however, such an approach misses important aspects of individual lived experiences, as well as glossing over the characteristic Roman habit of enslaving educated men.

These two case studies reveal one further suggestive attribute of Tyrannio's and Timagenes' shared self-presentation; they were both quite outspoken by Roman standards and stressed their independence of thought and action.[135] While some of this behavior reflects cultural norms from their home environments, such as the political satire common in Ptolemaic Alexandria, one should also note that both men worked to stress their position as independent intellectuals, however heavily they had relied on Roman patrons at various times. Tyrannio agreed to organize Marcus Cicero's library but would not do the same for Quintus. Philologus helped Sallust amass a thesaurus of archaic Latin words but advised others, notably Asinius Pollio, against writing in Sallust's new "old-fashioned" style.[136] The lives of both younger captives, Philologus and Diokles, also reflect variations on many of these same themes.

7

Conclusion

GLIMPSES OF EDUCATED MEN WHO HAD BEEN ENSLAVED

> "The goal of Hermippus was not, however, to write a purely biographical work, but to demonstrate that a slave is in no way inferior to a freeborn in his mental capacities: thus Hermippus' ultimate aim was to celebrate education as power."
>
> MATTHAIOS 2015, 235.

AFTER SURVEYING THE CAREERS and relationship networks of the individuals treated in these case studies, it is natural to ask how many of these enslaved or formerly enslaved intellectuals there were in the households of the intelligentsia in Rome and at their various villas in the countryside. Yet, at the same time, it will immediately be clear that this question is impossible for us to answer based on the surviving evidence. Such men surely represented only a tiny fraction amid the overall number of enslaved persons, a number that grew steadily over the second and first centuries.[1] That general enslaved population forms the background to this investigation. It is challenging to try to take a step or even two steps back from a biographical focus in order to survey a wider landscape, either in a single historical milieu or across the generations. In that sense, any discussion of highly literate freedmen inevitably ends up being primarily a qualitative, not a quantitative, endeavor.

Enter Hermippus of Berytus. This freedman, who seems to have been living at least partly in Rome at the time of Trajan and Hadrian, produced a two-volume work in Greek entitled *About Slaves who Excelled in Learning* (*Peri ton en paideia(i) diaprepsanton doulon*).[2] Unfortunately, no fragments or ancient descriptions allow further insights into the scope or nature of this lost book. Hermippus' project fits logically within the widespread interest in biography that emerged in the early imperial period. This trend is exemplified for us by

Plutarch's paired biographies of Greeks and Romans, by the biographies of Suetonius, notably in this context the *De Grammaticis et Rhetoribus* that probably dates to the early second century AD before Hermippus was writing, and by the third century AD biographies published by Philostratus, including his life of the Pythagorean philosopher Apollonius of Tyana, as well as his *Lives of the Sophists*. The latter, which is also in two books, has sometimes been taken as a possible parallel for Hermippus. Meanwhile, modern scholars have tended to see Hermippus' project as more ambitious and much more theoretically grounded than Suetonius' loosely assembled series of short biographies of teachers and rhetoricians.[3] However that may have been, Hermippus' work is significant if only because it suggests that not so long after Suetonius was writing, much more detailed information was available about many more of these individuals within a broad Mediterranean context beyond the city of Rome.

Our main access to glimpses of Hermippus' text seems to be through the *Suda*, a Byzantine encyclopedia of the tenth century AD, but in this case by way of an intermediary source, Hesychius of Miletus, who lived in Constantinople in the time of the emperor Justinian.[4] Some of the material in the *Suda* is clearly garbled, as has already been discussed in chapter 6. Yet its level of detail about the lives of these intellectuals (but none who lived beyond the reign of Hadrian) is a striking and suggestive feature. Hermippus, the hypothetical ultimate source for much of this material, seems to have been a careful researcher who went well beyond what we see in Suetonius. The very fact that he could fill two papyrus roll volumes with this kind of material shows that there was indeed an abundance of evidence available in his day. Such a realization seems somewhat at odds with the evidence we have about the household of Cicero, to mention just one obvious example from an earlier period. Cicero does not name many educated slaves or freedmen in his household and often needs to borrow an expert from outside his own group.[5] But ultimately, we should not be surprised that different ancient sources allow for varying interpretations of this elusive topic, especially over time.

Hermippus is interesting not only as a researcher and author but also because his own life story, attested again mainly in the *Suda*, reflects a path similar to that of many of his subjects. He also was born into slavery and later emerged as a prolific writer on a range of subjects after manumission.

> Ἕρμιππος, Βηρύτιος, ἀπὸ κώμης μεσογαίου, μαθητὴς Φίλωνος τοῦ Βυβλίου: ὑφ' οὗ ᾠκειώθη Ἐρεννίῳ Σευήρῳ ἐπὶ Ἀδριανοῦ τοῦ βασιλέως, ἔκδουλος ὢν γένος, λόγιος σφόδρα: καὶ ἔγραψε πολλά. ἔγραψε καὶ περὶ ὀνείρων.
>
> E 3045

> Hermippus of Berytus, from a village inland, a pupil of Philo of Byblos, by whom he was introduced into the household of Herennius Severus in the

time of Hadrian's reign, was born from an enslaved mother [and] very learned. And he wrote a great deal. He wrote about dreams.

Hermippus is described as coming from Berytus (Beirut), an ancient flourishing intellectual hub on the coast of the Roman province of Syria. Berytus, one of the most Romanized cities in the East, was one of the few urban centers in the Middle East where the Latin language was widely used. Berytus was where Hermippus will have been educated, eventually becoming a pupil of the well-known Philo of Byblos, a native of a nearby city. Hermippus, however, came from a small village inland that is not named by the *Suda*, where he had been born into a condition of enslavement.[6] It seems from his name that the person who manumitted him was not a Roman citizen. His teacher Philo, who did enjoy citizen status, introduced Hermippus to his own patron, the prominent Roman senator Herennius Severus, through whose help Hermippus was evidently able to spend time in Rome in the household of Herennius.[7]

Hermippus, therefore, had himself experienced some of the stark changes of fortune that other enslaved intellectuals had endured over the centuries. Born under what were probably reduced circumstances in an agricultural setting, he was moved (perhaps sold) away from his mother and native culture to a sophisticated urban center, where he was given an advanced education in the Greek tradition (and perhaps also in Latin?) by a person of means who was evidently not himself a Roman citizen. Hermippus' close relationship with his prominent teacher Philo created further opportunities for him, including an introduction to a leading Roman politician. Hermippus was a prolific author on a range of fashionable topics including dreams and their interpretation (in five books) and the number seven, perhaps a study of the seven-day week. He also wrote a separate series of biographies of famous doctors, which may have been used by Soranus of Ephesus. He seems to have been an original thinker. The biographies of learned freedman will presumably have been his own particular project rather than a commission, an ambitious collection of much information that will have required detailed research to assemble. Hermippus thought that the individual lives and identities of these (formerly) enslaved men mattered and that he could find an audience who would appreciate reading about their careers just as other biographies were now popular with the reading public.[8]

A consideration of Hermippus' publication about intellectual slaves suggests that they were a significant group that could be identified; but, at the same time, it is clear that most of this information is lost to us. Whereas Suetonius' *De Grammaticis et Rhetoribus* can seem to be a narrow collection of somewhat random facts that have been compressed from other sources, a broader world of learning and scholarly activity extended well beyond the classrooms of the *grammatici* in Rome. Meanwhile, even if we try to make allowances for this lost material, it remains easy to underestimate or misunderstand the lived experiences of enslaved intellectuals and the impact they had on the literary scene, either as editors and advisers to others or as authors in their own right. None of these considerations mean that any aspect of the Roman system of enslavement was necessarily superior to other historical examples of forced labor of various kinds in which education was much less common or even forbidden. In fact, it can be argued that the habit of exploiting the labor of the educated reveals that the Romans were more systematic than other societies since they extended enslavement to virtually every task and activity that existed in their premodern community, from the most menial to the most complex, specialized, and intellectual.

As noted in the introduction, comparanda from other slave societies can be hard to come by, so the comparative element is often largely absent from any analysis.[9] One nineteenth-century example that can perhaps be profitably adduced is the highly unusual life story of Nicholas Said (born Mohammed Ali ben Sa'id in the Borno kingdom of Nigeria in the mid-1830s).[10] Kidnapped by slave traders as a young boy and transported across the Sahara, Said was sold and resold across the Ottoman Empire and eventually freed after he had been taken to Russia by Prince Alexander Sergeyevich Menshikov, who had acquired him in Istanbul. Said was a gifted linguist who mastered many languages (Kanuri, Mandara, Arabic, Turkish, Russian, German, Italian, French, English, and some Armenian) and later became a free man as an Orthodox Christian in Russia. Subsequently, he emigrated to the United States of his own free will, where he fought with distinction on the Union side in the Civil War. It was his intellectual gifts that made him a valuable possession but also a precious item that was soon sold off when economic hard times arrived. In his initial five years of enslavement, he was sold eight times. His potential led each one of his enslavers to advance his education even as each hoped to gain from this type of investment. His own account of his early years before his new life in Russia suggests some of the many kinds of uncertainties, misfortunes, and startling opportunities that Said experienced during enslavement. Comparisons with the Roman slave trade are suggestive in the case of Said and of some of the fellow captives he mentions in his autobiographical writings.

As the Romans could appreciate, a worker who was literate was able to perform more tasks than one who was not; and a man who was highly educated was in a special category all his own. Consequently, the labor of the educated enslaved was pervasive, as we have seen in the case studies explored in this book, at least for those who could afford to exploit it. There was no branch of learning that was off-limits to the enslaved, nor any genre of ancient writing that can be shown to be reserved exclusively for the freeborn. Such educated workers could be children born into slavery who were trained from an early age for these tasks, either for use within the household or in order to be sold for profit in a market that put a high monetary value on literary culture and on all types of learning. Alternatively, such a person might be a foreigner, particularly someone captured in war, who had been educated elsewhere. Within the setting of the Hellenistic Mediterranean such an educated freeborn person had often already traveled for advanced study in the great centers of learning such as Rhodes or Alexandria before their enslavement. Such a person, once transported to Rome, brought particular skills and knowledge that might not be readily available in a local classroom or lecture hall. Interestingly, the market for educated young men also had its own effect on the illegal enslaving of *expositi*, Roman citizen infants who were not being raised by their birth parents for various reasons of need or of choice.

Most if not all of the writers discussed in this study will themselves have made use of literate slaves, both for menial and probably also for less menial tasks. The sheer volume of publications that many of these men are associated with, along with the teaching, advising, socializing with patrons, and other activities they were called upon to perform, indicates the nature of the self-renewing cycle that they had become an integral part of. Their need to produce texts, either as a requirement or for pay in order to make a living, will itself have produced a corresponding dependence on literate helpers of various kinds.

Manumission, according to the Roman custom, regularly was bestowed upon the educated, yet neither as a matter of course nor according to a predictable schedule. Some patrons were eager to manumit for a variety of motives, most to do with their own social prestige or economic advantage. Others waited, again to serve a particular purpose they had in mind. At the same time, it will have been relatively much harder for a highly educated enslaved person to save enough money to buy their own freedom in a highly competitive market for luxury goods. In this sense, the educated were no less dependent on their primary patron(s), perhaps sometimes even more so, than others who had less direct contact with the householder.

Most of the educated individuals we know of were indeed eventually manumitted and some went on to lead relatively more independent lives as new citizens, partly by making money from teaching, writing commissions, and specialized library consulting, while accessing a broader network of patrons, some of whom they had known before they were freed. Manumission provided a person with opportunities for self-determination, for having a legally recognized family, and for engaging in many more types of activities in society. However, this new status also came with obligations to a patron, especially in cases where manumission had been a gift from that person. More and different services could now be requested, which created (at least potentially) a range of new situations of exploitation and (inter)dependence.

A number of distinct factors emerge as vital to creating and sustaining the use of educated enslaved labor. Above all it was the cultural prestige of literary knowledge and production among Rome's wealthiest citizens (both senators and equestrians) that gave rise to most of the conditions that shaped the lives of enslaved and manumitted intellectuals. These individuals produced a commodity that was valued in a way that made them into commodities themselves. Second, the labor of the enslaved had already been and continued to be pervasive in Roman society, already well before the period under discussion in this study. Romans progressively expanded the uses they made of enslavement. As a logical result, an increasing number of different and more complex tasks were assigned to the enslaved or manumitted, rather than to free men hired for pay. Third, from the beginning of the second century and subsequently a significant number of freeborn war captives with advanced skills in varying fields arrived from the Hellenistic East. These individuals, and probably others like them in earlier periods, themselves exemplified the skilled and educated person subject to forced labor. They were recognized as bringing with them specialized knowledge that was potentially profitable. Intellectuals, therefore, formed a small but often highly valued subgroup of people arriving in Rome as newly enslaved captives.

Wealthy Romans acquired increasingly larger households and access to far greater resources. Many of them were serious about bilingualism in Greek and about the acquisition of cultural knowledge from the Greek East. Literary culture was one area of special expertise that was highly esteemed, alongside medical and technical knowledge, artistic and musical expertise, as well as so many other fields of inquiry. Books and material objects were brought back to Rome in large numbers as the fruits of empire. But people were just as important, if not even more vital, in the quest to explore what could be learned from other cultures and societies.

Meanwhile, a large population of enslaved children was educated in Roman schoolrooms created specifically for them, in order to make them useful in various ways. In more affluent households, the curriculum made available to and imposed on these children will not have been so different from what the sons of the elite were required to learn, initially at the level of basic literacy and numeracy, and then also at a more advanced level for those chosen to go on. Increasingly high prices paid for the educated also created a particular market that was fed by entrepreneurs, who trained children to sell for profit rather than for their own use within their households. Within this economic system, an intellectual could be treated as a commodity auctioned off to the highest bidder or as a spectacular gift presented to a person of influence or as a precious loan at a time of particular need or as a desirable prize distributed or requested as booty in war. In other words, these individuals represented a particular form of currency for elites and for those aspiring to closer relationships with the intelligentsia in the city. Freely manumitting a highly educated man could also attract prestige and publicity, at the same time as creating a lifelong obligation.

All the prominent authors and politicians we know of during this time period made use of educated slaves and freedmen, whether members of their own households or of those of their close friends, to help them produce the texts we study and so many others now lost to us. These productions included speeches delivered in a variety of venues, letters to social equals and to employees or business associates, and literary works in any and every genre of prose and poetry. Indeed, appreciating at least some of the contributions made by such men affords us a relatively more nuanced and realistic picture of the lives and writings of the Romans we know most about. In this context, the topic of intellectuals in enslavement should not be an exclusively niche inquiry but more central to the field of Roman culture, at least as we can access it through surviving texts. The rather particular environment in which Latin literary texts were produced differed from the settings in other cultures, for example medieval or Renaissance Europe, communities in which authors did not have access to a range of enslaved helpers. At the same time, personal relationships between enslavers and enslaved with shared intellectual interests will have added a further dimension to their literary collaborations. The highly educated were not simply like writing tools or databases to be used by their patrons.

It is important to keep in mind that both educated freedmen and their patrons lived and worked in a society where literacy among the freeborn population was limited and universal schooling was far from being a norm. While estimates of functional literacy in antiquity range widely, and increasing evidence from graffiti on Roman walls does raise many questions about who wrote what for whom to read in a casual, everyday setting, it seems safe to say that most of the population in the city of Rome was either not literate or only literate in basic ways. It is beyond the reach of this study to explore this vital question in the detail that it deserves. Yet, it seems essential at least to take note again of the relatively singular situation of the fully literate, whether during enslavement or after manumission. They were not unexpected inhabitants of large households, and yet, at the same time, their knowledge was indeed special and especially prized for being relatively rare, prestigious, and useful. Their learning made them subject to a whole range of demands, to produce and curate information, to help read and write new texts, to entertain the learned and those pretending to more culture than they actually had access to. After manumission these freedmen might also sometimes achieve lives of some independence, both financially and intellectually, if they were fortunate.

NOTES

Introduction: Intellectual Pursuits and the (Formerly) Enslaved

1. All dates in this book are BC unless otherwise indicated.

2. For Daphnis, see chapter 3 and Flower 2022b.

3. The individuals treated in this study are the following: Licinius, Chilon, Paccius, Quintio, Philotimus, Eros, Dionysius, Alexis, Phemius, Epirota, Daphnis, Archias, Panurgus, Eros, Opillus, Epicadus, Melissus, Gnipho, Tyrannio the Elder, Tyrannio the Younger, Philologus, Timagenes, and Hermippus. Treggiari 1969a notes the following associations of learned patrons and freedmen in pairs: Daphnis and Catulus, Epicadus and Sulla, Lenaeus and Pompey, Diochares and Julius Caesar, Cilix and Phamea and Appius Claudius, Tiro and Cicero, Alexis and Atticus.

4. For Suetonius *Gram. et rhet.*, see Kaster's text in the *Oxford Classical Texts* and his commentary (1995). Christes 1979 is effectively an explication of this text. For a new discussion with a focus on subalternity, see Richlin 2024, especially 152 table 8.1.

5. Houston 2014 offers the most accessible recent introduction to book production and care. See also Winsbury 2009 and Blänsdorf 2016, 108–11.

6. Blake 2012 and 2016 uses Pliny and other imperial evidence to reconstruct reading and writing habits of literate Romans. For Pliny's slaves, see now Froehlich 2023, who uses Geertz's method of thick description. The forthcoming study *Slavery and the Roman Book* by Joseph Howley will offer a detailed treatment of enslavement and book production.

7. For slave jobs, see Blänsdorf 2016, 157–64.

8. See now Moss 2021, 2023, and 2024 on the possible use of slave labor in the composition and copying of New Testament texts.

9. For an overview of Roman education, see Wolff 2015 with earlier bibliography.

10. Gurd 2012 provides a fascinating examination of literary revisions in the period from Cicero to Pliny, within a broader literary context. The present study argues that his conclusions about the social function of literary revision had a wider societal context than the group of social equals whom he focuses on. See Benferhat 2020, 65, on multiple edits and revisions discussed in Pliny *Ep.* 7.12: "this becomes a case of a piano for four hands so to speak, even if the friend has to choose between two variants written by Pliny who remains the only author."

11. Benferhat 2020 offers a thought-provoking discussion of copyright and authorship with a focus on Pliny (*Ep.* 7.12.4–5 and 9.11.1).

12. Blake 2012 is an example of a study that is full of insights but that ultimately reduces literate staff to tools little different from the pen or the papyrus roll. Even if (some) Romans treated their assistants in this way, we should try not have our own view limited to theirs because it will

cause us to underestimate or even miss the intellectuals who are the subject of this study. For slaves with special skills, see Blänsdorf 2016, 90–118.

13. Suetonius *Iul.* 56 gives us a booklist for Julius Caesar that includes the war commentaries, his work on analogy, a poem, some speeches, his letters to the senate and to friends, as well as various juvenilia that Augustus suppressed.

14. For the role of the enslaved in business and commerce, see Craver 2010, 140; and Mouritsen 2011, 206–47. McNelis 2007 discusses the social status of grammarians and rhetors. Tomlin 2016, 4.2 pp. 152–59, offers an interesting example from one of the new Bloomberg writing tablets discovered in London that mentions a freedman with the unusual name Tibullus. He will presumably have been named after the famous elegist of the early Augustan period.

15. For Epictetus (c. AD 50–135), see *PIR*[2] E 74 with Inwood in *OCD* and Millar 2004.

16. Bradley 1994, 174–78. He discusses Epictetus' engagement with questions of freedom in his philosophy.

17. For Gaius Musonius Rufus, see Inwood in *BNP*.

18. There is little evidence for women in these roles. Note, however, Memmia Timothoe, who is attested as a poet living at the time of Ennius (Isidore *Orig.* 1.39. 17 with Suerbaum 2002, 327 no. 152). Her name suggests she might be a freedwoman of the Memmii. Nevertheless, since Roman women from affluent backgrounds were usually themselves literate, it is not unreasonable to imagine that they also felt the need for literate female slaves.

19. For slaves as part of dowry goods (*servus dotalis*), see Forschner 2020.

20. For P. Terentius Afer (*RE* 36, Jachmann), see Blänsdorf (*BNP*); Brown (*OCD*); Richlin 2024, 147–49; and Braund (*Oxford Bibliographies Online*) for bibliography. Most of the details about his life come from Suetonius' biography.

21. Suetonius records extensive ancient debates about how Terence came to be enslaved and then arrived in Rome. Palmer 1997 discusses the relations between Rome and Carthage in times of peace. See 134–35 for Terence. For Africans (*Afri*) living in Rome, including especially in the neighborhoods of the *vicus Africus* and the *vicus Sobrius*, see 22, 25–27, 45–46, 60, and 74–79.

22. For P. Terentius Lucanus, see *RE* 56 (Münzer) and also a coin possibly minted by this same man (*RRC* 217). Palmer 1997, 134–35, suggests Terentius Culleo, who had spent time at Carthage.

23. Suetonius *Vita Ter.* 5.

24. An obvious example is the freedman of Atticus named Epirota, who was born a *verna* in Tusculum but named "the man from Epirus." See chapter 2 for detailed discussion of his origins and career. For the naming patterns of vernae in Rome, see Bruun 2013. Afer was in fact a *cognomen* used by a prominent Roman orator of the early imperial period, Gnaeus Domitius Afer (*RE* 14 Kappelmacher and Wissowa), who had been born at Nîmes in the South of France. For a study of *cognomina*, see Kajanto 1982.

25. Lepore 2013, 344.

26. Treggiari 2007.

27. Treggiari 2019.

28. Scheid 2007, xxvii: "S'il faut donc admirer quelque chose dans les Res Gestae, c'est le savoir-faire du secrétariat d'Auguste." (If it is necessary to admire something in the *Res Gestae*, it is the skill of Augustus' secretariat.) Scheid does allow Augustus some influence on the text's

design and final draft but does not see him as an author in a traditional sense, even among a group of authors.

29. For an exploration of the concept of ghostwriters in antiquity, see now Moss 2024.

30. See now Richlin 2024.

1. Licinius the Flute Player and Gaius Gracchus the Orator

1. Gaius Sempronius Gracchus: tr. pl. 123, 122, *RE* 47 Münzer, *ORF*^{4} no. 48 and Manuwald 2019, no. 48. See Cicero *Brut.* 100, 104, 125 with Suerbaum 2002, no. 180 pp. 500–504, who stresses the survival of texts of his speeches even into late antiquity. For discussion see Sciarrino 2007, 60–67; and van der Blom 2016, 69–112. M. Porcius Cato: cos. 195, cens. 184, *RE* 9 Münzer, *ORF*^{4} no. 8 and Manuwald 2023a, F 17–254A. For discussion, see Suerbaum 2002, 380–418 and *FRHist.* no. 5 (Cornell) with Astin 1978, 137–44; Sciarrino 2007, 55–60; and Sciarrino 2011. The fragments can also be found in Cugusi and Sblendorio Cugusi 2001.

2. Licinius is described by Münzer as originally enslaved by Gaius Gracchus and as a Greek, not a *verna* (*RE* 5). For Licinia, see *RE* 180 (Münzer); Liubimova 2020; and Flower forthcoming. The flute he played seems to have been a special pitch pipe, not an ordinary reed flute or panpipe (Wille 1967, 453–54). For further discussion of his flute/pipe, see Morgan 2023, 110–15. Daube 1965, 204, 207, doubted that Licinia was legally able to manumit, although Münzer assumed she could. Epigraphical evidence indicates that women could and did regularly manumit in the second century, for example: *CIL* 1^2. 978 = 6.167 = *ILS* 3682a = *ILLRP* 97 (*MNR* Terme inv. no. 72575).

3. If he was a freedman of Licinia or of her father Publius, his new *praenomen* may also have been Publius. Epigraphical evidence, which is often hard to date precisely, tends to suggest that freedmen regularly started taking their manumitter's *praenomen* only around the time of Sulla (Salomies 1987, 230–38; and Salomies 2014, 156). For earlier examples with differing *praenomina*, see, for example, *CIL* 1^2. 1351 = 6.38697 = *ILLRP* 95 from Rome and *ID* 1753 (113) and 1754 from Delos.

4. For the fragments of Gaius Gracchus' speeches, see *ORF*^{4} no. 48; and Manuwald 2019, no. 48. Twenty-three speeches are attested and fourteen testimonia speak about the powerful effects of Gaius' oratory. For a list of his speeches in chronological order, see van der Blom 2016, 290–95. For discussion, see Münzer *RE* 47; Stockton 1979, 217–25; David 1983; and Courtney 1999, 124–33. For Gaius' bills and laws, see Williamson 2005, 459–60; and Elster 2020, nos. 19, 20, 21, 22, 23, 24, 25, 26, 28, 30, 31, 32, 33, 34, 35, 37, 38.

5. For example, Wille 1967, 453–54: "a musician;" Fantham 2004, 297 and 307: "a flute-player"; Morstein-Marx 2004, 270; Sciarrino 2007, 61–64; van der Blom 2016, 72, 92, 107; and Morgan 2023, 110–15, who stresses our uncertainty about Licinius' flute.

6. For insightful and thorough discussion, see Schulz 2020 and especially Morgan 2023, 104–15, who places Gracchus within the larger context of music and republican political culture.

7. M. Licinius Crassus: cos. 95, cens. 92, *RE* 55 Häpke, *ORF*^{4} no. 66 with Manuwald 2019. He was considered the outstanding orator of his age, together with M. Antonius (*ORF*^{4} no. 65), and is one of the main participants in Cicero's *De Oratore*. He does not, however, seem to have published many of his speeches.

8. Cicero *De or.* 3.214. See Cicero's view that an orator should be able to evoke a variety of emotions in his audience and move them from one to another within the same speech.

9. Quoted in the epigraph of this chapter. Quintilian *Inst.* 12.10.27 compares Gaius' simplicity with that of Lysias. Tacitus *Dial.* 18.2 thinks Gaius was the best orator, a better speaker even than Cato the Elder. Cicero *De or.* 3.227 advises: *sed fistulatorem domi reliquetis* (but you should leave the fluteplayer at home).

10. David 1983, 114, thinks Gellius misunderstands Licinius' role. See also Holford-Strevens 2003, 195–97.

11. Note Gellius' well-known attack on Cicero's trusted freedman Tiro (*NA* 6.3 = *ORF*[4] no. 8 F 163–69) with careful discussion in *FRHist.* vol. 3, 132–36 and Howley 2018, 174–90. Tiro can be considered the most visible educated freedman in our surviving evidence.

12. Given Cato's long and productive life, this was a relatively easy case to make. Holford-Strevens 2003, 196, notes that Gellius prefers Cato even to Cicero. 209: Gellius quotes Cicero and Cato as much as Vergil and Varro.

13. For the *rostra*, see Coarelli (*LTUR*) and Morstein-Marx 2004, figures 1 and 2 with map 2.

14. See Wille 1967, 453–54; and David 1983, 115, for Dio's misunderstanding of Licinius' role.

15. For Tiberius as an orator, see *ORF*[4] no. 34 and especially Livy *Per.* 60; Velleius Paterculus 2.6.1; Plutarch *Ti. Gracch.* 2.2–6 with Linke 2005, 26–27; and Flower 2012. Suerbaum 2002, T 8 notes that both brothers studied oratory with Carbo.

16. For Gaius in Numantia with Aemilianus (134–133), see Plutarch *C. Gracch.* 2.9 and 13.1. He will surely have returned with his commanding officer, not before as argued by Münzer in *RE* 47. See now Ljung 2022 for a decisive argument that Gaius was not in Rome at the time of his brother's death.

17. For Gaius' military service, see Münzer (*RE* 47), who has him start at the age of 16 and go to Spain on campaign before the final siege of Numantia. Two of his speeches in 124 are relevant to his extensive military service, one before the censors (Manuwald 2019, F 23–25) and one before the people (Manuwald 2019, F 26–28). He explained that he left Sardinia before his commanding officer because he had served well beyond the 10 campaigning seasons required before standing for election to political office (cf. Polybius 6. 19).

18. For Gaius and the *salutatio*, see Seneca *Ben.* 6.33.3–34; Plutarch *C. Gracch.* 29.3–30.1 with Goldbeck 2010, 191 and 217–24; and Flower forthcoming. Plutarch *QR* 81 notes that tribunes of the plebs were expected to keep their doors open at all times during daylight hours, so that they could be ready to help needy citizens. Licinius may have played a role at these regular, elaborate receptions when Gaius was in town.

19. For Cornelia, her literary interests, and the education of her children, see Plutarch *Ti. Gracch.* 1.3 with Stockton 1979, 25–26; and Dixon 2007, 40. The fragments of her letters to him reflect a close relationship. Hemelrijk 2004 provides a fundamental overview of Roman women and education.

20. For Cornelia's villa at Misenum on the Bay of Naples, see Plutarch *C. Gracch.* 19 with D'Arms 1970, 22; and Dixon 2007, 43–48.

21. For the Roman general's *consilium*, see Johnston 2008. For the military *contio*, see Pina Polo 1989.

22. For P. Cornelius Scipio Aemilianus, the second son of Aemilius Paullus (*ORF*[4] no. 12) who had been adopted by a son of Africanus, see *RE* 335 and *ORF*[4] no. 21. Cicero considered

him an outstanding orator and gives him an important role in *De Re Publica*. Gellius *NA* 3.4.1 is useful. Astin 1967 remains the classic treatment of his life in English.

23. Gaius' first public speeches are probably his defense of Vettius Sabinus in 132 (Plutarch *C. Gracch.* 1.3) and a speech in 131 in support of Carbo's bill proposing that reelection to the tribunate be allowed. See van der Blom 2016, 290. He may also have had a chance to ask questions of Aemilianus at a *contio*.

24. For mentions of Tiberius in Gaius' speeches, see Cicero *de Div.* 1.26.56; Plutarch *C. Gracch.* 1; and especially Florus 2.3.1.

25. For the commission of 3 men set up by Tiberius' agrarian law, see Livy *Per.* 58; Appian *B Civ.* 1.55; and Dio F 83.8 with Roselaar 2010, 221–89.

26. For the Gracchan boundary stones, see *II* 3.3.1; Gargola 1995, 147–74; and Campbell 2000, 452–53.

27. For Sempronia, sister of the Gracchi and wife of Aemilianus, see *RE* 99 (Münzer) with Harders 2008, 128–37; and Beness and Hillard 2016.

28. For Aemilianus and the Italians, see Astin 1967 *ad loc.* and Beness 2005 and 2012.

29. Gaius' sympathy for the plight of the Italian landowners and eventual support for extending Roman citizenship both make sense in the context of extensive contact with communities in Italy over many years.

30. Our sources do not indicate anything about the date of manumission, which could have been either during Gaius' lifetime or after his death (Cicero *De or.* 3.225 and Valerius Maximus 8.10.1).

31. For the confiscation of Gaius' property, see Plutarch *C. Gracch.* 17.5; and Orosius 5.12.9 with Flower 2006, 77–78.

32. Licinia's lawsuit was for losses to her dowry goods (*Digest* 24.3.66 pr). It is perhaps possible but seems unlikely that an enslaved person who was legally considered part of Licinia's dowry would have been confiscated. If that happened, the individual(s) would have been returned to her automatically because the dowry was legally her property. Her lawsuit indeed implies that the state had indeed already recognized her legal right to her dowry. Subsequently, she sued for damages caused by looters, probably to her house on the Palatine. Plutarch *C. Gracch.* 17.2 is incorrect in stating that her dowry was confiscated. See Flower forthcoming for a full discussion.

33. For dowry and enslavement, see Forschner 2020. Note the large dowries attested in the second century. Cornelia, Licinia's mother-in-law, and her sister are the most famous examples (Polybius 31.27 with Etcheto 2012, no. 25, 175–76, 282–87; McClintock 2013; and Valentini 2016). Cicero (*Rep.* 3.17) refers to the huge inheritance a daughter of Mucianus could expect. Alternatively, Licinius could have been still part of Mucianus' household and assigned by him to help Gaius. This seems less likely because Licinius is described as still being enslaved for at least some of the time that he was working with Gaius, which would have been after Mucianus had died. It is also possible that Licinia could have inherited Licinius from her father, which would not have made him part of her dowry but still have allowed her to manumit him at a later date.

34. Since the marriage to Licinia was probably very recent, it seems unlikely (but of course not impossible) that Licinius went to Spain with Gaius in 134–33. He seems a less plausible candidate to have been chosen for military service.

35. For Mucianus (cos. 131), see *RE* 72 Münzer. He was a son of P. Mucius Scaevola (cos. 175, *RE* 16 Münzer), adopted by an unidentified Licinius. His brother was P. Mucius Scaevola (cos. 133, *RE* 17 Münzer, *ORF*[4] no. 69).

36. Mucianus is no. 31 in *ORF*[4] and Manuwald 2019. A single *testimonium* is provided by Cicero *Amic.* 96. See also Cicero *De or.* 1.170, 216, 240.

37. For various more or less heroic versions of Mucianus' death in Asia, see Valerius Maximus 3.2.12, Frontinus 4.5.16, Florus 5, and Orosius 5.10.3.

38. See the chronological list of Gaius' attested speeches in van der Blom 2016, 290–95.

39. The first Licinius Crassus we know of to use the additional *cognomen* Dives (rich man) was P. Licinius Crassus cos. 205, *RE* 69 Münzer; and Marshall 1973.

40. In the first century, two Liciniae, daughters of L. Licinius Crassus (*RE* 55) and his wife Mucia were described as learned and well spoken (*RE* 183 and 184, Münzer) by Cicero (*Brut.* 211 and *De or.* 3.134).

41. Cicero *Amic.* 96 on Gaius Licinius Crassus, tr. pl. 145, *RE* 52 Münzer. He is not mentioned by Malcovati in *ORF* or Manuwald 2019, but he clearly was an innovative and possibly influential orator. Coarelli (*LTUR*: *rostra* of the republican era) also overlooks Licinius and has Gaius Gracchus as the first orator to face the Forum crowd.

42. See note 7.

43. The smaller pre-Sullan *rostra* is hard to reconstruct. It is important to keep in mind that Gaius was not speaking from the same platform used by Cicero and his contemporaries. See note 13.

44. Since Licinius fulfilled an energetic and even athletic role in his work with Gaius and then seems to have survived him by several decades, he appears to have been around Gaius' age or perhaps even a bit younger (closer in age to Licinia herself?). Gaius was about 20 in 134, the year in which he may have married before leaving for Numantia with Aemilianus.

45. Plutarch *C. Gracch.* 17.2 is incorrect in stating that Licinia had her dowry confiscated as part of postmortem sanctions imposed on Gaius. See Flower forthcoming.

46. The looting of Gaius' and Fulvius Flaccus' houses is recorded in Appian *B Civ.* 1.119. See Eck in *LTUR*. Grosso 1968, 206, imagines many slaves may have been killed or wounded in the attack of this mob.

47. For Gaius' move from the Palatine to Forum area, see Plutarch *C. Gracch.* 12.1. Flower forthcoming argues that Gaius went to live in a family house on the Vicus Tuscus near the Basilica Sempronia, a house that belonged to his mother, Cornelia, who seems also to have been staying in Rome at that time.

48. For Gaius' death, see Plutarch *C. Gracch.* 17, Appian *B Civ.* 1.115–18, and Orosius 5.12.8–9 (from Livy *Per.* 61). For the lucus Furrinae, see Calzini Gysens (*LTUR*). For the pons Sublicius, Rome's oldest bridge, see Coarelli (*LTUR*).

49. Q. Lutatius Catulus, cos. 102, *RE* 7, *ORF*[4] no. 63 with Manuwald 2019. We do not know how long Licinia lived after Gaius' death; she may have been only about 30 years old at the time. A son seems to have survived, according to Liubimova 2020.

50. Diophanes: (*RE* 4) Münzer sees him as a Stoic philosopher in exile from Mytilene, who was patronized by the Mucii Scaevolae. See Plutarch *Ti. Gracch.* 8.4–5 and 20, Cicero *Brut.* 104, and Strabo 13.617. For Blossius, see *RE* 1 Klebs. He was also a Stoic and a pupil of Antipater of Tarsus, who dedicated a book to him. He had, therefore, studied in the Greek East. Fantham 2004, 81, argues that there were no Greek teachers of rhetoric in Rome before the generation of the Gracchi.

51. Cicero *Amic.* 37 and Plutarch *Ti. Gracch.* 8.17.

52. Cornelia's speech: Cicero *Brut.* 211 in the mouth of Atticus.

53. For the death of Diophanes, see Cicero *Brut.* 104, Strabo 13.617, and Plutarch *Ti. Gracch.* 8.20. For the death of Blossius, see Cicero *Amic.* 37, *Brut.* 104, Valerius Maximus 4.7.1, and Plutarch *Ti. Gracch.* 8.6 and 20.4–7. D'Arms 1970, 292 and 317, discusses Blossius' family connections at Puteoli.

54. It does not seem likely that Licinius was ever part of Cornelia's household. Rather, he came into contact with Gaius after the marriage alliance with Licinia.

55. For Menelaus of Marathos (*RE* 12 Kroll), see Cicero *Brut.* 100 with Rawson 1985, 76; Scholz 2011, 132–33, Wisse 2013b, 183; and Eckert 2018, 19.

56. For Gaius Fannius, see *ORF*[4] no. 32, especially F 1 = Cicero *Brut.* 99–100.

57. Quintilian *Inst.* 11.3.7–8 makes the same point about Hortensius' delivery, which he claims to be unable to recreate from the texts of his speeches. For Q. Hortensius Hortalus, *RE* 13 and *ORF*[4] no. 92 with Manuwald 2019.

58. *Lex Aufeia*: F 44 = Gellius *NA* 11.10.1–6.

59. Cato did not name magistrates in his *Origines*. For discussion, see Cornell in *FRHist.* vol. 1, no 5.

60. See also F 49 = Gellius *NA* 10.3.5 from the same speech by comparison.

61. Cf. Cicero *Mur.* 88; Quintilian *Inst.* 11.3.115; Iulius Victor, RLM, p.443.3–4.

62. Euripides *Medea* 502–600.

63. Ennius *Medea* F 227–28 Jocelyn = Cicero *De or.* 3.217 with Fantham 2004, 293–94.

64. References to family members: For Cornelia, see Plutarch *C. Gracch.* 25.5–6; Seneca *Dial.* 12.16.6; Charis. GL 1 p. 102.20–103.1 = Manuwald 2019, no 48 F 65a, 65b, 66 with Dixon 2007, 22; and van der Blom 2016, 73.

65. See Adherbal's speech to the senate in Sallust *Iug.* 14 (written around 40), which is also based on this same rhetorical strategy and may be designed to recall Gaius' final days. For discussion, see Fowler 1987; Dué 2000; Fantham 2004, 293–94; and van der Blom 2016, 103–8.

66. L. Opimius (cos. 121, *RE* 4, Münzer) does not have an entry in *ORF* or in Manuwald 2019. M. Fulvius Flaccus (cos. 125, *RE* 58) is *ORF*[4] no. 40, but no fragments of any speeches survive. Cicero *Brut.* 108 provides the single piece of evidence that describes Fulvius as a mediocre orator.

67. My analysis is based on Malcovati in *ORF*[4] and Manuwald 2019. *The Fragments of the Roman Republican Orators* will provide many new insights into republican oratory.

68. For Mucianus as an orator, see notes 32–34, *ORF*[4] no. 31 with Manuwald 2019, and especially Cicero *De or.* 1.170, *Brut.* 98, and Gellius *NA* 1.13.9–10.

69. For P. Decius (tr. pl. 120, praetor 115, *RE* 9), see *ORF*[4] no. 36 with Manuwald 2019 (one testimonium and two fragments). Cicero *Brut.* 108: *ut vita sic oratione etiam turbulentus* (as in his life so in his public speaking [he was] unruly).

70. For L. Calpurnius Piso Frugi (tr. pl. 149, cos. 133, censor 120 or 108, *RE* 96), see *ORF*[4] no. 37 with Manuwald 2019 (one testimonium and two fragments).

71. See *FRHist.* no. 9 for his *Annales* with introduction and commentary by Mark Pobjoy.

72. For M. Livius Drusus (tr. pl. 122, cos. 112, censor 109, *RE* 17), see *ORF*[4] no. 42 with Manuwald 2019 (two testimonia and four fragments, all from the year of his tribunate).

73. For Drusus' unnamed associates, see Plutarch *C. Gracch.* 2.4 = *ORF*[4] no. 42 F 6 with Manuwald 2019, which records criticism of Gaius spending 1,250 drachmas per pound for silver dolphins. Cf. Pliny *HN* 33.147.

74. Other tribunes of 122:? M'. Acilius Glabrio (*RE* 37), Cn. Marcius Censorinus (*RE* 45), M. Fulvius Flaccus (*RE* 58), C. Rubrius (*RE* 2 cf. 9). The latter two were, however, supporters of Gaius. Rumors also circulated independently of public meetings; see Rosillo-López 2020 and 2022.

75. For Q. Aelius Tubero (tr. pl. 129, *RE* 155), see *ORF*[4] no. 45 with Manuwald 2019 (one testimonium and no fragments = Cicero *Brut.* 117–18). Tubero, a grandson of L. Aemilius Paullus (*RE* 12) and a nephew of Scipio Aemilianus (*RE* 21), was a prominent Stoic.

76. For M. Iunius Pennus (tr. pl. 126, subsequently aedile, RE 123), see *ORF*[4] no. 46 with Manuwald 2019 (one testimonium = Cicero *Brut.* 109). Cf. Festus 362. The clash between Pennus and Gaius suggests that Gaius may already have been circulating speeches in written form as quaestor.

77. Gaius was apparently not expecting to be tribune of the plebs in 122 since he was planning an extended trip to Africa.

78. For Gaius Fannius (cos. 122, *RE* 7), see *ORF*[4] no. 32 with Manuwald 2019 (seven fragments). This Fannius is not the same man as the historian, as argued by Cornell in *FRHist.* no. 12 and accepted by Manuwald 2019.

79. See *ORF*[4] no. 32 with Manuwald 2019, F 1–5 (Cicero, Iulius Victor, Charisius, Priscian). F 3: *si Latinis civitatem dederitis, credo, existimatis vos ita, ut nunc constititis, in con[ten]tione habituros locum aut ludis et festis diebus interfuturos? Nonne illos omnia occupaturos putatis?* (If you were to give citizenship to the Latins, in my opinion, do you think that you would still have a place to stand at public speeches or that you would be able to be spectators the games, as you now do? Do you not think that they would take up all the places?)

80. See Appian *B Civ.* 1.100 with van der Blom 2016, 100–101; and Elster 2020 no. 38, pp. 126–32. For the situation of the Italians in general, see now the thorough and detailed treatment in Roselaar 2019.

81. F 1 = Cicero *Brut.* 99–100. Atticus suggests that either C. Persius or many unnamed *nobiles* working together could be the author(s) of this speech.

82. For C. Papirius Carbo (tr. pl. 131 or 130, cos. 120, *RE* 33), see *ORF*[4] no. 35 with Manuwald 2019 (six testimonia and five fragments).

83. For Carbo on the commission to redistribute public land under Tiberius' law, see Cicero *Brut.* 103, 159; Livy *Per.* 59; and Appian *B Civ.* 1.18.73–74.

84. He was implicated by some in the sudden and much-debated death of Aemilianus (129), whom he had challenged in a *contio* after the murder of Tiberius (Diod. 34/35.33.7 with Pina Polo 1996, 50; and Mouritsen 2001, 53). Cicero *De or.* 2.170, *Fam.* 9.21.3. Cf. Cicero *QFr.* 2.3.3, *Mil.* 16, *Fat.* 18, *Fam.* 9.21.3, *Amic.* 12, Orosius 5.10.9.

85. F 8–11 (one of which may come from a different speaker). Decius was the prosecutor; see note 69.

86. Cic. *De or.* 2.170.

87. F 11 = Cicero *De or.* 2.169: *si Gracchus nefarie, praeclare Opimius* (if Gracchus [acted] wickedly, Opimius [acted] splendidly).

88. For Carbo's suicide, see Cicero *Verr.* 2.3.3, *De or.* 1.40 and 154, *Brut.* 103, *Fam.* 9.21.3, *Leg.* 3.35, Tacitus *Dial.* 34.7. For M. Licinius Crassus (cos. 95, *RE* 55) see *ORF*[4] no. 66 with Manuwald 2019, especially F 13–14.

89. There was no permanent, stone theater in Rome before the one dedicated by Pompey in 55. The increasing number of dramatic performances and games were staged in a variety of

temporary venues (Bernstein 1998). For example, the steps of large temples could serve as seating for the audience (Goldberg 1998 on the Palatine in the second century). Near the end of his life, Gaius had made a gladiatorial performance in the Forum accessible by removing the wooden seats, for which tickets were being sold (Plutarch *C. Gracch.* 12.3–4).

90. For Q. Roscius (Gallus?), see Von der Mühll (*RE* 16) with Treggiari 1969b, 139; Leppin 1992, 241–44; and Čulík-Baird 2022, 188–98. Nicolet 1966–74, no. 300n3 has him born into the equestrian rank. His sister married the equestrian P. Quinctius (Cicero *Quinct.* 77). For Roscius' book, see Macrobius *Sat.* 3.14.12, which is not mentioned by Bardon 1952, the exhaustive treatment of lost works of Latin literature. Sciarrino 2007, 64, argues that Cato the Elder already used theatrical techniques, including gestures and metrical patterns like those in Plautus.

91. For the *infamia* attached to actors, see Cicero *Rep.* 4.10 and Nepos pr.1.5.1 with Edwards 1993, 125–26; and Čulík-Baird 2022, 186–88.

92. Mostly enslaved: in general, see Leppin 1992 and Richlin 2017a and 2017b. For Roscius' free birth in Lanuvium, see Cicero *Nat. D.* 1.79. It is possible that he was the son of a (wealthy) freedman, which might explain his somewhat liminal status, but there is no explicit evidence about his family.

93. For Sulla and Roscius' equestrian census status, see Cicero, *Fam.* 10.32.2 and Macrobius *Sat.* 3.14.13 cf. 2.7.8 with Leppin 1992, 241–44. For his decision to forego his formerly high fees, see Cicero *QRosc.* 23, *Fam.* 9.22.1, *Arch.* 17, *Brut.* 290, Pliny *HN* 7.128, Tacitus *Dial.* 20, and Gellius *NA* 5.8.4.

94. For Q. Hortensius Hortalus' speaking style (cos. 69, *RE* 13, *ORF*^{4} no. 92), see especially Valerius Maximus 8.10.2 with Dyck 2008. For a chronological list of his attested speeches, see Bardon 1952, 214–16. Hortensius also wrote a treatise on oratory (Ovid *Tr.* 2.441), as well as erotic poems and *Annales* in prose (Velleius Paterculus 2.16.3 and *FRHist.* no. 31 Drummond).

95. Gellius *NA* 1.5.2–3.

96. The trial of P. Sulla (*RE* 385, Münzer, a nephew of the dictator) took place in the summer of 62 under the *lex Plautia de vi.* Cicero and Hortensius spoke for the defense, with Hortensius appearing first. The opposing lawyer, who is here dismissed as an uncouth person lacking in Greek cultural refinement, was Cicero's young friend L. Manlius Torquatus (praetor 49, *RE* 80, *ORF*^{4} no. 146 with Manuwald 2019). A son of the consul of 65 and Pompey's brother-in-law, Torquatus was an Epicurean, who appears as a character in Cicero's *De Finibus* (45). Torquatus also wrote poetry (Pliny *Ep.* 5.3.5) and is the dedicatee of Catullus poem 61, so hardly a stranger to Greek literature, philosophy, and culture.

97. For audience reactions in the theater, Nicolet 1976, 479–94, remains the classic discussion. Cicero asked M. Caelius Rufus to report to him regularly about audience reactions while he was away from Rome as governor of Cilicia in 51.

98. Pliny *Ep.* 2.11 with Sherwin-White 1966 and Whitton 2013 *ad loc.*

99. *Ep.* 2.11.

100. *Ep.* 4.16.3 attests Pliny speaking for seven hours. He had been very ill in AD 97.

101. Whitton 2013 *ad loc.* imagined that Trajan might be seated near Plinius so that he could speak to him directly.

102. Talbert 1984, 156, interprets this Plinius' presence as an exceptional concession to Pliny's fragile health. Whitton 2013 *ad loc.* suggests the occasion follows the custom of the law courts, where freedmen attendants were more usual. See Dio 60.16.3 for freedmen of the emperor present in the senate.

2. In the Households of Cato the Censor and Atticus the Businessman

1. The Latin word *familia* often refers primarily or even exclusively to the enslaved members of the household.

2. For Cato the Elder, see *RE* 9; and Suerbaum 2002, no. 162. For shorter introductions, see Briscoe and Spurr (*OCD*), Kierdorf (*BNP*), and now especially Cornell (*FRHist.* no. 5). The classic treatment of his life in English remains Astin 1978. A new edition of his works other than the *De Agricultura* is provided by Manuwald in two volumes (2023a and 2023b).

3. Cato was married twice and had a son named Marcus by each wife. His first wife was a Licinia (*RE* 177, Münzer), from the prominent family of the Licinii Crassi. Since his older son, nicknamed Licinianus (*RE* 4, Miltner, died as *praetor designatus* in 152), was born by c. 192, the marriage is usually dated a couple of years before, around the time of Cato's consulship in 195. Licinia died before her son married Aemilia Tertia (*RE* 180, Klebs) around 162 (Plutarch, *Cato Mai.* 24). Cato then married a Salonia, the young daughter of his former *scriba*, Salonius (Plutarch *Cato Mai.* 24), probably in the late 160s or early 150s. Salonius, as his name indicates, was not Cato's freedman, but perhaps a freedman or the son of a freedman connected to the senatorial family of the Salonii. His daughter Salonia was most probably freeborn. Her son, known as Salonianus (*RE* 15, Miltner), was born around 154, when Cato was 80 years old. See Plutarch *Cato Mai.* 24 and Gellius *NA* 13.20.

4. For the fragments of Cato's speeches, see *ORF*[4] no. 8, Sblendorio Cugusi 1982, Courtney 1999, Cugusi and Sblendorio Cugusi 2001, and Manuwald 2023b. For the *Origines* (in seven books), see Beck and Walter 2001, Chassignet 2002, *FRHist.* no. 5 (Cornell), and Manuwald 2023a.

5. Livy on Cato's self-praise: Livy 34.15.9. See also Plutarch *Cato Mai.* 14.2 and *De se ipsum citra invidiam laudando* 14.

6. For Cato's triumph, see Itgenshorst 2005, no. 172 (194).

7. For Cato as an author, see conveniently the overview by Cornell in *FRHist.* vol. 1, no. 5; and the introduction in Manuwald 2023a.

8. For M. Pomponius Atticus (*RE* Suppl. Vol. 8, 102, Feger), see Badian (*OCD*), Kierdorf (*BNP*), Drummond (*FRHist.* no. 33), and Hillard and Beness (*BNJ* no. 189).

9. Nepos *Atticus* 13 is quoted on page 52.

10. For Atticus' works, see Drummond *FRHist.* no. 33. They included *Imagines*, a Greek work on Cicero's consulship, and especially his *Liber Annalis*, dedicated to Cicero. He also wrote family histories, often on the request of prominent friends. Dortmund 2001 shows that he did not have a publishing business on anything like a commercial scale.

11. For Nepos' biography, see the commentary by Horsfall 1989. For Cicero's letters to Atticus, see the commentaries by Shackleton-Bailey in seven volumes (1965–71), as well as his Loeb edition. Shackleton-Bailey 1965, 1–45, remains the most detailed exposition of the friendship between Cicero and Atticus, as well as the best guide to the chronology and movements of each person.

12. For Atticus' father, see Nepos *Att.* 1 with Horsfall 1989 *ad loc.*

13. Atticus' move to Athens: Nepos *Att.* 2. Horsfall 1989 *ad loc.* stresses Atticus' humble start in Athens, which he dates to immediately after Sulla's victory.

14. Marshall 1999, 62, argues that Atticus will have served with Sulla and Lucullus in the Social War. She has him move east early and specifically to support Sulla's expedition against

Mithridates. But there is no evidence for Atticus leaving Rome before Sulla captured Athens. The help he offered various people, including young Marius, suggests he was still in Rome in 87.

15. For Anicia and Sulpicius, see Nepos *Att.* 2 with Horsfall 1989 *ad loc.* Anicia's mother will have been a sister of Atticus' father. Marshall 1999, 63, elucidates the ways in which Atticus was connected both to the tribune Sulpicius and to Sulla in 88. See also Cicero *Amic.* 2. This painful, early experience of being in the middle of civil conflict seems to have been formative for Atticus.

16. Given how much information we do have about Atticus, it seems unlikely that an earlier marriage was never mentioned by Cicero or Nepos or any other source. Rather Atticus remained unmarried until he married Pilia on February 12, 56, at the age of 54. Horsfall 1989, 65, speculates about a first marriage.

17. Atticus' business dealings have been much discussed. See especially Perlwitz 1992, Welch 1996, Jones 1999, and Marshall 1999.

18. For the Epirus estate (now in southern Albania), see the detailed discussion in Perlwitz 1992, 66–78, with a map. He argues for a very extensive property (c. 15,000 hectares), which could have been acquired earlier than the first references in 68.

19. Shackleton-Bailey 1965, 12, dates Atticus' return to Rome to January 64.

20. Atticus' adoption in the will of Q. Caecilius took place in September 58, at a time when Cicero had gone into exile. He kept his *cognomen* Atticus.

21. Pilia (*RE* 3, Münzer) is never mentioned by Nepos but often receives greetings from Cicero and other members of his family. The Pilii were an established family from Cora in Latium (*CIL* 1^2 1509). See Syme 1986, 314n9; and Horsfall 1989, 65–66.

22. For Atticus' neutrality, see for example Millar 1988 and now Volk 2021, 104–8.

23. For the military service of Cato's father and grandfather, see Plutarch *Cato Mai.* 1.

24. For the young Cato working on the land, see Plutarch *Cato Mai.* 2–3.

25. Plutarch *Cato Mai.* 3 and 4.

26. For the young Cato and his servant in the army, see Plutarch *Cato Mai.* 1.

27. Interestingly, Cato would later instruct his staff never to share any information about his life or movements with anyone outside the household (Plutarch *Cato Mai.* 21.1). One wonders what had changed in the intervening years.

28. For the development of slavery in second century, see Čulík-Baird 2019; and Flower 2022a with earlier bibliography. Note also Sallust *BJ* 85.39 where Marius is described as complaining that his political rivals criticize him for not having expensive slaves in his house in Rome: *sordidum me et incultis moribus aiunt, quia parum scite convivium exorno neque histrionem ullum neque pluris preti coquom quam uilicum habeo* (They say I am vulgar and uncultivated in my way of life because I do not know how to put on an elaborate dinner party, I have not a single actor in my household, and I do not own a cook who cost more than a farm manager). Cicero *Pis.* 27.67 alleges that Piso had shabby slaves serve at table.

29. The job of the *vilicus* is described in detail at *De Agric.* 5. Section 5 is especially relevant here. Carlsen 1995 offers a discussion in a broader context with attention to epigraphical evidence.

30. For the *De Agricultura*, see Suerbaum 2002, no. 162.3, p. 400–409.

31. For Cato at Tarraco in 195, see Astin 1978, 42.

32. See the fragments of Cato's speech against Q. Minucius Thermus (cos. 193) in 190 attacking his harsh treatment of the Bruttians (Cugusi 2001; F42 = *ORF*[4] 8; F58 = Gellius *NA* 10.3.17 = Manuwald 2023b, F 58). See Cugusi and Sblendorio Cugusi 2001, 277–83. Thermus was denied a triumph. One may also note the speech attacking a certain P. Furius (*In P. Furium pro Hispanis de frumento*) in Cugusi and Sblendorio Cugusi 2001, 109–11 of 171 (Livy 43.2), which discusses the greed and arrogance (*superbia*) of Roman magistrates who treat allies as if they were enemies. Huemoeller 2021 discusses who was and was not enslaved among prisoners of war.

33. For Cato's tax on young slaves during his censorship, see Livy 39.44.3 and Plutarch *Cato Mai.* 18. For Roman concepts of luxury in general, see now Berno 2023.

34. See especially Cato's disapproval at some young men paying a talent for a young boy, Diodorus 31.24.

35. *FRHist.* 5 F88 = Peter F95b = Chassignet F3b = Cugusi F101 = *ORF*[4] 8 F164 = Manuwald 2023b F 164: *ne sub solo imperio nostro in seruitute nostra essent* (in order not to be under our sole dominion enslaved to us).

36. The next sentence reads: *Libertatis suae causa in ea sententia fuisse arbitror* (It was for the sake of their freedom that they had this opinion, I think).

37. Cato here effectively negates the vocabulary of *amicitia* so often used by Romans to mask a variety of power relationships. For further analysis of this speech, see Flower 2020.

38. For Cato regularly buying young captives, see Plutarch *Cato Mai.* 21.1.

39. Plutarch *Cato Mai.* 4.4 and Gellius *NA* 13.24.

40. Plutarch *Cato Mai.* 2 with Astin 1978, 159–60, who argues that Cato learned Greek young and was certainly fluent by 191. Much discussion has centered on Cato's familiarity with Greek literature. But his early travels to Greek-speaking locations (Sicily and southern Italy) and his interest in acquiring prisoners after wars suggest that he will have found learning to speak the contemporary version of the language useful, if not essential.

41. For Chilon, see Plutarch *Cato Mai.* 20, 3–4 with Astin 1978, 342.

42. Cato's elder son Marcus, who died in late 152 after being elected praetor for the following year (*praetor designatus*), is usually thought to have been born in 192 or 191. See Astin 1978, 54; and Cornell in *FRHist.* no. 5.

43. For the sixth-century Spartan politician and elegiac poet Chilon, see Cartledge (*OCD*) and Welwei and Furley (*BNP*) with further bibliography.

44. For Cato and Greek culture, see Astin 1978, 157–81; and Gruen 1992.

45. For the legal position of the *vicarius*, see Kirschenbaum 1987, 31–88; and Reduzzi Merola 1990. Plutarch could have missed this option. Mouritsen 2013 elucidates household structure.

46. Sick 1999, 337–38, gives an alternative reconstruction that does not convince because he has the slaveowners do everything at Cato's expense and then "give" (rather than "sell") him the boys at the end of the year.

47. For the *peculium* (a fund of money controlled by anyone who was not legally independent, including women, minors, children with living fathers, and enslaved persons), see now Gamauf 2023 with earlier bibliography. Almost all the surviving sources are from legal texts; they are mostly prescriptive rather than descriptive.

48. See especially Mouritsen 2013 for the Statilii Tauri of the first century AD. The majority of enslaved individuals attested by inscriptions in this family's tomb were owned by other members of the household, not directly by the family. Some of these enslaved or manumitted slaveowners had many slaves they had acquired.

49. See also a scheme involving sex for pay in Cato's household, described by Plutarch at *Cato Mai.* 21.2. As Astin notes (1978, 263), the Greek text is ambiguous about who receives the fees paid by male slaves for sex with female slaves within the household. Allowing women (who chose to participate?) to be paid in this way would have given them an opportunity to save money for themselves. It is hard to see how this would have operated on a farm, however, since the one described by Cato in *De Agricultura* only has one woman (the *vilica*) living there, who is not obviously enslaved. This seems, therefore, to be a description of practices in Cato's town house in Rome. Again, it is Cato who fixes the price for transactions within his household. He also benefits since any child born to a woman enslaved by him (regardless of who the father was) will also be his *verna*.

50. For Cato in Spain in the years 195 and 194, see Livy 34 and 35 and Plutarch *Cato Mai.* 10–11 with Astin 1978, 28–50.

51. His five personal attendants will have represented the staff Cato brought with him at his own expense, which could have included both current members of his household and freedmen, whose jobs will have ranged from domestic chores, to looking after the horses, to administrative tasks. As praetor in Sardinia, he made use of only one attendant at public expense (*dēmosios*), who is a different category of attendant (Plutarch *Cato Mai.* 6), probably a public slave (*servus publicus*). The precise details may have escaped Plutarch, who was living in a different time.

52. For Paccius, see Plutarch *Cato Mai.* 10.5. He is explicitly said to be one of the five "servants" (*therapontes*). Plutarch seems not to know exactly who this man was.

53. Cato is explicit about his staff and friends not profiting from his command. This policy fits into a much larger context of not wanting a general to have so much control over war booty of various kinds (especially *manubiae*).

54. This fact, as well as his name (*nomen*), suggests that Paccius was someone else's freedman, who was not necessarily expecting to interact regularly with Cato after returning from Spain, where he would have traveled on a special assignment. The Paccii were not, however, a prominent family in the second century. It is interesting to see what looks like a documented case of Cato employing a freedman from a different household, presumably for a special administrative skill.

55. See chapter 6 for the story of Dymas and Diokles.

56. For Quintio, see Plutarch *Cato Mai.* 21.5–6; and Astin 1978, 250–51, 263.

57. Plutarch strongly disapproves of maritime loans. Cato's arrangement is designed to work around the *lex Claudia* (Elster 2003, no. 83, from the year 218) that specifically forbade senators from themselves owning anything except a small ship.

58. For Cato's *vilicus*, see *Agr.* 5.

59. For the *vilica*, see *Agr.* 143 with Roth 2004 and Hallett 2021.

60. Plutarch claims Cato preferred and even fostered disharmony among his household (*Cato Mai.* 21), but Cato's own instructions to a *vilicus* to create a harmonious community are clear and make much more practical sense (*Agr.* 5). Cato's custom of allowing the household to judge a fellow slave when his life was at stake also looks like a shrewd if sinister co-opting move, treating the household almost like a *consilium* (Plutarch *Cato Mai.* 21). Cato wants to avoid a situation where he puts an enslaved person to death and the staff then turn against him. Rather he aims to unite them against the wrongdoer.

61. For Cato's writings, see notes 2 and 7.

62. For the *Origines*, see note 4.

63. The history for the son (*libri ad filium*) is mentioned by Plutarch *Cato Mai.* 20. See Astin 1978, 332–40; and Manuwald 2023b, 276–95. This work in its original form may not have been meant for wider circulation.

64. See *ORF*[4] no. 8, F 173 = Manuwald 2023b, F 173 with Sciarrino 2007, 65.

65. For the variety of Roman writing tablets, see conveniently the *Roman Inscriptions of Britain* (https://romaninscriptionsofbritain.org), which includes the Vindolanda and Bloomberg tablets.

66. Cato and Greek literature, see Astin 1978, 157–81; and Flower 2020.

67. His small house is commented on by Plutarch *Cato Mai.* 24.

68. *Agr.* 2.7: *patrem familias vendacem, non emacem esse oportet* (A head of household should be a producer of goods to be sold, not a consumer).

69. See the detailed instructions about raising sheep attributed to Atticus as a speaker in book 2 of Varro's *De Re Rustica* (written in 37, set in 67). For Atticus as a slaveholder, probably a demanding one, see Iris Samotta in *HAS*, 271–75.

70. For Atticus' businesses, see Horsfall 1989, 61–63 and 91–93; Perlwitz 1992, 34–85; Welch 1996; and Marshall 1999.

71. For Atticus' literary interests, see Rawson 1985 *ad loc* and Drummond in *FRHist.* no. 33 and Philipp Fondermann in *HAS*, 275–76. Cicero does, on occasion, refer to him as a *grammaticus* (*Att.* 1.14.3 and 7.32.10). Tyrannio's book on Greek meter was dedicated to Atticus.

72. Mouritsen 2017, 222n25, provides a complete list.

73. For Atticus' houses, see Marshall 1999, 59–60. According to Nepos *Att.* 14.3 he also owned land at Arretium in Etruria.

74. Attested interests are in Sicyon, Macedonia, Delos, Corcyra, and Sybota but there were surely many more since our sources are not detailed on this subject. For discussion, see Horsfall 1989, 92; and Perlwitz 1992, 43–44, 47. Jones 1999 discusses epigraphical evidence for Atticus' connections with Ephesus.

75. This house on the Quirinal had belonged to one of the Baebii Tamphili. Horsfall 1989, 87–88, identifies its site as the Palazzo della Consulta, facing the main entrance to the Quirinal Palace. A Pomponius is still on an inscription here from the time of Trajan (*CIL* 6.1492). If this is a freedman, he is descended from someone who was manumitted before Atticus inherited the house. See also Eck in *LTUR*.

76. Shackleton-Bailey 1965, 1–45, remains the most detailed reconstruction of Atticus' movements. See p. 4 and 6 for his regular trips to Rome for elections.

77. Horsfall 1989, 67: "Who was to call Atticus a legacy-hunter?" The story in Valerius Maximus (7.8.5) that the Roman populace reacted negatively because Caecilius was expected to leave his money to Lucius Licinius Lucullus seems exaggerated and implausible but may still perhaps suggest that people were surprised at the time that Atticus inherited so much from his mother's brother.

78. Nepos *Att.* 1.1.

79. For Atticus as a possible early editor of Cicero's letters (although perhaps not for publication), see Perlwitz 1992, 20–29.

80. Samotta (*HAS*, 272–74) offers an incisive picture of Atticus as a demanding slaveholder.

81. For literacy rates in Rome, see Harris 1989, who estimates overall literacy at only about 10 percent of the population. Woolf 2011 offers a thoughtful discussion of how to use inscribed

objects and economic relations to explore the expansion of literacy within the Roman imperial context. Houston 2014, 16, describes all Atticus' staff as "copyists."

82. For Attica's birth in 51, see Horsfall 1989, 84. She does not appear in Cicero's letters to Atticus until book 5, but is then a regular topic. Her parents married in February 56, so she will in any case not have been born before the end of that year at the earliest.

83. Other ways to acquire slaves included through legacies, for example, of which Atticus will surely have received many from his friends over the years. Alternatively, enslaved persons might be sold together with the animals they cared for, for example a herd of sheep. Varro (*RR* 2.9) speaks of a herd of sheep purchased with their sheepdogs but without their shepherds by P. Aufidius Pontianus of Amiternum. As a result, the loyal dogs leave the sheep to follow their shepherd-masters all the way back home to Umbria. The implication is that the same shepherds should have been retained as part of a team with the dogs and probably also the sheep.

84. Nepos *Att.* 2 with Horsfall 1989, *ad loc.*

85. Marshall 1999 argues that Atticus owned land in Epirus, possibly inherited, before 68, but there is no ancient evidence. She sees him as much richer earlier in life as a result of inherited property and investments in Greece and in Asia. Her reconstruction has not, however, attracted many followers.

86. Nepos on household accounts: *Att.* 13. Horsfall 1989, 90, thinks that Nepos has not actually seen these accounts himself. The monthly expenditure should presumably be expressed in sesterces, not in asses.

87. For Atticus and Octavian, see Nepos *Att.* 19 with Horsfall 1989, 103, who describes *elegantia* as "a quality of mind as well as of taste." Suetonius *Aug.* 73.1 comments on the studied simplicity of Augustus' lifestyle. Both men had a deep interest in Roman customs and antiquarianism, as well as in the promotion of a national literature in Latin.

88. Atticus' gladiators are mentioned by Cicero (*Att.* SB 78 = 4.4a, 346 = *Att.* 13.37.4).

89. Edmondson 2016 provides a thorough and revealing analysis. Cicero comments to his brother that gladiators are changing hands rapidly (*QFr.* 2.5.3 = SB 9). Pompey broke up Caesar's gladiator troop in 49 (*Att.* 4.4a.2).

90. Cicero *Att.* 4.4a = SB 78.

91. Edmondson 2016, 46, traces some subsequent purchasers of gladiators once owned by Atticus during the mid to late-50s. These enslaved fighters presumably also reveal that Atticus was an active participant in the slave trade, rather than simply a trainer of *vernae* as gladiators.

92. Treggiari 1969a and 1969b Appendix 3, 253–64; and Mouritsen 2017.

93. For M. Tullius Tiro (*RE* 52), see Treggiari 1969b, 259–63; Zelzer (*BNP*); Badian (*OCD*); McDermott 1972; Tempest in Wiley's *Encyclopedia of Ancient History* (2012); and Blänsdorf 2016, 126–34.

94. Mouritsen 2017 offers an incisive analysis of Cicero's household in town. He estimates that Atticus and many others will have had larger domestic staffs. See also Daubigny 1976; and Blänsdorf 2016, 87–90. At *Fam.* 14.7.3 Cicero talks about the need to move his household to his estate in Arpinum when food prices spike. This may suggest that he has many mouths to feed.

95. Treggiari 1969b, 253–55, lists 10 freedmen connected with Cicero's household (including Terentia's freedman Philotimus). By comparison, her list of Cicero's own freedmen contains 8 named individuals, plus a further 6 who may still be enslaved or could be manumitted. See Mourtisen 2017, 222n25, who lists the references to the 23 named members of Atticus' household mentioned in Cicero's surviving letters.

96. See *Att.* 16.20 for Tiro cataloging Cicero's library at Tusculum, with Hurka in *HAS*, 3082–83.

97. Library workers helping Tyrannio: *Att.* 4.4a = SB 78 and 4.8 = SB 79.

98. Cicero *Att.* 4.8.2 with Rawson 1985, 41.

99. For Terentius Philotimus, see Fündling (*BNP*) with Treggiari 1969b, 263–64 no. 9; and Blänsdorf 2016, 102–3. For marriage without *manus*, see Treggiari 1991, 16–36, especially 32–36, 442–46, 459–61.

100. Suspicions and complaints are voiced at Cicero *Att.* 5.8, 5.17.1, and 7.1.9; *Fam.* 4.2.1. Tiro was also familiar with the accounts (*Fam.* 16.24.1)

101. For Eros, presumably by now manumitted by Atticus, see Cicero *Fam.* 7.23.3 with Blänsdorf 2016, 104.

102. For Philotimus' slaves, see Cicero *Att.* 10.15.1. For his role at the *Lupercalia*, see Cicero *Att.* 12.5.1.

103. For Publilia, see Treggiari 2007, 134–35, 140–42.

104. Tullia's divorce from Dolabella took place late in the year 46 (Treggiari 2007, 131).

105. Other accountants who appear in the letters are Quintus Cicero's Statius and Atticus' Philogenes (*Att.* 5.13.2 and 7.7.2 with Mouritsen 2011, 236; and Blänsdorf 2016, 105).

106. For Dionysius, see Kierdorf (*BNP*); Treggiari 1969b, 119–21; Christes 1979, 107–15, Rawson 1985, 70–71; Guard 2011, 37–39; Blänsdorf 2016, 123, 135–37; and Mouritsen 2017, 215–16. Warwick's (2024) argument that this Dionysius, freedman of Atticus, should be equated with Cicero's slave of the same name is unconvincing, if only for chronological reasons.

107. He is first mentioned in *Att.* 4.8a = SB 82 (November 17, 56?). As already argued by Shackleton-Bailey 1965, 183, it is not plausible to see this same man as the Dionysius who is gluing the books at Antium in the spring of 56 (*Att.* 4.4a.1 = SB 78 and 4.8.2 = SB 79). The Dionysius who is close to Cicero had taken his *praenomen* before 58.

108. Dionysius is waiting for Cicero in mid-November 55 (*Att.* 4.13 = SB 87).

109. For Cicero and Dionysius, see the detailed reconstruction of their interactions in Christes 1979, 107–15; and the overview in Rawson 1985, 70–71. Mouritsen 2017, 216, draws attention to their reconciliation by the year 45.

110. Dionysius in Cilicia: *Att.* 5.9.3, 6.1.12, 6.2.3, 7.3.10.

111. For the stand-off in 49, see *Att.* 7.4.1, 7.7.1, and 7.18.3.

112. *Att.* 8.4.1, 9.12.2, 10.2.2, 10.16.1.

113. Christes 1979, 111n25, tries to reconstruct the whole encounter between Dionysius and Cicero at Formiae based on *Att.* 8.5.1.

114. Atticus and Dionysius: *Att.* 9.15.5, 13.33a.1. Cicero does not ask Atticus to compel Dionysius to return to him. Presumably it was not legal for him to do so.

115. *Att.* 7.18.3.

116. See chapter 6 for the possibly similar situation of L. Ateius Philologus.

117. Rawson 1985, 70, calls him irritable and "capable of self-assertion."

118. *Sanctus* (venerable, distinguished, holy): *Att.* 6.1.12 and 7.4.1. The only other person so described in the correspondence is P. Nigidius Figulus (*Fam.* 4.13.3), who is much closer to being Cicero's social equal.

119. Dionysius' wealth: *Att.* 8.10.

120. For Dionysius' son, see *Att.* 13.26 and 13.33a.2 with Seneca *Controv.* 1.4.11 and Rawson 1985, 71n23.

121. For Philotimus' enthusiastic support of Pompey, see Cicero *Att.* 9.7.6 and 10.9.1.

122. For mentions of other freedmen, including greetings sent to them from Cicero, see Mouritsen 2017, 222n90.

123. For Alexis, see Cicero *Att.* 5.20.9 = SB 113 (December 19, 51), 7.2.3 = SB 125 (Brundisium, November 25, 50), 7.7.7 = SB 130 (Formiae, December 19, 50), 12.10.1 = SB 247 (Tusculum, summer or autumn 46), and 16.15.1 = SB 426 (Arpinum, after November 12, 44).

124. Alexis' handwriting: *Att.* 7.2.3 = SB 125 and 16.15.1 = SB 426, separated by about six years. Suetonius (*Aug.* 64) notes that Augustus had his grandsons Gaius and Lucius trained to imitate his own handwriting.

125. Atticus' malaria is analyzed as a typical case by Salares 2002, 131–32.

126. For Phemius, see *Att.* 5.20.9. 5.21.9, 6.1.13 with the insightful discussion by Morgan 2019. Samotta (*HAS*, 274) argues that Phemius' horn was an example of Atticus' expenditure on a luxury item. But it is possible that Cicero was expected to cover the cost as a favor to his friend.

127. For Q. Caecilius Epirota (*PIR*^{2} C 42), see Kaster's 1995 commentary on Suetonius' *Gram. et rhet.* 16; Kaster (*OCD* and *BNP*); Treggiari 1969b, 11, 123, 248; Christes 1979, 61–64; and Rawson 1985, 46–47, 69, 75, 102–3, 317.

128. Pomponia's marriage to Quintus Cicero had taken place by the early 60s. It is impossible to know who Epirota's father was.

129. Cicero *Att.* 1.14.7.

130. The adornment of Cicero's Tusculan villa is already a topic in some of his earliest letters to Atticus in 68 and 67, for example *Att.* 1.5 = SB 1 (November 68).

131. Varro *RR* 2.2.1.

132. For the naming of *vernae*, see especially Bruun 2013 with analysis of around 600 relevant inscriptions from the city of Rome. It is not surprising to see that Atticus kept a careful record of his human property, even when loans to family members were involved. In this case the loan bore fruit that he reclaimed.

133. Was Epirota forced to leave his mother young in order to enter Atticus' training program? Or did his mother return to Atticus after her (possibly lengthy) stay with Pomponia at Tusculum?

134. The date of Attica's marriage is suggested by her own age and by the fact that her daughter Vipsania Agrippina was born in 36. Vipsania was first married to Tiberius, the future emperor, and then to a son of Asinius Pollio. For this daughter of Agrippa, see *ILS* 165 and 8540; Tacitus *Ann.* 1.12, 3.19, 4.61; Suetonius *Tib.* 7; Dio 58.3 with *PIR* V 462; Raepsaet-Charlier 1987, p. 632 no. 811; and Syme 1986, 314. See now Zhang 2024 for a detailed discussion of the marriage.

135. The scandal involving Epirota and Attica must be dated between the time of her marriage to Agrippa (in 37) and Cornelius Gallus' departure for the East, perhaps in 31. It seems to have happened while Atticus was still alive (therefore before the end of March 32). A date in 36 or 35 seems plausible. It certainly happened well before Agrippa's marriage to Marcella in c. 28, by which time Attica, if she was still alive, would surely have been too old for a tutor in any case. See also Rohr Vio 2000, 77n202 and 150–51, who thinks Gallus was already in Egypt at the time and that Epirota fled there in order to escape from Rome.

136. No one stood to benefit from a scandal like this one, let alone one that was so talked about outside the household. Epirota had clearly been deemed completely trustworthy but (was

perceived to have) failed. The blame was put entirely on him because of Attica's young age and female sex.

137. Private tutors for women: Plutarch *Pomp.* 55 and Hemelrjik 2004.

138. For C. Cornelius Gallus (*RE* 164, *PIR*[2] C 1369) an equestrian from Forum Iulii, see Courtney (*OCD*); Stroh (*BNP*); Hollis 2007, 219; and Kaster 1995 *ad loc.* all with extensive bibliography, including on the papyrus fragments of Gallus' poetry and the epigraphical evidence for his remarkable career in Egypt, on which see now Myers 2018.

139. The exact reasons for Gallus' disgrace are not essential to the present discussion. See Suetonius *Aug.* 66.2; Ovid *Tr.* 2.446; Dio 53.23 with Rohr Vio 2000, 147–69; and Flower 2006, 125–29, figures 19–21, 316.

140. Horsfall 1989, 104, assumes that Agrippa divorced Attica to marry Marcella. But no direct information survives. Reinhold 1972 argues that Attica survived and had a daughter, who went on to marry P. Quinctilius Varus.

141. If Epirota had traveled east with Gallus in the armies of Octavian, it is less surprising that Augustus knows who he is in 27 or 26. The perceived arrogance of each of these two close friends may have affected the reputation of the other.

142. For the schools of the *grammatici*, see Christes 1979 and Kaster 1995.

143. For Epirota's teaching style, see Jocelyn 1988, 59; Goldschmidt 2014, 31; and especially Kaster 1995, 187: "It was the first of E's innovations that he not only gave a gramm.'s typical lectures, tied to the line-by-line expository reading of poetry (*praelectio*), but also engaged in extempore lectures or discussions (on literary texts, or on other grammatical subjects) of a freer and less formal sort, perhaps with give-and-take between himself and his pupils."

144. Epirota may, in fact, not have been seriously short of money at all by this stage of his life, as suggested by Christes 1979, 64.

145. Kaster 1995 *ad loc.* notes Suetonius' apparent misinterpretation of this quotation, which suggests that Epirota produced poets through his teaching rather than simply teaching poetry. Christes 1979, 64, speculates that Ovid could have been one of his pupils.

146. For the neoteric poets in Rome, see Crowther 1970 and Lyne 1978.

147. For Epirota and the teaching of Vergil in schools, see Christes 1979, 63–64; Horsfall 1995; and Goldschmidt 2014, 31.

148. For Parthenius of Nicaea, see Williams (*OCD*) and Fornaro (*BNP*) with Lightfoot 1999 and Francese 2001. For Maecenas, see chapter 5 in the section on Melissus.

149. New attention to graffiti from the Bay of Naples raises questions about who could read and who could write in the years before the eruption of Vesuvius in AD 79.

3. The Homegrown and the Immigrant: Quintus Lutatius Daphnis the Freedman and Archias of Antioch the Greek Poet

1. See also chapter 6 for educated war captives, some of whom were not so young when they came to Rome.

2. The Roman colony was established in 184 (Livy 39.44.10 and Velleius Paterculus 1.15.2). For Daphnis, see also an earlier version of this discussion in Flower 2022b.

3. In contrast to Daphnis, Licinius was probably never sold, let alone at a public auction.

4. See Pliny *HN* 7.128 and Suetonius *Gram. et rhet.* 3.5–6, both quoted and discussed in the next section.

5. Cicero's *QRosc.* 28 and 29 suggests a sum that may be as high as HS 600,000 for a trained comedian but the text is uncertain. The price could instead be HS 100,000.

6. Habinek 2005 issues a challenge to scholars to consider the role of enslaved labor in the production of Latin literary texts. See already Bardon 1952, 122; Treggiari 1969b, 110 and 119; and now especially Fitzgerald 2000; Joshel 2011; and Blake 2012.

7. For *grammatici*, the classic treatment remains Christes 1979, to be supplemented by Rawson 1985, 66–76; Kaster 1995 on Suetonius' *De Grammaticis et Rhetoribus*; and more succinctly McNelis 2007.

8. For Roman *vernae* in general, see Herrmann-Otto 1994, but she does not discuss highly educated individuals in any detail. See Bradley 1985 for the roles of skilled slaves. Temin 2013, 129 and 133, argues for education as the defining factor in shaping the labor market for both free and unfree in the larger Roman economic context. For a fascinating inscription that records the education of a young slave in Pisaurum in the second century AD, see now Vesperini 2022.

9. M. Aemilius Scaurus (*RE* 140 Klebs) was a patrician, probably born in the late 160s, who was consul in 115, *princeps senatus* in Africa in 112 and 111, censor in 109, and died in late 90 or very early 89. See Suerbaum 2002, no. 170 with *FRHist.* no. 18 (Christopher Smith).

10. Cicero *Font.* 24 offers an idealized picture of Scaurus as an all-powerful politician.

11. For Q. Lutatius Catulus' career (*RE* 7 Münzer), see Suerbaum 2002 no. 172 and *FRHist.* no. 19 (Christopher Smith).

12. For the 12 surviving fragments (with commentary), see Chassignet 2004, xvi–xxii, and no. 2 under the entry for Catulus; Walter 2009; and *FRHist.* no. 32 (Christopher Smith). The citing authors are Probus, Servius, *Origo Gentis Romae*, Lydus, Solinus, *Fasti Praenestini*, and Varro. The subjects cover the following: F1 Apollo Musagetes; F2 Baiae is named after Aeneas' companion Euxinus' nurse Boia; F3 Aeneas and the miraculous sow; F4 Aeneas becomes king of the Latins after killing Turnus; F5 name of the river Albula; F6 Neapolis' foundation; F7 Janus; F8 Aeneas betrays Troy to the Greeks; F9 the date of Rome's founding; F10 Romulus' staff found on Palatine; F11 aetiology of the Lacus Curtius; F12 aetiology for the name of the island Prochyta.

13. See Christopher Smith and Tim Cornell in *FRHist.* vol. 1, 96–101, for a discussion of this text as a source for much earlier historiographical material.

14. See Chassignet 2002, xxii, for the various theories that have been put forward.

15. For Cato's *Origines*, see Beck and Walter 2001 no. 3, p. 148–224; Chassignet 2002; and *FRHist.* no. 5 (Cornell).

16. See Bardon 1952, 121–22; and Smith in *FRHist.* vol 1. no. 32, p. 343.

17. See Jahn 1843 followed by Peter 1877 (although Peter changed his mind later when he was editing the fragments of the Roman historians).

18. See *FRHist.* nos. 19 and 32 (Christopher Smith). Smith identifies Lutatius the historiographer as Q. Lutatius Daphnis (with full bibliography). By contrast, Chassignet 2004, xxi; and Walter 2009 attribute the fragments to Q. Lutatius Catulus his patron, partly because of the very Roman and Italian subject matter.

19. See *FRHist.* no. 32 F 8 = *OGR* 9.2-5 = Chassignet 2002, F2. Through his mother's marriage to Lucius Julius Caesar, Catulus had two half brothers who were Julii Caesares.

20. See also, for example, the confusion of the elder and younger Plinys, which is elegantly highlighted by Gibson 2020, 1–3.

21. For example, Suetonius *Gram. et rhet.* 17 (with Kaster 1995) discusses the career of M. Verrius Flaccus without mentioning his ground-breaking and hugely influential alphabetical

Latin dictionary *De Verborum Significatu* or his *Fasti*, fragments of which have been rediscovered in an inscription from Praeneste (Palazzo Massimo alle Terme, *MNR* 10062, *II* 13.2.17 = *ILS* 8744a).

22. See Beck and Walter 2001, 27, and Walter 2004 for a broader consideration of the ways in which Romans thought about and represented their past, in texts and other media.

23. See Kay 2014, 202–6, on the markets for luxury items in Rome. Holleran 2012, 239: "Conspicuous consumption is about more than just expenditure and ostentation: it is a means of communicating with a particular audience." For Roman *luxuria*, see now Berno 2023.

24. For the Roman slave supply, see Jongman 2003 and Scheidel 2005 with chapter 6.

25. For prices in a broader context, see Duncan-Jones 1982, 348–50; and Scheidel 2005, 7–8, who suggests a benchmark price of about HS 2000. Temin 2013, 137–38, discusses prices in relation to education.

26. See Treggiari 1975 and Horsfall 1989, 88–89.

27. See the complaints of Cato the Elder discussed in chapter 2.

28. For the house of Scaurus, see *LTUR* (Papi) with Carandini 1988, 370 figure 2 (the extensive slave quarters); and Carandini 2017, 227 and 232, table 66. For the house of Catulus, see *LTUR* (Coarelli) with Carandini 2017, 235, table 68.

29. See McKeown 2007 for an introduction to the bibliography. Kay 2014, 178–82 and Temin 2013, 114–38, provide essential economic background.

30. For two case studies of education within the household, see chapter 2.

31. Unfortunately, the fragmentary nature of Cicero's speech and its uncertain date (c. 72–70) make the legal case, which was brought many years after Panurgus' death (perhaps in the time of Sulla's dictatorship or earlier in the 80s), very obscure. For discussion, see the edition of Hinard and Benferhat 2006; Lintott 2008, 60–67; and now especially Čulík-Baird 2022.

32. *QRosc.* 28: *facies non erat, ars erat pretiosa* (it was not his looks, it was his art/skill that was valuable); *ex artificio comico aestimabat* (he was valued for his skill as a comedian). See Leppin 1992, 47. *QRosc.* 30 mentions Eros, perhaps also an enslaved or recently freed actor, who trains with Roscius but at his own request (and expense?). Eros appears not to have a patron and begs Roscius to be taken on as his pupil. Cf. Cicero *Fam.* 13.16 = SB 316 (c. 45) for the quest of Apollonius, a learned freedman of Crassus, who needed to seek support from new patrons after Crassus' death in battle at Carrhae some years before. Axer 1979 tries to make sense of the numbers in Cicero's speech.

33. For chronological overviews, see Bang 2008, 202; Kay 2014, 189–213; and Tan 2017, 6–9.

34. For the status and census rating of an *eques*, see Davenport 2019, 34–38, 66–67, 204–6.

35. According to Cic. *Rep.* 7.17, this silver, presumably mostly in the form of household or decorative items, was worth HS 3.36 million.

36. Nepos *Att.* 14.1–2 is suggestive of Atticus' lifestyle and expenditures. See chapter 2 for a more detailed analysis.

37. Diodorus 37.3.2–5 with Kienast 1954, 77. Cato spoke frequently about the high price of slaves (fragments of speeches, *ORF*[4] no. 8 with Polybius 31.25.4–5 and Diodorus 31.24 and 37.3.5).

38. Zanda 2011 provides a thorough discussion and collection of the evidence.

39. But in fact, Pliny the Elder already seems to be making this same observation in the 70s CE. Prices for the educated may well have stabilized by the time Pliny was writing, over 150 years later.

40. Pliny *HN* 7.128 quoted on page 67.

41. See Suetonius *Iul.* 47 quoted in the epigraph.

42. See Asconius 23, 24, and 26 St., Valerius Maximus 4.4.11, *de vir ill.* 72.1. His humble beginnings were discussed in his autobiography.

43. Sallust *Iug.* 15.4–5, 29.2–3 represents Scaurus as corrupted by money. Cf. Livy *Per.* 64 and *de vir ill.* 72.4. Shatzman 1975 no. 39 claims there was "nothing exceptional" in Jugurtha's presents to Scaurus and other leading Romans.

44. Pliny *HN* 36.116 and even Cicero *De or.* 2.283. Valerius Maximus 3.7.8 and 8.1. abs. 10 mentions money received from Mithridates while Scaurus was serving as a legate in Asia Minor.

45. See Scheidel 2005, especially 3, table 1. Harper 2010 gives a long view.

46. For educated slaves, see Booth 1979; Habinek 2005; and Maurice 2013, 111–42.

47. One myth has Daphnis as the Sicilian shepherd who invented pastoral poetry (Howatson 2011, s.v. Daphnis). A possible mention of the Hellenistic pastoral poet Theocritus is suggestive as a literary reference in a name chosen for an enslaved baby born in Italy the 130s. Accius was known for his Hellenizing interests (Feeney 2016, 160–61).

48. See Pliny *HN* 7.128 quoted on page 67.

49. For the Attii/Accii, see Cicero *Brut.* 271 and Jerome *Chron.* 1878 (139, in the 160th Olympiad) with Suerbaum 2002, 158.

50. Accius was born in 170. For his background and social setting, see Conte 1994, 105–9; Suerbaum 2002, no. 122; and Baldarelli 2004, 11–45. Manuwald 2011, 216–25; and Feeney 2016, 160–61, note that he was the first dramatist to write literary treatises.

51. We have the titles of 45 tragedies and 2 *fabulae praetextae*. He is also cited as the author of: *Didaskalia* (at least 9 books that mixed prose and verse), *Pragmatica* (at least 2 books), *Parerga* (at least 2 books), *Sotadica* (at least 2 books), *Annales* (27 books or more), *Praxidicus*, and possibly a separate work on spelling conventions. See also the Budé edition of the fragments by Dangel (1995/2002).

52. Decimus Iunius Brutus Callaicus, *RE* 57, Münzer (180–113, consul 138) was Accius' patron.

53. Conte 1994, 112–30.

54. For Quintus Lutatius Catulus (*RE* 7 Münzer, c. 150–87, consul in 102), see Suerbaum 2002, no. 172 and *FRHist.* no. 19 (Christopher Smith). For his speeches, see ORF^4 no. 63. His poetry: Cicero *De or.* 2.44 with Flower 1996, 122; Hillard 2001; and Courtney 2003, 75–78.

55. Cicero *Arch.* 5 and McDonnell 2006, 264.

56. See Flower 2014 for Catulus' artistic and cultural interests and his memoirs.

57. See Shatzman 1975 no. 61. Pliny *HN* 36.109 says Catulus owned the grandest house in Rome in his day that cost over HS 6 million. For his villa, see Cicero *De or.* 2.12–13. Craver 2010 offers an overview of urban real estate in late republican Rome.

58. Lucilius F 750 Marx = 741; Christes and Garbugino 2015. This fragment, in which Lucilius makes fun of Catulus' extravagance, dates to late in the 130s when Catulus was a young man. It refers to him buying something for a high price. But this is surely too early to be a reference to Daphnis, who may only have been a baby or young child at this time.

59. Suetonius *Gram. et rhet.* 3.4–5 quoted on page 67–68.

60. *De vir ill.* 72 probably reproduces details from Scaurus' autobiography.

61. Caecilia Metella (*RE* 134, Münzer) was a daughter of L. Caecilius Metellus Delmaticus (*RE* 91, cos. 119, cens. 115). Her children by Scaurus are *RE* 137, 141, 154. She subsequently married Sulla and also had (at least) three more children by him.

62. Suetonius *Gram. et rhet.* 3.4 with Kaster 1995 *ad loc.*

63. See Courtney 2003, 75–78, who dates the poem around 100. Roscius (c. 126–62) was probably younger than Daphnis. He wrote a treatise on oratory and acting (Cicero *QRosc.* 29 with Lintott 2008, 60–67). Was Roscius himself also a freedman (although Cicero seems to imply otherwise)? Treggiari 1969b, 139; and Leppin 1992, 40 and 116–17, argue that he was freeborn, although the majority of attested actors were not, as is discussed by Richlin 2017a and Čulík-Baird 2022.

64. In the second century, some Romans did pay relatively high prices for young slave boys for sexual purposes, as Cato attests. For discussion, see chapter 2.

65. For an example of the mythical Daphnis in art, see a marble statue group from Pompeii showing Pan and Daphnis, a copy of an earlier work by Heliodorus (Naples Archaeological Museum, Collezione Farnese, inv. 6329, 1.58 m high, https://commons.wikimedia.org/wiki/File:Pan_and_Daphnis.jpg).

66. See Cicero *Brut.* 132 and Fronto 124–25 (Van den Hout 1988) with Chassignet 2004, 170–71, xcvii–xcix; and Scholz et al. 2013, 71–79. Flower 2014 offers a re-dating that puts Catulus first among the memoirists and argues that he wrote two works in different styles, rather than the single work that has been posited in every modern edition of the fragments.

67. For Scaurus' memoirs, see Chassignet 2004, 161–63, lxxxviii–xciii; and Scholz and Walter 2013, 49–58.

68. For Archias, see Cameron (*OCD*) and Selzer (*BNP*) with *RE* 20 (Reitzenstein).

69. See Cicero *Pro Archia* with the insightful and thorough commentary by Coşkun 2009 and 2010. His detailed introduction is particularly helpful. Archias was accused by a certain Grattius under the *lex Papia de peregrinis* of 65, for which see Coşkun 2010, 54–59, 109; and now the masterly reinterpretation by Chillet 2019. This law targeted persons who pretended to be Roman citizens, at a time when a census was due to take place. The extent of the penalties, other than removal from the city and its community, are unclear.

70. If Archias was 20 (for example) when he arrived in Rome in 102, he could have been about a decade younger than Daphnis. But both men may well have been older. Coşkun 2010, 25, has Archias born around 120, which would make him only 18 when he arrived in Rome. Vretska and Vretska 1979 imagine him a couple of years older. For Archias and Catulus, see Cicero *Arch.* 5, 6, and 19 with Bardon 1952, 123, and Coşkun 2010, *ad loc.*

71. For Scaurus and Archias, see Cicero *Arch.* 6. Scaurus was the man who had enslaved Daphnis and had sold him on to Catulus.

72. For dependent poets including Archias, see the classic discussions of Treggiari 1977 and Wiseman 1982.

73. For manumission, see Fabre 1981; Mouritsen 2013 and 2016; and the essays in Bell et al. 2024. Mouritsen 2019 examines the high rate of manumission in Herculaneum, which suggests a reliable supply of the (newly) enslaved.

74. Daphnis could have been about 70 years old in 62, if he was still alive by then.

75. Cicero surely knew Archias during his early years in Rome, although there is no reason to label him Cicero's teacher in a formal sense. Archias is not mentioned in other accounts of Cicero's youth, notably the *Brutus*. See Dugan 2005, 21–54, for Cicero's use of Archias to construct an image of himself.

76. For the historical value of the *Pro Archia*, see Coşkun 2010.

77. Bellemore 2002 has not found many followers for her proposal to date the speech to the spring of 56. See Coşkun 2010, 26–28.

78. For Petrarch and the *Pro Archia*, see especially Čulík-Baird 2020. The many surviving manuscripts of this speech demonstrate its immediate popularity after its rediscovery.

79. The principal issues addressed in modern scholarship on the *Pro Archia* have been (1) the politics of 62 and the clash between Lucullus and Pompey; (2) Cicero's own self-representation; (3) how Roman citizenship spread in Italy during and after the Social War; and (4) the role of Cicero's encomium of literature, especially in Greek, in republican political culture.

80. An immediate publication date for *Pro Archia* is suggested by the fact that Cicero still thinks Archias is going to write a poem about his consulship, a prospect that was dismissed by the middle of the following year (*Att.* 1.16.15 = SB 16 of July 61). The speech does not refer to Pompey's magnificent, third triumph in 61 (Itgenshorst 2005, no. 258, cf. nos. 246 and 253 for his two earlier celebrations).

81. *Arch.* 7 with Coşkun 2010, 43–50.

82. For Q. Caecilius Metellus Pius (pr. 89, cos. 80), see *RE* 98. He was a first cousin of the Luculli brothers, whose mother was a Caecilia. For Heraclea, see Camassa (*BNP*).

83. It is interesting to note that in 89 Archias adopted the *praenomen* Aulus, which was not a name used by the Licinii Luculli. Three Licinii with the *cognomen* Nerva are called Aulus, but none seems connected to Archias. This name could refer to the adoption of Marcus Licinius Crassus by an Aulus Terentius Varro, a change of status (in the 90s?) that Marcus apparently later regretted (so Wiseman 1982, 32). However, all the evidence indicates that this man continued to use the name Marcus, which was also a common one for a Terentius Varro. The *praenomen* Aulus should, therefore, indicate a special closeness to another patron, whom Cicero does not identify. None of the other patrons Cicero mentions in the speech is named Aulus. See Arnott 1971 for the rather implausible suggestion that Aulus is simply a translation of the Greek *aulos* (flute). See chapter 2 for Pomponius Dionysius called Marcus after Cicero, rather than Titus after his manumitter Atticus.

84. As already suggested, Daphnis seems to have been manumitted by Catulus around the turn of the century or in the early 90s. Archias may well, therefore, have first met Daphnis while he was still enslaved and could have been present in Rome at the time of his highly publicized manumission by Catulus.

85. Cicero calls Archias *praetextatus* at the time when he arrived in Rome (*Arch.* 5). This cannot be taken as a literal statement, since Archias was never a Roman boy who wore a *toga praetexta*. As argued here, Cicero's language is metaphorical, perhaps even humorous. For various rhetorical reasons, Cicero is creating an image of Archias as a boy genius who arrived early in Rome and is steeped in Roman culture, before he goes on to portray him as the ideal Greek poet. See chapter 6 for Ateius Philologus, who may have been called Praetextatus as a nickname.

86. For example, *Arch.* 5.

87. *Arch.* 4. For Antioch in Syria in the second century, see Liebeschuetz 1972; Wittke (*BNP*); and De Giorgi and Asa Eger 2021.

88. For multiple honorary citizenships in Greek cities, especially for athletes but also for artists, see Lomas 2002 and van Nijf 2012.

89. See *Arch.* 5 with Coşkun 2010 *ad loc.*

90. Cicero *Arch.* 4 claims that Archias was born *loco nobili*, which is usually translated as a reference to his family's social status as prominent in society at Antioch. The Latin could, however, also refer more generally to the city of Antioch, the once and future provincial capital of Syria. The punctuation adopted by most editions opts for the former translation. In any case, Cicero passes over Archias' time in Antioch rapidly, in a single sentence, and without providing details.

91. The question of Archias' ethnicity has been raised by Čulík-Baird 2020. If Archias' father did not use a Greek name, then his omission is no surprise in this context.

92. *Arch.* 5.

93. Pr. urb. 104. See the insightful discussion in Coşkun 2010, 66–67.

94. For L. Licinius Lucullus (pr. 104), father of Lucius and Marcus, see Nadig (*BNP*) and *RE* 103.

95. L. Licinius Lucullus (cos. 74, *RE* 104) and his brother M. Licinius Lucullus (cos. 73, *RE* 109), also known as M. Terentius Varro Lucullus after being adopted at an unknown date. These boys would, however, have been too young to have been initial patrons of Archias when he first arrived. For the self-representation of the Luculli, see Coarelli 1981.

96. For L. Lucullus' exile in Heraclea, see the thorough discussion in Kelly 2006, 83, and 176–78. If Lucullus moved to Heraclea, he is the last Roman exile we know of to settle in Italy.

97. See Tröster 2008 for an analysis of Plutarch's biography of Lucullus, with full bibliography. Chapter 6 discusses educated prisoners of war.

98. Plutarch is focused on the philosopher Antiochus of Ascalon (and the pupils who traveled with him) as Lucullus' most important intellectual companion and adviser. But this choice could reflect Plutarch's own interests rather than the relative importance of Archias and Antiochus to Lucullus at the time. See Tröster 2005, 100–102, for discussion of Lucullus' various friends.

99. For Roman politics at the end of the second century, see Flower 2010, 61–97, and Steel 2013, 42–61.

100. Archias clearly made many connections with leading Romans, specifically in the 90s. See Coşkun 2010, 65–73. Meanwhile, it is possible that Archias also continued to spend at least some time in southern Italy, as he had before. He may have traveled from Rome to Sicily with Marcus, or he could have met him in the South and simply returned to Rome with him from Heraclea after their visit to Sicily.

101. See Tröster 2008, 33, who sees Lucullus as decisively influenced by Archias from an early and impressionable age.

102. *Arch.* 6 with Coşkun 2010, *ad loc.*

103. Archias' older patrons mentioned in the speech include Q. Caecilius Metellus Numidicus (cos. 109, *RE* 97), M. Aemilius Scaurus (cos. 115, cens. 109, *RE* 140), Q. Lutatius Catulus (cos. 102, *RE* 7), L. Licinius Crassus (cos. 95, cens. 92, *RE* 55), M. Livius Drusus (tr. pl. 91, *RE* 18), possibly also Cn. Octavius (cos. 87, *RE* 20) and M. Porcius Cato (tr. pl. 99?, *RE* *14, father of Cato Uticensis). Others may be implied in plural family names. See Coşkun 2010, 93–94.

104. Note the *lex Licinia Mucia de civibus redigundis* of 95, see Cicero *Off.* 3.11.47, *Sest.* 13.30 with *Schol. Bob.* 129 St., *Brut.* 16.63, *Balb.* 21.48 and 24.54. Asconius 67C, with Elster 2003, no. 95.

105. *Arch.* 6 with Coşkun 2010, *ad loc.* The text is problematic around the area of the *praenomen* that indicates which Lucullus went to Sicily with Archias in the 90s. Marcus is the favorite

candidate. This identification is also confirmed by the fact that he is the witness at the trial who claims to have been at Heraclea when Archias became a citizen. Coşkun 2010, 102, dates this visit to 92/91, so that Archias' name would have appeared on the most recent local census lists compiled immediately before the Social War.

106. The only official witnesses Cicero mentions are Marcus Licinus Lucullus and an unnamed and unspecified number of delegates (*legati*) from Heraclea. It remains unclear who else among Archias' circle might have attended the trial in order to support him. Damon 1997, 268–76, argues that Lucius deliberately stayed away from the trial.

107. Coşkun 2010, 102, believes that there was enough unrest in Lucania to make the fire in Heraclea seem credible without any supporting evidence from another ancient source.

108. Heraclea is several days journey from Rhegium (about 200 miles even on a modern road), which would presumably have been the starting point for Marcus and Archias on their way back from Sicily.

109. For the Social War and the enfranchisement of Italians, see Mouritsen 1998 and Bispham 2007 and 2018.

110. For Lucius' career, see *RE* 104 (Gelzer); Keaveney 1992; Badian (*OCD*); Will (*BNP*); *FRHist.* no. 23 (Smith); Beness and Hillard (*BNJ* no. 185); with the detailed and compelling discussion in Lundgreen 2019. *CIL* 1^2. 196 = 11.1832 = *ILS* 60 = *II* 13.3.84 is an Augustan *elogium* from Arretium in Etruria that focuses on Lucius' military exploits as proconsul.

111. For Lucius and Sulla's memoirs, see Plutarch *Sulla* 6.5–6 and *Luc.* 1.4 and 4.5. In general, see Calabi 1951; Valgiglio 1975; Lewis 1991; Behr 1993; Thein 2002, 359–63, and 2009; Scholz 2003; Smith 2009; and Scholz and Walter 2013. Smith (*FRHist.* 23) does not think that Lucius will have followed through with publishing Sulla's memoirs in Greek.

112. Coşkun 2010, 94, notes this important omission but does not discuss the close relationship that must have existed in the 80s and perhaps throughout Archias' time in Rome, given the intimate friendship of Sulla with the Luculli, as well as the literary interests Sulla shared with them and with Archias himself.

113. For Sulla's first march on Rome, see Livy *Ep.* 77; Velleius Paterculus 2.19; and Appian *B Civ.* 1.60 with Flower 2010, 91–94.

114. For Mithridates VI Eupator Dionysus (120–63), see Olshausen (*BNP*); McGing (*OCD*); McGing 1986; and especially Mayor 2009.

115. For L. Cornelius Epicadus (*RE* 150, Goetz) and Aurelius Opillus (*RE* 176, Goetz) and P. Rutilius Rufus (cos. 105, *RE* 34, Münzer), see chapter 4.

116. There is no specific evidence for the movements of Archias between his return to Rome with Lucius in c. 80 and his renewed departure with him in late 74 or early 73, but he obviously stayed close to the Luculli brothers. Lucius and Marcus were aediles together in 79. Lucius was praetor the following year. His consulship was in 74; Marcus was consul the following year, presumably with his brother having presided over his election.

117. Lucius was in Africa as propraetor in 77–76 (Cicero *Acad.* 2.1 and *vir ill.* 74.3).

118. For Archias' official salary, see *Arch.* 11 with Coşkun 2010, *ad loc.*

119. Archias' epic is mentioned by Cicero, *Arch.* 21. Plutarch does not cite Archias as a source, but some of his more stylized descriptions, especially of battles, may have been inspired by the poem, for example, *Luc.* 27 and 28. For discussion, see Reinach 1890 and Wiseman 1982, 33, who attributes Aphrodite's hexameter line (*Luc.* 12.1) to Archias. Coşkun 2010, 69, has Archias

possibly write his epic in response to Theophanes of Mytilene's praise of Pompey. Yet Archias was surely commissioned to write his poem many years previously.

120. For the continuing rivalry between Lucius and Pompey in 66–63, see now Lundgreen 2019, 94–110. Cicero shrewdly avoids drawing attention to or taking sides in the clash between two leading men whom he wanted to stay on good terms with and whom he both praises.

121. For Lucius' triumph over Mithridates that was finally celebrated during Cicero's consulship, see Itgenshorst 2005, no. 256. Archias will presumably have played a part in the celebrations.

122. For a succinct overview of the 60s, Wiseman 1992 remains an essential read.

123. *Contra* (for example) Dominic Berry 2004, 291, who describes Archias as "of no political or social importance whatsoever," or Andrew Sillett (Oxford Bibliographies: Cicero's *Pro Archia*, 2019), who calls this "a short speech defending a man of relatively little importance on a charge of no great gravity." A different view is expressed by Haley 1983, 3: "in many ways Archias was an obvious choice" to be targeted for prosecution in a political trial. See also Tröster 2005, 105.

124. The cost of travel from Heraclea to Rome will not have been insignificant. In addition, the delegation will have incurred food and lodging expenses in the city, although the trial itself probably only lasted one day.

125. As noted, it is not easy to calculate how much time Archias had actually spent in Rome since he became a Roman citizen. Even if he was only away while on campaign with Lucius (87–80 and 73–66), that would amount to more than half the intervening 27 years. He could easily have been absent for more time and may, in fact, regularly have spent part of the year elsewhere, as many other inhabitants of the city did. Coşkun 2010 offers a complex reconstruction that has Archias missing the census in Rome, but also being absent for local census taking in the various cities where he held honorary citizenships. Hence, his need to follow Lucius left him in a situation of being largely undocumented.

126. Coşkun 2010, 114–15.

127. *Arch.* 11.

128. Haley 1983 presents a compelling argument.

129. *Arch.* 28. The way in which Cicero connects a hypothetical poem about his consulship with Archias' work on the recent Mithridatic war suggests that he is thinking in terms of an epic, also in several books.

130. *Att.* 1.16.15 = SB 16. Archias has now been commissioned by the Caecilii Metelli. Cicero was not able to come up with another poet to fill in for Archias.

131. Cf. Atticus' freedman Dionysius in 49, discussed in chapter 2.

132. Archias could not have foreseen the way in which Lucius would be replaced by Pompey as commander of the war. His assignment of writing about the war will have seemed much less politically fraught at its inception.

133. For the Luculli and Cicero after 62, see Lundgreen 2019, 96–98.

134. Cicero *Arch.* 18 with Coşkun 2010, 119–20. See also *De or.* 3.194 and Quintilian 10.7.19; and Hardie 1983, 22, 24, 75–85.

135. *Arch.* 5 and 19 may imply verses written separately for each consul in the Cimbric War, perhaps epigrams, or alternatively a more extended poem. Cicero is noticeably vague about Archias' earlier works, both oral and written.

136. For Lucullus' writing, see Plutarch *Luc.* 41–42 with Beness and Hillard (*BNJ* no. 185) and *FRHist.* no. 23 (Smith). For his Hellenism, see Tröster 2008, 27–47. Tiro is also said to have

written in different genres (Cicero *Fam.* 16.18.3; Pliny *HN* 2.106; Gellius *NA* 6.3.10, 10.1.7; 13.9.100). For M. Tullius Tiro (*RE* 52, Groebe), see *Fam.* 16 with Badian (*OCD*); Zelzer (*BNP*); and especially Tempest in Wiley's *Encyclopedia of Ancient History* (2012); and Stefan Knoch and Florian Hurka in *HAS*, 3080–83.

137. Some of Archias' epigrams may be included in the *Palatine Anthology* among the poems collected by Meleager. See Law 1936, who attributes eight of these surviving poems to this Archias on the basis of style. However, none are directly ascribed specifically to an Archias from Antioch.

138. One may note a poem he wrote in honor of the actor Roscius, probably an epigram or other short composition (Cicero *Div.* 1.79).

139. *Arch.* 6 mentions M. Aemilius Scaurus "listening to" Archias in phrasing that may suggest a lecture but could also simply refer to a public performance of his poetry, whether improvised or not.

140. The written versions are specifically referred to by Cicero (*Arch.* 18). Steel 2001, 82–98, plays down Archias' poems, both in terms of quality and of quantity.

141. Polybius had already shown the way in the second century.

142. *Contra* Berry 2004, who describes Archias as a teacher of young boys much like many others in Rome.

143. Wiseman 1982, 33: "It is likely enough that Archias and Antipater [of Sidon], along with Catulus' learned freedman Daphnis, helped him with these works in much the same way that Tiro helped Cicero."

144. See, for example, the mid-second-century AD epitaph from Ostia of thirteen-year-old Melior, a *verna* who is described as a learned *calculator* (bookkeeper), *CIL* 14.472 with Eckardt 2017, 130.

145. See Horsfall 1989, 88. Pliny the Younger's letters provide many insights into the households, both in town and in various country locations, of a wealthy man with literary pretensions in the age of Trajan (Blake 2016). Houston 2014 is an invaluable overview of book production, book collecting, and library maintenance.

146. Seneca *Ep.* 27.5–7: Calvisius Sabinus paid HS 100,000 each for 11 men, each of whom knew by heart the works of one Greek poet (Homer, Hesiod, and the 9 lyric poets).

147. There have been sharply differing views as to the caliber and type of literary work produced by freedmen. See, for example, Treggiari 1969b, 110 and 119, as opposed to Christes 1979, 4.

148. Pliny *Ep.* 9.36: *mox cum meis ambulo, quorum in numero sunt eruditi. Ita variis sermonibus uespera extenditur, et quamquam longissimus dies bene conditur.* "Soon (after dinner) I go for a walk with my slaves [and freedmen?], among whose number there are learned men. In this way the evening is drawn out with [intellectual] conversation on a variety of topics, and even the longest day has a good ending." A world of emotional and intellectual interactions lies behind Pliny's evening walks and the way in which he recalls them so fondly.

4. Multitaskers: Aurelius Opillus and Lucius Cornelius Epicadus

1. Blänsdorf 2016, 118–42, offers an insightful discussion of trust in the context of such relationships.

2. Epitaphs in family tombs are commonly found from the age of Augustus onward. For discussion, see Joshel 1992; Hasegawa 2005; Mouritsen 2013; and Borbonus 2014. Groen-Vallinga 2024

discusses the value assigned to labor within the household based on evidence from family tombs.

3. For the household of Livia, see the classic discussion in Treggiari 1975, with Bradley 1994, 61–63, table 3.

4. Carandini 1988 is a seminal discussion, which also includes identification of extensive quarters for enslaved domestics in the basement of Roman houses from the later republican period.

5. For autobiographies written in Latin, see Badian 1966; Suerbaum 2002 no. 169.1; Walter 2003; Baier 2005; Smith and Powell 2009; Candau 2011; Tatum 2011; Scholz et al. 2013, 20–37; and *FRHist.* nos. 18 (Scaurus), 19 (Catulus), 21 (Rutilius), 22 (Sulla), and 23 (Lucullus).

6. M. Aemilius Scaurus (*RE* 140, Klebs) was a patrician, probably born in the late 160s, who was consul in 115, *princeps senatus* in Africa in 112 and 111, censor in 109, and died in late 90 or early 89. See Suerbaum 2002, no. 170 with *FRHist.* no. 18 (Christopher Smith). His wife Caecilia Metella (*RE* 134, Münzer) was daughter of L. Caecilius Metellus Delmaticus (*RE* 91, cos. 119, cens. 115). Her children by Scaurus are *RE* 137, 141, 154. She subsequently married Sulla and had (at least) three more children by him. For a history of the debate about her identity, see Smith in *FRHist.* vol. 3, 292.

7. For Aurelius Opillus, see *RE* 176 (Goetz); *BNP* (Schmitz); *OCD* (Kaster); and Suerbaum 2002, no. 193.2, p. 559–60 with Bardon 1952, 144; Christes 1979, 17–20; Rawson 1985, 7, 23; Kelly 2006, 90. Damaggio 2011 offers an introduction to a new edition of the fragments of the grammarians. See also the website *Grammatici disiecti* at https://gradis.hypotheses.org/62 (entry for Opillus by Julie Damaggio, 2016).

8. *Gram. et rhet.* 6 with the commentaries of Kaster 1995 and Vacher 2003 *ad loc.*

9. Opillus is apparently a Latinized version of the Oscan man's name Upils, attested in a Campanian inscription. See Rix 2002; Cm 33; Sa 53; tSa12; and Cp31, 32; with Weiss 2010, 369; and O'Brien 2021, 15.

10. For the fragments of Opillus, see Funaioli 1907, 86–95. Twenty-eight fragments have survived, which puts him in second place among the grammarians of the period before Varro (who himself cites Opillus six times). By far the largest number of Opillus' fragments (15) come from Festus.

11. Symmachus *Ep.* 1.20.2 mentions Rutilius and Opillus in a list of famous earlier pairs of teachers and ungrateful pupils, a list that is historically inaccurate since most of the pairs were not pupils and teachers. See the commentary of Salzman and Roberts 2011 *ad loc.* Contra Rawson 1985, 67, who seems to take Symmachus out of context.

12. Münzer (*RE* 34) opts for 154, followed by Chassignet 2004. Badian 1966 posits 160, while Smith (*FRHist.* No. 22) reckons Rutilius cannot have been born any later than 158. This discussion uses the year 158, partly for convenience.

13. Opillus' Roman *praenomen* is not securely attested; it might have been Decimus or Sextus (Suerbaum 2002, 560). But note that the Oscan name Upils, from which his *cognomen* seems to derive, was itself employed as a *praenomen*. See note 9.

14. *Gram. et rhet.* 6: *Huius cognomen in plerisque indicibus et titulis per unam L litteram scriptum animadverto, verum ipse id per duas effert in parastichide libelli, qui inscribitur Pinax.* (I notice that this man's *cognomen* is written with one L in most book labels and titles, but he himself records it with two LLs in an acrostic in the book that is entitled *Catalogue.*)

15. For Rutilia, wife of M. Aurelius Cotta, see Münzer in *RE* 38; and Kelly 2006, 136, 183–84. In an unusual move, she went into exile to Athens for some years with her son C. Aurelius Cotta (Kelly 2006, no. 28). Rutilius did not opt to join them there. One of her freedwomen seems to be attested in an inscription on travertine from Rome (*CIL* 1^2 1209 = 6. 33919a = *ILLRP* 821 = *ILS* 7703).

16. Gaius Aurelius Cotta, cos. 75 and *pontifex* (*RE* 96, Klebs) was a well-known orator. He was one of the exiles who returned to Rome with Sulla, unlike his uncle Rutilius.

17. For Epictetus, see the suggestive discussion in Bradley 1994, 174–78, who highlights the ways in which the life of Epictetus brings out some of the stark paradoxes inherent in Roman enslavement and manumission. For Tiberius Claudius Epaphroditus, see *RE* 4 Stein; *PIR*[2] E 69 and Mancioli in *LTUR* for his gardens (*horti*); with *ILS* 9505; and Eck 1976. Epictetus is also discussed in the preface.

18. See Cicero *Brut.* 113–16; and *Off.* 3.10 with Meier 1980^2, 318–20.

19. For Rutilius as the Roman Socrates, see especially the analysis of Suerbaum 2002, no. 171.

20. *Gram. et rhet.* 6: *composuitque variae eruditionis aliquot volumina.* (He wrote several books with a broad range of learning.)

21. Funaioli 1907 F 9 from Festus 162 L: *necessarium ait esse Opillus Aurelius, in quo non sit cessandum, aut sine quo vivi non possit, aut sine quo non bene vivatur, aut quod non possit prohiberi quin fiat.* (Aurelius Opillus says that a necessary thing is something one cannot give up, or without which one cannot live, or without which one cannot live well, or that which cannot be prohibited from being.)

22. For Panaetius in Rome, see *BNP* (Inwood) and Griffin 1989. He seems to have left Rome soon after the sudden death of his patron Scipio Aemilianus in 129, at a time when he succeeded Antipater as head of the Stoic School in Athens.

23. *Gram. et rhet.* 6: *philosophiam primo, deinde rhetoricam, novissime grammaticam docuit.* (First he taught philosophy, then rhetoric, lastly grammar.)

24. For further discussion of Opillus' teaching career, see Christes 1979, 17–18; Kaster 1995; and Vacher 2003 *ad loc.*

25. *Gram. et rhet.* 4.4: *Veteres grammatici et rhetoricam docebant, ac multorum de utraque arte commentarii feruntur.* (The earlier grammar teachers were also teaching rhetoric, and commentaries on both subjects by many of them are extant.)

26. Opillus' age is assumed to be close to that of Rutilius because Suetonius (*Gram. et rhet.* 6) describes him as growing old with Rutilius in Smyrna (*consenuit* / grew old together). An echo of this same language can be found in Orosius 5.17.13 (*qui Zmyrnam conmigrans litterarum studiis intentus consenuit,* who emigrated to Zmyrna and spent his old age there focused on literary pursuits), although the name of Rutilius' companion has fallen out in this passage.

27. Astin 1967, 88–89, sees Rutilius as a client of Aemilianus.

28. In his praetorian edict, Rutilius limited the claims of a *patronus* (manumitter/patron) on the services of his freedman to an *actio operarum* (suit for service) and his inheritance claim to half of the legacy. See *Digest* 38.2.1 (Ulpian) with Watson 1970; and Masi Doria 1999, 52–58 and 99–130.

29. *Gram. et rhet.* 6: *Dimissa autem schola, Rutilium Rufum damnatum in Asiam secutus, ibidem Zmyrnae simul consenuit.* (But he closed his school and followed Rutilus Rufus to Asia after his conviction; there he grew old together with him at Smyrna.)

30. Crawford et al. 2011 show the extent of Oscan in the epigraphic record of Italy both before and after the Social War.

31. For Rutilius' trial and conviction, see Cicero *Brut.* 115; *Orat.* 1.53; *Font.* 17; *In Pis.* 39; Livy *Per.* 70; Velleius Paterculus 2.13; Valerius Maximus 2.10.5; Quintilian *Inst.* 11.1.12; Dio fr. 97; Orosius 5.17.12 with Gruen 1966, 53–55; and Alexander 1990, no. 94. Elster 2020 no. 82, 245–50, outlines the extortion law of Servilius Glaucia under which Rutilius was convicted. Kelly 2006, no. 25, places the exile in 92. Kallet-Marx 1990 argues for an earlier date, in 94, which would (presumably) have resulted in Rutilius and Opillus spending more time in exile in Mytilene before the outbreak of the war with Mithridates.

32. For Scaevola and Rutilius in Asia, see Badian 1956 and Morrell 2017, 12–14. For the date of their activity in Asia, see *MRR* 3.145–6 with Ferrary 2000, 163–65.

33. For Rutilius' penalty, see Shatzman 1975, no. 71, who believes he lost all his property; and Alexander 1990, no. 94, with Cicero *ND* 3.86 for the estate at Formiae.

34. For Scaevola's financial support of Rutilius, see Valerius Maximus 2.10.5 and Dio F 97.4.

35. For Rutilius' wife Livia (*RE* 34), see Val. Max. 8.13.6 and Pliny *NH* 7.158. She was probably the daughter of the consul of 147, sister of the consul of 112 and tribune of 122, aunt of the tribune of 91, and great-aunt of Livia Drusilla, the wife of Augustus. Frontinus *Strat.* 4.1.12 records a son who is described as grown up at the time of Rutilius' consulship in 105. See Münzer *RE* 34, col. 1276.

36. The warm welcome received by Rutilius in Asia is recorded by Dio 28 fr. 97.4. It must remain unclear, however, whether he eventually had access to the same kinds of financial resources as he had had before his own property was confiscated. While it was not unusual to go into exile in a province where one had served before (Kelly 2006, 69), Rutilius' account of his exile may have contained a degree of exaggeration in painting a rosy picture of universal accolades for Rutilius not long before a widespread revolt from Rome.

37. For Rutilius in Mytilene, see Cicero *Rab. Post.* 27, Dio 28 fr. 97.

38. For Mithridates in Asia, see the detailed introduction in Goukowsky 2001. Appian *Mithr.* 21 records the continued resistance of Mytilene to Rome even after the Peace of Dardanus. See also Livy *Per.* 89 and Plutarch *Luc.* 4.2–3. As noted by Kallet-Marx 1995, 157, even a city like Ephesus that had seen a particularly brutal massacre of Romans, was eager to renew its alliance with Rome by the winter of 86/85. For a convenient overview, see Keaveney 2005, 189–93.

39. Rutilius claims to have taken off his toga and assumed a disguise: see Cicero *Rab. Post.* 10.27 and Dio 24 fr. 95.3–4 with Amiotti 1980 and Ferrary 2002. Heskel 1994, 136, argues that Cicero distorts the account of Rutilius' escape for his own purposes. Kelly 2006, 148n44, explains that Roman exiles were expected to continue to wear Roman dress abroad, but one wonders how many did and on what occasions, especially in cases where citizenship had been lost.

40. For an economic reading of the Ephesian Vespers, see McGing 1986, 113–18, 126–30. Goukowsky 2001 sees Appian's interpretation of the massacre as being more due to hatred of Rome than fear of Mithridates as an oversimplification. See already Kallet-Marx 1995, 153–60, who draws attention to the ways in which so many cities were soon able to renew their alliances with the Romans. Other discussions include Millar 2004; Isayev 2017, 49–56; and Vervaet 2023, 123–26. For the foreign policy of Mithridates VI in general, see Cicero *Leg. Manil.* 3.7, 5.11; Pliny *NH* 2.209; Tacitus *Ann.* 4.14; Appian *Mithr.* 17–27; and Dio fr. 101 with McGing 1986; Mastrocinque 1999; and Mayor 2009, especially 13–26.

41. Mithridates was presented with Manius Aquillius (cos. 101) in Mytilene. Amiotti 1979 examines the various traditions about the death of Aquillius.

42. Posidonius *FGH* 87 F 36.50 (= Athenaeus 213B) describes other Romans taking off their togas in order to disguise their identities. For Rhodes as a refuge, see Appian *Mithr.* 24.94 with Goukowsky 2001, *ad loc.* No ancient source specifies how many Romans and Italians made their way to Rhodes, as opposed to returning to Italy or finding another refuge from Mithridates and his allies. See *Syll.*^{3} 741 (*INysa* 8 and 9) for two letters written by Mithridates in 88 to his satrap Leonippos that describe the resistance against the king organized by Chairemon, son of Pythodorus, who had taken refuge in the Temple of Artemis at Ephesus. Chairemon had arranged for an unspecified number of Romans to escape to Rhodes, together with his own two sons.

43. Their arrival in Smyrna is mentioned by Dio 28 fr. 97, who has Rutilius go to Smyrna from Mytilene and then from Smyrna to meet Sulla. This journey is accepted by Münzer (*RE* 34).

44. Smyrna had sided with Mithridates soon after his invasion, but revolted against him, together with Ephesus, in the fall of 86. Magie 1950, 223–25, remains the classic discussion.

45. A somewhat similar scenario is suggested by Philippe Labro's autobiography entitled *Le petit garçon* (Paris, 1990), which describes how his parents hid a Jewish family in their home at the same time as they were housing German officers who had been billeted on them during the Second World War. The presence of the high-ranking officers meant that the house was subject to fewer searches.

46. Their hiding place(s) elsewhere may never have been revealed, perhaps in order to protect their friends or to obscure other matters that Rutilius did not want to share in his autobiography. He had a lot to explain (away). For a detailed discussion of the chronology of Mithridates' invasion of Asia in 89–88, see now Leydold 2020.

47. For Theophanes of Mytilene, see *BNJ* no. 188 F 1 (= Plutarch *Pomp.* 37.1–3) with Gold 1985; Anastasiadis 1999; Yarrow 2006, 57; and Santangelo 2015 (Italian edition of the fragments) and 2018.

48. Plutarch *Pomp.* 37.3 with Santangelo 2015 and 2018.

49. For Rutilius with Sulla, see Appian *Mithr.* 60 with Goukowsky 2001 *ad loc.*

50. Dio 28 fr. 97.

51. For Sulla as a *hostis,* subjected to a penalty he himself had imposed on his enemies, see the detailed discussion in Allély 2012, 21–33.

52. For Flaccus, Fimbria, and Sulla, see Livy *Per.* 85; Vell. Pat. 2.24; Plutarch *Sulla* 25; Appian *Mithr.* 59–60; Orosius 6.2.11; and *De vir ill.* 70 with Keaveney 2005, 189–93. More sources are listed by Greenidge and Clay 1960, 185–89.

53. For Rutilius in Smyrna, see Cicero *Balb.* 11.28, Suetonius *Gram. et rhet.* 6, Tacitus *Ann.* 4.43, and Orosius 5.17.12–13 with Keaveney 2005, 192–193. For Rutilius' well-known refusal(s) to return to Rome, see Ovid *Pont.* 1.3.63–64, Val. Max. 6.4.4, Seneca *Ep.* 24.4, *Ben.* 6.37.2, *Dial.* 1.3.7, and Quintilian 11.1.13. A recent discussion can be found in Flaig 2019, 70–74, who stresses Rutilius' decision to become a citizen of Smyrna, thus giving up any claim to recover his Roman civic identity. Ovid (*Pont.* 1.3.61–66) idealizes Smyrna as a place to live, but in comparison with his own place of exile in Tomis on the Black Sea.

54. For Q. Servilius Caepio (*RE* 49) in Smyrna, see Kelly 2006, no. 17. Caepio also had become a citizen of Smyrna, according to Cicero (*Balb.* 28). He seems still to have been alive at

the time of Rutilius' conviction. Kelly 2006, 83, sees Caepio's choice of Smyrna as an indication that he was not hopeful of a recall from exile. It is unknown whether he survived the massacre of 88 and was still alive when Rutilius and Opillus arrived in Smyrna.

55. For Cicero and Rutilius in the 70s, see Cicero *Rep.* 1.13.17, *Brut.* 85–89, and *ND* 3.80.

56. See also Keaveney 2005, 192–93, who points out ambiguities in the surviving evidence about how Smyrna behaved during the war and in its immediate aftermath. He does, however, posit that the Smyrnaeans had saved the life of Rutilius.

57. For the fragments of Rutilius' history in Greek, see Chassignet 2004, 2–5; and Beck in *BNJ* (2011) no. 815 with full bibliography.

58. For Rutilius' autobiography, see Chassignet 2004, no. 1, 164–69; Scholz et al. 2013, 59–70; and *FRHist.* no. 21 (Christopher J. Smith) with Suerbaum 2002, no. 171; Hendrickson 1933; Badian 1966; Amiotti 1991; and Flower 2023.

59. See Chassignet 2004, CIX, for the authors who quote Rutilius, in comparison with the other memoirists. These are Cicero, Plutarch, Appian, and the later grammarians Charisius, Diomedes, Isidore, and Granius Licinianus. Pelling 2009, 73–75, sees Rutilius as much less influential than (for example) Badian 1966 does. For further discussion, see Mastrocinque 1999, 62–64; Scholz 2003, 175–76; many essays in Welch 2015; and Flower 2023.

60. Two further wars were fought with Mithridates after Sulla's treaty. They happened in c. 83–81 and 74/73–63.

61. Aulus Gellius *NA* 17.17 on Ennius' *tria corda: Quintus Ennius tria corda habere sese dicebat, quod loqui Graece et Osce et Latine sciret.* (Quintus Ennius used to say that he had three hearts, because he knew how to speak Greek and Oscan and Latin.)

62. Epicadus was considerably younger than Opillus, while Rutilius was probably at least 20 years older than Sulla (who was born in 138).

63. For Sulla and the actors, see Plutarch *Sulla* 2.3 and 37.1.

64. For Sulla and Rutilius, see note 49.

65. For Epicadus (*RE* 150 Goetz), see Suetonius *Gram. et rhet.* 12 with Kaster 1995 and Vacher 2003 *ad loc.*; *BNP* (Elvers); Christes 1979, 49–52; Suerbaum 2002 no. 173, Lit. 3; Scholz et al. 2013, 85–86; and Marshall 2019, 135–36. There is no entry for him in the *Oxford Classical Dictionary*. Santangelo 2007, 94, with note 30 argues that this Epicadus is not the same man whose name appears on some amphora stamps from this period. Syme 2016, 116, calls him "not a thug, but a scholar and author." Chassignet 2004, p. C, calls Epicadus a "Greek" freedman.

66. For the 10,000 Cornelii, see Appian *B Civ.* 1.100, 104, and *ILLRP* 353 = *ILS* 871 with Flower 2010, 125–26.

67. For Cicero and Atticus' households, see chapter 2.

68. For Chrysogonus (*RE* 101 Münzer), with Cicero *Rosc. Am.* 6, 35, 58, 60, 135–36, 138, 140, Pliny *HN* 35.200, Plutarch *Cic.* 3.2, *BNP* (Elvers) and *OCD* (Badian). Most of our information about him is connected to his alleged role in the prosecution of the younger Sextus Roscius in 80. Needless to say, Cicero sets out to paint as black a picture of Chrysogonus as possible. Interestingly, Sallust (*Hist.* 1.55.22) does not mention either Chrysogonus or Epicadus in his negative portrayal of Sulla's other freedmen, Tarula and Scirtus. For discussion, see Syme 2016 and Santangelo 2007, 88–99.

69. For Chrysogonus' house on the Palatine, see Cicero *Rosc. Am.* 133f. and *LTUR* (Eck).

70. *Gram. et rhet.* 12 with Christes 1979, 9 and 182.

71. This argument is put forward by Vacher 2003, 126, who notes the chronological break in Suetonius' work at the beginning of section 12 and the corruption of the text in section 13. She suggests that these chapters became damaged and were abbreviated before being reinserted in the wrong place in the manuscript.

72. The name Epicadus is Illyrian. See Fraser and Matthews in *LGPN* iii. A p. 146: the name was common in inscriptions in northwest Greece (33 examples across a broad time period). For earlier Illyrians with this name, see Livy 44.30 (168). For later examples in Latin inscriptions, see, for example, *ILS* 7164, 9411, 9412. Syme 2016, 116–18, assumed Epicadus was a POW captured by Sulla's armies in northern Greece in 85. Christes 1979, 177, also sees him as an Illyrian. Kaster 2003, 164, calls him a Greek.

73. As in the case of Atticus' freedman, Caecilius Epirota (see chapter 2), a name that contains a geographical reference does not necessarily indicate that the individual in question was from that place.

74. Faustus' age can be calculated most securely from his first public office, the quaestorship that he held in 54 (*MRR* vol. 2 *ad loc.*). There is no reason to assume that his career was delayed. Consequently, he (and his twin sister) would have been born in 85 or 84, after his mother, Caecilia, rejoined her husband in Greece, not before Sulla's departure for the East (early in 87).

75. For the public orator at Sulla's funeral, see Plutarch *Sulla* 37.4.

76. *Gram. et rhet.* 12: *Cornelius Epicadus, L. Cornelii Syllae dictatoris libertus calatorque in sacerdotio augurali, filio quoque eius Fausto gratissimus fuit; quare numquam non utriusque se libertum edidit.* (Cornelius Epicadus, freedman of L. Cornelius Sulla the dictator and his assistant in his augural priesthood, was also most dear to his son Faustus. For that reason, he always called himself the freedman of both men.)

77. See the detailed discussion of Kaster 1995, 164.

78. For Sulla's library, see Strabo 13.1.54 with Cicero *Att.* 4.10.1 and Plutarch *Cic.* 27.2.

79. *Gram. et rhet.* 12: *Cornelius Epicadus, L. Cornelii Syllae dictatoris libertus calatorque in sacerdotio augurali. . . . Librum autem, quem Sylla novissimum de rebus suis imperfectum reliquerat, ipse supplevit.* (Cornelius Epicadus, freedman of L. Cornelius Sulla the dictator and his assistant in his augural priesthood . . . himself completed/edited the final book of his memoirs that Sulla had left unfinished.)

80. For named calatores, see Rüpke's 2008 catalog, and especially the appendix (39–50) about the inscribed lists naming calatores in AD 101–102. See Scheid 1990b, 467, for the calatores named in the Arval records, of whom there are only nine.

81. For the calatores who worked with Roman priests, see *RE calatores* (Samter); *ThesCRA* vol. 5 p. 115; Scheid 1990b, 619–23 and 649–54; Rüpke 2008, 12; and Rüpke and Santangelo 2017. The calatores, who appear as freedmen of the priest they serve, are often classed, as in these discussions, as belonging to the broader category of *apparitores*, although this classification includes them with others of lower rank whose jobs were more menial and less technical.

82. For the *lapis niger* from the sacred area near the *comitium* in the Roman Forum, dated between 580 and 550, see *CIL* 6.36840 = 1.1 = *ILS* 4913 = *ILLRP* 3 = Terme 2012 p. 95–99 (Coarelli) = EDR 071720 with Wachter 1987, 66–69; Battaglini 2009; Rocca 2016; Morandi 2017; Licandro 2020; and Coarelli in *LTUR* (sepulchrum Romuli).

83. For a *calator* performing functions similar to a herald, see Servius auctus *Georg.* 1.268: the *pontifices* send their *calatores* ahead to clear the way for them and to prevent inauspicious

interruptions as they set out to perform a sacrifice. Paul Fest. p. 38 claims that all slaves were at one time termed *calatores* because they were continually on call. Charisius *Gram.* 1.106.20: Verrius Flaccus calls a *nomenclator* a *calator.* For early attestations of *calator* as a trusted slave, see Plautus *Pseud.* 1009; *Rud.* 335; and *Merc.* 852. In sum, *calator* is derived from *calare* (announce, call, summon), but was variously explained over time as referring to one who is summoned or one whose job it is to summon. See *TLL ad loc.* for a list of relevant inscriptions and passages.

84. For the *praeco* of a priest, see *ThesCRA* vol. 5, p. 115, where the heralds are discussed together with the *lictors* and the *viatores* (messengers), but separately from the *fictores* (bakers), *accensi velati* (more senior attendants), the musicians who played various kinds of wind instruments (*tibicines, aenatores, tubicines, liticines, cornicines*), the freeborn children involved in rituals (*pueri patrimi matrimique, camilli*), and the persons who actually performed an animal sacrifice (*victimarii, popae, cultrarii*). Not every priest made use of each kind of attendant; many of these attendants were enslaved but some were freedmen or freeborn citizens of high rank.

85. See Rüpke 2008, 11, on the technical skills of priestly assistants. He cites Cicero *Leg.* 3.48 on the expertise of *apparitores* in general.

86. For the Arval *acta*, see the edition of the inscriptions by Scheid 1998 with introduction and full commentary.

87. For the *calatores* of the Arval brothers, see Scheid 1990a, 467, and 1998 with index.

88. A dispute over an entrance fee is attested in AD 121 (Scheid 1998, no. 69 with commentary on p. 214). On this occasion, the priests decided that only a one-time entry fee was due, which was payable when the priest and his first *calator* took office, but that this fee was not refundable in cases where another *calator* was later substituted, if the first one was still alive. This discussion suggests that the issue had not come up much before and consequently no existing guideline was in place. The priest and his *calator* are essentially treated as a ritual unit or team in the Arval context.

89. The incense donated to honor Matidia's consecration weighed 50 Roman pounds = 16.3 kg and was recorded separately from the fragrant oil contributed by the priests themselves. See Scheid 1998, no. 69, lls. 5–7 with commentary *ad loc.*

90. In this context, Scheid 1998, 214, stresses the term *accessio.*

91. For the *tuscanicae*, see Scheid 1990a, 648–50, who interprets these as special Etruscan *ollae* (jars) used for ritual purposes.

92. Children and public slaves are frequent participants in ritual: Scheid 1998, nos. 58, l. 47, no. 69 lls. 32 and 53, no. 80 l. 26, no. 81.II l. 8, with commentary *ad loc.*

93. For expiatory rituals involving blades entering or leaving the grove, see Scheid 1998, nos. 48, 55, 65, 69, 91, 99a and 99b, 105b with commentary *ad loc.*

94. Linderski 1986 argues in detail for books of augural rituals. By contrast, Rüpke 2011, 29, claims that there were no manuals and that priestly records were protocols by date, not systematic collections of practices or beliefs. See Cicero *ND* 7.10–11 for Tiberius Sempronius Gracchus (cos. 177) consulting unspecified books to see if he made a ritual mistake in conducting the consular elections.

95. *CIL* 6.2187 = 7445 = *ILS* 4973 = *EDR* 107848 (Musei Vaticani, Galleria Lapidaria, 8, 18, inv. 5664) with Negroni 2001, 176. The inscription itself is not easy to date since the stone has been cut down for mounting in the wall and the letters have been redrawn in red paint. On purely epigraphic grounds, there is no reason this could not be a republican text, although

Degrassi did not include it in *ILLRP*. By comparison, see *CIL* 6.3878 = 6244 = 32447 = *ILS* 4974 = *EDR* 112875 (*MNR*, Terme inv. 30541) for the much more modest epitaph of T. Statilius Epaphra, freedman of (T.?) Statilius Corvinus, *calator XVvir* (*calator* to a *quindecemvir*). His patron was presumably Taurus Statilius Corvinus, cos. ord. AD 45 (*PIR*[2] S 822, *RE* 17, *BNP* Eck), see Rüpke 2008, no. 3130, who proposes that he became a *quindecemvir sacris faciundis* under Caligula, if not earlier. This man may be the father of Statilia Messalina, third wife of Nero.

96. *Dispensator* is another Latin term that can cover many functions, including steward, *procurator* (administrator), administrator of goods or crops, and *a rationibus* (accountant). All these jobs focus on financial and accounting expertise but in different contexts.

97. Paris' patron has been identified as Lucius Iunius M. f. D. n. Silanus (*PIR*[2] I 827), who is attested under Augustus. *CIL* 9. 332 has him as a praetor in c. 24 and *augur* but this inscription is now lost. Alternatively, another, earlier family member could also have held this same priesthood. Lucius is not a common *praenomen* among the Iunii Silani, which raises the further possibility that Paris' *praenomen* might not have matched that of the man who manumitted him.

98. *Calatores* are attested for the following priests: *pontifices, augurs, quindecemviri, sacerdotes Titalium Flavialium,* and the *Marciani Antoniniani.*

99. *CIL* 6. 2188 and 2189 = *ILS* 4976 = *EDR* 151260 (Rome, Villa Albani inv. 276) is inscribed on a large marble funerary altar of very uncertain date. The inscription on the front reads: *Q. Caecilio / Feroci / kalatori sacerdotii / Titialium Flavialium / studioso / eloquentiae / vixit annis XV / mense I diebus XXIIII / filio optimo ac / reverentissimo / M. Gavius Charinus.*

100. The association of *calatores* was known as the *kalatores pontificum et flaminum* (*CIL* 6. 712.900 = *ILS* 4970, *CIL* 6. 2186, *CIL* 6.31034 and 32445. See also *CIL* 6.31426 and 37167 with Bollmann 1998, 256–57, and Scott in *LTUR* (*schola: kalatores pontificum et flaminum*) who concludes that the southwest annex of the Regia could have served the *kalatores* as their meeting space in the late republic, at the time of Epicadus.

101. For some impressive monuments dedicated by one or more *calatores*, see *CIL* 6.2184 = 32445 = *ILS* 4971 (AD 101), *CIL* 6. 2185 = 31034 (AD 102), and *CIL* 6.40684 (AD 227–235). See also *AE* 1936, 95 = EDR073311 (found inside the church of S. Maria in Aracoeli on the Capitoline hill), for the gift by a group of *calatores* of a public banquet in honor of Jupiter (28th May AD 98).

102. For T. Tettienus Felix, *calator pontificum*, see *CIL* 10.531 (now in Salernum but discovered in Rome at the Vatican around 1470) = *ILS* 3593 = EDR 105782 with *CIL* 6.32455a and 31034. Discussion can be found in Eck 1978, 48n23, and Hartmann 2020, A.176 p. 161. This man seems exceptional in his degree of upward mobility, but it is not clear if he was himself a freedman or perhaps the son of a freedman. For his patron T. Titienus Serenus (suff. cos. AD. 81), see *PIR*[2] T 133 with *CIL* 6.1984 and 2185.

103. For the *scribae*, see now Hartmann 2020, with a full analysis and a catalog of known *scribae*.

104. Of course, Epicadus was not inevitably Sulla's first and only *calator*. A previous *calator* who is not attested could have died young.

105. For the debate about Sulla's augurate, a priesthood that is only directly attested by Suetonius' chapter on Epicadus, see *MRR* vol. 2 for 88; Badian 1968; Frier 1967, 1969; Keaveney 1982; Martin 1989; Vervaet 2004; Drummond 2008; North 2011; and Rosenblitt 2019, 125–30.

106. See Rüpke 2008 and 2011. Rüpke 2011, 30: "generally the rule that a person held only one priesthood at a time applied," and p. 31 table 2 shows that throughout Roman history the overall chance of any Roman *augur* holding a second priesthood was only 0.89 percent. There is no evidence for a second priesthood in the first century before Julius Caesar.

107. See Appian *B Civ.* 1.79 with commentary by Gabba 2021 (originally 1958/1967) *ad loc.*, who argues that this demand shows Sulla was already an *augur* before his departure for the East in 87. If this is not the augurate that Sulla was asking for, then another priesthood must be assumed, for which there is no evidence at all. But then we are left with a situation in which Sulla either goes on to be the first Roman to hold two priesthoods at the same time or he changes his mind when the augurate becomes available and somehow drops the priesthood he was asking for before his return. Gabba already proposed the most economical and logical explanation for this passage in Appian.

108. For Sulla, who invented the designation *hostis* before himself being subjected to this penalty, see Allély 2012, 21–33. It should be noted that this unprecedented status of being categorized as a "foreign enemy," first attested in the 80s, cannot be equated with traditional exile, which had often allowed a Roman to retain a priesthood, since priesthoods were customarily held for life.

109. Smith (*FRHist.* vol. 1 no. 22) thinks Sulla was both *augur* and *pontifex* at the same time but has no ancient evidence to support this hypothesis. Rüpke 2008, no. 1390, calls Sulla's priesthoods "among the most disputed of questions." He rules out a pontificate and instead proposes that Sulla had been *decemvir s.f.*, after his return from the war in Numidia. This was a priesthood held by other family members recently, probably from the late second century onward.

110. See Frier 1969 and especially the detailed treatment by Drummond 2008. North 2011 is unconvincing in his attempt to demolish Drummond's arguments. The long-disputed question as to whether two members of the same family could legally be represented in a single priestly college seems to be a distraction in Sulla's case. As North, 2011, 50, himself shows, there are several examples of this very situation in the 70s and 60s, before Labienus' law of 63 (Dio 37.37.1).

111. For Sulla's coin, see *RRC* 359 (84) with Noble 2014, 169–73. Ultimately, the jug and *lituus* depicted on this coin could refer to the office of *augur* or to Sulla's auspices as a general with *imperium* or to both conditions. This coin was minted in Greece (probably in Athens) in preparation for Sulla's invasion of Italy (Hollstein 2000a, 489–90, 2000b, 136; Pobjoy 2006, 68–69).

112. For Faustus' coin, that depicts augural symbols in association with other emblems that commemorate his father, see *RRC* 426 of 56.

113. Brennan 1992 offers the best reconstruction of Sulla's career in the 90s. Sulla may have been away from Rome between 97 and 92.

114. Note, however, that Marius may have been co-opted as *augur in absentia* in 98 or 97, which would show that this practice was possible at the time.

115. Rüpke 2008, no. 1390, has argued that this time frame would fit in with Sulla's career and status as a patrician but imagines him joining a different college of priests as a young man. See note 109.

116. Rüpke 2008, no. 2389, notes that "the *homo novus* was not accepted into a priesthood until he had served six consulates (in the years 107, and 104–100)."

117. For Faustus Sulla, see *RE* 377 (Münzer), *BNP* (Elvers) and *OCD* (Badian). He did not advance on the usual career beyond the office of quaestor (54) but clearly benefited from having married Pompey's daughter.

118. For example: if Sulla was chosen as *augur* in 92, a 20-year-old Epicadus would have been born in 112. Consequently, Epicadus would have been 58 when Faustus was quaestor in 54. By contrast, if Sulla became augur in 107, on the same model Epicadus (born in 127) would have been 73 in 54. Either model is possible; Epicadus could also have undertaken the role of *calator* at a younger age, while still in his teens, which would help explain why he outlived Sulla by so many years.

119. See Rüpke 2011, 29, table 1, on Roman priests as authors. The *augurs* are attested as the most likely of all the pagan priests to be engaged in literary pursuits.

120. *Contra* Kaster 1995, 163, assumes that there would have been no role for a *calator* during the years 87 to 83 while Sulla was a *hostis*. The reverse situation makes more sense, especially in light of Sulla's behavior overall.

121. Linderski 1986 remains the essential introduction to augural practice. See now also Santangelo 2013 and Driediger-Murphy 2019. There can be no doubt that the *augurs* were central to Roman religion.

122. For Sulla and religion, see Peter 1914, cclxxvi–vii, who already collected the signs. For Sulla and the gods, see Keaveney 1983; Fadinger 2002; Sumi 2002; Giardina 2008, especially 80–81; and Mann 2008. For the dreams (from the memoirs), see Kragelund 2001, 92–95. *FRHist.* vol. 1, 284 (Christopher Smith), notes "the deep overlay of religious symbolism and portentous prophecy that is clear at every stage." See also Flower 2015a and 2015b for further discussion. The issue of Sulla's belief was debated by Alföldi 1976 and Keaveney 1983. Mann 2008, 543–44, is excellent. See also Wiseman 2009.

123. For Sulla's memoirs, see Chassignet 2004, 172–84 with lxxxvi–vii and xcix–civ; Scholz and Walter 2013, 80–135 with full bibliography; and *FRHist.* no. 22 (Christopher Smith) vol. 1, 282–86, vol. 2, 472–91, vol. 3, 289–99. See also Engels 2007, 114–15; and Smith 2009.

124. For the consensus view that the last section of Plutarch's biography reflects the cutting-off point of Sulla's own narrative in 81, see Lewis 1991, 519; and Giardina 2008, 67.

125. For religion in Sulla's memoirs, see note 122.

126. A total of 22 books (= papyrus roles) would comprise a very extensive text; many more may have been planned.

127. For Sulla's habit of referring to detailed notes, see especially *RDGE* no. 23, lines 31 and 58 (85) that cites tablets containing these records.

128. Sulla's retirement took place early in 79, immediately following his second consulship.

129. For Lucullus and Sulla's memoirs, see Plutarch *Sulla* 6.5–6 and *Luc.* 1.4 and 4.5. Plutarch *Sulla* 6.10 = F8 Chassignet = *FRHist.* 22 F 14 refers to L. Licinius Lucullus (cos. 74, *RE* 104 Gelzer). Plutarch *Luc.* 4.5 notes his closeness to Sulla. Lucullus also wrote memoirs in a similar style; for the fragments, see *FRHist.* 23 (vol. 1, 287, and vol. 2, 492–93: Smith).

130. For the dreams associated with Sulla's death, see Appian *B Civ.* 1.105 with Gabba 2021 *ad loc.*; Weber 2000, 429–32; and Flower 2015a. For Sulla's funeral, see Plutarch *Sulla* 38 and Appian *B Civ.* 1.105–6, both full of precise details.

131. See already Flower 2015a and 2015b.

132. Sulla's slow death is described with some relish by Plutarch *Sulla* 36. This narrative is presumably a response to the idealized picture of Sulla at the end of his life to be found in the memoirs.

133. See Appian *B Civ.* 1.105 with Gabba 2021 *ad loc.* Flower 2015b discusses other incidents in Appian that seem to come from the memoirs but that are not found in Plutarch.

134. For *De Cognominibus,* see Charisius 110,3 = Funaioli 1907, p. 104 F 1. The paraphrase for Epicadus relates to the *cognomen* Sulla being derived from the Sibyl, which may reflect an etymology developed within the family of the Cornelii.

135. For *De Metris,* see Victorinus p. 209,9 = Funaioli 1907, p. 104 F 2.

136. Varro *LL* 5.148 = Funaioli 1907, 105 F 3 on the origins of the Lacus Curtius in the Roman Forum. This fragment seems to be shared with Daphnis.

137. For Augustine and Sulla, see Rawson 1987.

138. For Faustus Cornelius Sulla as *augur,* see *MRR* vol. 2 *ad loc.*

5. Foundlings: A Genial "Miser" and a Librarian who Collected Old Jokes

1. For *servus,* see the *OLD* and Lewis and Short.

2. For *verna,* see conveniently Horace *Ep.* 2.2.5 (*domi natus*) with Herrmann-Otto 1994.

3. For exposure as a Roman custom, see the overviews in Harris 1994; Corbier 2001; and Duboulez 2014.

4. Harris 1994 argues strongly for the widespread practice of exposure, most commonly for economic reasons, and its frequent resulting in the death of the infant. At the same time, he sees exposure as making a substantial contribution to the number of slaves overall. See already Ramin and Veyne 1981, 475. Other evidence for ancient conversations about exposure comes from the Stoic philosopher Gaius Musonius Rufus (first century AD), who opposed this practice, which he describes as not uncommon, and from Longus' Greek novel *Daphnis and Chloe* (second century AD) whose two protagonists are both *expositi.* The central question of how many *expositi* survived to be enslaved inevitably remains unanswered. Later authors claim that many exposed babies survived (Justin *First Apol.* 27.29 and Tertullian *Ad nat.* 1.16).

5. For Gnipho, see *RE* 59 (Goetz) with Kaster (*BNP* and *OCD*). For Melissus see *RE* Melissus (Wessner) and *PIR*² M 38 with Schmidt (*BNP*) and Brown (*OCD*).

6. Gnipho's dates were c. 114—c. 64 (Goetz in *RE* 59), while Melissus has sometimes been dated as late as c. 50 BC to c. AD 20 (Christes 1979, 87), but could have been born in the late 60s.

7. Soranus *Gyn.* 2.10 with Flemming 2021, 901.

8. For *patria potestas* and exposure, see Ramin and Veyne 1981; Corbier 2001, 58–60; Evans-Grubbs 2010, 297; and Flemming 2021, 906.

9. Harris 1994 lists deformity, illegitimacy, hard times, and evil omens (or despair) as the four principal reasons for exposure. Some of these would presumably make a baby less attractive to pick up. He thinks that girls were more likely to be exposed than boys. See now Flemming 2021, 903, for a nuanced approach to the question of sex-selection at birth. *P.Oxy.* IV, 744 (June 17, 2, Rowlandson 1998, p. 295, no. 230), is a much-cited letter from Hilarion to his wife Alis instructing her to expose her baby if she has a girl but keep the child if it is a boy.

10. Corbier 2001, 53–58.

11. See Shaw 2001, especially 56–77, on the father's right of life and death.

12. For a discussion of attested places of exposure in Roman towns, see Corbier 2001, 62.

13. For formal fostering, a practice linked to the Latin term *alumnus/a* (foster child), see Sigismund-Nielsen 1987 and 2013 and Bellemore and Rawson 1990. Flemming 2021 juxtaposes a discussion of exposure with fostering and formal adoption, the latter an alternative option

regularly practiced by prominent Roman families who were short of their own biological sons. Corbier 2001, 70–71, sees foster children (*alumni*) as a relatively rare phenomenon.

14. Evidence is available from wet nurse contracts on papyri from Egypt, some specifically for an exposed child who has been picked up (*anairetos*). *P.Kellis* 8 (AD 362, Rowlandson 1998, p. 274, no. 212) records the sale of a slave girl who is explicitly described as having been exposed at birth. See Evans-Grubbs 2010, 305–6, who argues that it would have been cheaper to pay for a baby's upkeep than to buy an older slave. Obviously, it is hard to generalize across time periods and geographical regions about such relative costs of child-rearing.

15. For the four instances of exposure in Suetonius, see *Aug.* 65.4, *Claud.* 27.3, *Gram. et rhet.* 7 and 21 with Corbier 2001, 60–62. Suetonius *Calig.* 5 records examples of despairing Romans allegedly exposing babies born at the time when Germanicus died. See also Dio 61.16.2 for a child exposed in the Forum in protest at Nero's murder of his mother, Agrippina the younger. A label (*pinakion*) was attached to the baby stating that the parents did not want to raise it in case it killed its mother.

16. Evans-Grubbs 2010 offers a detailed consideration of the evidence from the *Digest.* Most legal sources date from much later than republican Rome and may not reflect earlier conditions.

17. *Dig.* 40.4.29 records an exceptional case from the Antonine period of a son who retained his father's name even after exposure and was eventually reinstated within his birth family. He clearly lived locally and was known to his family. See Evans-Grubbs 2010 for discussion with a special focus on exposed children who were raised within their birth communities.

18. For the *vindex libertatis,* see Gardner 1986; Evans-Grubbs 2010, 297–99; and Flemming 2021, 906–7.

19. The lawsuit brought by Melissus' mother, discussed in detail later in this chapter, provides the principal extant example.

20. See *Dig.* 40.12.1–2 with Gardner 1986 and Evans-Grubbs 2010, 298. Strictly speaking, the *expositus* could obviously not be a witness to what had happened at the time of his birth. Yet, his complete removal from the case is an interesting development in Roman law, since testimony could be taken from enslaved persons in other lawsuits, albeit often under torture. The alleged *expositus,* therefore, exists in a kind of legal vacuum during a lawsuit brought about his original status at birth. His status appears to be separate from his person and his lived experience.

21. Cato the censor had already complained about the wrongful abuse of certain Italians, as if they were slaves, in the early second century (*ORF*[4] no. 8 F 58 = Manuwald 2023b F 58). More explicit evidence is provided by an exchange of letters between the emperor Trajan and Pliny (*Ep.* 10.65 and 66 cf. 72 and 73 with Sherwin-White 1966 *ad loc.* who refers to *threptoi* in inscriptions from Bithynia and Pontus) about a significant number of provincials who claimed to have been exposed and reared by another (*threptoi*). These people (or their parents?) now filed to change their status to that of Roman citizens. This correspondence shows that by the early second century AD many people were involved in these provinces and that their legal status was relevant to the way in which social status was understood to operate on a general level beyond the merits of their individual cases.

22. Dio Chrysostom mentions tokens left with exposed babies (4.25).

23. See Evans-Grubbs 2010, 307–10. For slave traders, see Bodel 2005.

24. For Melissus, freedman of Maecenas, see *RE* Melissus (Wessner) and *PIR*[2] M 38; Schmidt (*BNP*); Brown (*OCD*) with Christes 1979, 86–91; Kaster 1995, 214–22; Le Doze 2014b, 102 and 132; Chillet 2016, 405–7; and Gowers 2024, 41, 70–71, 96–97, 150.

25. For introductions to Augustan culture, see conveniently Galinsky 1996 and 2005; Wallace-Hadrill 2008; Morrell et al. 2019; and Le Doze 2020.

26. Kaster 1995 *ad loc.* provides the essential commentary.

27. Introductions to his publications could have included some of these autobiographical details, such as the age at which he started writing the *Ineptiae.*

28. For Spoletium, see *PECS* 858.

29. See *BGU* IV, 1104 (Rowlandson 1998, p. 171, no. 129, 8 BC), for a pregnant widow who is explicitly allowed to expose her infant and remarry, without owing anything more to her deceased husband's family.

30. The name Melissus might refer to a mythical king of Crete (Lactantius 1.22.19 and 28) or to a philosopher from Samos (Cicero *Acad.* 2.37.118). Alternatively, there could be a simpler reference to bees and beekeeping or to the sweetness associated with bees and their honey. Melissus is said to have been the author of a work on bees (Servius *ad Aen.* 7.66)

31. An enslaved war captive from Syria originally named Diokles was educated at the expense of a freedman named Dymas and given as a present to a certain Terentia. This case, whose chronology is uncertain, is discussed in detail in chapter 6.

32. An alternative scenario would have the *educator* be someone like the freedman Dymas (see chapter six), a self-made man who was seeking or repaying the favor of the great Maecenas with a costly and carefully chosen present. The hypothetical reconstruction suggested here imagines the *educator* as much closer to Maecenas himself in social and economic status. The 30s were a time of great political and economic turmoil; a number of reconstructions are surely possible in this time of societal transition.

33. On the Stanford University *ORBIS* site (https://orbis.stanford.edu) the following times are suggested for a journey in good weather from Spoletium to Rome: fast carriage (1.7 days), oxcart (9.3 days), walking (3.7 days). In other words, a range between 2 and 10 days seems likely for such a trip, which would represent a significant journey for a newborn under any conditions.

34. No discussion so far has raised the possibility that the woman who brought the suit and Melissus conspired together to put pressure on Maecenas with what was essentially a fraudulent lawsuit.

35. One may compare Melissus to Daphnis (discussed in chapter 3), who seems to have been enslaved for at least 10 years after completing his advanced education.

36. See Kaster 1995 *ad loc.* for Suetonius *Gram. et rhet.* 21 for this important observation.

37. See note 20.

38. Evans-Grubbs 2010, 298, posits that the mother withdrew her lawsuit to fit in with Melissus' preference to stay enslaved within the household of Maecenas. Kaster 1995, 217–18, points out that this is only one possible explanation. It is purely speculative to try to imagine how Melissus himself felt about the woman who claimed to be his mother and who seems to have been blaming his (now-deceased) father for the decision to expose him at the time of their divorce.

39. Why bring a case in the knowledge that the person in question was opposed to it? As presented by Suetonius, the failure of the lawsuit suggests that Melissus and his mother were not fully cooperating at that time.

40. For judges skeptical of false claims, see Dio 40.12.14 and 40.13.3.

41. If Melissus had been recognized as a free man, he would have owed his mother both the customary *pietas* of a biological son and presumably also the gratitude due to a personal benefactor or savior.

42. For manumission, see Mouritsen 2011 and 2016. Melissus' name (Gaius Maecenas Melissus) shows that he was manumitted by Maecenas.

43. In this chapter of *Gram. et rhet.*, Suetonius calls the emperor by the name Augustus. It is not evident, however, that this should be taken literally to indicate that Melissus was only introduced to his future patron in or after the year 27, when Octavian took his new name. The compressed nature of Suetonius' account and the fact that Melissus evidently went on to work for Augustus in the 20s and beyond could easily have led to an elision of the chronology here.

44. For C. Maecenas, see *RE* 6 (Stein and Kappelmacher) with Elvers (*BNP*) and Gowers (*OCD*). For an introduction to the extensive bibliography, see the entry by Philippe Le Doze in the Oxford Bibliographies online (https://www-oxfordbibliographies-com.ezproxy.princeton.edu/display/document/obo-9780195389661/obo-9780195389661-0395.xml?rskey=V7pjEi&result=203). For biographical treatments, see especially Le Doze 2014b; Chillet 2016; Mountford 2019; and now Gowers 2024. For the fragments of Maecenas' own poems, see Courtney 2003, 276–81; Hollis 2007, 314–25; Costa 2014; and Le Doze 2014b, 281–83. For Maecenas' name, see Simpson 1996; and Le Doze 2014b, 12–13.

45. As already noted by Stein (*RE* 6), Maecenas' many freedmen and slaves are attested by numerous inscriptions from Rome: *CIL* 6. 4610, 7245–7256, 10295, 17762, 21771–21785, 34134, 35756, 35757, and also by *CIL* 10.2687. See now Chillet 2016, 498–515, table 2 (74 inscriptions, including those of descendants of this household), and 395–410 for discussion. Two separate tombs have been found in Rome (Baccini Leotardi *LTUR Suburbium: Maecenatis familiae monumentum* with Cantarelli and Gautier di Confiengo 2012, 30–33, 52–58; and Cossu 2014).

46. Was Melissus a child favorite (*delicius*) of Maecenas, suggesting that he was exploited for sexual purposes? Maecenas was known for his attachment to attractive young boys. See Seneca *Ep.* 19.9, 101.10–13, and especially 114 for negative moralizing traditions about Maecenas' luxurious lifestyle. Maecenas was probably born between 74 and 68 (Le Doze 2014b, 13), which would make him at least a decade older than Melissus, perhaps more. For a thought-provoking discussion of literate, enslaved children and sexual exploitation, see now Beckmann 2023.

47. For the political scandal that has been associated with Maecenas withdrawing from a political role in 23, see Suetonius *Aug.* 66.3 with Syme 1961, 28–29; Williams 1990; White 1991; Rohr Vio 2000, 285–96; Le Doze 2009; and Rohr Vio 2011, 57–69. Le Doze 2014a and 2014b, 73–112, argues that Maecenas stepped back from his former political role already in 29, soon after the triple triumph and well before Octavian took the name Augustus. It remains unclear, however, to what extent Maecenas' personal relationship with Augustus was changed by either the disgrace and execution of his brother-in-law A. Terentius Varro Murena in 23 or by his own wife Terentia's (subsequent?) intimate relationship with the princeps (Dio 54.19.3, 16 BC). Le Doze argues in detail against disgrace or loss of friendship. Alternatively, perhaps Augustus was quick to secure the services of Melissus at a moment when Maecenas was no longer in as strong a position to object? See Chillet 2016, 373–78, on the marriage of Maecenas and Terentia.

48. One may cite the example of the learned and prolific Gaius Julius Hyginus, a captive originally from Alexandria, who became the head of the Palatine library adjacent to Augustus'

house on the Palatine (Suetonius *Gram. et rhet.* 20) with Kaster 1995 *ad loc.* and *FRHist.* no. 63 (Levick and Cornell).

49. For Maecenas' "circle," see Gold 1987, 115–41, 221–32; White 1993; Le Doze 2014a, 2014b, 229–43, and 2019; and Chillet 2016. A list of poets and others associated with Maecenas includes Virgil, Horace, M. Varius Rufus, Propertius, Plotius Tucca, Quintilius Varus, Aristius Fuscus, Domitius Marsus, Fundanius, Valgius Rufus, Aemilius Macer, and Sabinius Tiro.

50. For the portico of Octavia, see Ovid *AA* 1.69, Livy *Per.* 138, Velleius Paterculus 1.11, Vitr. 3.2.5, Pliny *HN* 36.42, Suetonius *Aug.* 29, Fest. 178, Dio 49.43. For the library named in memory of Marcellus, see Plut. *Marc.* 30 and Ovid *Tr.* 3.1.69; for the curia Octaviae, see Pliny *HN* 36 28; for the *schola(e)*, see Pliny *HN* 35.114 and 36.22. For discussion and bibliography, see Viscogliosi in *LTUR* (both the porticus Metelli and the porticus Octaviae) and Petruccioli in Haselberger 2002, 206. The library is also attested in the epitaph of one of its subsequent library staff, a public slave named Philoxenus Iulianus (*CIL* 6.2348 = *ILS* 1972 = *ILMN* no. 66 p. 84). Le Doze 2014b, 102, argues that Melissus was hired for the job at the library after 23 and that this shows the continuing close connections of Maecenas' household with the *domus Augusta*. See also Houston 2014, 222, for Melissus as a librarian.

51. For the fragments of Melissus' works, see Funaioli 1907, 537–40.

52. The second-century playwright Terence, who was said to have coauthored some of his comedies with his aristocratic backers, is discussed in the preface. Horace calls Melissus' patron Maecenas *iocosus* in a poem (*Epod.* 3.20 with Le Doze 2014b, 273–76) composed in or before the year 30.

53. See *CIL* 6.5715 for the tomb inscription of [Q.] Poppaedius Gnipho, who may also be a freedman.

54. For Gnipho, see *RE* 59 (Goetz), *HLL* no. 279, and Kaster (*BNP* and *OCD*) with Treggiari 1969b, 5, 114–15; Christes 1979, 21–15; and Rawson 1985, 16, 35, 52, 67, 74, 76n43, 118, 121–22, 269. For the fragments of his works, see Funaioli 1907, 98–100.

55. Kaster 1995, 122, argues that Philologus meant works written by some of Gnipho's students were later attributed to him. Alternatively, the students may have circulated versions of notes they had taken from his lectures, classes, or oratorical declamations. Epictetus' discourses were recorded by his pupil Arrian of Nicomedia. A tentative comparison could perhaps also be made with *The Blue and Brown Books* that reproduced notes taken from lectures delivered by Ludwig Wittgenstein at Cambridge in 1933–35.

56. See Kaster 1995, 116.

57. Suetonius' account of Gnipho's life stresses his *comitas* throughout.

58. For L. Ateius Philologus (*RE* 11, Goetz), see Kaster (*BNP* and *OCD*). According to Suetonius *Gram. et rhet.* 10, he picked the name Philologus (scholar, fond of learning, learned) for himself. He is discussed in chapter 6.

59. But is it possible that this Gallic location was outside the Roman sphere of direct control? Was Gnipho trafficked as a baby across the boundary of the Roman province of Narbonensis (for example)? In this case, the term *expositus* would be claiming free Gallic birth beyond the borders of the Roman empire.

60. Treggiari 1969b, 5, opts for Gallia Transalpina and posits that Gnipho will have shared a Mediterranean Hellenized cultural background with scholars such as Tyrannio of Amisus and Publilius the Syrian. By contrast, Rawson 1985, 35, places Gnipho's origin in Cisalpine Gaul, the

region that would go on to produce so many writers including Catullus and Vergil. Kaster 1995, 117, also opts for northern Italy.

61. For Alexandria as a cultural center, see especially the classic treatment by Fraser 1972. Maehler 1983 gives a succinct overview of the last Ptolemies.

62. Kaster 1995, 118, clarifies the grammar and meaning in Suetonius' text.

63. In a subsequent generation, young Romans did travel to Egypt for educational purposes, as was the case with the several acquaintances who hosted the ambassador Dio of Alexandria in 56 BC. See Cicero *Cael.* 10 and 21 with Dyck 2013 *ad loc.* with the discussion of Timagenes of Alexandria in chapter 6. A freedman accompanied Cicero's son Marcus to Athens, partly to make sure that he received his allowance in installments (*Att.* 5.15.4).

64. As Kaster 1995, 117, explains, it would have been the usual norm for a person to be fully educated before manumission. Suetonius may, therefore, simply be varying his word order. Alternatively, as explored here, the distance of Egypt from Rome could have created special conditions in which an early manumission for Gnipho made sense.

65. M. Antonius (cos. 99, cens. 97, *RE* 28 Klebs) was celebrated as a great orator by Cicero, especially in *De Oratore* and *Brutus* (*Brut.* 138–440). None of his speeches seem to have been published (*ORF*[4] no. 65). His (attested) sons were M. Antonius Creticus (*RE* 29 Klebs, pr. 74) and C. Antonius Hybrida (*RE* 19 Klebs, cos. 63). Ironically, he was said to have been betrayed to the Marians by the carelessness of a slave (Appian *B Civ.* 1.72).

66. For the relationship between the Julii and the Antonii, see Creticus' marriage to a Julia (*RE* 543, Münzer, daughter of L. Caesar, cos. 90, *RE* 142, Münzer and of Fulvia, daughter of M. Fulvius Flaccus, cos. 125), which produced the triumvir Marc Antony (*RE* 30, Groebe), as well as his two brothers Gaius (*RE* 20, Klebs) and Lucius (*RE* 23, Klebs), and (perhaps also) a sister (*RE* 111, Klebs). Mark Antony, one of Caesar's closest friends, was, therefore also related to him. Antony named a son by his own wife Fulvia Iullus Antonius (*RE* 22, Groebe) in honor of the Julii and then went on to marry Octavia, sister of the future emperor Augustus and great-niece of Caesar (his sister's granddaughter). These marriage and kinship ties will have affected both the family members themselves and the members of their households.

67. For Julius Caesar's studies on Rhodes, see Rawson, 1985, 110, with Plutarch *Caes.* 2.2. Hall 2009 offers an especially insightful contextualization and argument that Caesar used language for political and national purposes.

68. Macrobius *Sat.* 3.13.6.

69. Suetonius notes that Gnipho died in his fiftieth year, which is generally taken to be soon after Cicero was praetor in 66. Yet Gnipho must have taught the young Caesar at the end of the 90s and in the early 80s, if Caesar was born in 100. Consequently, his lifetime seems to be closely defined by these specific indicators.

70. For Caesar as an author, see Suetonius *Iul.* 56 and now conveniently the essays in Grillo and Krebs 2018, with full recent bibliography. For Caesar as an orator, see *ORF*[4] no. 121 with Manuwald 2019, vol. 2, no. 121.

71. See Wiseman 1998 for the definitive argument showing that the *De Bello Gallico* was published in annual installments, rather than as a single text in the late 50s. Fronto (Parth. 9 p. 224, 12–17, van den Hout 1988) notes that Caesar was working on these several publications at the same time and while waging war in Gaul.

72. Caesar is included in this category on the website *Grammatici Disiecti*: https://gradis.hypotheses.org. Such an identification was already hinted at by the *Suda* (K 1196) but is rejected by Garcea 2012, 28, in his edition of the fragments as an "oversimplification."

73. For contemporary debates about the Latin language, see the very detailed introduction (pp. 1–124) to Garcea's 2012 edition of the fragments of Caesar's *De Analogia* with Hall 2009, especially 23, 37n133; Krebs 2013 and 2017. Garcea argues for Philodemus as the decisive intellectual influence on Caesar. It seems likely that Caesar was influenced by many intellectuals of his day, while still building on the foundational knowledge he had acquired from Gnipho.

74. For Opillus and Epicadus, see chapter 4.

75. For Caesar as a brilliant orator, see Cicero *Brut.* 252–53, 261–62; Quintilian *Inst.* 10.1.114, 12.10.11; Tacitus *Dial.* 25.3–4; and Suetonius *Iul.* 55.1–3. But before 66, Caesar had spoken mainly and not always successfully in the lawcourts. In addition, one may note that he spoke in favor of the *lex Plautia* at someone else's *contio* in 70 (Suetonius *Iul.* 5, Gellius *NA* 13.3.5) and delivered funeral orations for his aunt Julia, widow of Marius, and for his wife Cornelia, daughter of Cinna, in 69, the year he was quaestor (Suetonius *Iul.* 6). In 66 he spoke again at a *contio* in favor of the *lex Manilia* (Dio 36.43.2) and was elected as curule aedile for the following year. In other words, most of his famous speeches still lay ahead of him.

76. Maecenas died in September 8 at the same time as Horace, after some years of ill health (Suetonius *vit. Hor.*).

77. For Roman *cognomina* in general, see Kajanto 1982. The Antonii whom Gnipho interacted with also had mocking nicknames attached to them, including Creticus (the Cretan) and Hybrida (half-breed). See Bruun 2013 for the names of *vernae* within the household.

78. For slave traders, see Bodel 2005.

6. Intellectual Prisoners Captured in War: Two Tyrants, a Literary Scholar, and a Fierce Critic

1. Already in Homer the fate of a captured city is unambiguous and undisputed; many of its surviving inhabitants would be enslaved after a siege.

2. The term "prisoner of war" is sometimes applied specifically to combatants rather than to civilians, but in other contexts it is used to designate anyone captured or interned in an armed conflict. In the case of the captives discussed in this chapter, it seems unlikely both that they never took up arms in the face of war or that the Romans would have classified men of fighting age as noncombatants through a detailed analysis of their actual roles in the conflict.

3. For Archimedes' death in the Roman sources, see Livy 25.31 with Jaeger 2013, 126 and 131, and 2008, 77–99, with full references.

4. Appreciating the learning of an educated individual and exploiting him for that same learning were often, if not usually, two sides of the same coin.

5. For Tyrannio of Amisos, see Wendel (*RE* 2); Forbes, Browning, and Wilson (*OCD*); Baumbach (*BNP*); Haas 1977, 93–96 with 16 *testimonia*; Christes 1979, 27–38; and Rawson 1985, 40–43, 52, 67, 69, 111. The main source for his life is the *Suda* at T 1184 (see note 24). Amisos, a town originally settled by Ionian Greeks from Miletus, subsequently a colony of Athens in the fifth century, is now the major Turkish Black Sea port named Samsun.

6. For the siege of Amisos, see Cicero *Leg. Man.* 8.21, Memnon of Heraclea (*BNJ* 434) 30, Plutarch *Luc.* 14, 15, 19 and Appian *Mithr.* 83. For the war overall, see Appian *Mithr.* 72–83 with commentary by Goukowsky 2001. Will 1982, 83–74 and 490–92, discusses Murena's exploits during the war.

7. For the Roman province(s) of Bithynia and Pontus, see Storey 1999; Marek 2003; and Harris 2019.

8. Strabo *Geogr.* 12.3.16 and 13.1.54. He calls Tyrannio *philaristoteles* (a lover of Aristotle).

9. For example, Baumbach (*BNP*) simply notes that Tyrannio was "probably" working in Rome from c. 68, without any explanation for his move. Such an elision demonstrates, once again, how easy it is for us to focus on the intellectual career of an individual at the expense of lived experience. See note 133 for more examples. Other educated men certainly were drawn to Rome as immigrants, in the way that Archias had come already in 102.

10. For the destruction of the city, see Plutarch *Luc.* 19 and especially Appian *Mithr.* 83 where Lucullus destroys and repopulates Amisos, whose inhabitants are said to have fled by sea.

11. How many societies did the Romans come across that did not use some form of enslaved labor? Hardly any, and certainly none in the Hellenized Eastern Mediterranean.

12. For Plutarch's biography of Lucullus, see Tröster 2008 for a detailed analysis, especially 36–37.

13. For L. Licinius Lucullus (cos. 74, *RE* 104 Gelzer), see Badian (*OCD*); Will (*BNP*); Smith (*FRHist.* no. 23); and Beness and Hillard (*BNJ* no. 185) with ample bibliography.

14. For the fragments of Lucullus' history of the Social War, see *FRHist.* 23 (vol. 1, 287 and vol. 2, 492–93: Smith). Fantham 2013, 8, identifies a memoir by Lucullus as an important source for Plutarch. Such a work is also imagined by Chassignet 2004, p. C n. 522, but not mentioned by Tröster 2008; Scholz and Walter 2013; or *FRHist.* (2013).

15. For Sulla's memoirs, see Chassignet 2004, 172–84 with lxxxvi–vii and xcix–civ; Scholz and Walter 2013, 80–135, with full bibliography; and *FRHist.* no. 22 (Christopher Smith) vol. 1, 282–86, vol. 2, 472–91, vol. 3, 289–99. See also Engels 2007, 114–15; Smith 2009; and Flower 2015a and 2015b.

16. For direct speech, see Plutarch *Luc.* 19.5.

17. At Plutarch *Luc.* 19.5 Lucullus weeps over the city in the way that Aemilianus did over Carthage at the end of the Third Punic War. He tells his friends that Sulla was fortunate to be able to save Athens after the siege (!) while he himself will be thought of simply as a second Mummius (who destroyed Corinth), although he had wanted to save Amisos. One may also note that this episode is similar in some ways to Josephus' description (written in the 70s AD) of Titus' vain attempts to save the Temple in Jerusalem from being burned by his troops, who ignore his desperate instructions (*BJ* 6.4). Plutarch was writing well after Josephus.

18. For the Athenian citizens in Amisos, see Plutarch *Luc.* 19.6 with Christes 1979, 29.

19. See by comparison Plutarch *Luc.* 12.5 for Lucullus requesting that his soldiers bring Marcus Marius (quaestor 76) to him so that he could torture him to death. Because Marius had lost an eye fighting with Sertorius in Spain, Lucullus ordered his soldiers to spare all men with only one eye so that his victim could be identified among them. See also Appian *Mithr.* 77 and Orosius 6.2.22.

20. For L. Licinius Murena, see *RE* 123, Münzer; Frigo (*BNP*); Badian (*OCD*); and Fantham 2013, 6–8. He was consul in 62.

21. Münzer (*RE* Licinius 123) has the siege start in the spring of 72 and not conclude until later in 71. Regardless of the exact timeline, it seems to have been hard fought.

22. For an overview of Roman manumission, see Mouritsen 2011, 2013, and 2016.

23. For Murena's movements, see Cicero *Mur.* 20 and 89; and Plutarch *Luc.* 15 for the early stages of the war. After the fall of Amisos in 71, Murena campaigned in Armenia (Plutarch *Luc.* 25 6f.) and spent time at Tigranokerta (Plutarch *Luc.* 27.2). He subsequently returned to Rome in 68 (Cicero *Att.* 13.6.4). His return could, therefore, have been as long as three years after the initial capture of Tyrannio.

24. *Suda* T 1184: Τυραννίων, Ἐπικρατίδου καὶ Λινδίας Ἀλεξανδρίνης, Ἀμισηνός. ἐχρημάτιζε δὲ Κορύμβου, γεγονὼς ἐπὶ Πομπηΐου τοῦ μεγάλου καὶ πρότερον, μαθητὴς ἄλλων τε καὶ Ἑστιαίου τοῦ Ἀμισηνοῦ, ὑφ' οὗ καὶ Τυραννίων ὠνομάσθη, ὡς κατατρέχων τῶν ὁμοσχόλων, πρότερον καλούμενος Θεόφραστος. εἶτα διήκουσε καὶ Διονυσίου τοῦ Θρᾳκὸς ἐν Ῥόδῳ. ἀντεσοφίστευσε δὲ Δημητρίῳ τῷ Ἐρυθραίῳ: ἤχθη δὲ εἰς Ῥώμην, ληφθεὶς αἰχμάλωτος ὑπὸ Λουκούλλου, ὅτε κατεπολέμησε Μιθριδάτην, τὸν Πόντου βασιλεύσαντα. διαπρεπὴς δὲ γενόμενος ἐν Ῥώμῃ καὶ πλούσιος ἐκτήσατο καὶ βιβλίων ὑπὲρ τὰς τρεῖς μυριάδας. ἐτελεύτησε δὲ γηραιός, ὑπὸ ποδάγρας παραλυθείς, ὀλυμπιάδι ριη' ἐν τῷ γ'ἔτει τῆς ὀλυμπιάδος. (Tyrannio from Amisos, son of Epikratides and of Lindia, a woman from Alexandria. But he used to call himself son of Korybos. He lived at the time of Pompey the Great and before. He was a student of other teachers and of Hestiaios of Amisos, by whom he was also given the name of "Tyrant," because he was in the habit of criticizing his fellow students. Previously he was called Theophrastus. Then he studied with Dionysius the Thracian on Rhodes. He was a rival sophist to Demetrius of Erythrai [*RE* 105]. He came to Rome after being taken as a prisoner of war by Lucullus when he defeated Mithridates, the king of Pontus. Once he became illustrious and wealthy at Rome, he acquired over 30,000 books. He died as an old man, crippled by gout, in the 118th Olympiad, in the third year of that Olympiad.) The Olympiad year is clearly wrong here and is usually emended to the 188th = 26. Christes 1979, 27, sees this information as derived from Hermippos of Berytus, who is discussed in chapter 7. See also Blänsdorf 2016, 111–12.

25. Haas 1977, 93, explains that Korymbos is a pun on Epicratides, his father's name.

26. For Dionysius Thrax, who taught at Rhodes, see Linke 1977 and Haas 1977, 96. For Aristarchus of Samothrace, see *Suda* S 3892 with Schironi 2018, especially 3–6.

27. See Diogenes Laetius 5.84 with Haas 1977, 94.

28. For all the *testimonia*, see Haas 1977.

29. Haas 1977, 95, suggests Tyrannio was born c. 110–100 and lived into the 20s.

30. It is, of course, possible that Tyrannio already had a personal library in Amisos that was seized and accompanied him into the possession of Murena, but this seems less likely. For Tyrannio and libraries, see Rawson 1985, 40–43; and Houston 2014.

31. In 59 Cicero was seeking advice from Tyrannio about writing a geographical work (*Att.* 2.6.1).

32. *Suda* S 643 for Caesar and Tyrannio's book on the meter of the *skolion*, with Christes 1979, 37–38, and Rawson, 1985, 111 and 125. For the reading at Atticus' house, see Cicero *Att.* 12.6.2 with Rawson 1985, 52.

33. See Haas 1977 for discussion and fragments. By contrast, Christes 1979, 38, argues that Tyrannio did not publish much himself and was mainly famous as a teacher.

34. For Sulla's library, see Strabo *Geogr.* 13.1.54 and Plutarch *Sulla* 26.1–3 with Houston 2014, 34–37.

35. For the books of Apellicon, see the critical discussion of Lindsay 1997, who argues that Apellicon, who was a bibliophile rather than a scholar, exaggerated the contents and rarity of his collection. Regardless of the exact nature and value of these papyri, Tyrannio identified and put them in order and gained considerable recognition as a result.

36. For Cicero's library reorganization in 57–56, see *Att.* 4.4a.1, 4.8.2 with Johnson 2012; Houston, 2014, 218; Blänsdorf 2016, 110; and Moss 2024, 155–56. Cicero's latest preserved references to Tyrannio are in 46 (*Att.* 12.2.2 and 12.6.2).

37. Houston 2014, 219–20. For the library organizing software named for Tyrannio of Amisos, see Tyrannioware, http://www.panix.com/~asl2/software/Tyrannio/.

38. For Quintus and Tyrannio, see Cicero *Q fr.* 3.4.5 and 3.5.6 in 54. Tyrannio's reason for refusing this assignment is not revealed.

39. For Diokles, see Wendel (*RE* 3); Baumbach (*BNP*); Forbes and Wilson (*OCD*); Haas 1977, 96–97; Christes 1979, 64–67; and Rawson 1985, 17 and 69.

40. *Suda T 1185:* Τυραννίων, ὁ νεώτερος, Φοίνιξ, πατρὸς Ἀρτεμιδώρου, μαθητὴς Τυραννίωνος τοῦ πρεσβυτέρου· διὸ καὶ ὠνομάσθη Τυραννίων, πρότερον καλούμενος Διοκλῆς. αἰχμάλωτος δὲ γενόμενος καὶ αὐτὸς ἐπὶ τοῦ πολέμου Ἀντωνίου καὶ Καίσαρος ὑπό τινος Δύμαντος ὠνήθη, τοῦ Καίσαρος ὄντος ἀπελευθέρου, εἶτα ἐδωρήθη Τερεντίᾳ τῇ τοῦ Κικέρωνος γυναικί. ἐλευθερωθεὶς δὲ ὑπ' αὐτῆς ἐσοφίστευσεν ἐν Ῥώμῃ. καὶ ἔγραψε βιβλία πρὸς η' καὶ ξ', ὧν καὶ ταῦτα· Περὶ τῆς Ὁμηρικῆς προσῳδίας, Περὶ τῶν μερῶν τοῦ λόγου, ἐν ᾧ λέγει, ἄτομα μὲν εἶναι τὰ κύρια ὀνόματα. θεματικὰ δὲ τὰ προσηγορικά, ἀθέματα δὲ τὰ μετοχικά· Περὶ τῆς Ῥωμαϊκῆς διαλέκτου ὅτι ἐστίν ἐκ τῆς Ἑλληνικῆς, ἐκ τοῦ Ἀντιγένους ὅτι ἀντιγένης ἡ Ῥωμαϊκὴ διάλεκτος, Ὅ τι διαφωνοῦσιν οἱ νεώτεροι ποιηταὶ πρὸς Ὅμηρον, Ἐξήγησιν τοῦ Τυραννίωνος μερισμοῦ, Διόρθωσιν Ὁμηρικήν, Ὀρθογραφίαν. (Tyrannio the younger, a Phoenician, his father was Artemidorus, he was a pupil of the older Tyrannio. For this reason, he was named Tyrannio, having before been called Diokles. Having been captured as a prisoner of war himself also in the war between Antony and Caesar, he was bought by a certain Dymas, a freedman of Caesar, and then he was given as a present to Terentia, the wife of Cicero. After being manumitted by her, he was a sophist in Rome. He wrote about 65 books, including *On Homeric Language, About the Parts of Speech* [in which he says that proper nouns are indivisible and that appellatives can form the basis of derivatives, but particles cannot], *On the Roman Dialect* [which he derives from Greek, not from a local language?], *The Disagreement of the New Poets with Homer, Exegesis of Tyrannio's Parts of Speech, Textual Criticism of Homer, Spelling.*) There is some corruption in the title of the work on the Latin language.

41. Since nothing else is known about Dymas, the date of his manumission is also lost. He will presumably have received his new status as a citizen before his patron took the name Augustus, but probably not before the Ides of March and the posthumous adoption of C. Octavius by his great-uncle Julius Caesar. Consequently, his Roman citizen name was probably C. Julius Dymas, rather than C. Octavius Dymas.

42. The debate about when Diokles arrived in Rome was already well underway when Wendel wrote his entry in *RE* in the 1940s. He argued forcefully for keeping the dating to after Actium as indicated by the *Suda*. Haas 1977, 96–97, agrees; since this chronology is possible, we should not try to emend it. By contrast, Treggiari 2007, 143–44, opts for the war between Caesar and Pompey, following Christes 1979, 64–67. This higher dating would make Dymas a freedman of Julius Caesar who acquired Diokles in the early 40s, rather than in the late 30s, a difference of almost 20 years.

43. Christes 1979, 30–32, presents a nuanced argument for the earlier date. According to his timeline, Tyrannio of Amisos would have died in the mid-40s and been succeeded then by Diokles. He posits that there were never two Tyrannios active as teachers at the same time.

44. For the family of the Terentii, see Münzer *RE* Terentius. The scholar Varro was the most prominent member of the family.

45. For Terentia, first wife of Cicero, see Weinstock (*RE* 95), *PIR*^{2} T 75, Strothmann (*BNP*), Flower (*OCD*), Dixon 1986, and especially Treggiari 2007. Treggiari 2007, 143–44, sees Cicero's wife as the recipient of Diokles but is surprised by the gift. Her conclusion on p. 144 is valid regardless of which Terentia was involved and when the donation took place: "If a freedman of Caesar gave her a scholar as a present, he must have thought the gift would be welcome."

46. For Terentia, wife of Maecenas, see Stein (*RE* 96), *PIR*^{2} T 76, and Strothmann (*BNP*). Hillscher 1892, 375, was the first to suggest that she should be identified as the recipient of Diokles. Horace *Od.* 2.12 may be dedicated to her.

47. For her divorce from Maecenas, see Trebatius in *Digest* 24.1.64 with Le Doze 2014b, 197–200; and Chillet 2016, 373–78.

48. Le Doze 2014a and 2014b, 73–112, has reconstructed their complex relationship in detail. See now Gowers 2024, 2–3, 5, 155, 233.

49. For a detailed discussion of the foundling Melissus, see chapter 5.

50. For Augustus' personal relationship with Terentia, see Dio 54.19 and 55.7.5. Even if these were simply rumors, they nevertheless attest to the close association that continued between Terentia and her husband and the princeps over many decades.

51. See Haas 1977; and Christes 1979, 35–38 and 66–67.

52. For Archias, see chapter 2.

53. For Dymas' full name, see note 41.

54. For Cato in Spain, see Plutarch *Cato Mai.* 10–11 with the discussion in chapter 2.

55. If Dymas had himself also been a pupil of Tyrannio, that relationship could have made it easier for him to arrange for Diokles also to study with the great master. Christes 1979, 178–80, imagines that a freedman like Dymas might himself have been a *grammaticus.* He draws attention to the pattern shared by Daphnis, Diokles, and others of an initial patron of lower social status, followed by a much more prominent one.

56. For L. Ateius Philologus (*RE* 11, Goetz), see Kaster (*BNP* and *OCD*); Treggiari 1969b, 5, 121–22; Christes 1979, 43–48; and Rawson 1985, 8–9 and 73–74. Much of what we know about him can be found in Suetonius *Gram. et rhet.* 10 (with commentary by Kaster 1995, *ad loc.*).

57. Rawson 1985, 73n31, raised the possibility that Philologus had already been enslaved and was not a citizen. It would be much less likely, however, for him to have received an advanced education in Athens under these social circumstances.

58. For L. Ateius the centurion, see Tacitus *Ann.* 3.75.1 and Plutarch *Sulla* 14.3 with the *Fasti Capitolini* for AD 5 (*II* 13.1.61) and Kaster 1995, 138.

59. L. Ateius Capito (suff. cos. AD 5, *RE* 8 Jörs, *PIR*^{2} A 1279) the prominent jurist was probably born in the 40s. The fact that he remarks on Philologus' skills in various areas may also provide evidence for Philologus' long life into the Augustan age.

60. For an example of a swift auction of prisoners, see Cicero in Cilicia (*Att.* 5.20.5 = SB 113, December 19, 51). This auction in the Roman camp at Pindenissum raised HS 120,000 in total. For the habit of such sales, see Livy 23.37 and Tacitus *Ann.* 13.39.7 with Huemoeller 2021.

61. In calculating Philologus' lifespan, it is generally assumed that he was about 20 years old when captured in 86 (a birthdate of c. 106 would make him the same age as Cicero). He clearly outlived Sallust (who died in 35) and may well have survived into the 20s. He would have been about 80 years old in 27. For Tyrannio's timeline, see note 29.

62. For the brilliant and personable Gnipho, see chapter 5.

63. For Pollio at school, see Suetonius *Gram. et rhet.* 10.2 with the textual reading of Kaster 1995, 140–1: *praetextatis nobis grammaticus Latinus* (a Latin teacher at the time when we were schoolboys).

64. For the brothers, both apparently called Appius Claudius Pulcher (*RE* 298 and 299), see Suetonius *Gram. et rhet.* 10.3 with commentary by Kaster 1995, 143–45, who explains their identification as sons of C. Claudius Pulcher (pr. 56, *RE* 303), who was governor of Asia (55–53). Philologus will have traveled through Greece and spent these years with the Claudii in Asia.

65. For "Praetextatus" in the text of Suetonius at 10.2, see Lebek 1970; and Kaster 1995, 141. The alternative text (Robinson 1925) reads: *Ateius Praetextatus nobilis grammaticus Latinus* (Ateius Praetextatus a prominent Latin teacher) as opposed to *Ateius praetextatis nobis grammaticus Latinus*. See note 63.

66. For freedmen wearing the *toga praetexta* at Compitalia, see Flower 2017, 166.

67. For the semantic range of the adjective and related noun *praetextatus*, see *TLL ad loc.*

68. For Philologus and Sallust, see Suetonius *Gram. et rhet.* 10.6 with Kaster 1995, *ad loc.*

69. For Philologus and Pollio, see Suetonius *Gram. et rhet.* 10.6 with Kaster 1995, *ad loc.*

70. For the fragments of Philologus' works, see Funaioli 1907, 136–41. Suetonius, who had read at least some of what Philologus wrote, claims that by his day most of Philologus' works were lost.

71. It is Charisius (p. 127, 17) who mentions a separate work entitled *An amaverit Didun Aeneas*. There remain faint traces of a special relationship between Anna and Aeneas in Vergil's version (*Aen.* 4.421–22).

72. *Gram. et rhet.* 10.2: *inter grammaticos rhetorem, inter rhetores grammaticum*. As Kaster 1995, 140, notes, it is not easy to catch the precise tone of this remark. It seems to place Philologus in a category all his own, too skillful with language to be a *grammaticus*, but not quite eloquent or learned enough to be an orator or teacher of rhetoric.

73. *Gram. et rhet.* 10.3 with Kaster 1995, *ad loc.* The letters Suetonius cites were addressed to a certain Laelius Hermas, an otherwise unknown freedman in the circle of Philologus.

74. Rawson 1985, 8, identifies three major figures who came to Rome as enslaved captives during the Mithridatic wars: Tyrannio of Amisos, Alexander Polyhistor, and Parthenius of Nicaea.

75. For Timagenes, see Laqueur (*RE* 2), Meister (*BNP*), and especially the updated entries in Capponi (*OCD*) and McInerney and Roller (*BNJ* no. 88). Especially influential discussions can also be found in Fraser 1972, 518–19; Sordi 1982; Alonso-Núñez 1982; Muccioli 2009 and 2012; Wisse 2013a; Capponi 2017, 42–57, and 2018.

76. For Daphnis, reputedly the most expensive *verna* sold at auction, see chapter 3.

77. For Gabinius' controversial military operation in Egypt, see conveniently Siani-Davies 1997. For more general background from an Egyptian point of view, see Maehler 1983; Manning 2010; Morrell 2019; Osgood 2019; and Rich 2024.

78. See especially Bowersock 1965, 123–27; Sordi 1982; Malitz 1983, 52–53; Engels 1999, 229–42; Muccioli 2009 and 2012; and Mehl 2014, 111–12. Capponi 2018, 42, calls him the most

important historian writing in Greek in this period. McInerney and Roller (*BNJ* no. 88) describe him as "one of the most significant scholars of the latter 1st century and an important figure in the transfer of Greek intellectual culture to Rome."

79. The nineteenth-century notion that Pompeius Trogus largely reproduced Timagenes has now been discredited (Fraser 1972, 519; and Sordi 1982, 777–78). Jacoby in his introduction already noted (no. 88 in 1926) that Timagenes has loomed much larger in scholarship than the 15 slim fragments of his work (many from Ammianus Marcellinus) would normally have inspired. Timagenes has been posited as an inspiration and source for Strabo, Plutarch, Appian, and Pausanias (see, e.g., Fraser 1972, 746n202; and Westall 2015).

80. For Evagoras of Lindos, see Jacoby (*RE* 12), who suggested that Evagoras had himself been a student of Timagenes; Radicke (*BNJ* no. 1055); and Moyer (*OCD*) with Muccioli 2012, 378–79.

81. *Suda* T 588.

82. Fraser 1972, 746–47n203: "a money-changer is likely to have been a person of humble position."

83. Timagenes was probably born somewhere between 100 and 90 and certainly lived into the 20s, and perhaps to the end of the century. Asinius Pollio, his last Roman patron, died in AD 4. Fraser calls Timagenes "an elusive figure" (1972, 518).

84. Noy 2004 provides an invaluable discussion of Egyptians and their self-identification in Rome. He points out that in the inscriptions and papyri individuals tend to label themselves either as Alexandrians or as Egyptians, not both. Plautus (*Merc.* 413) attests to a regular, if probably modest, trade in enslaved Egyptians at the end of the third century. See Ricci 1993 for an overview of the epigraphical evidence for Egyptians in Rome during the imperial period.

85. For C. Rabirius Postumus (*RE* 6, von der Mühll), see Cicero's speech in his defense with commentary by Siani-Davies 2001, especially 38–65.

86. *CIL* 6.2246 = *ILS* 4404 = *SIRIS* 437 = *RICIS* vol. 2 no. 501/160 = *EDR*103440 (*MNR*, Palazzo Massimo inv. 196633) found on the via Appia in Rome. Rabirius' two freed people are identified as C. Rabirius Post(umi) l(ibertus) Hermodorus and Rabiria Demaris. The other female has perhaps been added later; she is Usia Prima, a priestess of Isis. Her relationship to the two Rabirii is not specified but an Egyptian connection clearly remains. All three people are represented by half-length portraits facing front; see Kleiner 1977, 231n63.

87. Alexandrian politics had been and remained divisive and violent for centuries—see Fraser 1972, 86–92 and 124–26; and especially Siani-Davies 1997, 316–19. Diodorus was an eyewitness to the unrest (1.44.1; 1.83.8–9), which is also remarked upon by Plutarch *Pomp.* 49.6 and *Cato Min.* 35.2.

88. For Cyprus and the Romans, see conveniently Siani-Davies 2001, 16–18.

89. For Auletes' revenge on his political enemies, see Strabo 17.1.11 and Dio 39.58.3 with Siani-Davies 1997, 334n108 and 338.

90. For the embassy from Egypt to Rome in 57, see Canali de Rossi 1997, 595–97n650 for *testimonia*, bibliography, and commentary. Related Egyptian delegations to Rome in the 50s are nos. 645 (59), 649 (earlier in 57 than Dio's mission), 651 (56), 653 (54), and 656 (c. 51 announcing the death of Auletes and the contents of his will).

91. For the poisoning of Dio(n) the Academic Skeptic philosopher (*RE* 14 von Arnim and Ameling in *BNP*) while he was staying in Rome, see Cicero *Har. Resp.* 34; *Cael.* 10 and 21 with

commentary by Dyck 2013 *ad loc.*; and Capponi 2017, 30. See also Strabo 17.1.11 and Dio 39.13–14, who both imply that Pompey was involved.

92. The attack at Puteoli is mentioned by Cicero *Cael.* 23 but its details have been obscured by Cicero's desire to disassociate Caelius from this unfortunate episode.

93. Dyck 2013, 3–4: "Such brutality, though not uncommon in Alexandria, provoked outrage in Rome, against both Ptolemy and his Roman supporters, the most prominent of whom was Pompey." See also Capponi 2017, 30.

94. Suggested as a possibility by Capponi 2018, 50.

95. For Auletes' debts, see Siani-Davies 2001, 1–38. He effectively borrowed from Roman businessmen to bribe Roman politicians; 6,000 talents had allegedly already changed hands in 59 and his restoration to the throne in 56 apparently cost at least another 10,000 talents. As a result, the *publicani* in Rome were keen for him to be restored to power so that they could be repaid, with interest. For the burden placed on the Egyptian population by higher taxation at every level of society, see Cicero *Att.* 2.16.1, Suetonius *Iul.* 54, Dio Chrysostom 32.70, Dio 39.12.1–2 and evidence from papyri (*BGU* 8. 1773, 1782, 1821, 1825, 1828, 1846, *BGU* 14. 2314).

96. For Faustus Cornelius Sulla, see *RE* 377 (Münzer), *BNP* (Elvers) and *OCD* (Badian). He did not advance on the usual career beyond the office of quaestor (54).

97. For Faustus' library and others based on book collections looted during the Mithridatic wars, see especially Houston 2014, 34–37.

98. For Marcus Antonius, the *triumvir*, see conveniently Pelling 1988, 10–18; and especially now Welch (*OCD*).

99. For Antony's early career in Egypt, see Plutarch *Ant.* 3 with commentary by Pelling 1988 *ad loc.* Plutarch is keen to stress the early successes of Antony in Egypt, the location of his ultimate defeat and death.

100. For Timagenes as a political adviser, especially on Egyptian affairs, see Fraser 1972, 518.

101. Plutarch *Ant.* 72 with Pelling 1988 *ad loc.* Cf. Josephus *BJ* 1.393 and *Ant.* 15.197–98.

102. For Cleopatra's visits to Rome (notably the extended stay in 45–44), see Muccioli 2012, 366. Plutarch (*Ant.* 72) refers to Timagenes as one of his sources for the death of the queen, which portrays her in a positive light overall. For discussion, see Capponi 2018, 50–51, who sees Timagenes as an influential source sympathetic to the last Ptolemaic pharaoh.

103. It is not directly attested when Timagenes moved from Antony's circle to that of his rival Octavian. But this seems to have happened before Actium and on friendly terms.

104. For Timagenes and Octavian, see Seneca *Ira* 3.23.4–8 with Bosworth 1972, who comments (445): "The incident [the quarrel between Augustus and Timagenes] had no political importance. Augustus' withdrawal of *amicitia* meant only that a prominent Greek literary figure needed a fresh patron, and Pollio adopted him as a client, as he had done with L. Ateius Philologus after the death of Sallust." See also Fear 2010 for a different reading from a more cultural and less political perspective. Consequently, Timagenes is not included in Rohr Vio's 2000 discussion of political opponents of Augustus, whom she describes as voices of dissent.

105. The dating of this episode is based on Horace *Ep.* 1.19.15–16, which warns against Timagenes' free speech. See Mayer 1994, 10–11, who dates this book to 20 or 19. Horace provides telling evidence that Timagenes' witticisms also inspired others to try the same satirical tone, at least before his fall from favor. The *Suda* also has him expelled from his school for his

outspokenness. For the row itself, see Seneca *Controv.* 10.5.22 (who probably knew Timagenes) and Seneca *Ira* 3.23.4–8 (*BNJ* no. 88 T 2 and 3 with commentary by McInerney and Roller).

106. The younger Seneca stresses Augustus' forbearance (*tulit . . . patienter*, he bore it patiently) with Timagenes, mentioning the fact that Augustus gave Timagenes a series of warnings to tone down his public statements before he broke off their relationship permanently. The mention of the whole *domus* as Timagenes' target could include other relatives (Julia?), as well as servants and even other resident dependents.

107. Note especially the incisive discussion of Engels 1999, 234–39. Greek speakers in Rome were quite willing to write contemporary history at a time when Roman senators were much less eager to do so under the new regime.

108. It is suggestive that Timagenes chose not to return to Alexandria to live after the death of Faustus, either in the time of Cleopatra VII when he himself was under the patronage of Antony, nor once Alexandria flourished again as the capital of Roman Egypt under Augustus as the new pharaoh. Many factors such as his health, his political enemies in Alexandria, or a preference for his situation in Rome could all have played into this choice, which was different from that of others whose homeland had been destroyed.

109. For political satire at the expense of the Ptolemies, see Seneca *Dial.* 12.19.6 and Dio 39.58.1–2 with Roy 1998; Biffi 2001; and Capponi 2017, 53–54. Tyrannio's comments may have been much more satirical and humorous than is often imagined, as is suggested by Biffi 2001. In this context, one may also note the harsh personal invective that had been exchanged between Octavian and Antony during the triumviral period (see Borgies 2016). By contrast, Leppin 2022, 107, draws attention to what Dio characterizes as Octavian's care in how he addressed Antony (Dio 45.6.1). The new "Augustan" age soon called for a different, more civil tone.

110. Seneca *Controv.* 10.5.22: *cum illi multis de causis iratus Caesar interdixisset domo . . .* (when Caesar, angry with him for many reasons, forbade him from entering his house . . .). Seneca *Ira* 3.23.5: *saepe illum Caesar monuit, moderatius lingua uteretur: perseveranti domo sua interdixit* (Caesar often warned him to use more moderate language; when he [Timagenes] persevered he [Augustus] forbade him from entering his house). Augustus banned Timagenes from his house in what was an entirely private gesture toward a man who had no political standing in Rome. This direct evidence does not support the *Suda*'s claim that he was also removed from teaching at his own school.

111. For C. Asinius Cn. f. Pollio (cos. 40, *RE* 25, Groebe), see *PIR*[2] A 1241, Schmidt (*BNP*), McDonald and Spawforth (*OCD*), Ferriès 2007 no. 17, and especially Drummond (*FRHist.* no. 56) with Morgan 2000. Pollio had been a supporter of Antony for many years and possibly as late as 32. For his relationship with Timagenes, which makes sense in the context of Antony's circle of acquaintances, see now the sophisticated discussion in Allen 2019, especially 103–7.

112. Seneca *Ira* 3.23.6: *tota civitate direptus est: nullum illi limen praeclusa Caesaris domus abstulit* (He was cultivated by the whole community. No house was closed to him except that of Caesar) with Alonso-Núñez 1982, 133; and Engels 1999, 230. *Contra* Sordi 1982, who sees Timagenes as an outcast who had to leave the city. Timagenes' long stay with Pollio and the positive picture of him in later writers, including Quintilian and Ammianus Marcellinus, all demonstrate that his public statements and writings could not have been "anti-Roman" in a more general political sense.

113. For Varro and Tyrannio, see Lehmann 1988, who identifies a significant influence.

114. Seneca *Ira* 3.23.6: *libros acta Caesaris Augusti continentis in igne posuit . . .* (He burned the books that contained the deeds of Caesar Augustus). *BNJ* no. 88 T 3 with commentary.

115. Seneca *Contr.* 10.5.22. This gesture has been much discussed—see (for example) Bowersock 1965, 125; Alonso-Núñez 1982, 132–33; Sordi 1982, 777; and Engels 1999, 230. Capponi 2018, 48, argues that he must have been forced to burn his books, but this interpretation misses the effect of Timagenes' revenge against Augustus.

116. *Theriotropheis* is a rare Greek word that suggests Augustus was able to respond in kind to Timagenes' jokes about him. He implies that Pollio himself will eventually be attacked by the "wild animal" he is harboring in his home. In this same context, he urges his friend to make the most of Timagenes' company while it lasts (*fruere*)—another highly ironic comment.

117. For a subtle analysis of this passage within a more general Augustan political and cultural landscape, see Feeney 2021, 22–25 (first published in 1992).

118. *"Hoc me," inquit, "putas facturum, cum ego vos in gratiam reduxerim?"* (Do you think I would do that, when I was the one who restored your good relationship?) Augustus' response to Pollio has been much less discussed than Pollio's initial question, but it demonstrates that the *princeps*, in fact, did not want to ruin Timagenes or drive him out of Rome or even cause a rift between him and Pollio. Both Augustus and Pollio knew how difficult a character Timagenes could be on a personal level.

119. For *On Kings* (*Peri Basileon*), see McInerney and Roller (*BNJ* no. 88 with full bibliography) with Mazzarino 1966, 407–8; Malitz 1983, 52–53; Engels 1999, 231–42; Muccioli 2009 and 2012; and Mehl 2014, 111–12. We do not know how many books it was in nor what its chronological range covered. The 15 fragments in *BNJ* no. 88 (some of which may come from other works) are cited by Strabo, Josephus, Pliny the Elder, Quintilian, Plutarch, Q. Curtius Rufus, Pseudo-Plutarch, Ammianus Marcellinus, and Stephanus of Byzantium.

120. See Quintilian *Inst.* 1.10.9–10, 10.1.75, Ammianus Marcellinus 15.9.2, 15.10.9, 15.12.1–4 with Marincola 1997, 255. The hostility of the Senecas to Timagenes was exceptional.

121. *P. Oxy.* 37.2820 and *P.Oxy.* 73.4940 have been identified as possible fragments of Timagenes' history. See also *P.Oxy* 71.4890 and *SB* 22.15203 with Capponi 2017, 54–57, and 2018, 52–53, for discussion and bibliography.

122. Muccioli 2012, 371, shows how simplistic it is to characterize Timagenes as a political opponent of Augustus. By contrast, Whitmarsh 2018, 366, firmly describes Timagenes as an anti-Roman historian ("an obvious example"). Bowersock 1965, 110, is surely correct that there would have been much opposition to Roman expansion among Greek intellectuals, as well as prophecies of disaster for the Romans, but virtually none of this material has survived.

123. Timagenes was compared to Clitarchus, the historian of Alexander, by Quintilian *Inst.* 10.1.75. For commentary, see McInerney and Roller (*BNJ* no. 88 T6). There is no reason, however, to interpret a focus on other cultures as necessarily "anti-Roman" or "pro-barbarian," especially given the very slim evidence available. See Muccioli 2007 for Timagenes and the representation of the Parthians in Greek and Roman historiography.

124. See *BNJ* no. 88 T 8 for incisive commentary and further bibliography. See Biffi 2001 for a closer analysis and for the notion that this was the kind of remark made in conversation at the Atrium Libertatis.

125. *Suda* T 588.

126. *Suda* P 2165 names Asinius of Tralles (*RE* 23, Schwartz). See *BNJ* no. 88 T 4 (McInerney and Roller) and *BNJ* no. 193 (Dowden) with Bosworth 1972, 445n30; and Bowie 2022. The fact that a freedman of Pollio's seems to have taken over Timagenes' school is another indication of the closeness these two men enjoyed over many years.

127. See *Suda* T 588 for the mention of Tusculum and the Alban hills.

128. For Octavia, sister of Augustus, see *RE* 96 (Hammond) and *PIR*[2] O 66 with Fischer 1999.

129. See Plutarch, *Ant.* 87; and Dio, 51.15.5. Octavia had stayed on in Antony's house until she was compelled by him to leave. She then took the children with her.

130. For literary culture in the age of Augustus, see Galinsky 1996 and Wallace-Hadrill 2008.

131. Muccioli 2009, 60, creates a nuanced picture of a possible middle position for Greek writings, neither as an apology for Roman imperialism nor as an anti-Roman diatribe.

132. Timagenes was remembered for his detailed and sympathetic accounts of both Hasmonean and Celtic histories. See *BNJ* no. 88 F 2, 5, 6, 13, and 15.

133. McInerney and Roller provide an obvious example in their biographical sketch in *BNJ* no. 88 ("He soon entered the household of Faustus Cornelius Sulla"). Capponi (*OCD*) has him "ransomed and subsequently set free" by Faustus. Meister in *BNP* also has him "ransomed." Engels 1999, 230, names Antony as Timagenes' first patron in Rome, thus omitting the whole episode of Faustus purchasing Timagenes. Capponi 2017 contains a striking self-contradiction: on p. 33 Timagenes comes to Rome of his own accord (to escape the vendettas of Auletes!) but on pp. 43 and 52 he is brought as a prisoner. These examples of oversight or euphemism are all the more striking given Seneca the Elder's vituperative characterization of Timagenes (*Controv.* 10.5.22) as someone who been employed in menial jobs such as cook and litter-bearer while enslaved. Although Seneca's assertion seems highly unlikely, even simply on chronological terms (so already Laqueur *RE* 2 in 1936), its attempt to associate Timagenes with the characteristic taint of menial enslavement is still telling. Both Senecas had negative feelings about Timagenes.

134. Treggiari 1969b, 220: "a distinguished man like Tyrannio of Amisos should never have been admitted to be a slave." Rawson 1985, 69: "The elder Tyrannio is a well-known example of a man forced, though only technically, to pass through slavery."

135. For a sophisticated history of free speech (*parrhesia*) across different cultures in antiquity, see now Leppin 2022, who represents Augustus (102–103) as highly tolerant of free speech, in a republican tradition (41–45). The Greek term *parrhesia* can be translated as either *libertas* or *licentia* in Latin (Leppin 2022, 196–99).

136. *Cum sibi sciat nihil aliud suadere quam ut noto civilique et proprio sermone utatur vitetque maxime obscuritatem Sallusti et audaciam in translationibus.* (Since he knew that Philologus had given him no other advice than that he should use common, current, and correct language and should avoid above all the obscurity of Sallust and his outlandish metaphors; Suetonius *Gram. et rhet.* 10.6.) This is a rare attestation of a personal opinion expressed by a learned freedman who was writing a specialized book on commission, but one that he evidently would not have wanted to write for himself in his own time.

7. Conclusion: Glimpses of Educated Men who had been Enslaved

1. For overall slave population figures, see Scheidel 1997, 2005, and 2011.

2. For Hermippus of Berytus (modern Beirut, *RE* 8, Heibges, not to be confused with the much earlier Hermippus of Smyrna), see Sartori 1981; Ippolito in *LGGA* with an edition of the fragments (2005); Radicke (*BNJ* no. 1061); and Matthaios 2015, 233–35.

3. See Christes 1979, 137–40; and Matthaios 2015, 233–35.

4. For Hesychius of Miletus, see Kaldellis 2005. The *Suda* is available with an introduction online at https://www.cs.uky.edu/~raphael/sol/sol-html/.

5. For discussion, see chapter 2.

6. The Greek does not indicate that the village inland was also called Berytos, as Ippolito (*LGGA*) suggests. Rather, Hermippus' epithet naturally recalled the famous urban center where he had been educated.

7. For Herennius Severus, a Spanish senator possibly of consular rank and a friend of Pliny the younger; see *RE* 45, Groag and *PIR*^{2} H 130.

8. Matthaios 2015 (quoted in the epigraph to this chapter) sees a larger, more theoretical purpose in Hermippus' writing. But this must remain a hypothesis in the present state of the evidence about his text.

9. Luraghi 2022 (*BMCR* review of Vlassopoulos 2021): "the underlying comparison with the social and economic structures of New World slavery has created a straitjacket that too many scholars have been incapable of recognizing" and "the moral urgency that has driven the study of ancient slavery in a comparative direction has fundamentally hindered our understanding of the phenomenon itself and especially of its intrinsic diversity in space and time."

10. Calbreath 2023 is the most recent treatment, which includes previous bibliography and references to Said's own account of his life.

BIBLIOGRAPHY

Abbreviations

Abbreviations of journal titles follow the conventions of *L'Année philologique*.
Abbreviations of ancient authors follow the conventions of *The Oxford Classical Dictionary*.

ANRW = *Aufstieg und Niedergang der römischen Welt. Geschichte und Kultur Roms im Speigel der neueren Forschung,* Hildegard Temporini, ed. Berlin, 1972–.

BGU = *Berliner griechische Urkunden,* Fabian Reiter, ed. Berlin.

BNJ = *Brill's New Jacoby,* Ian Worthington, ed. https://referenceworks.brillonline.com/browse/brill-s-new-jacoby

BNP = *Brill's New Pauly Online,* H. Cancik and H. Schneider, eds. https://referenceworks.brill.com/display/db/npoe

CIL = *Corpus Inscriptionum Latinarum,* Berlin, 1862–: https://cil.bbaw.de/en/

CLE = *Carmina Latina Epigraphica,* 2 vols. F. Buecheler, ed. Leipzig, 1895–1897.

FRHist. = *The Fragments of the Roman Historians,* 3 vols. T. J. Cornell, ed. Oxford, 2014.

HAS = *Handwörterbuch der Antiken Sklaverei,* Mainz, 2006–: https://www.adwmainz.de/index.php?id=313

II = *Inscriptiones Italiae,* Rome, 1931–

ILLRP = *Inscriptiones Latinae Liberae Rei Publicae,* 2 vols. A. Degrassi, ed. Florence, 1957–1963.

ILMN = *Le iscrizioni latine del Museo Nazionale di Napoli, I Roma e Latium,* Naples, 2000.

ILS = *Inscriptiones Latinae Selectae,* 2nd ed., 5 vols., H. Dessau, ed. Berlin, 1954–1955.

LGGA = *Lexicon of Greek Grammarians of Antiquity,* F. Montanari, L. Pagani, and F. Montana, eds. 2015–: https://referenceworks.brill.com/display/db/lgga

LGPN = *A Lexicon of Greek Personal Names,* 5 vols., P. M. Fraser and E. Matthews, eds. Oxford, 1987–2010.

LTUR = *Lexicon Topographicum Urbis Romae,* 6 vols., E. M. Steinby, ed. Rome, 1993–2000.

OCD = *Oxford Classical Dictionary,* 5th ed., T. Whitmarsh, ed. Oxford, https://oxfordre.com/classics

ORF^{4} = *Oratorum Romanorum fragmenta liberae rei publicae,* 4th ed. E. Malcovati, ed. Turin.

PECS = *Princeton Encyclopedia of Classical Sites,* R. Stillwell, W. MacDonald, L. McAlister, and M. Holland, eds. Princeton, NJ, 1976.

RE = *Paulys Realencyclopädie der Classischen Altertumswissenschaft,* G. Wissowa ed. Stuttgart, 1894–1978.

RICIS = *Recueil des Inscriptions concernant les cultes Isiaques*, http://ricis.huma-num.fr/exist/apps/RICIS/index.html
SIRIS = *Sylloge inscriptionum religionis Isiacae et Sarapiacae*, L. Vidman, ed. Berlin, 1969.
ThesCRA = *Thesaurus Cultus et Rituum Antiquorum*, 5 vols. Los Angeles, 2004–2006.

Works Cited

Alexander, M. C. 1990. *Trials in the Late Roman Republic: 149 to 50 BC*. Toronto.

Alföldi, A. 1976. "*Redeunt saturnia regna*: Zum Gottesgnadentum des Sulla." *Chiron* 6:143–58.

Allély, A. 2012. *La déclaration d'hostis sous la république romaine*. Bordeaux.

Allen, J. 2019. "C. Asinius Pollio and the Politics of Cosmopolitanism." In *The Alternative Augustan Age*, edited by K. Morrell, J. Osgood, and K. Welch, 96–112. Oxford.

Alonso-Núnez, J. M. 1982. "L'opposizione contro l'imperialismo Romano e contro il principato nella storiografia del tempo di Augusto." *RSA* 12:131–41.

Altman, W. H. F. 2017. "The Egyptian Question in Roman Politics (65–30 BC)." *Calíope: presença classica* 5:4–25.

Amiotti, G. 1979. "La tradizione sulla morte di Manio Aquillio." *Aevum* 53:72–7.

Amiotti, G. 1980. "I Greci ed il massacre degli Italici nell' 88 a. C." *Aevum* 54:132–39.

Amiotti, G. 1991. "A proposito dell' immagine di P. Rutilio Rufo." *L'immagine dell uomo politico: vita pubblica e morale nell'antichità*, edited by M. Sordi, 159–67. Milan.

Anastasiadis, V. 1999. "Inventing a *kakoetheuma*: A Propagandistic Attack against P. Rutilius Rufus." *Parola del Passato* 304:48–68.

Arnott, G. 1971. "The *Praenomen* of Archias." *Hermes* 99 (2): 254–55.

Astin, A. E. 1967. *Scipio Aemilianus*. Oxford.

Astin, A. E. 1978. *Cato the Censor*. Oxford.

Axer, J. 1979. "I prezzi degli schiavi e le paghe degli attori nell'orazione di Cicerone pro Q. Roscio comoedo." *Actes du colloque sur l'esclavage Nieborow 2–6, XII 1975*. 217–25. Warsaw.

Badian, E. 1956. "Q. Mucius Scaevola and the Province of Asia." *Athenaeum* 34:104–23.

Badian, E. 1966. "The Early Historians." In *Latin Historians*, edited by T. A. Dorey, 1–38. London.

Badian, E. 1968. "Sulla's Augurate." *Arethusa* 1:26–46.

Badian, E. 1970. *Lucius Sulla. The Deadly Reformer*. Seventh Todd Memorial Lecture. Sydney.

Baier, T. 2005. "Autobiographie in der späten römischen Republik." In *Antike Autobiographien. Werke—Epochen—Gattungen*, edited by M. Reichel, 123–42. Köln.

Balconi, C. 1993. "Rabirio Postumo dioiketes d'Egitto in P. Med. Inv. 68.53?" *Aegyptus* 73:3–20.

Balconi, C. 1994. "Rabirio Postumo dioiketes d'Egitto: prima testimonianze papirea." In *Proceedings of the 20th International Congress of Papyrologists*, 219–22. Copenhagen.

Baldarelli, Beatrice. 2004. *Accius und die vortrojanische Pelopidensage*. Paderborn.

Balsdon, J. P. V. D. 1951. "Sulla Felix." *JRS* 41:1–10.

Bang, P. Fibiger. 2008. *The Roman Bazaar: A Comparative Study of Trade and Markets in a Tributary Empire*. Cambridge.

Bardon, H. 1952. *La littérature latine inconnue, vol 1: L'époque républicaine*. Paris.

Battaglini, S. 2009. *Il complesso del Niger Lapis nella storia della prima Roma. Note sull'iscrizione e i monumenti*. Rome.

Beck, H., and U. Walter. 2001. *Die frühen römischen Historiker*, vol. 1. Darmstadt.

Beck, H., and U. Walter. 2004. *Die frühen römischen Historiker*, vol. 2. Darmstadt.

Beckmann, Sarah E. 2023. "The Naked Reader: Child Enslavement in the Villa of the Mysteries Fresco." *AJA* 127 (1): 55–81.

Behr, H. 1993. *Die Selbstdarstellung Sullas. Ein aristokratischer Politiker zwischen persönlichem Führungsanspruch und Standessolidarität*. Frankfurt.

Bell, S. W., D. Borbonus, and R. Maclean, eds. 2024. *Freed Persons in the Roman World: Status, Diversity, and Representation*. Cambridge.

Bellemore, J. 2002. "The Date of Cicero's *Pro Archia*." *Antichthon* 36:41–53.

Bellemore, J., and B. Rawson. 1990. "Alumni: The Italian Evidence." *ZPE* 83:1–19.

Beness, L. 2005. "Scipio Aemilianus and the Crisis of 129 BC." *Historia* 54 (1): 37–48.

Beness, L. 2012. "Another Voice against the 'Tyranny' of Scipio Aemilianus in 129 BC?" *Historia* 61.3:270–81.

Beness, L. 2013. "Insulting Cornelia, Mother of the Gracchi." *Antichthon* 47:61–79.

Beness, L., and T. Hillard. 2016. "Wronging Sempronia." *Antichthon* 50:80–106.

Benferhat, Y. M. 2020. "All About Money? Authorship and Copyright in Ancient Rome." *Forum Prawnicze* 54–66.

Berno, Francesca R. 2023. *Roman Luxuria: A Literary and Cultural History*. Oxford.

Bernstein, F. 1998. *Ludi Publici: Untersuchungen zur Entstehung und Entwicklung von öffentlichen Spiele im republikanischen Rom*. Stuttgart.

Berry, D. H. 2004. "Literature and Persuasion in Cicero's *Pro Archia*." In *Cicero the Advocate*, edited by J. Powell and J. Patterson, 291–312. Oxford.

Biffi, N. 2001. "Timagenes sugli incendi a Roma (nota a Sen. *Ep.* 91.13 = *FGHist.* 88 T8)." *InvLuc* 23:15–25.

Bispham, E. 2007. *From Asculum to Actium: The Municipalization of Italy from the Social War to Augustus*. Oxford.

Bispham, E. 2018. "Sulla and the *populi Italici*." In *L'età di Silla*, edited by M. T. Schettino and G. Zecchini, 1–44. Rome.

Blake, S. 2012. "Now You See Them: Slaves and Other Objects as Elements of the Roman Master." *Helios* 39:193–211.

Blake, S. 2016. "*In Manus*: Pliny's Letters and the Arts of Mastery." In *Domestic Politics, Revolutionary Poetics, Civic Spectacle*, edited by Alison Keith and Jonathan Edmondson, 89–107. Toronto.

Blänsdorf, J. 2016. *Das Thema der Sklaverei in den Werken Ciceros*. Forschungen zur Antiken Sklaverei 42. Stuttgart.

Bodel, J. 2005. "*Caveat Emptor*: Towards a Study of Roman Slave Traders." *JRA* 18:181–95.

Bodel, J. 2015. "The Publication of Pliny's Letters." In *Pliny the Bookmaker: Betting on Posterity*, edited by I. Marchesi, 13–108. Oxford.

Bollmann, B. 1998. *Römische Vereinshäuser: Untersuchungen zu den Scholae der römischen Berufs-, Kult- und Augustalen-Kollegien in Italien*. Mainz.

Booth, A. D. 1979. "The Schooling of Slaves in First Century Rome." *TAPA* 109:11–19.

Borbonus, D. 2014. *Columbarium Tombs and Collective Identity in Augustan Rome*. Cambridge.

Borgies, L. 2016. *Le conflit propagandiste entre Octavien et Marc Antoine: de l'usage politique de la uituperatio entre 44 et 30 a. C.* Brussels.

Bosworth, A. B. 1972. "Asinius Pollio and Augustus." *Historia* 21:441–73.

Bowersock, G. W. 1965. *Augustus and the Greek World*. Oxford.

Bowie, E. 2022. "Greek High Culture in Hellenistic and Early Imperial Bithynia: Towards a Prosopography of Practitioners of Greek Culture in Bithynia Down to the Middle of the Third Century AD." *Mnemosyne* 75 (1): 73–112.

Bradley, K. 1985. "Child Labor in the Roman World." *Historical Reflections* 12:311–30.

Bradley, K. 1994. *Slavery and Society at Rome*. Cambridge.

Brenk, F. 1977. *In Mist Apparelled: Religious Themes in Plutarch's Moralia and Lives*. Leipzig.

Brennan, T. C. 1992. "Sulla's Career in the Nineties: Some Reconsiderations." *Chiron* 22:102–58.

Bruun, C. 2013. "Greek or Latin? The Owner's Choice of Names for *Vernae* in Rome." In *Roman Slavery and Roman Material Culture*, edited by M. George, 19–42. Toronto.

Calabi, I. 1951. "I commentarii di Silla come fonte storica." *Atti dell'Accademia Nazionale dei Lincei: Memorie, Classe di Scienze morali, storiche e filologiche*, 3:247–302.

Calbreath, D. 2023. *The Sergeant: The Incredible Life of Nicholas Said, Son of an African General, Slave of the Ottomans, Free Man under the Tsars, Hero of the Union Army*. New York.

Campbell, B. 2000. *The Writings of Roman Land Surveyors: Introduction, Text, Translation and Commentary*. *JRS* monograph 9. London.

Canali de Rossi, F. 1997. *Le ambasciere dal mondo Greco a Roma in età repubblicana*. Rome.

Candau, J. M. 2011. "Republican Rome: Autobiography and Political Struggle." In *Political Autobiographies and Memoirs in Antiquity. A Brill Companion*, edited by G. Marasco, 121–59. Leiden.

Capponi, L. 2017. *Il ritorno della Fenice: intellettuali e potere nell'Egitto romano*. Pisa.

Capponi, L. 2018. "A Disillusioned Intellectual: Timagenes of Alexandria." In *Intellectual and Empire in Greco-Roman Antiquity*, edited by Philip R. Bosman, 1–19. London.

Carandini, A. 1988. *Schiavi in Italia: gli strumenti pensanti dei Romani fra tarda repubblica e medio impero (Studi NIS archeologia vm)*. Rome.

Carandini, A., with P. Carafa, 2017. *The Atlas of Ancient Rome: Biography and Portraits of the City*. 2 vols. Princeton, NJ.

Carlsen, J. 1995. *Vilici and Roman Estate Managers until AD 284*. Rome.

Chassignet, M. 1986/2002. *Les origines (fragments). Caton*. Paris.

Chassignet, M. 2004. *L'annalistique romaine 3: l'annalistique récente, l'autobiographie politique*. Paris.

Chillet, C. 2016. *De l'Étrurie à Rome : Mécène et la fondation de l'Empire. EFR* 373. Rome.

Chillet, C. 2019. "La *lex Papia* de 65 avant J.-C. sur 'l'usupation de citoyenneté.'" *Revue Internationale des Droits de L'Antiquité* 66:33–62.

Christ, K. 2002. *Sulla. Eine römische Karriere*. Munich.

Christes, J. 1979. *Sklaven und Freigelassene als Grammatiker und Philologen im Antiken Rom*. Wiesbaden.

Christes, J., and G. Garbugino, 2015. *Lucilius: Satiren, lateinisch und deutsch*. Darmstadt.

Coarelli, F. 1981. "Alessandro, i Licinii e Lanuvio." In *L'art décoratif à Rome à la fin de la république et au début du principat*, 229–84. Rome.

Conte, G. B. 1994. *Latin Literature: A History*. Baltimore, MD.

Corbier, M. 2001. "Child Exposure and Abandonment." In *Childhood, Class and Kin in the Roman World*, edited by S. Dixon, 52–73. London.

Coşkun, A. 2009. *Bürgerrechtsentzug oder Fremdenausweisung? Studien zu den Rechten von Latinern und weiteren Fremden sowie zum Bürgerrechtswechsel in der römischen Republik.* Stuttgart.

Coşkun, A. 2010. *Cicero und das römische Bürgerrecht. Die Verteidigung des Dichters Archias.* Göttingen.

Cossu, V. 2014. "Un columbario di liberti e di liberte di Mecenate: alcune considerazioni." *Archeologia Classica* 65: 461–71.

Costa, S. 2014. *Mecenate: frammenti e testimonianze latine.* Milan.

Courtney, E. 1999. *Archaic Latin Prose.* Atlanta, GA.

Courtney, E. 2003. *The Fragmentary Latin Poets.* Revised edition. Oxford.

Craver, S. E. 2010. "Urban Real Estate in Late Republican Rome." *MAAR* 55:135–58.

Crawford, M. with W. M. Broadhead, J. P. T. Clackson, F. Santangelo, S. Thompson, M. Watmough, E. Bissa, and G. Bodard. 2011. *Imagines Italicae: A Corpus of Italic Inscriptions. BICS* Suppl. 10. 3 vols. London.

Crowther, N. B. 1970. "*ΟΙ ΝΕΩΤΕΡΟΙ, poetae novi,* and *cantores Euphorionis.*" *CQ* 20:322–27.

Cugusi, P., and M. T. Sblendorio Cugusi, 2001. *Opere di Marco Porcio Catone Censore,* vol. 1. Turin.

Čulík-Baird, H. 2019. "Staging Roman Slavery in the Second Century BCE." *Ramus* 48 (2): 174–97.

Čulík-Baird, H. 2020. "Archias the Good Immigrant." *Rhetorica* 38 (4): 382–410.

Čulík-Baird, H. 2022. "The Portrait of the Actor in Cicero's *Pro Roscio comoedo.*" *TAPA* 152 (1): 183–209.

D'Arms, J. H. 1970. *Romans on the Bay of Naples: A Social and Cultural Study of the Villas and their Owners from 150 BC to 400 AD.* Cambridge, MA.

Damaggio, J. 2011. "Un corpus des premiers fragments grammaticaux à Rome." *Eruditio Antiqua* 3:23–55.

Damon, C. 1997. *The Mask of the Parasite: A Pathology of Roman Patronage.* Ann Arbor.

Dangel, J. 1995/2002. *Accius, oeuvres et fragments.* Paris.

Daube, D. 1965. "Licinnia's Dowry." In *Studi in onore di Biondo Biondi,* 197–212. Milan.

Daubigny, A. 1976. "Contribution à l'étude de l'esclavagisme. La propriété esclavagiste chez Cicéron." In *Texte, politique, idéologie: Cicéron,* 13–71. Paris.

Davenport, C. 2019. *A History of the Roman Equestrian Order.* Cambridge.

David, J.-M. 1983. "L'action oratoire de C. Gracchus: l'image d'un modèle." In *Demokratia et Aristokratia - à propos de Caius Gracchus: mots grecs et réalités romaines,* edited by C. Nicolet, 103–16. Paris.

De Giorgi, A., and A. Asa Eger. 2021. *Antioch: A History.* London.

Dix, T. K. 2000. "The Library of Lucullus." *Athenaeum* 88 (2): 441–64.

Dixon, S. 1986. "Family Finances: Terentia and Tullia." In *The Family in Ancient Rome: New Perspectives,* edited by B. Rawson, 93–120. Ithaca, NY.

Dixon, S. 2007. *Cornelia, Mother of the Gracchi.* Abingdon.

Dortmund, A. 2001. *Römisches Buchwesen um die Zeitwende. War T. Pomponius Atticus (110–32 v. Chr.) Verleger?* Wiesbaden.

Driediger-Murphy, L. 2019. *Roman Republican Augury: Freedom and Control.* Oxford.

Drummond, A. 2008. "The Ban on *Gentiles* Holding the Same Priesthood and Sulla's Augurate." *Historia* 57 (4): 367–407.

Duboulez, J. 2014. "Présence et absence des enfants exposés dans le droit romain (1er—3e siècles)." In *Enfants perdus, enfants trouvés. Dire l'abondon en Europe du XVI au XVIII siècles*, edited by F. Magnot-Ogilvy and J. Valls -Russell, 57–72. Paris.

Dué, C. 2000. "Tragic History and Barbarian Speech in Sallust's *Jugurtha*." *HSCP* 100:311–25.

Dueck, D. 2000. *Strabo of Amasia: A Greek Man of Letters in Augustan Rome*. London.

Duff, T. 1997. "Moral Ambiguity in Plutarch's *Lysander-Sulla*." In *Plutarch and His Intellectual World*, edited by J. M. Mossman, 169–87. London.

Dugan, J. 2005. *Making a New Man: Ciceronian Self-Fashioning in the Rhetorical Works*. Oxford.

Duncan-Jones, R. 1982. *The Economy of the Roman Empire*. Oxford.

Dyck, A. R. 2008. "Rivals into Partners: Hortensius and Cicero." *Historia* 57 (2): 142–73.

Dyck, A. R. 2013. *Cicero Pro Marco Caelio*. Cambridge.

Eck, W. 1976. "Neros Freigelassener Epaphroditus und die Aufdeckung der pisonischen Verschwörung." *Historia* 25 (3): 381–84.

Eckardt, H. 2017. "Writing Power: The Material Culture of Literacy as Representation and Practice." In *Materialising Roman Histories*, University of Cambridge Museum of Classical Archaeology Monograph 3, edited by A. Van Oyen and M. Pitts, 23–30. Oxford.

Eckert, A. 2018. "Roman Orators between Greece and Rome: The Case of Cato the Elder, L. Crassus and M. Antonius." In *Reading Republican Oratory. Reconstructions, Contexts, Reception*, edited by Christa Gray, Andrea Balbo, Richard Marshall, and Catherine Steel, 19–32. Oxford.

Edmondson, J. 2011. "Slavery and the Roman Family." In *The Cambridge World History of Slavery, vol. 1: The Ancient Mediterranean*, edited by P. A. Cartledge and K. R. Bradley, 337–61. Cambridge.

Edmondson, J. 2016. "Investing in Death: Gladiators as Investment and Currency in the Late Republic." In *Money and Power in the Roman Republic*, edited by H. Beck, M. Jehne, and J. Serrati, 37–52. Brussels.

Edwards, C. 1993. *The Politics of Immorality in Ancient Rome*. Cambridge.

Elster, M. 2003. *Die Gesetze der mittleren römischen Republik. Text und Kommentar*. Darmstadt.

Elster, M. 2020. *Die Gesetze der späten römischen Republik, von den Gracchen bis Sulla (133–80 v. Chr.)*. Göttingen.

Engels, D. 2007. *Das römische Vorzeichenwesen: Quellen, Terminologie, Kommentar, historische Entwicklung*. Stuttgart.

Engels, J. 1999. *Augusteische Oikumenegeographie und Universalhistorie im Werk Strabons von Amaseia*. Stuttgart.

Etcheto, H. 2012. *Les Scipions. Famille et pouvoir à Rome à l'époque républicaine*. Bordeaux.

Evans-Grubbs, J. 2010. "Hidden in Plain Sight: *Expositi* in the Community." In *Children, Memory, and Family Identity in Roman Culture*, edited by V. Dasen and T. Späth, 293–310. Oxford.

Fabre, G. 1981. *Libertus. Recherches sur les rapports patron-affranchi à la fin de la république romaine*. EFR 50. Rome.

Fadinger, V. 2002. "Sulla als *imperator felix* und *Epaphroditos* (= Liebling der Aphrodite)." In *Widerstand-Anpassung-Integration: die griechische Staatenwelt und Rom. Festschrift für Jürgen Deininger zum 65. Geburtstag*, edited by N. Ehrhardt and L.-M. Günther, 155–88. Stuttgart.

Fantham, E. 2004. *The Roman World of Cicero's De Oratore*. Oxford.

Fantham, E. 2013. *Cicero's* Pro Murena Oratio. Oxford.

Fear, T. 2010. "*Interdictiones Domo et Ingenio*: Timagenes and Propertius: A Reading in the Dynamics of Augustan Exclusion." *Arethusa* 43 (3): 429–38.

Feeney, D. C. 2016. *Beyond Greek: The Beginnings of Latin Literature*. Cambridge, MA.

Feeney, D. C. 2021. "*Si licet, si fas est*: Ovid's *Fasti* and the Problem of Free Speech under the Principate." In *Explorations in Latin Literature*, vol. 2, 15–36. Cambridge.

Ferrary, J.-L. 2000. "Les gouverneurs des provinces romaines d'Asie Mineure (Asie et Cilicie) depuis l'organisation de la province d'Asie jusqu' à la première guerre de Mithridate (126–88 av. J.-C.)." *Chiron* 30:161–93.

Ferrary, J.-L. 2002. "La création de la province d'Asie et la présence italienne en Asie Mineure." In *Les Italiens dans le monde grec*, edited by C. Müller and C. Hasenohr, 133–46. Athens.

Ferriès, M.-C. 2007. *Les partisans d'Antoine: des orphelins de César aux complices de Cléopâtre*. Paris.

Fischer, R. A. 1999. *Fulvia und Octavia. Die beiden Ehefrauen des Marcus Antonius in den politischen Kämpfen der Umbruchszeit zwischen Republik und Principat*. Berlin.

Fitzgerald, W. 2000. *Slavery in the Roman Literary Imagination*. Cambridge.

Flaig, E. 2019. "Zum Verlieren und Scheitern römischer Senatoren. Überlegungen an den Rändern der historischen Kulturwissenschaft." In *Verlierer und Aussteiger in der "Konkurrenz unter Anwesenden": Agonalität in der politischen Kultur des antiken Rom*, edited by K.-J. Hölkeskamp and H. Beck, 55–80. Stuttgart.

Flemming, R. 2021. "Fertility Control in Ancient Rome." *Women's History Review* 30 (6): 896–914.

Flower, H. I. 1996. *Ancestor Masks and Aristocratic Power in Roman Culture*. Oxford.

Flower, H. I. 2006. *The Art of Forgetting: Disgrace and Oblivion in Roman Political Culture*. Chapel Hill.

Flower, H. I. 2008. "Remembering and Forgetting Temple Destruction: The Destruction of the Temple of Jupiter Optimus Maximus in 83 BC." In *Antiquity in Antiquity: Jewish and Christian Pasts in the Greco-Roman World*, edited by G. Gardner and K. L. Osterloh, 74–92. Tübingen.

Flower, H. I. 2012. "Beyond the *Contio*: Political Communication in the Tribunate of Tiberius Gracchus." In *Community and Communication: Oratory and Politics in Republican Rome*, edited by C. Steel and H. van der Blom, 85–100. Oxford.

Flower, H. I. 2014. "Memory and Memoirs in Republican Rome." In *Memoria Romana: Memory in Rome and Rome in Memory* (*Memoirs of the American Academy in Rome* supplement 10), edited by Karl Galinsky, 27–40. University of Michigan Press.

Flower, H. I. 2015a. "Sulla's Memoirs as an Account of Personal Religious Experiences." *Religion in the Roman Empire* 1:297–320.

Flower, H. I. 2015b. "The Rapture and the Sorrow: Characterization in Sulla's Memoirs." In *Fame and Infamy: Essays for Christopher Pelling on Characterization in Greek and Roman Biography and Historiography*, edited by R. Ash, J. Mossman, and F. B. Titchener, 209–23. Oxford.

Flower, H. I. 2020. "The Freedom of the Rhodians: Cato the Elder and Demosthenes." In *Libertas and Res Publica in the Roman Republic*, edited by Catalina Balmaceda, 84–103. Leiden.

Flower, H. I. 2022a. "Periodization in Perspective: Further Thoughts about the Second Century BCE." In *A Community in Transition: Rome Between Hannibal and the Gracchi*, edited by M. Balbo and F. Santangelo, 339–58. Oxford.

Flower, H. I. 2022b. "The Most Expensive Slave in Rome: Quintus Lutatius Daphnis." *Classical Philology* 117 (1): 99–119.

Flower, H. I. 2023. "Self-Representation in a Time of Civil Strife: Publius Rutilius Rufus' *de vita sua*." In *A Culture of Civil War? Bellum Civile in the Late Republic and Early Empire*, edited by H. Börm, U. Gotter, and W. Havener, HABES 65, 159–75. Stuttgart.

Flower, H. I. forthcoming. "Women's Property Rights and Political Crisis in Republican Rome: The Dowry of Licinnia, Wife of Gaius Gracchus." In *Women's Wealth and Power in Republican Rome*, edited by Catherine Steel and Lewis Webb. Cambridge.

Forschner, B. 2020. *Servus dotalis. Der Sklave in der Ordnung des klassischen römischen Mitgiftrechts*. Forschungen zur antiken Sklaverei vol. 44. Stuttgart.

Fowler, R. L. 1987. "The Rhetoric of Desperation." *HSCP* 91:5–38.

Francese, C. 2001. *Parthenius of Nicaea and Roman Poetry*. Frankfurt am Main.

Fraser, P. M. 1972. *Ptolemaic Alexandria*. Oxford.

Frier, B. 1967. "Augural Symbolism in Sulla's Invasion of 83." *ANSMusN* 13:111–18.

Frier, B. 1969. "Sulla's Priesthood." *Arethusa* 2 (2): 187–99.

Froehlich, S. 2023. "Geschichte schreiben als 'dichte Beschreibung'. Der jüngere Plinius und seine Sklaven." *Klio* 105 (2): 624–45.

Funaioli, G. 1907. *Grammaticae romanae fragmenta*, vol. 1. Leipzig.

Gabba, E. 2021. *Appiani Bellorum Civilium liber primus*, 3rd ed. (with introduction by F. Santangelo), Bari. Earlier editions in 1958 and 1967.

Galinsky, K. 1996. *Augustan Culture: An Interpretive Introduction*. Princeton, NJ.

Galinsky, K. 2005. *The Cambridge Companion to the Age of Augustus*. Cambridge.

Gamauf, R. 2023. "*Peculium*: Paradoxes of Slaves with Property." In *The Position of Roman Slaves: Social Realities and Legal Differences*, edited by M. Schermaier, 87–124. Berlin/Boston.

Garcea, A. 2012. *Caesar's* De Analogia. Oxford.

Gargola, D. 1995. *Lands, Laws, and Gods: Magistrates and Ceremony in the Regulation of Public Lands in Republican Rome*. Chapel Hill, NC.

Giardina, A. 2008. "*Metis* in Rome: A Greek Dream of Sulla." In *East and West: Papers in Ancient History Presented to Glen W. Bowersock*, edited by T. C. Brennan and H. I. Flower, 61–83. Cambridge, MA.

Gibson, R. 2020. *Man of High Empire. The Life of Pliny the Younger*. Oxford.

Gold, B. K. 1985. "Pompey and Theophanes of Mytilene." *AJP* 103:312–27.

Gold, B. K. 1987. *Literary Patronage in Greece and Rome*. Chapel Hill, NC.

Goldbeck, F. 2010. *Salutationes. Die Morgenbegrüßungen in Rom in der Republik und der frühen Kaiserzeit*. Berlin.

Goldberg, S. 1998. "Plautus on the Palatine." *JRS* 88:1–20.

Goldschmidt, N. 2014. *Shaggy Crowns: Ennius' Annales and Virgil's Aeneid*. Oxford.

Goukowsky, P. 2001. *Appien, histoire romaine livre XII, la guerre de Mithridate*. Paris.

Gowers, E. 2024. *Rome's Patron: The Lives and Afterlives of Maecenas*. Princeton, NJ.

Greenidge, A. H. J., and A. M. Clay. 1960. *Sources for Roman History 133–70 B.C.*, 2nd ed. Oxford.

Griffin, M. T. 1989. "Philosophy, Politics and Politicians at Rome." In *Philosophia Togata: Essays on Philosophy and Roman Society*, edited by M. T. Griffin and J. Barnes, 1–37. Oxford.

Grillo, L., and C. Krebs eds. 2018. *The Cambridge Companion to the Writings of Julius Caesar*. Cambridge.

Groen-Vallinga, M. J. 2024. "The Value of Work: Work and Labour within the Roman Upper-Class Household." In *Valuing Labour in Greco-Roman Antiquity*, edited by M. Flohr and K. Bowes, 169–90. Leiden.

Grosso, G. 1968. "P. Mucio Scaevola tra il diritto e la politica." *Archivio Giuridico* 44:204–11.

Gruen, E. S. 1966. "The Political Prosecutions in the 90s B.C." *Historia* 15:32–64.

Gruen, E. S. 1968. *Roman Politics and the Criminal Courts 149–78 BC*. Cambridge, MA.

Gruen, E. S. 1974. *The Last Generation of the Roman Republic*. Berkeley.

Gruen, E. S. 1992. "Cato and Hellenism." In *Culture and National Identity in Republican Rome*, 52–83. Ithaca, NY.

Guard, T. 2011. "Affection et humanitas dans les relations maître-esclave d'apès la correspondance de Cicéron." In *Sklaverei und Zwangsarbeit zwischen Akzeptanz und Widerstand*, edited by E. Hermann-Otto, 29–41. Hildesheim.

Gurd, S. A. 2012. *Work in Progress: Literary Revision as Social Performance in Ancient Rome*. APA American Classical Studies vol. 57. Oxford.

Haas, W. 1977. *Die Fragmente der Grammatiker Tyrannion und Diokles. Sammlung griechischer und lateinischer Grammatiker*, vol. 3, 79–184. Berlin.

Habinek, T. 2005. "Slavery and Class." In *A Companion to Latin Literature*, edited by Stephen J. Harrison, 385–93. Malden, MA.

Haley, S. P. 1983. "Archias, Theophanes, and Cicero: The Politics of the *Pro Archia*." *CB* 59:1–4.

Hallett, J. 2021. "*Vilicus* and *Vilica* in the *De Agricultura*: The Elder Cato's Script for a Farming Couple." In *Married Life in Greco-Roman Antiquity*, edited by C.-E. Centlivres Challet, 60–75. London.

Harders, A.-C. 2008. *Suavissima soror: Untersuchungen zu den Bruder-Schwester-Beziehungen in der römischen Republik*. Munich.

Hardie, A. 1983. *Statius and the* Silvae*: Poets, Patrons, and Epideixis in the Greco-Roman World*. Liverpool.

Harper, K. 2010. "Slave Prices in Late Antiquity (in the very Long Term)." *Historia* 59:206–38.

Harris, B. F. 2016. "Bithynia: Roman Sovereignty and the Survival of Hellenism." *ANRW* 2.7.2:857–901.

Harris, W. V. 1989. *Ancient Literacy*. Cambridge, MA.

Harris, W. V. 1994. "Child-Exposure in the Roman Empire." *JRS* 84:1–22.

Harris, W. V. 2009. *Dreams and Experience in Classical Antiquity*. Cambridge, MA.

Hartmann, B. 2020. *The Scribes of Rome: A Cultural and Social History of the Scribae*. Cambridge.

Hasegawa, K. 2005. *The Familia Urbana during the Early Empire: A Study of Columbaria Inscriptions*. Oxford.

Haselberger, L. 2002. *Mapping Augustan Rome*. Portsmouth, RI.

Hemelrijk, E. A. 2004. *Matrona Docta: Educated Women in the Roman Elite from Cornelia to Julia Domna*. London.

Hendrickson, G. L. 1933. "The Memoirs of Rutilius Rufus." *CP* 28:153–75.

Herrmann-Otto, E. 1994. *Ex ancilla natus. Untersuchungen zu den "hausgeborenen" Sklaven und Sklavinnen im Westen des römischen Kaiserreiches (Forschungen zur antiken Sklaverei, B XXIV)*. Stuttgart.

Heskel, J. 1994. "Cicero as Evidence for Attitudes to Dress in the Late Republic." In *The World of Roman Costume*, edited by J. L. Sebesta and L. Bonfante, 133–45. Madison.

Hillard, T. 2001. "Popilia and *laudationes funebres* for Women." *Antichthon* 35:45–63.

Hillscher, A. 1892. "Hominum litteratorum Graecorum ante Tiberii mortem in urbem Roma commoratorum historia critica." *Jahrbücher für klassische Philologie Suppl. Bd.* 18, 355–444.

Hinard, F. 1985a. *Les proscriptions de la Rome républicaine*. Paris.

Hinard, F. 1985b. *Sylla*. Paris.

Hinard, F., and Y. Benferhat. 2006. *Cicéron, Discours 1.2: Pour Sextus Roscius*. Paris.

Holford-Strevens, L. 2003. *Aulus Gellius: An Antonine Scholar and His Achievement*. Oxford.

Holleran, C. 2012. *Shopping in Ancient Rome: The Retail Trade in the Late Republic and Principate*. Oxford.

Hollis, A. S. 2007. *Fragments of Roman Poetry c. 60 BC—AD 20*. Oxford.

Hollstein, W. 2000a. "Die Stempelstellung—ein ungenutztes Interpretationskriterium für die Münzprägung der Römischen Republik." XII. In *Internationaler Numismatischer Kongress: Berlin 1997*, edited by B. Kluge and B. Weisser, 487–91. Berlin.

Hollstein, W. 2000b. "Exkurs: Die Bedeutung der Stempelstellung für die Münzprägung der Römischen Republik." In *Metallanalytische Untersuchungen an Münzen der Römischen Republik*, edited by W. Hollstein, 133–36. Berlin.

Horsfall, N. 1989. *Cornelius Nepos: A Selection including the Lives of Cato and Atticus*. Oxford.

Horsfall, N. 1995. *A Companion to the Study of Vergil*. Leiden.

Houston, G. W. 2014. *Inside Roman Libraries: Book Collections and Their Management in Antiquity*. Chapel Hill, NC.

Howatson, M. ed. 2011. *The Oxford Companion to Classical Literature*. Oxford.

Howley, J. A. 2018. *Aulus Gellius and Roman Reading Culture: Text, Presence, and Imperial Knowledge in the* Noctes Atticae. Cambridge.

Howley, J. A. forthcoming. *Slavery and the Roman Book*.

Huemoeller, K. P. D. 2021. "Captivity for All? Slave Status and Prisoners of War in the Roman Republic." *TAPA* 151 (1): 101–25.

Hurlet, F. 1993. *La dictature de Sylla: monarchie ou magistrature républicaine? Essai d'histoire constitutionelle*. Brussels.

Isayev, E. 2017. *Migration, Mobility and Place in Ancient Italy*. Cambridge.

Itgenshorst, T. 2005. *Tota illa pompa. Der Triumph in der römischen Republik*. Göttingen.

Jaeger, M. 2013. *Archimedes and the Roman Imagination*. Ann Arbor.

Jahn, O. 1843. *Auli Persii Flacci Satirarum Liber*. Leipzig.

Jocelyn, H. 1988. "Studies in the Indirect Tradition of Plautus' *Pseudolus* III: The 'Archaising Movement', Republican Comedy and Aulus Gellius' *Noctes Atticae*." In *Vir bonus et discendi peritus: Studies in Celebration of Otto Skutsch's Eightieth Birthday*, edited by N. Horsfall, 57–72. London.

Johnson, W. A. 2012. "Cicero and Tyrannio: *Mens addita videtur meis aedibus*." *CW* 105 (4): 471–77.

Johnston, P. D. 2008. *The Military Consilium in Republican Rome*. Piscataway, NJ: Gorgias Press.

Jones, C. P. 1999. "Atticus in Ephesus." *ZPE* 124:89–94.

Jongman, W. 2003. "Slavery and the Growth of Rome: The Transformation of Italy in the 2nd and 1st Centuries BCE." In *Rome the Cosmopolis*, edited by Catherine Edwards and Greg Woolf, 100–22. Cambridge.

Joshel, S. 1992. *Work, Identity and Legal Status: A Study of the Occupational Inscriptions*. Norman, OK.

Joshel, S. 2011. "Slavery and Roman Literary Culture." In *The Cambridge World History of Slavery vol.1: The Ancient Mediterranean World*, edited by K. Bradley and P. Cartledge, 214–40. Cambridge.

Kajanto, I. 1982. *The Latin Cognomina*. Helsinki.

Kaldellis, A. 2005. "The Works and Days of Hesychios the Illoustrios of Miletos." In *Greek, Roman, and Byzantine Studies* 45:381–403.

Kallet-Marx, R. M. 1990. "The Trial of Rutilius Rufus." *Phoenix* 44:122–39.

Kallet-Marx, R. M. 1995. *Hegemony to Empire: The Development of the Roman Hegemony in the East from 148 to 62 BC*. Berkeley.

Kaster, R. A. 1995. *C. Suetonius Tranquillus, De grammaticis et rhetoribus*. Oxford.

Kay, P. 2014. *Rome's Economic Revolution*. Oxford.

Keaveney, A. 1982. "Sulla augur: Coins and the Curiate Law." *AJAH* 7:150–71.

Keaveney, A. 1983. "Sulla and the Gods." In *Studies in Latin Literature and Roman History* 3, edited by C. Deroux, 44–79. Brussels.

Keaveney, A. 1992. *Lucullus: A Life*. London.

Keaveney, A. 2005. *Sulla, the Last Republican*. 2nd ed. London.

Kelly, G. P. 2006. *A History of Exile in the Roman Republic*. Cambridge.

Kienast, Dieter. 1954. *Cato der Zensor: seine Persönlichkeit und seine Zeit. Mit einem kritisch durchgesehenen Neuabdruck der Redefragmente Catos*. Heidelberg.

Kirschenbaum, A. 1987. *Sons, Slaves and Freedmen in Roman Commerce*. Washington, DC.

Kleiner, D. 1977. *Roman Group Portraiture: The Funerary Reliefs of the Late Republic and Early Empire*. New York.

Kragelund, P. 2001. "Dreams, Religion and Politics in Republican Rome." *Historia* 50:53–95.

Krebs, C. B. 2013. "Caesar, Lucretius, and the Dates of the *De Rerum Natura* and the *Commentarii*." *CQ* 63 (2): 772–79.

Krebs, C. B. 2018. "A Style of Choice." In *The Cambridge Companion to the Writings of Julius Caesar*, edited by L. Grillo and C. Krebs, 110–14. Cambridge.

Law, H. H. 1936. "The Poems of Archias in the Greek Anthology." *CP* 31 (3): 225–43.

Le Doze, P. 2009. "Aux origines d'une retraite politique: Mécène et la *res publica restituta*." In *Le principat d'Auguste. Réalités et représentations du pouvoir. Autour de la* res publica restituta, edited by F. Hurlet et B. Mineo, 101–17. Rennes.

Le Doze, P. 2014a. *Le Parnasse face à l'Olympe. Poésie et culture politique à l'époque d'Octavien/Auguste*. Rome.

Le Doze, P. 2014b. *Mécène: ombres et flamboyances*. Paris.

Le Doze, P. 2019. "Maecenas and the Augustan Poets: The Background of a Central Ambition." In *The Alternative Augustan Age*, edited by K. Morrell, J. Osgood, and K. Welch, 231–46. Oxford.

Le Doze, P. 2020. *Auguste: prince républicain*. Rome.

Lebek, W. 1970. "Eine pollionische Bemerkung Suet. *Gramm.* 10.1 und der Name des Ateius Philologus." *Hermes* 98 (1): 127–28.

Lehmann, Y. 1988. "Varron et le grammarien Tyrannion: l'apport doctrinal de l'aristotélisme." *Ktema* 13:179–86.

Lepore, Jill. 2013. *Book of Ages: The Life and Opinions of Jane Franklin*. New York.

Leppin, H. 1992. *Histrionen. Untersuchungen zur sozialen Stellung von Bühnenkünstlern im Westen des römischen Reiches zur Zeit der Republik und des Principats*. Bonn.

Leppin, H. 2022. *Paradoxe der Parrhesie: eine antike Wortgeschichte.* Tübingen.

Lewis, R. G. 1991. "Sulla's Autobiography: Scope and Economy." *Athenaeum* 79:509–19.

Leydold, M. 2020. "Wann eroberte Mithridates die Provinz Asia?" *Klio* 102 (2): 579–600.

Licandro, O. 2020. *Ius scriptum. Lineamenti di epigrafia e papyrologia.* Rome.

Liebeschuetz, J. H. W. G. 1972. *Antioch: City and Imperial Administration in the Later Roman Empire.* Oxford.

Lightfoot, J. L. 1999. *Parthenius of Nicaea: The Poetical Fragments and the Erotika Pathemata.* Oxford.

Linderski, J. 1986. "The Augural Law." *ANRW* II.16.3, 2146–312.

Lindsay, H. 1997. "Strabo in Apellicon's Library." *RhM* 140:290–8.

Linke, B. 2005. *Die römische Republik von den Gracchen bis Sulla.* Darmstadt.

Linke, K. 1977. *Die Fragmente des Grammatikers Dionysios Thrax. Sammlung griechischer und lateinischer Grammatiker,* vol. 3, 1–77. Berlin.

Lintott, A. 2008. *Cicero as Evidence: A Historian's Companion.* Oxford.

Liubimova, O. 2020. "The Mother of Decimus Brutus and the Wife of Gaius Gracchus." *Mnemosyne* 1–26.

Ljung, E. 2022. "A Third Gracchus Brother? Revisiting Plutarch's Account of the Death of Tiberius Sempronius Gracchus." *CW* 115 (4): 399–415.

Lomas, K. 2002. "The *Polis* in Italy: Ethnicity, Colonization, and Citizenship in the Western Mediterranean." In *Alternatives to Athens: Varieties of Political Organization and Community in Ancient Greece,* edited by R. Brock and S. Hodkinson, 167–86. Oxford.

Lundgreen, C. 2019. "Lucullus und die politische Kultur der römischen Republik. Konkurrenz und Distinktion zwischen Feldherrn, Feinschmeckern und Fischteichbesitzern." In *Verlierer und Aussteiger in der 'Konkurrenz unter Anwesenden.' Agonalität in der politischen Kutur des antiken Rom,* edited by K.-J. Hölkeskamp and H. Beck, 81–126. Stuttgart.

Lyne, R. O. M. 1978. "The Neoteric Poets." *CQ* 28 (1): 167–87.

Maehler, H. 1983. "Egypt under the last Ptolemies." *BICS* 30:1–19.

Magie, D. 1950. *Roman Rule in Asia Minor to the End of the Third Century after Christ.* 2 vols. Princeton, NJ.

Malitz, J. 1983. *Die Historien des Poseidonios.* Munich.

Mann, C. 2008. "Sulla und die Götter des Orients." *Med Ant.* 11:541–51.

Manning, J. 2010. *The Last Pharaohs: Egypt under the Ptolemies, 305–30 BC.* Princeton, NJ.

Manuwald, G. 2011. *Roman Republican Theater.* Cambridge.

Manuwald, G. 2019. *Fragmentary Republican Latin 3, Oratory.* 3 vols. Cambridge, MA.

Manuwald, G. 2023a. *Cato: Testimonia. Origines.* Cambridge, MA.

Manuwald, G. 2023b. *Cato: Orations, Other Fragments.* Cambridge, MA.

Marasco, G., ed. 2011. *Political Autobiographies and Memoirs in Antiquity, A Brill Companion.* Leiden.

Marek, C. 2003. *Pontus et Bithynia: die römischen Provinzen im Norden Kleinasiens.* Mainz.

Marincola, J. 1997. *Authority and Tradition in Ancient Historiography.* Cambridge.

Marshall, A. M. 1999. "Atticus and the Eastern Sojourn." *Latomus* 58 (1): 56–68.

Marshall, B. A. 1973. "Crassus and the *Cognomen Dives.*" *Historia* 22:459–67.

Marshall, R. M. A. 2019. "Suetonius the Bibliographer." In *Scholastic Culture in the Hellenistic and Roman Eras: Greek, Latin, Jewish,* edited by S. A. Adams, 119–48. Berlin.

Martin, T. R. 1989. "Sulla *imperator iterum*, the Samnites and Roman Republican Coin Propaganda." *Schweizerische Numismatische Rundschau* 68:19–44.

Masi Doria, C. 1999. Civitas, operae, obsequium*: tre studi sulla condizione giuridica dei liberti.* Naples.

Mastrocinque, A. 1999. *Studi sulle guerre Mitridatiche.* Historia Einzelschrift 124. Stuttgart.

Matthaios, S. 2015. "Greek Scholarship in the Imperial Era and Late Antiquity." In *Brill's Companion to Ancient Greek Scholarship, vol. 1*, edited by F. Montanari, S. Matthaios, and A. Rengakos, 184–296. Leiden/Boston.

Maurice, L. 2013. *The Teacher in Ancient Rome: The* Magister *and His World.* Lanham, MD.

Mayer, R. 1994. *Horace Epistles Book 1.* Cambridge.

Mayor, A. 2009. *The Poison King: The Life and Legend of Mithradates, Rome's Deadliest Enemy.* Princeton, NJ.

Mazzarino, S. 1966. *Il pensiero storico classico*, vol. 2.1. Bari.

McClintock, A. 2013. "The *Lex Voconia* and Cornelia's Jewels." *RIDA* 60:183–200.

McClintock, A. 2022. *La ricchezza femminile e la 'lex Voconia'.* Napoli: Jovene.

McDermott, W. C. M. 1972. "Cicero and Tiro." *Historia* 21:259–86.

McDonnell, M. 2006. *Roman Manliness.* Virtus *and the Roman Republic.* Cambridge.

McGing, B. 1986. *The Foreign Policy of Mithridates VI Eupator, King of Pontus.* Leiden.

McKeown, N. 2007. *The Invention of Ancient Slavery?* London.

McNelis, C. 2007. "Grammarians and Rhetoricians." In *A Companion to Roman Rhetoric in Society and Literature*, edited by W. J. Dominik and J. Hall, 285–96. Malden, MA.

Meier, C. 1980. *Res Publica Amissa. Eine Studie zu Verfassung und Geschichte der späten römischen Republik.* 2nd ed. Berlin.

Millar, F. G. B. 1988. "Cornelius Nepos, 'Atticus' and the Roman Revolution." *G and R* 35 (1): 40–55.

Millar, F. G. B. 2004. "Epictetus and the Imperial Court." In *Rome, the Greek World, and the East*, vol. 2, edited by H. M. Cotton and Guy M. Rogers, 105–14. Chapel Hill, NC.

Millar, F. G. B. 2006a. "The Phoenician Cities: A Case Study of Hellenization." In *Rome, the Greek World and the East*, vol. 3, edited by F. Millar, H. M. Cotton, and G. M. Rogers, 32–50. Chapel Hill, NC.

Millar, F. G. B. 2006b. "The Roman *Coloniae* of the Near East: A Study of Cultural Relations." In *Rome, the Greek World and the East*, vol. 3, ed. F. Millar, H. M. Cotton, and G. M. Rogers, 164–222. Chapel Hill, NC.

Morandi, A. 2017. *Epigrafia Italica* 2. Rome.

Morgan, H. 2019. "A Horn for Phemius: Cicero, Atticus, and the Musical Culture of the Late Republican Elite." *Mnemosyne* 72:250–72.

Morgan, H. 2023. *Music, Politics, and Society in Ancient Rome.* Cambridge.

Morgan, L. 2000. "The Autopsy of Asinius Pollio." *JRS* 90:51–69.

Morrell, K. 2017. *Pompey, Cato, and the Governance of the Roman Empire.* Oxford.

Morrell, K. 2019. "Who Wants to Go to Alexandria? Pompey, Ptolemy and Public Opinion, 57-56 BC." In *Communicating Public Opinion in the Roman Republic*, edited by C. Rosillo López, 151–74. Stuttgart.

Morrell, K., J. Osgood, and K. Welch, eds. 2019. *The Alternative Augustan Age.* Oxford.

Morstein-Marx, R. 2004. *Mass Oratory and Political Power in the Late Roman Republic.* Cambridge.

Moss, C. 2021. "Between the Lines: Looking for the Contributions of Enslaved Literate Laborers in a Second Century Text, P.Berol. 11632." *Studies in Late Antiquity* 5:432–52.

Moss, C. 2023. "The Secretary: Enslaved Workers, Stenography, and the Production of Early Christian Literature." *The Journal of Theological Studies* 14:20–56.

Moss, C. 2024. *God's Ghostwriters: Enslaved Christians and the Making of the Bible*. Boston.

Mountford, R. 2019. *Maecenas*. London.

Mouritsen, H. 1998. *Italian Unification: A Study in Ancient and Modern Historiography*. London.

Mouritsen, H. 2001. *Plebs and Politics in the Late Roman Republic*. Cambridge.

Mouritsen, H. 2011. *The Freedman in the Roman World*. Cambridge.

Mouritsen, H. 2013. "Slavery and Manumission of the Roman Elite: A Study of the *Columbaria* of the Volusii and Statilii." In *Roman Slavery and Material Culture*, edited by M. George, 43–68. Phoenix suppl. 52. Toronto.

Mouritsen, H. 2016. "Manumission." In *The Oxford Handbook of Roman Law and Society*, edited by P. J. du Plessis, C. Ando, and K. Tuori, 402–15. Oxford.

Mouritsen, H. 2017. "Cicero's *'familia urbana'* and the Social Structure of Late Republican Rome." In *Politische Kultur und soziale Struktur der römischen Republik: Bilanzen und Perspektiven*, edited by M. Haake and A-C. Harders, 215–30. Stuttgart.

Mouritsen, H. 2019. "Slavery and Manumission in Imperial Italy: The Album from Herculaneum Revisited." In *Popolazione, riscorse, e urbanizzazione nella Campania antica. Dall'età preromana alla tarda antichità*, edited by M. Maiuro and M. Balbo, 211–31. Bari.

Muccioli, F. 2007. "La rappresentazione dei Parti nelle fonti tra ii e i secolo a. C. e la polemica di Livio contro i *levissimi ex Graecis*." In *Incontri tra culture nell'Oriente ellenistico e romano. Atti del convegno di studi, Ravenna 11–12 Marzo 2005*, edited by T. Gnoli and F. Muccioli, 87–115. Milan.

Muccioli, F. 2009. "Letterati greci a Roma nel I secolo a. C.: Elementi per una riconsiderazione di Alessandro Poliistore e Timagene." In *Stranieri a Roma. Atti del convegno internazionale di studi*, edited by S. Conti and B. Scardigli, 59–84. Ancona.

Muccioli, F. 2012. "Timagene. Un erudito tra Alessandria e Roma. Nuove riflessioni." In *Tradizione e trasmissione degli storici greci frammentari II. Atti del Terzo Workshop Internazionale. Roma 24–26 febbraio 2011*, edited by V. Costa, 365–88. Tivoli.

Myers, M. Y. 2018. "Import/Export. Empire and Appropriation in the Gallus Papyrus from Qasr Ibrim." In *Rome, Empire of Plunder. The Dynamics of Cultural Appropriation*, edited by M. P. Loar, C. MacDonald, and D. Padilla Peralta, 214–36. Cambridge.

Negroni, A. 2001. "Aggiunte e correzioni al *CIL* VI. Alcune revisioni nella Galleria Lapidaria (settori 6, 8, 10, 12)." *Bolletino, Monumenti Musei e Gallerie Pontificie* XXI:171–80.

Nicolet, C. 1966–74. *L'ordre équestre à l'époque républicaine (313–43 av. J-C.)*. 2 vols. Paris.

Nicolet, C. 1976. *Le métier de citoyen dans la Rome républicaine*. Paris.

Noble, F. M. 2014. "Sulla and the Gods: Religion, Politics, and Propaganda in the Autobiography of L. Cornelius Sulla." PhD diss. Newcastle.

North, J. A. 2011. "Lex Domitia Revisited." In *Priests and State in the Roman World*, edited by J. H. Richardson and F. Santangelo, 39–61. Stuttgart.

Noy. D. 2004. "Being an Egyptian in Rome: Strategies of Identity Formation." In *Christians as a Religious Minority in a Multicultural City*, edited by J. Zangenberg and M. Labahn, 47–54. London.

O'Brien, D. 2021. *Lexicon of Oscan Inscriptions from Campania, Pompeii, Capua and the Rest of Campania.* https://www.academia.edu/35883898/Oscan_Lexicon_of_Campania_2021_03_01

Osgood, J. 2019. "Dio and the Voice of the Sibyl." In *Cassius Dio and the Late Roman Republic,* edited by J. Osgood and C. Baron, 197–214. Leiden.

Palmer, R. E. A. 1997. *Rome and Carthage at Peace.* Historia Einzelschrift 113. Stuttgart.

Pelling, C. B. R. 1988. *Plutarch Life of Antony.* Oxford.

Pelling, C. B. R. 1997. "Tragical Dreamer: Some Dreams in the Roman Historians." *Greece and Rome* 44:197–213.

Pelling, C. B. R. 1999. "Modern Fantasy and Ancient Dreams." In *Writing and Fantasy,* edited by C. Sullivan and B. White, 15–31. London.

Pelling, C. B. R. 2009. "Was There an Ancient Genre of 'Autobiography? Or, Did Augustus Know What He was Doing?" In *The Lost Memoirs of Augustus and the Development of Roman Autobiography,* edited by C. J. Smith and A. Powell, 41–64. Swansea.

Perlwitz, Olaf, 1992. *Titus Pomponius Atticus. Untersuchungen zur Person eines einflußreichen Ritters in der ausgehenden römischen Republik.* Hermes Einzelschrift 58. Stuttgart.

Peter, H. 1877. "Q. Lutatius Catulus und Lutatius Daphnis." *NJPhP* 115:751.

Peter, H. 1914. *Historicorum romanorum reliquiae.* 2nd ed. Stuttgart.

Pina Polo, F. 1989. *Las contiones civiles y militares en Roma.* Zaragoza.

Pina Polo, F. 1996. *Contra arma verbis: der Redner vor dem Volk in der späten römischen Republik.* Stuttgart.

Pobjoy, M. 2006. "Epigraphy and Numismatics." In *A Companion to the Roman Republic,* edited by N. Rosenstein and R. Morstein-Marx, 51–80. Oxford.

Probert, Philomen. 2019. *Latin Grammarians on the Latin Accent: The Transformation of Greek Grammatical Thought.* Oxford.

Purcell, N. 1993. "*Atrium Libertatis.*" *PBSR* 61:125–55.

Raepsaet-Charlier, M.-Th. 1987. *Prosopographie des femmes de l'ordre sénatorial (Ier—IIe siècles),* 2 vols., Louvain.

Ramin, J., and P. Veyne. 1981. "Droit romain et société: les hommes libres qui passent pour esclaves et l'esclavage volontaire." *Historia* 30 (4): 472–97.

Rawson, E. 1985. *Intellectual Life in the Late Roman Republic.* Baltimore.

Rawson, E. 1987. "Sallust on the 80s." *CQ* 37:163–80.

Reduzzi Merola, F. 1990. *Servo parere. Studi sulla condizione giuridica degli schiavi vicari e dei sottoposti a schiavi nelle esperienze greca e romana.* Naples.

Reinach, T. 1890. *De Archia poeta.* Paris.

Reinhold, M. 1972. "Agrippa's Son-in-Law P. Quinctilius Varus." *CP* 67:119–21.

Ricci, C. 1993. "Egiziani a Roma nelle fonti epigrafiche di età imperiale." *Aegyptus* 73:71–91.

Rich, J. 2024. "Corruption, Power, and an Oracle in the Late Roman Republic: The Restoration of Ptolemy Auletes." In *Money, Warfare, and Power in the Ancient World: Studies in Honour of Matthew Freeman Trundle,* edited by J. Armstrong, A. J. Pomeroy, and D. Rosenbloom, 219–44. London.

Richlin, A. 2017a. *Slave Theater in the Roman Republic: Plautus and Popular Comedy.* Cambridge.

Richlin, Amy. 2017b. "The Traffic in Shtick." In *Empire of Plunder: The Dynamics of Cultural Appropriation,* edited by M. Loar, C. MacDonald, and D. Padilla Peralta, 169–93. Cambridge.

Richlin, A. 2024. "Subalternity in the Roman Metropole." In *The Routledge Handbook of Classics, Colonialism and Postcolonial Theory*, edited by K. Blouin and B. Akrigg, 142–67. London.

Riggsby, A. 2006. *Caesar in Gaul and Rome: War in Words*. Austin, TX.

Riggsby, A. 2008. "Memoir and Autobiography in Republican Rome." In *A Companion to Greek and Roman Historiography*, edited by J. Marincola, 266–74. Oxford.

Rix, H. 2002. *Sabellische Texte. Die Texte des Oskischen, Umbischen und Südpikenischen*. Heidelberg.

Rocca, G. 2016. "Nuova lettura dell'iscrizione sul cippo del Foro." *Alessandria, Rivista di glottologia* 10:3–6.

Rohr Vio. F. 2000. *Le voci del dissenso: Ottaviano Augusto e i suoi oppositori*. Padua.

Rohr Vio. F. 2011. *Contro il principe: congiure e dissenso nella Roma di Augusto*. Bologna.

Roselaar, S. 2010. *Public Land in the Roman Republic: A Social and Economic History of* Ager Publicus *in Italy, 396–89 BC*. Oxford.

Roselaar, S. 2019. *Italy's Economic Revolution: Economic Relations and the Integration of Republican Italy*. Oxford.

Rosenberger, V. 1998. *Gezähmte Götter: das Prodigienwesen der römischen Republik*. Stuttgart: Steiner.

Rosenblitt, J. A. 2019. *Rome after Sulla*. London.

Rosillo-López, C. 2020. "Informal Political Communication and Network Theory in the Late Roman Republic." *Journal of Historical Network Research* 4:90–113.

Rosillo-López, C. 2022. *Political Conversations in Late Republican Rome*. Oxford.

Roth, U. 2004. "Inscribed Meaning: The *Vilica* and the Villa Economy." *PBSR* 72: 101–24.

Rowlandson, J. 1998. *Women and Society in Greek and Roman Egypt*. Cambridge.

Roy, J. 1998. "The Masculinity of the Hellenistic King." In *When Men Were Men: Masculinity, Power and Identity in Classical Antiquity*, edited by L. Foxhall, 111–35. London.

Rüpke, J. 2008. *Fasti Sacerdotum: a Prosopography of Pagan, Jewish, and Christian Religious Officials in the City of Rome, 300 BC to AD 499*. Oxford.

Rüpke, J. 2011. "Different Colleges—Never Mind?" In *Priests and State in the Roman World*, edited by J. H. Richardson and F. Santangelo, 25–38. Stuttgart.

Rüpke, J., and F. Santangelo, 2017. "Public Priests and Religious Innovation in Imperial Rome." In *Beyond Priesthood: Religious Entrepreneurs and Innovators in the Roman Empire*, edited by R. Gordon, G. Petridou, and J. Rüpke, 15–47. Berlin.

Salares, R. 2002. *Malaria and Rome: A History of Malaria in Ancient Italy*. Oxford.

Salomies, O. 1987. *Die römischen Vornamen: Studien zur römischen Namengebung*. Helsinki.

Salzman, M. R., and M. Roberts, 2011. *The Letters of Symmachus, Book 1*. Atlanta.

Santangelo, F. 2007. *Sulla, the Elites and the Empire*. Leiden.

Santangelo, F. 2015. *Teofane di Mitilene: testimonianze e frammenti*. Rome.

Santangelo, F. 2018. "Theophanes of Mytilene, Cicero and Pompey's Inner Circle." In *Institutions and Ideology in Republican Rome: Speech, Audience, and Decision*, edited by H. van der Blom, C. Gray, and C. Steel, 128–46. Cambridge.

Sartori, F. 1981. "Ermippo di Berito, sciavo e storiografo." *Index* 10:260–70.

Sblendorio Cugusi, M. T. 1982. *M. Porci Catonis Orationum Reliquiae*. Turin.

Scheid, J. 1990a. *Romulus et ses frères. Le collège des frères Arvales, modèle du culte public dans la Rome des empereurs*. Rome.

Scheid, J. 1990b. *Le collège des frères Arvales. Étude prosopographique du recrutement (69–304)*. Rome.

Scheid, J. 1998. *Commentarii Fratrum Arvalium qui supersunt. Les copies épigraphiques des protocoles annuels de la Confrérie Arvale (21 av.–304 ap. J. C.)*. Rome.

Scheid, J. 2007. *Res Gestae Divi Augusti = Hauts faits du divin Auguste*. Paris.

Scheidel, W. 1997. "Quantifying the Sources of Slaves in the Early Roman Empire." *JRS* 87:156–69.

Scheidel, W. 2005. "Human Mobility in Roman Italy, II: The Slave Population." *JRS* 95:64–79.

Scheidel, W. 2011. "The Roman Slave Supply." In *The Cambridge World History of Slavery, 1: The Ancient Mediterranean World*, edited by K. Bradley and P. Cartledge, 287–310. Cambridge.

Schermaier, M. 2023. "Without Rights? Social Theories meet Roman Law Texts." In *The Position of Roman Slaves: Social Realities and Legal Differences*, edited by M. Schermaier, 1–24. Berlin.

Schironi, F. 2018. *The Best of the Grammarians: Aristarchus of Samothrace on the* Iliad. Ann Arbor.

Scholtz, P. 2003. "Sullas *commentarii*—eine literarische Rechtfertigung. Zu Wesen und Funktion der autobiographischen Schriften in der späten römischen Republik." In *Formen römischer Geschichtsschreibung von den Anfängen bis Livius. Gattungen, Autoren, Kontexte*, edited by U. Eigler, U. Gotter, N. Luraghi, and U. Walter, 172–95. Darmstadt.

Scholz, P., U. Walter, and C. Winkle, 2013. *Fragmente römischer Memoiren*. Heidelberg.

Schulz, V. 2020. "The Music of Words in Roman Rhetoric." In *A Companion to Ancient Greek and Roman Music*, edited by T. Lynch and E. Rocconi, 365–77. Hoboken, NJ.

Sciarrino, E. 2007. "Roman Oratory before Cicero: The Elder Cato and Gaius Gracchus." In *A Companion to Roman Rhetoric*, edited by W. Dominik and J. Hall, 54–66. Malden, MA.

Sciarrino, E. 2011. *Cato the Censor and the Beginnings of Latin Prose: From Poetic Translation to Elite Transcription*. Columbus, OH.

Shackleton-Bailey, D. R. 1965. *Cicero's Letters to Atticus*, vol. 1. Cambridge.

Shatzman, I. 1971. "The Egyptian Question in Roman Politics." *Latomus* 30:363–69.

Shatzman, I. 1975. *Senatorial Wealth and Roman Politics*. Brussels.

Shaw, B. D. 2001. "Raising and Killing Children: Two Roman Myths." *Mnemosyne* 54:31–77.

Sherwin-White, A. N. 1966. *The Letters of Pliny: A Historical and Social Commentary*. Oxford.

Siani-Davies, M. 1997. "Ptolemy XII Auletes and the Romans." *Historia* 46:306–40.

Siani-Davies, M. 2001. *Cicero's Speech* Pro Rabirio Postumo. Oxford.

Sick, D. H. 1999. "Ummidia Quadratilla: Cagey Businesswoman or Lazy Pantomime Watcher?" *CA* 18:330–48.

Sigismund-Nielsen, H. 1987. "*Alumnus*: A Term of Relation that Denotes Quasi-adoption." *C&M* 38:142–88.

Sigismund-Nielsen, H. 2013. "Slave and Lower-class Roman Children." In *The Oxford Handbook of Childhood and Education in the Classical World*, edited by J. Evans-Grubbs and T. Parkin, 286–301. Oxford.

Simpson, C. 1996. "Two Small Thoughts on 'Cilnius Maecenas.'" *Latomus* 55 (2): 394–98.

Smith, C. 2009. "Sulla's Memoirs." In *The Lost Memoirs of Augustus and the Development of Roman Autobiography*, edited by C. Smith and A. Powell, 65–85. Swansea.

Smith, C. J., and A. Powell, eds. 2009. *The Lost Memoirs of Augustus and the Development of Roman Autobiography*. Swansea.

Solin, H. 1996. *Die stadtrömischen Sklavennamen: ein Namenbuch*. Stuttgart.

Sordi, M. 1982. "Timagene di Alessandria: uno storico ellenocentrico e filobarbaro." *ANRW* 2.30.1:775–97.

Spawforth, A. J. S. 2012. *Greece and the Augustan Cultural Revolution*. Cambridge.

Stadter, P. 1992. "Paradoxical Paradigms: Lysander and Sulla." In *Plutarch and the Historical Tradition*, edited by P. Stadter, 41–55. London.

Steel, C. 2001. *Cicero, Rhetoric, and Empire*. Oxford.

Steel, C. 2013. *The End of the Roman Republic, 146–44 BC: Conquest and Crisis*. Edinburgh.

Stockton, D. 1979. *The Gracchi*. Oxford.

Storey, S. J. 1999. "Bithynia: History and Administration to the Time of Pliny the Younger." MA thesis, University of Alberta.

Suerbaum, W., ed. 2002. *Die archaische Literatur. Von den Anfängen bis Sullas Tod. Handbuch der lateinischen Literatur der Antike 1*. Munich.

Sumi, G. 2002. "Spectacles and Sulla's Public Image." *Historia* 51:414–32.

Swain, S. 1992. "Plutarch's Characterization of Lucullus." *RhM* 135:307–17.

Syme, R. 1961. "Who Was Vedius Pollio?" *JRS* 51:23–30.

Syme, R. 1986. *The Augustan Aristocracy*. Oxford.

Syme, R. 2016. "Satellites of Sulla." In *Approaching the Roman Revolution: Papers on Republican History*, edited by R. Syme and F. Santangelo, 111–18. Oxford.

Talbert, R. A. 1984. *The Senate of Imperial Rome*. Princeton, NJ.

Tan, J. 2017. *Power and Public Finance at Rome, 264–49 BCE*. Oxford.

Tansey, P. 2003. "The Death of M. Aemilius Scaurus, cos. 115 BC." *Historia* 52:378–83.

Tatum, J. 2011. "The Late Republic: Autobiographies and Memoirs in the Age of the Civil Wars." In *Political Autobiographies and Memoirs in Antiquity*, edited by G. Marasco, 161–88. Leiden.

Temin, P. 2013. *The Roman Market Economy*. Princeton, NJ.

Thein, A. G. 2002. "Sulla's Public Image and the Politics of Civic Renewal." PhD Diss, UPenn.

Thein, A. G. 2009. "*Felicitas* and the Memoirs of Sulla and Augustus." In *The Lost Memoirs of Augustus and the Development of Roman Autobiography*, edited by C. Smith and A. Powell, 87–109. Swansea.

Thomas, Y. 1996. *'Origine' et 'commune patrie'. Étude de droit public romain (89 av. J.-C. ~ 212 ap. J.-C.)*. Rome.

Tomlin, Roger. 2016. *London's First Voices: Writing Tablets from the Bloomberg London Excavations 2010–14* (MOLA Monograph Series 72). London.

Treggiari, S. 1969a. "The Freedmen of Cicero." *G and R* 16 (2): 195–204.

Treggiari, S. 1969b. *Roman Freedmen During the Late Republic*. Oxford.

Treggiari, S. 1975. "Jobs in the Household of Livia." *PBSR* 43:48–77.

Treggiari, S. 1977. "Intellectuals, Poets, and their Patrons in the First Century BC." *EMC* 21 (1): 24–29.

Treggiari, S. 1991. *Roman Marriage: Iusti Coniuges from the Time of Cicero to the Time of Ulpian*. Oxford.

Treggiari, S. 2007. *Terentia, Tullia, and Publilia: The Women of Cicero's Family*. Abingdon.

Treggiari, S. 2019. *Servilia and Her Family*. Oxford.

Tröster, M. 2005. "Lucullus, his Foreign *Amici*, and the Shadow of Pompey." In *Roms auswärtige Freunde in der späten Republik und im frühen Prinzipat*, edited by A. Coşkun, H. Heinen, and M. Tröster, 91–111. Göttingen.

Tröster, M. 2008. *Themes, Character, and Politics in Plutarch's Life of Lucullus: The Construction of a Roman Aristocrat.* Stuttgart.

Tweedie, F. 2015. "Appian's Characterization of Scipio Aemilianus." In *Appian's Roman History: Empire and Civil War*, edited by K. Welch, 169–84. Swansea.

Vacher, M.-Cl. 2003. *Suétone: grammairiens et rhéteurs.* Paris.

Valentini, A. 2016. *Matronae tra novitas e mos maiorum. Spazi e modalità dell'azione pubblica feminile nella Roma medio repubblicana.* Venice.

Valgiglio, E. 1975. "L'autobiografia di Silla nelle biografie di Plutarco." *StudUrb* 49:245–81.

Van den Hout, M. P. J. 1988. *M. Cornelii Frontonis Epistulae.* Leiden.

van der Blom, H. 2016. *Oratory and Political Career in the Late Roman Republic.* Cambridge.

van Nijf, O. 2012. "Athletes, Artists, and Citizens in the Imperial Greek City." In *Patrie d'origine et patries électives: les citoyennetés multiples dans le monde grec d'époque romaine*, edited by A. Heller and A.-V. Pont, 175–94. Bordeaux.

Vervaet, F. 2004. "The Lex Valeria and Sulla's Empowerment as Dictator (82–79 BCE)." *Cahiers du Centre Gustave Glotz* 15:37–84.

Vervaet, F. 2023. *Reform, Revolution, Reaction: A Short History of Rome from the Origins of the Social War to the Dictatorship of Sulla.* Zaragoza.

Vesperini, P. 2022. "Les savoirs et les plaisirs d'un jeune esclave lettré, Pétronius Antigénidès." *Cahiers des études anciennes* LIX:1–18.

Volk, K. 2021. *The Roman Republic of Letters: Scholarship, Philosophy, and Politics in the Age of Cicero and Caesar.* Princeton, NJ.

Vretska, H., and K. Vretska, 1979. *Marcus Tullius Cicero:* Pro Archia poeta. *Ein Zeugnis für den Kampf des Geistes um seine Anerkennung.* Darmstadt.

Wachter, R. 1987. *Altlateinische Inschriften: Sprachliche und epigraphische Untersuchungen zu den Dokumenten bis etwa 150 v. Chr.* Bern.

Wallace-Hadrill, A. 2008. *Rome's Cultural Revolution.* Cambridge.

Walter, U. 2003. "*Natam me consule Romam.* Historisch-politische Autobiographien in republikanischer Zeit—ein Überblick." *Der Altsprachliche Unterricht* 46 (2): 36–43.

Walter, U. 2004. *Memoria und res publica: zur Geschichtskultur im republikanischen Rom.* Frankfurt.

Walter, U. 2009. "Die *Communes Historiae* des Lutatius: Einleitung, Übersetzung, Kommenar." *Göttinger Forum für Altertumswissenschaft* 12:1–15.

Warwick, R. 2024. "Escaping Cicero: 'Dionysius' and the Limits of the Archive." *CP* 119 (1): 94–110.

Watson, A. 1970. "The Development of the Praetor's Edict." *JRS* 60:105–19.

Weber, G. 2000. *Kaiser, Träume und Visionen in Prinzipat und Spätantike.* Stuttgart.

Weiss, M. 2010. "Two Sabellic *Praenomina.*" In *Ex Anatolia Lux: Anatolian and Indo-European Studies in Honor of H. Craig Melchert on the Occasion of his sixty-fifth Birthday*, edited by R. Kim, N. Oettinger, E. Rieken and M. Weiss, 363–75. Ann Arbor.

Welch, K. E. 1996. "T. Pomponius Atticus: A Banker in Politics?" *Historia* 45 (4): 450–71.

Welch, K. E., ed. 2015. *Appian's Roman History: Empire and Civil War.* Swansea.

Westall, R. 2015. "The Sources for the *Civil Wars* of Appian of Alexandria." In *Appian's Roman History: Empire and Civil War. Roman Culture in an Age of Civil War*, edited by K. Welch, 125–67. Swansea.

White, P. 1991. "Maecenas' Retirement." *CP* 86.2:130–38.

White, P. 1993. *Promised Verse: Poets in the Society of Augustan Rome.* Cambridge, MA.

Whitmarsh, T. 2018. "How to Write Anti-Roman History." In *How to Do Things with History,* edited by D. S. Allen, P. Christesen, and P. Millett, 365–90. Oxford.

Whitton, C. 2013. *Pliny the Younger: Epistles, Book II.* Cambridge.

Will, E. 1982. *Histoire politique du monde hellénistique.* 2nd ed., 323–30 av. J.-C., vol. 2. Nancy.

Wille, G. 1967. *Musica Romana.* Amsterdam.

Williams, G. 1990. "Did Maecenas Fall from Favor? Augustan Literary Patronage." In *Between Republic and Empire,* edited by K. Raaflaub and M. Toher, 258–75. Berkeley.

Williamson, C. 2005. *The Laws of the Roman People. Public Law in the Expansion and Decline of the Roman Republic.* Ann Arbor.

Winsbury, R. 2009. *The Roman Book.* London.

Wiseman, T. P. 1982. "*Pete nobiles amicos*: Poets and Patrons in Late Republican Rome." In *Literary and Artistic Patronage in Ancient Rome,* edited by B. K. Gold, 28–49. Austin, TX.

Wiseman, T. P. 1992. "The Senate and the Populares: 69–60 BC." In *The Cambridge Ancient History 9²: The Last Age of the Roman Republic 146–43 BC,* edited by J. A. Crook. Andrew Lintott, and Elizabeth Rawson, 327–67. Cambridge.

Wiseman, T. P. 1998. "The Publication of the *De Bello Gallico.*" In *Julius Caesar: The Artful Reporter,* edited by K. Welch and A. Powell, 1–9. Swansea.

Wiseman, T. P. 2009. "Augustus, Sulla, and the Supernatural." In *The Lost Memoirs of Augustus and the Development of Roman Autobiography,* edited by C. Smith and A. Powell, 111–23. Swansea.

Wisse, J. 2013a. "Remembering Cremutius Cordus. Tacitus on History, Memory, and Tyranny." *Histos* 7:299–361.

Wisse, J. 2013b. "The Bad Orator: Between Clumsy Delivery and Political Danger." In *Community and Communication: Oratory and Politics in Republican Rome,* edited by C. Steel and H. van der Blom, 163–94. Oxford.

Wolff, Catherine. 2015. *L'éducation dans le monde romain: Du début de la République à la mort de Commode.* Antiquité synthèses 16. Paris.

Woolf, G. 2011. "Literacy or Literacies in Rome?" In *Ancient Literacies: The Culture of Reading in Greece and Rome,* edited by W. A. Johnson and H. N. Parker, 46–68. Oxford.

Yarrow, L. 2006. *Historiography at the End of the Republic: Provincial Perspectives on Roman Rule.* Oxford.

Zanda, Emanuela. 2011. *Fighting Hydra-Like Luxury: Sumptuary Regulation in the Roman Republic.* London.

Zecchini, G. 1990. "La storiografia lagide." In *Purposes of History: Studies in Greek Historiography IV-II Century BC,* edited by G. Schepens, 213–32. Leiden.

Zhang, X. 2024. "T. Pomponius Atticus, M. Vipsanius Agrippa, and the Marriage between Caecilia Attica and Agrippa." *AJP* 145 (3): 375–406.

INDEX

Page numbers in italics refer to maps. Page numbers followed by an n refer to notes.

Accius, Lucius, 50, 52, 73–75, 83, 183n7
accountants, 46, 55
actors: influences of, 31; theaters, 122, 170–171n89; theatrical techniques and, 171n90
adoption, 173n20, 200–201n13
Aeficius Calvinus, 68
Aelius Tubero, Quintus, 29, 30
Aemilia Tertia, 172n3
Aemilius Paullus, Lucius, 166n22
Aemilius Scaurus, Marcus: autobiography of, 110; career of, 100; Daphnis and, 71–78; household system of, 69; oratory and, 67; Pliny the Elder on, 73; widow of, 91, 102
Aeneas, 68, 144
Aeneid (Vergil), 62, 144
Aeschylus, 17
Aesopus, 32
Africa, 29
Akhisar, 99
Alexander the Great, 151
Alexandria: destruction of, 152; Gnipho and, 123–126, 128; influence of, 154, 155; Menelaus and, 26; study in, 160; Timagenes of Alexandria, 145–149; Tyrannio the Elder (of Amisus) and, 138
Alexas of Laodicea, 149
Alexis (Atticus' secretary), 58
Amisos, 132, 134–137, 206n5
Ammianus Marcellinus, 13, 20, 151
Anicia, 37
Annales (Accius), 74
Annius Milo, Titus, 54
Antiochus of Ascalon, 186n98
Antonius, Iullus, 205n66
Antonius, Marcus (consul 99 BC), 125, 126, 127
Antonius Creticus, Marcus, 205n65
Antonius Hybrida, Gaius, 205n65
Antony, Marc (triumvir), 38, 140, 153
Apellicon, 139
Apollonius of Tyana, 157
apparitores, 195n81
Appuleius, Lucius, 68
Appuleius Saturninus, Lucius, 21
Archias, Aulus Licinius (Archias of Antioch): career of, 7, 80; Cicero's defense of, 77–79, 82; citizenship of, 77–79, 80, 82, 87–88; education of, 80; name of, 79, 82; origins of, 79–80; patrons of, 81; poetry of, 83–85, 88; reputation of, 80; role in political and literary culture, 85; travels of, 80–83
Archimedes, 133–134
Aristarchus of Samothrace, 138
Aristonicus, 25
Aristotle, 139
Artemidorus, 132, 140
Arval brothers, 104–106
Asinius Pollio, Gaius, 3, 143–144, 149–152, 155, 212n83
Ateius, Lucius, 143
Ateius Capito, Lucius, 143

Athens: Atticus's household in, 37, 50, 52, 53, 57, 60; booty from, 139; capture of, 37, 83, 133–134, 145; Panaetius's return to, 94; Philologus and, 123, 132, 143; study in, 126; Timagenes and, 153
Attius of Pisaurum, 73
auctions, 210n60
audiences, 170–171n89
Aufidius Pontianus, Publius, 177n83
augurs, 104, 106, 108–109
Augustine, 112
Augustus: Atticus and, 53; Caesar and, 127; early principate under, 1; household system of, 90, 140; leadership of, 133; *libelli* and, 76; Melissus and, 122, 155; name of, 141; Philologus and, 144; priesthood and, 105; *Res Gestae*, 11; Timagenes and, 146, 149–153. *See also* Asinius Pollio, Gaius; Epirota, Quintus Caecilius; Livia Drusilla; Melissus, Gaius Maecenas; Octavian
Aulus (*praenomen*), 185n83
Aurelius Cotta, Gaius, 91, 93
Aurelius Symmachus, Quintus, 92
authors and authorship: household work of, 2–3; interpretation of, 11; nature of, 3; Pliny and, 163n11
autobiography, 91, 103, 110, 112, 135–136

Battle of Actium, 133, 141
bees and beekeeping, 202n30
Berytus (Beirut), 157
bilingualism, 161
Bithynia, 134
Bloomberg writing tablets, 164n14, 176n65
Blossius, Gaius, 25
Bradley, Keith, 6
Buthrotum in Epirus, 50, 53, 57, 60

Caecilia Attica, 38, 60–61
Caecilia Metella, 91, 102
Caecilii Metelli, 84
Caecilius, Quintus, 38, 50
Caecilius Atticus, Quintus. *See* Pomponius Atticus, Titus
Caecilius Metellus Delmaticus, Lucius, 183n61
Caecilius Metellus Pius, Quintus, 79
Caelius Rufus, Marcus, 147
Caesarion, 149
calatores, 104–106
Callimachus, 136
Calpurnius Piso Frugi, Lucius, 26, 29
Campania, 25, 111
Campus Martius, 76
captives. *See* war captives
Carthage, 8, 136
Cato the Elder. *See* Porcius Cato, Marcus (Cato the Censor)
children: education of, 161–162; exposure of. *See* exposure of infants
Chilon, 42–44, 62, 174n43
Chrysogonus, 102–103, 112
Cilicia, 55, 58
Cimbric War, 85
citizenship, 77–79, 80, 82, 87–88
Claudius Marcellus, Marcus, 118
Claudius Pulcher, Appius, 211n64
Cleopatra VII, 61, 126, 149, 150, 151
Clitarchus, 215n123
Clodius Pulcher, Publius, 54
cognomen, 8
coins, 108, 164n22
collaborators, 109, 113
comedies, 122
Commentarii (Caesar), 128
Communis Historia (*Shared History*) (Daphnis), 68, 74
conversations, literary projects and, 3–4
copyright, 163n11
Cornelia, 21, 25, 28
Cornelius Dolabella, Publius, 55
Cornelius Gallus, Gaius, 3, 61–62, 63
Cornelius Nepos, 37, 52, 68
Cornelius Scipio Aemilianus, Publius, 8, 31, 95, 136, 191n22

Cornelius Scipio Africanus, Publius, 21, 22, 166n22
Cornelius Sulla, Faustus: augur role of, 109; death of, 149; Epicadus and, 103–104, 112; library of, 139; Timagenes and, 148, 153
Cornelius Sulla Felix, Lucius: augur role of, 108–109; autobiography of, 91, 103, 110, 112, 135–136; capture of Athens, 37; career of, 109; citizenship of, 108; death of, 111; description, 57; Epicadus and, 102–103, 110–113; family of, 91; household system of, 102, 111, 113; leadership of, 71, 82, 102; library of, 139; military service of, 110, 143; Plutarch's biography of, 110–111; Rutilius and, 99, 100

Daphnis, Quintus Lutatius: career of, 67, 72–77, 87; Catulus and, 76–77; Catulus's affection for, 77; *Communis Historia*, 68, 74; education of, 67, 72–77; enslavement of, 1; as a luxury, 76; manumission of, 68; mockery of, 129; name of, 75; origins of, 65–66, 70, 73–74; *Origo Gentis Romanae*, 68; research challenges, 5; slave trade and, 67, 69, 71, 74, 86
De Agricultura (Cato), 39–40, 46
De Cognominibus (Epicadus), 112
De Grammaticis et Rhetoribus (Suetonius): description of Daphnis, 66, 68–69, 75; description of Epicadus, 89, 103, 104; description of Epirota, 59; description of Gnipho, 123–126; description of Melissus, 118–121; description of Opillus, 91–95, 101; description of Philologus, 144–145; description of Sulla, 108; focus of, 2; scope of, 157–158. *See also* Suetonius Tranquillus, Gaius
De Latino Sermone (Gnipho), 124, 126
De Metris (Epicadus), 112
De Natura Deorum (Cicero), 100
De Oratore (Cicero), 14–15, 24, 27
De Re Rustica (Varro), 53, 60
De Sermone Latino (Gnipho), 128
De Verborum Significatu (Flaccus), 181–182n21
De Vita Sua (Marcus Aemilius Scaurus), 77
Dea Dia cult, 105–106
Decius, Publius, 29
Demaris, 147
Demetrios of Erythrai, 138
Demosthenes, 49
Dido, 144
Dio (ambassador from Egypt), 147
Dio, Cassius: description of Licinius, 13, 19–20; on Rutilius, 99
Diokles (Tyrannio the Younger), 140–142, 155
Dionysios Scytobrachion, 125
Dionysius, Marcus Pomponius, 56–57, 63
Dionysius of Halicarnassus, 146
Dionysius Thrax, 138
Diophanes of Mytilene, 25
dispensatores, 107, 197n96
doctors, 55
Domitius Afer, Gnaeus, 164n24
Domitius Marsus, 62
dowries: of Licinia, 22, 24; size of, 167n32, 167n33; Terence and, 8; of Tullia, 55; use of, 6
Dymas (freedman of Augustus), 132, 140–143

Eclogues (Vergil), 62
education: of children, 161–162; of the enslaved, 6, 39–50, 159–160; of war captives, 160; of women, 61, 164n18
educators, 119–120
Egypt and Egyptians, 126, 133, 212n84
elegantia (term), 177n87
Ennius, Quintus, 101, 164n18
enslaved and formerly enslaved intellectuals: careers of, 6; contributions of, 162; *dispensatores*, 107, 197n96; education of, 6, 159–160; gladiators, 54, 170–171n89; interests of, 6; librarians, 118–119, 122, 129; lives of, 2–3; as luxuries, 71–72, 76, 86, 161; manumission of, 160; origins of, 7, 10; roles of, 3–4, 86; skills of, 3; studies of, 90; teachers, 121, 152; use of, 162; *vicarius*, 43; wet nurses, 116. *See also exposití*
Epaphroditus (freedman of Nero), 6

Ephesus, 98
Epicadus (name), 195n72
Epicadus, Lucius Cornelius: Archias and, 83; career of, 7; citizenship of, 91; *De Cognominibus*, 112; *De Metris*, 112; education of, 91, 108; manumission of, 104; name of, 103; Opillus and, 90–91, 102; origins of, 103; research challenges, 5; skills of, 112; Sulla and, 102–103, 110–113; writings of, 104, 112
Epicratides, 132, 138, 142
Epictetus: education of, 93; life story of, 6
Epicureanism, 93, 94
epigrams, 189n137, 189n138
Epirota, Quintus Caecilius, 58–62, 63, 164n24
Epirus, 50, 53, 57, 93
epitaphs, 90, 106–107
equestrians and equestrian status: Atticus, 36–38, 49, 59; equestrian census, 71; jury trials and, 93, 96; literary culture and, 161; Roscius, 32; *scribae*, 108
Eros, 55
ethnic names, 8
Euripides, 28, 32
Evagoras of Lindos, 146
exile, and confiscation of property, 96, 139
expositi, 114–118, 129–130. *See also* enslaved and formerly enslaved intellectuals; exposure of infants
exposure of infants: effects of the slave trade on, 160; reasons for, 200n9; Roman law and, 117, 201n20. *See also* expositi; Gnipho, Marcus Antonius; Melissus, Gaius Maecenas

familia (term), 172n1
family tombs, 90
Fannius, Gaius, 26, 30
Fannius Chaerea, Gaius, 71
Fasti (Flaccus), 181–182n21
Ferentinum, 27
Ficulea, 50
flamines, 107
Flavius, Quintus, 71
Flavius Fimbria, Gaius, 99
flute player. *See* Licinius (freedman)
Forum: gladiators in, 170–171n89; orators' orientation toward, 12, 23, 24
fostering, 200n13
Franklin, Benjamin, 9
Franklin, Jane, 9
freeborn writers, reliance on others, 5
freedmen: job titles of, 89–90; naming of, 69; patrons and, 89–90; services provided by, 86–87; skills of, 87. *See also* manumission and manumitted intellectuals
Fulvius Flaccus, Marcus, 28, 29, 30
Furius, Aulus, 77

Gabinius, Aulus, 132, 145
Gallia Cisalpina, 125
Gaul, 125
Gellius, Aulus: biases of, 18–19; description of Gracchus, 26–27; description of Licinius, 13, 17–18; *Noctes Atticae*, 101; on Opillus, 101
Georgics (Vergil), 62
ghostwriters, role of, 11
gladiators, 54, 170–171n89
Gnipho, Marcus Antonius: birth of, 116, 124; career of, 126; *De Latino Sermone*, 126; death of, 123, 127; easygoing nature of, 124; education of, 125, 126; exposure of, 115, 124, 125; influence on Caesar, 123, 125, 126–128; influence on Cicero, 127; *On the Latin Language*, 124; name of, 124–125, 129–130; origins of, 116, 124–125; Philologus and, 143; Suetonius's description of, 123–126; travels of, 126; writings of, 124, 126–127. *See also* exposure of infants
graffiti, 162, 180n149
grammar, 94, 139, 140
grammaticus (title), 119–120
Greek literature, 49
Grove of Furrina, 25

Hadrian, 105, 157
handwriting, 179n124
Hannibal, 36, 39
Heliodorus, 184n65
Heraclea, 82
heralds, 105
Herennius, Severus, 157–158
Hermippus of Berytus, 156–158
Hermippus of Smyrna, 216n2
Hermodorus, 147
Herodotus, 49
Hestiaios, 138
Hesychius of Miletus, 157
hetairiai, 147
historiography, 68, 69, 100, 145
Homer, 49
Horace, 62
horns, 58
Hortensius Hortalus, Quintus, 32
hostis designation, 198n108
households: of Atticus, 37, 52–54, 57, 63; of Augustus, 90; authorship and, 2–3; of Cato, 41, 43, 49; of Cicero, 57, 157; intellectual labor and, 2–4, 35; of Rutilius, 113; of Scaurus, 69; of Sulla, 102, 111, 113
humor, 76–77
Hyginus, Gaius Julius, 203n48
Hyle (Philologus), 144

illegal enslavement, 117, 143. *See also* enslaved and formerly enslaved intellectuals
Imagines (Atticus), 172n10
immigrants, 78
incense, 196n89
Ineptiae or *Ioci* (Trifles or Jokes) (Melissus), 76
infanticide, 116
infants: exposure of. *See* exposure of infants
instruments, Phrygian style horn, 58
intellectual culture, 3–4, 46, 161, 162, 164n18
intellectual property, concept of, 9
Italy, 50
Iunius Brutus Callaicus, Decimus, 74
Iunius Brutus, Marcus, 9
Iunius Pennus, Marcus, 29, 30

Jahn, Otto, 68
jobs for slaves: *dispensatores*, 107, 197n96; gladiators, 54, 170–171n89; librarians, 118–119, 122, 129; teachers, 121, 152; wet nurses, 116
jokes, 76–77, 122–123
Jugurtha (king of Numidia), 73
Julius Caesar, Gaius: Amisos and, 134; *Commentarii*, 128; *De Sermone Latino*, 128; friendship with Atticus, 38, 57; Gnipho's influence on, 123, 125, 126–128; influence of Tyrannio, 134, 139; interests of, 128; leadership of, 71; networks of, 3; slave trade and, 72–77; speeches, 128; Suetonius's description of, 127, 164n13
jury trials, 32, 93, 96
Justinian, 157

kalatores. *See calatores*
Korymbos, 138

Laelius, Gaius, 8
Laelius Herma, 145
Latin literature, 112–113
Latin political rhetoric, 29
Latium, 59, 75
legacies, 177n83
Lepore, Jill, 9
Lesbos, 25, 97–98
lex Aufeia, 26
lex Claudia, 175n57
lex Papia de peregrinis, 184n69
lex Plautia Papiria, 79
libelli, 76, 122
Liber Annalis (Atticus), 172n10
libraries and librarians: of Cicero, 55; Melissus, 118–119, 122, 129; organization of, 139; of Sulla, 104, 139; of Tyrannio, 139, 141
Licinia: dowry of, 22, 24; family of, 15, 22; Licinius and, 13; marriage to Gaius Gracchus, 22–23

Licinianus (Marcus Porcius Cato, elder son of Cato the Censor), 172n3
Licinii Crassi, 23–24
Licinius (freedman): career of, 14–20, 32; Cicero's description of, 14–15; Dio's description of, 19–20; education of, 23, 24, 32; Gellius's description of, 17–18; manumission of, 25, 32; Marcellinus's description of, 20; Valerius Maximus's description of, 15–16; origins of, 13, 22–23, 24; Plutarch's description of, 16–17; Quintilian's description of, 16; travels of, 24–25. *See also* pitchpipe and pipe music
Licinius, Aulus. *See* Archias, Aulus Licinius (Archias of Antioch)
Licinius Crassus Dives Mucianus, Publius, 22, 23, 24, 29
Licinius Crassus, Gaius, 23–24, 27
Licinius Crassus, Lucius, 168n40
Licinius Crassus, Marcus, 15, 24, 31
Licinius Crassus, Publius, 168n39
Licinius Lucullus, Lucius, 80–81, 134–138
Licinius Lucullus, Marcus: Archias and, 81–82; defense of Archias, 84
Licinius Murena, Lucius, 135–138
Lindia, 132, 138
literacy, 46, 162, 164n18
literary culture, 161
literary projects, 3–4, 9
Lives of the Sophists (Philostratus), 157
Livia Drusilla, 90, 97, 149, 150, 192n35
Livius Drusus, Marcus, 29, 71
Livy, narrative of Cato, 36
Lucilius, Gaius, 75, 95
Lutatius Catulus, Quintus (consul 102 BC): Archias and, 81; autobiography of, 91, 110; career of, 75; Daphnis and, 67–68, 75–77, 85; death of, 71; Licinius and, 25; mockery of, 129; self-representation of, 86
luxury: enslaved intellectuals as, 71–72, 76, 86, 161; war captives as, 136, 145
Lydia, 99
Maecenas, Gaius, 62, 118, 120–121, 122, 141
Manlius Torquatus, Lucius, 171n96
manumission and manumitted intellectuals: custom of, 160; naming patterns of, 69; reliance on others, 5; teachers and, 121. *See also* freedmen
Marius, Gaius, 21, 73, 75, 85, 92, 109
Marius, Marcus, 27
Marius Priscus, 33
market days, 127
Matidia, 105
Mecom, Jane Franklin, 9
Medea (Euripides), 28, 32
Melior, 189n144
Melissus, Gaius Maecenas: Augustus and, 122; birth of, 116, 119; career of, 118, 120–123, 129; citizenship of, 119, 121; on Daphnis, 68; education of, 119–120; exposure of, 119; *Ineptiae* or *Ioci*, 76; literary knowledge, 118; manumission of, 118; mother of, 120–121; name of, 129–130; research challenges, 5; Trifles or Jokes, 119; writings of, 122–123, 129. *See also* exposure of infants
Memmia Timothoe, 164n18
memoir, 91, 103, 110, 112, 135–136, 156
memorization, 3
Menelaus of Marathos, 25–26
Menshikov, Alexander Sergeyevich, 159
midwives, 115
Minucius Thermus, Quintus, 174n32
Mithridates VI (king of Pontus), 82, 91, 98–99, 100, 134
Mithridatic wars, 38, 85, 90, 110, 145
Mucii Scaevolae, 23
Mucius Scaevola, Pubius, 168n35
Mucius Scaevola, Quintus, 96–97
Musae (*Muses*) (Opillus), 101
music and musicians: Licinius, 14–20; Phemius, 58; Phrygian style horn, 58; pipe music, 12, 16, 17, 18, 20; priesthood and, 196n84
Musonius Rufus, Gaius, 6, 93
Mytilene, 97–98, 99

naming patterns of freedmen, 69
Narbonensis, 125
Nero, 6, 93
New Testament texts, 163n8
New World slavery, 159
newborns: exposure of. *See* exposure of infants
Nicolaus of Damascus, 146
Nigidius Figulus, Publius, 178n118
Noctes Atticae (Gellius), 101
Numidia, 109
nundinae, 127
nutritores, 125, 126

Octavia, 118, 153
Octavian: career of, 140–142; friendships of, 38; Timagenes and, 149. *See also* Augustus
Odyssey (Homer), 58
On Kings (Timagenes), 151
On the Latin Language (Gnipho), 124
Opillus (Oscan name), 190n9
Opillus, Aurelius: Archias and, 83; career of, 7, 93–97; citizenship of, 91, 97; education of, 91, 93; Epicadus and, 90–91, 102; interests of, 95, 101; *Musae*, 101; name of, 90, 91–93; origins of, 92–93; *Pinax (Tablet or Catalog?)*, 92, 101; research challenges, 5; resources of, 97; Rutilius and, 92–93, 95–96, 101; speeches, 94; writings of, 92, 101
Opimius, Lucius, 25, 28, 29, 31
oratory and orators: Cicero, 78–79; education of, 16; Gracchus, 16; Hortensius, 32; lessons on, 32, 124, 127, 129; Licinius and, 14–20; Philologus, 145; Scaurus, 67; skills and techniques of, 24, 26, 28–31. *See also* speeches
Origines (Cato), 47, 49, 68
Origo Gentis Romanae (Daphnis), 68
Oscan language, 101

Paccius, 45–46
Palatine, 21, 54, 75, 76
pamphlets, 122
Panaetius, 94
Panurgus, 70–71
Papirius Carbo, Gaius, 30, 31
Paris, Lucius Junius, 107
pastoral poetry, 183n47
patria potestas, 117, 120–121
patrons: freedmen and, 89–90; manumission and, 160
Peace of Apamea, 82
Peace of Dardanus, 98
peculium, 44, 174n47
Perseus (king of Macedon), 41
Persius, Gaius, 170n81
Petronius, 5
Phemius, 58
Philo of Byblos, 157–158
Philologus, Lucius Ateius: capture of, 143; career of, 143, 144–145; characterization of, 145; education of, 143; Gnipho and, 143; *Hyle*, 144; name of, 132, 143, 144; *Pinakes*, 144; travels of, 144; writings of, 124, 144. *See also* war captives
philosophy, 6, 25, 93–94
Philostratus, 157
Philotimus, 55, 57
Phrygian Hierapolis, 6
Phrygian style horn, 58
Pilia, 38, 50, 173n16
Pinakes (Philologus), 144
Pinax (Tablet or Catalog?), 92, 101
Pisaurum, 66
pitchpipe and pipe music: Gracchus's tone and, 18; Gracchus's use of, 12, 16, 17; sound of, 20
Plautus (Titus Maccius Plautus), 101
playwrights, 123
Plinius, 33–34
Pliny the Elder: authorship and, 163n11; on Daphnis, 1, 66; health of, 171n100, 171n102; on Scaurus, 73; slaves of, 163n6
Pliny the Younger, 33–34

Plutarch: biographies of the Gracchi brothers, 21; biography of Cato, 36, 39–40, 42–43, 45–46; biography of Lucullus, 81; biography of Sulla, 110–111; biography of Tyrannio, 134–137, 154; contributions of, 157; description of Licinius, 13, 16–17; description of politics, 83; on Rutilius, 99
poetry and poets: Archias, 77–86, 88; Catulus, 75; Cornelius Gallus, 61–62; enslaved intellectuals and, 162; pastoral poetry, 183n47; Vergil, 59
political clubs, 147
Polybius, 68, 152
Pompey, 71, 83–84, 140
Pomponia, 60, 72
Pomponius Atticus, Titus: assistants of, 139; career of, 49–50; chronological system used by, 68; Cicero's correspondence with, 37, 50, 54–55, 57–58; education of enslaved persons, 49–50, 52, 63; equestrian status of, 36–38, 49, 59; father of, 71; freedmen of, 56–62; friendship with Caesar, 38, 57; gladiators owned by, 54; household system of, 37, 52–54, 57, 63; *Imagines*, 172n10; influence of Tyrannio, 134, 139; influences of, 11; interests of, 37–38, 49–50; *Liber Annalis*, 172n10; life in Rome, 50; marriage to Pilia, 173n16; move to Athens, 37, 53; name of, 173n20; Nepos's biography of, 37, 52; origins of, 36–37, 49–50; real estate holdings of, 50, 51; Suetonius's description of, 58; writings of, 172n10
pontifices, 22, 107
Popilia, 75
Porcius Cato Licinianus, Marcus, 42, 172n3, 174n42
Porcius Cato, Marcus (Cato the Censor): career of, 36, 40, 142; *De Agricultura*, 26, 39–40, 46; documentation of, 36; education of enslaved persons, 39–49; family of, 38–39; farm work of, 39; Gellius and, 18; habits of, 39; household system of, 41, 43, 49; interests of, 37, 49; Livy's narrative of, 36; military service of, 36, 40; *Origines*, 47, 49, 68; origins of, 36–37; Plutarch's biography of, 36, 39–40, 42–43, 45–46; political aspirations of, 39; on sexual services, 73; slave trade and, 86; speeches by, 40, 47–48; theatrical techniques and, 171n90
Portico of Metellus, 122
Portico of Octavia, 129
Posidonius of Apamea, 95, 152
praecones, 105
priesthoods, 108, 196n84
Prima, Usia, 212n86
prisoners of war: use of term, 206n1. *See also* war captives
Pro Archia (Cicero), 185n78, 185n79, 185n80
Pro Roscio Comoedo (Cicero), 71
Prometheus Bound (Aeschylus), 17
Ptolemy X Alexander, 125
Ptolemy XII Auletes, 133, 145, 146, 147–148, 150
public speaking, 21, 24–25, 29, 31. *See also* speeches
publicani, 96. *See also* equestrians and equestrian status
Publilia, 55

Quinctilius Varus, Publius, 180n140
Quinctius, Publius, 171n90
Quintilian, 13, 16, 151
Quintio (freedman of Cato the Censor), 46
Quirinal, 38, 50, 52–53

Rabirius Postumus, Gaius, 147
Res Gestae (Augustus), 11
research challenges, 5
rhetoric: lessons on, 124, 127; production of, 9
rhetoric and rhetoricians: Gnipho, 123, 128–129; Gracchus and, 16, 25–31; Licinius and, 16; Opillus, 91–92, 94; Timagenes, 128–129, 147
Rhodes, 98, 138

Rhodians, 41
Roman culture, 162
Roman law: exposure of infants and, 117, 201n20; *lex Aufeia*, 26; *lex Claudia*, 175n57; *lex Papia de peregrinis*, 184n69; *lex Plautia Papiria*, 79
Roman market days, 127
Roman religion: Arval brothers, 104–106; augurs, 104, 106, 108–109; *flamines*, 107; *pontifices*, 22, 107; priesthood, 108, 196n84
Roman tax farmers (*publicani*), 96. *See also* equestrians and equestrian status
Roscius, Quintus, 31–32, 71, 76
Roscius, Sextus, 103
rostra, 168n43
Rutilius Rufus, Publius: autobiography of, 91, 110; Cicero and, 100; citizenship of, 96, 100; exile of, 83–84, 90–101; family of, 97; household system of, 113; Opillus and, 92–93, 95–96, 101; reputation of, 99; Scaevola and, 97; Sulla and, 99, 100; trial and conviction of, 96; writings of, 100

Said, Nicholas (Mohammed Ali ben Sa'id), 159
Sallust (Gaius Sallustius Crispus), 26, 144
Salonia, 172n3
Salonianus (Marcus Porcius Cato, younger son of Cato the Censor), 172n3
Salonius, 172n3
Sardinia, 21, 23, 36
Scheid, John, 11
Scirtus, 102
scribae, 107–108
Second Punic War, 35, 63
secretaries, 5
self-representation, 85, 86
Sempronia, 22, 36
Sempronius Gracchus, Gaius: career of, 13–15, 22; Cicero's appreciation of, 14–15, 18, 27; context of, 28–31; death of, 14, 25; education of, 21; family of, 20–21; Gellius's description of, 26–27; influences of, 25; marriage to Licinia, 22–23; military service of, 21; speaking style of, 15, 25–28; speeches by, 165n4, 165n17, 167n23; training of, 20
Sempronius Gracchus, Tiberius, 21, 22, 24, 25
Seneca the Younger, 152
Sergius Catilina, Lucius (Catiline), 127
Servilia, 9
Servilius Caepio, Quintus, 100
Seven Sages of Greece, 43
sexual services, 73, 175n49
Shakespeare, William, 8
Shared History (*Communis Historia*) (Daphnis), 68, 74
shepherds, 177n83
Sidicinum Teanum, 27
slave trade: auctions, 210n60; Daphnis and, 69; effects of, 160; enslaved intellectuals as luxuries and, 71–72; legacies and, 177n83; in the nineteenth-century, 159; prices, 74, 86; scholarship on, 70; in the second century, 173n28; sexual services and, 73
slaves. *See* enslaved and formerly enslaved intellectuals
Smyrna (or Zmyrna), 92, 96, 97, 99, 101
Social War, 79, 81–82, 92, 96, 143
sophists, 152
Soranus of Ephesus, 115, 157
Spain, 21, 40–41, 45
Spartan sage, 43
speeches: by Caesar, 128; by Cato, 40, 47–48; by Gracchus, 165n4, 165n17, 167n23; by Opillus, 94; *Pro Roscio Comoedo* (Cicero), 71. *See also* oratory and orators; public speaking
Spoletium, 118–120
Stoic school, 94
Stoicism, 6, 25, 93–94
Strabo of Amaseia, 134, 139, 146
Suda: description of, 157; description of Diokles, 140–141; description of Timagenes, 146; description of Tyrannio, 139

Suetonius Tranquillus, Gaius: description of Atticus, 58; description of Caesar, 127, 164n13; description of Daphnis, 1, 66, 68–69, 75; description of Epicadus, 103; description of Epirota, 59–60, 62; description of *expositi*, 117; description of Gnipho, 123–126; description of Melissus, 118–120; description of Opillus, 91–92, 94; description of Philologus, 144–145; description of Sulla, 108; description of Terence, 8
Sulpicius Rufus, Publius, 37
sumptuary legislation, 72
Syracuse, 133–134

Tarraco, 40
Tartula, 102
tax farmers, 96
taxes, 72
teachers: manumission of, 121; sophists, 152
Terence (Publius Terentius Afer), 8
Terentia (wife of Maecenas), 55, 57, 140–142
Terentius Lucanus, Publius, 8
Terentius Varro Murena, Aulus, 203n47
Tettienus Felix, Titus, 107
Tettienus Serenus, Titus, 107
Theater of Marcellus, 122
theaters, 170–171n89, 171n90
Theocritus, 183n47
Theophanes of Mytilene, 99, 187–188n119
Theophrastus, 139. *See also* Tyrannio the Elder (of Amisus)
Thyateira, 99
Tibullus, 164n14
Timaeus, 68
Timagenes of Alexandria: Augustus and, 150–153; capture of, 145, 146–147; career of, 145–146, 149, 152; enslavement of, 148; focus on, 7; influence of, 146; *On Kings*, 151; name of, 132; origins of, 146; Seneca the Younger's description of, 152; writings of, 151. *See also* war captives
Tiro (Marcus Tullius Tiro), 58, 166n11
Titius, Gaius, 101
toga praetexta, 144
tombs, 90
tonarion, 16
trabeatae, 119, 122
Trajan, 33
Treaty of Dardanus, 90, 101
Treggiari, Susan, 9
Trifles or Jokes (Melissus), 76, 119
Trimalchio (fictional character), 5
Troy, 69
Tullia, 55
Tullius Cicero, Marcus (consul 63 BC): appreciation of Gracchus, 14–15, 18; condemnation of Carbo, 31; correspondence with Atticus, 37, 50, 54–55, 57–58; *De Natura Deorum*, 100; *De Oratore*, 14–15, 24, 27; defense of Archias, 75, 77–79, 82, 84; defense of Sextus Roscius, 103; description of Archias of Antioch, 7; description of Crassus, 23–24; description of Gracchus, 27; description of Licinius, 13, 14–15; description of politics, 83; exile of, 139; family of, 9; Gnipho's influence on, 127; household system of, 57, 157; influence of Tyrannio, 134, 139; influences of, 11; library of, 139–140; networks of, 3; *Pro Archia*, 185n78, 185n79, 185n80; *Pro Roscio Comoedo*, 71; real estate holdings of, 60; speaking style of, 26
Tullius Cicero, Quintus, 60, 72
Tusculum, 59–60, 75
Tyrannio the Elder (of Amisus): Archias and, 83; capture of, 134–135, 136; career of, 7, 136, 138–139, 142; citizenship of, 137; education of, 138; enslavement of, 133, 134; influence of, 134, 139; manumission of, 137–138; name of, 137–138, 140; origins of, 133, 138; Plutarch's biography of, 134–137, 154; resources of, 139; skills of, 139; travels of, 138; writings of, 139. *See also* war captives
Tyrannio the Younger, 140–142. *See also* war captives

United States, 159
Upils (Oscan name), 190n9
Usia Prima, 212n86

Valerius Flaccus, Lucius, 36, 39
Valerius Maximus, description of Licinius, 13, 15–16
Varro (Marcus Terentius Varro): chronological system used by, 68; *De Re Rustica*, 53, 60; influence of Tyrannio, 134
Vergil, 62, 144
vernae (homeborn slaves), 37, 52, 67, 114
Verrius Flaccus, Marcus, 181–182n21
Vesuvius, 180n149
Vettius Sabinus, Titus, 167n23
vicarius, 43, 174n45
vilicus and *vilica*, 39, 46
Vindolanda writing tablets, 176n65
Vipsania Agrippina, 179n324
Vipsanius Agrippa, Marcus, 38, 59–61, 179n134, 179n135, 180n140

war captives: education of, 160; influence of, 153–155; as luxuries, 136, 145; skills of, 161; treatment of, 133–134. *See also* Philologus, Lucius Ateius; Timagenes of Alexandria; Tyrannio the Elder (of Amisus)
wet nurses, 116
women: education of, 61, 164n18; lives and contributions of, 9; role of, 5; studies of, 9
writing tablets, 164n14, 176n65

Xenophon, 49, 77

Zmyrna (or Smyrna), 92, 96, 97, 99, 101